IN SEARCH OF THE REPUBLIC

Public Virtue and the Roots of American Government

Revised Edition

Richard Vetterli
Gary Bryner

Rowman & Littlefield Publishers, Inc.

ROMAN & LITTLEFIELD PUBLISHERS, INC.

Published in the United States of America
by Rowman & Littlefield Publishers, Inc.
4720 Boston Way, Lanham, Maryland 20706

3 Henrietta Street
London WC2E 8LU, England

British Cataloging in Publication Information Available

Library of Congress Cataloging-in-Publication Data

Vetterli, Richard.
  In search of the republic : public virtue and the roots of American
government / Richard Vetterli, Gary Bryner.—Rev. ed.
  p. cm.
Includes index.
1. Political science—United States—History. 2. Republicanism—
United States—History. 3. Allegiance—United States—History.
4. Church and state—United States—History. 5. United States—
Constitutional history. I. Bryner, Gary C., 1951–   . II. Title.
JA84.U5V47   1995   172'.2'0973—dc20   95-26078

ISBN 0-8476-8173-4 (pbk. : alk. paper)

Printed in the United States of America

⊗™ The paper used in this publication meets the minimum requirements of
American National Standard for Information Sciences—Permanence of
Paper for Printed Library Materials, ANSI Z39.48–1984.

What a dreadful Spirit that Man possesses, who can put a private Appetite in balance against the universal Good of his Country, and of Mankind.

Cato

Contents

Acknowledgments

W E WISH TO EXTEND our sincere appreciation to the following persons with the understanding that the expression of our gratitude does not in any way suggest their endorsement of this book or any particular part of its content.

We appreciate the encouragement and support of succeeding deans of the college, Professors Martin Hickman and Stan Albrecht.

Professor and political science chair Dennis Thompson consistently extended welcome encouragement to us, generously provided us with departmental resources, and sought to assist us in our project in every way possible. Had it not been for his concern and assistance, the time required to produce this book would have been greatly extended. The previous chair, Professor F. LaMond Tullis, also gave valuable support as the project got underway.

To Professor Louis Midgley, for reading the manuscript several times and proferring invaluable suggestions, our thanks. His vast knowledge concerning the American Founding and his expertise concerning *The Federalist Papers* and the writings of Alexis de Tocqueville were freely extended to us. Furthermore, our discussions with Professor Midgley concerning the Founding and the concept of civic virtue and spanning more than a decade have been of inestimable value.

Professors Howard Christy (Senior Editor, Scholarly Publications), Neil York, Neil Flinders, Noel Reynolds, Carwin Williams, and especially Frank Fox, contributed their learned critiques of the manuscript. Too, we appreciate the many hours of discussion with Professor Hyrum Andrus, now retired, concerning the nuances in the ideas connected with the rise of Western civilization, and with Professor David Kirk Hart concerning the concepts of civic virtue and benevolence.

The help of the College Faculty Support Center was invaluable for professional assistance in every phase of manuscript development.

Numerous libraries across the nation helped provide us with books, journals, and other materials. We appreciate the cooperation of the Library of Congress and especially our University Library, whose employees went "the extra mile" on our behalf through the use of their own extensive resources and through interlibrary loans.

To our teaching assistants and readers James McLaren, Glenn Call, Drew Frogley, and particularly Cindy Ingersoll our special thanks.

Richard Vetterli
Gary Bryner

Foreword

CAN THE NATION'S GOVERNMENT as we know it today survive into the indefinite future? The system of government so many Americans take absolutely for granted has existed for but a brief, shining moment in recorded history. The modern form of representative government can perhaps be dated from Britain's Glorious Revolution of 1688–1689. But today's citizens would scarcely recognize the results of that upheaval, with its rigid class system and narrow suffrage, as being a close relative of our own. The United States and its unique Constitution came along about a century later, although it was not until the 1820s under Jacksonian populism that the political structure began to take on a shape that would be somewhat meaningful to a casually interested American today. Thinking of the brief time we have had in which to try to make representative democracy a lasting way of life and the tremendous pressures to which it is constantly subjected can easily shake one's faith in the future of our system. Can it survive beyond the "now" generation? If self-interest has truly deteriorated into sheer narcissism for some citizens, is recovery still possible? What happens to the quality of republican government when the nation experiences a secular downward trend in voter participation that has now extended for more than ninety years? The questions, each one more alarming than the previous, can be continued endlessly.

In which direction can we turn if we wish to strengthen the condition of the Republic? Richard Vetterli and Gary Bryner suggest that we reconsider one of the principal roots by which our Republic was originally nourished. It is the one that is quite surely the most neglected in everyday discourse about public leadership and decision-making today. Yet, as a nation, surely the concept and function of public virtue is the idea we can least afford to shunt aside. In this impressive volume, the authors review the ancient idea of public virtue, bring it through evolving conceptualizations, and show how it was centrally applied in the justifications for the prospects of the new Republic.

In order to preserve "virtue" as a meaningful term under the circumstances of a society in which class was deemphasized, in which the individual was central and self-interest was an acceptable, indeed a worthy line of pursuit, important modifications had to be made. In particular, expectations of human excellence had to be lowered and, if self-interest was not always to be condemned or seen as simply destructive of social good, it had to be conceptualized as coexisting in something of a symbiotic relationship with virtue.

The authors present evidence and powerful, closely reasoned arguments in defense of the position that the idea of public virtue was central to the political thought of the nation's founders. In the heroic tradition of political theory, they no doubt expect to encounter questions and vigorous arguments from some readers. Certainly there will be discussions about whether changes in the idea of virtue from classical and biblical through medieval and later times to the present, in fact, saves harmless the essential idea and political function of virtue. There is the question of whether the character of the American people or their willingness to devote a sufficient portion of their energies to the honoring of virtue's obligations is, in fact, a strong enough reed against which to anchor the Republic. And some will certainly challenge the conservative implications of what is argued here to be required in order to successfully blend virtue and liberty.

Still, debate as to what constitutes virtue and what is necessary to preserve it as well as the Republic, is the very kind of activity that will help to continue the existence of both. The authors frankly cite some of their own potential critics and discuss the arguments they have offered. They bring in impressive witnesses in support of their own interpretations. They show how ideas must and do change with the changing environment in which they exist. They reach their conclusions in an impressive display of erudition and close argument. This book could and should return an understanding of public virtue—and its critical importance—to a central place on the agenda of public debate and as a major topic in the political education of the young. Read it for yourself and see.

Charles R. Adrian
University of California,
Riverside
Professor of Political Science

Preface to the Revised Edition

A MONG THE MOST REPEATED TERMS used during the Revolutionary and early Constitutional eras were "moral sense," its expression in "virtue," and the "genius of the people." These were descriptive terms, widely understood at that time, and frequently employed by the Founders, the writers of newsprint, teachers in the classroom, and ministers from the pulpit—especially those selected to deliver the traditional "Election Sermons."

Central to the Founders' understanding was the belief that self-government presupposes what would now be called a "political culture" of at least moderate virtue, that a democratic republic requires a citizenry *capable* of exercising the kind of self-restraint and public-mindedness that would permit freedom to flourish. One of the great contributions of the American Founders was to articulate a modern understanding of "virtue" grounded in a realistic assessment of human nature, which recognized that certain primary institutions played an essential role in fostering and stimulating those "virtues." In so doing, the Founders neither deified nor degraded human beings, but concentrated on the notion that a broad spectrum of potential motivations drive human behavior, there being no simple "nature of man," either good or evil.

The Founders rejected the earlier republican concept that the political regime (or state) was the source of virtue, for virtue cannot be compelled through the coercive power of government. Government is quite limited in its ability to change individual or collective behavior. Attitudes and personal traits cannot be legislated. Instead, virtue is fostered by the primary institutions of society—family, neighborhood, religion, education, and other voluntary organizations. Virtue is something taught. It is educated habit, developed through practice. It is not produced merely through authoritative statements of law, although wise laws may be helpful in promoting consistency among the elements of virtue.

The Founders did endorse a government role in the formation of citizen character with the promotion of moral education and laws regulating public decency. According to political scientist Thomas G. West in *The Review of Politics*, they "regarded virtue as an indispensable condition of freedom, for without self-restraint in their private lives people would not be capable of governing themselves in public. But virtue was also judged intrinsically worthy, a necessary ingredient of human happiness." The ideal of *private virtue* preceded and merged with *public virtue*. "These two concerns, private and public, were often joined in important public documents."

Thus, while virtue did not essentially arise from government, self-government was dependent on its presence. The nature and function of government, the Founders believed, could not be created or maintained independently of the *genius*—the full character and experience—of the people. And the merging of private and public virtue ensured that their role would be significantly more important than mere participation in and support of the political system. History, tradition, beliefs, philosophies, experience, and expectations—the public culture—all shape the political and social environment and the prospects for self-government. Without this acknowledgment there is no way to establish or even define the "public good."

The structure of government—checks and balances, separation of powers, federalism, enumerated powers, rights, and other key elements of the Constitution—while vitally important, rested on a foundation of virtue. Structure was not sufficient to guarantee self-government. Process was not enough to check the ambition, greed, corruption, and factionalism that the Founders believed to be an inherent part of human nature. Government and the public culture were thus necessarily inextricably intertwined.

The wisdom and experience of the Founders taught them that a republic could not be sustained solely by virtue any more than it could by government structure alone. The two factors together, however, offered a subtle new expression, one that could *moderate* a regime. The combination of virtue and auxiliary precautions, reasoned Madison, would protect self-government from the threat of a single, overwhelming faction or partisan violence. Both the Federalists and the anti-Federalists agreed that virtue in the people was indispensable; their disagreements focused on how best to promote it. Republican government, wrote Madison in *Federalist* 55, *presupposes* the qualities of honor and virtue in the people and their leaders "in a higher degree than any other form."

In the study of the American Founding, one finds that "self-interest" is among the most misinterpreted and misapplied terms by writers on the Founding. The fact is consistently ignored that by the time of the Founding, the concept of self-interest had evolved beyond solely an overwhelming interest in survival and the voracious appetite for gain to a richer and more complicated subject. Self-interest, if moderated by a symbiotic relationship with virtue, can be beneficial. And one's self-interest in a growing number of choices and alternatives characteristic of the modern world might well be of benefit, not only for the individual but for the public as well. Tocqueville, who quickly perceived this phenomenon in his study of America in 1830, reported in his *Democracy in America* that self-interest can be "enlightened."

In Search of the Republic follows this delicate relationship through the philosophy of the Founding, including its association with what the Founders called the "Commercial Republic." Madison believed that factions and interests—which are also the issue of commerce—will begin to check, balance, and moderate each other as the system grows. Nevertheless, we are reminded that this process, too, begins with the assumption of a moderately virtuous people. No market system can be sustained solely by regulating devices any more than one could expect a moderately enlightened public virtue to uphold the political system alone.

In Search of the Republic traces the concepts of virtue and self-interest from the Classical philosophers, such as Plato, Aristotle, and Cicero; through Italian scholars such as the first of the great representatives of Renaissance Humanism, Francisco Petrarch (1304–1374); through the vanguard of the English Renaissance, "The Oxford Circle," in the sixteenth century; and later the "Cambridge Platonists" in the seventeenth century, to become an important part of the Scottish Enlightenment.

It was during the period beginning with the Renaissance humanists that the cardinal virtues of the Classical Greeks were wedded to the Pauline virtues and other Biblical elements. *In Search of the Republic* attempts to show that the impact of this union was eventually to affect dramatically the moral philosophy and "language" of the American Founding. Yet this conduit of the Enlightenment has been almost ignored in modern commentary.

Nevertheless, the search for the republic goes on. As the years passed after the Founding period, politics became more expansive and powerful, and the role of private interest became more organized and directed, strong forces have struggled over the meaning of the Constitution and the role of government. Periodic calls for reform dot the historical passage. During the period from 1880 to 1914, for example, numerous reform and radical movements opposed constitutionally imposed checks against majority rule. These were angered by late nineteenth-century scholarship concerning the Founding, which they claimed was Constitution worship, veneration of the

Founders, and support of the *status quo*. According to Martin Diamond in *The Founding of the Democratic Republic*, "reformers began to search about for feet of clay, to show that the Founders were not disinterested patriots but men rigging a constitution to protect their own interests. Debunking the Founders would emancipate the present from the moral claim of the past and open the way for drastic reform proposals."

Historian Charles A. Beard's *An Economic Interpretation of the Constitution* became a classic formulation of the attempt to question the motives of the Founders. Beard insisted that every facet of Constitutional development—from the convention through to ratification— had an economic core and was made in accordance with the Founders' own interests and those of their class. Beard contended that the Founders were representatives of property interests, including public securities, manufacturing, trading, and shipping, and that these subrational forces that undermine inquiry have a decisive influence on people's perceptions and thinking. Since economic activity determines human thought in general, according to Beard, it is reasonable to assume that the American Founders represented and were motivated solely by economic interests. He rejected the involvement of any possible notion of virtue. Ideas, Beard emphasized, were reduced to interest and class. This view subordinates interests and then makes them relative to time and place. There can be no universal purposes or timeless truths. Truth is but an entirely willful creation of time-bound beings.

Although Beard properly reintroduced economic concerns into the study of the Founding, subsequently many scholars have demonstrated that his research was faulty and did not support his larger thesis. Numerous reviews, articles, and books have recorded the many weaknesses in his evidence, especially his inferences. However, Beard's emphasis on economic determinism and what he thought to be antidemocratic tendencies are still influential. This influence caused a waning of interest in the concept of virtue in scholarship on the Founding; and fewer pages were dedicated to this period in American government textbooks.

New revisionist accounts of the Constitutional era began to appear. Building on subtle modifications of Beard's thesis, a number of acclaimed historians, including Gordon S. Wood (*The Creation of the American Republic*) and John Patrick Diggins (*The Lost Soul of American Politics*), concluded that a fundamental transformation of political culture had taken place in the philosophy of the Founders between 1776 and 1787. These writers, emphasizing their concept of collectivism, claim that while republicanism had previously, and properly, diminished the individual in the name of the "common good,"

Madison and his colleagues had rejected this and virtually all of the classical world for one that was "recognizably modern" and would not countenance establishment of regimes whose purpose it was to transcend the peculiar interests of citizens. Instead, argued Wood, they established an essentially aristocratic regime, one intended to check the democratic tendencies of the period and forfeit the "ideal good" to the tangible interests of a society composed of distinct classes.

Furthermore, these writers insisted that moral philosophy and concern for virtue had no impact on the outcome of the new government. The Constitution, they wrote, was made up merely of mechanical devices, was intended to control self-interest, and made no demands on virtue. Politics, we are told in these accounts, is reduced to ideology, which ultimately represents unrestrained interests.

The continuing popular impact of Beard's account of the Founding, and later that of Wood and Diggins, merged with the rapidly developing academic popularity of the doctrines of moral and philosophical relativism. A number of texts began to appear that questioned the philosophy and the efforts of the Founders. Scholars built their reputations on similar portrayals of the Founding period.

During the sixties this demeaning of the Founding ignited into what Isaac Kramnick, in his "Republican Revisionism, Revisited" for *The American Historical Review*, describes as a "fundamental reinterpretation of Anglo-American eighteenth century social and political thought," replacing in historical and political philosophy "the liberal individualist heritage preoccupied with [individual] rights." Instead, the revisionist emphasis would be "citizenship and public participation, a tradition with roots deep in the classical and renaissance worlds." Called "civic humanism," and said to be based on the writings of Aristotle, Cicero, and Machiavelli, this utopian ideology "conceives of man as a political being whose self-realization occurs only through participation in public life, through active citizenship in a republic." This intense political activity—which specifically includes participation in the military—is to be directed toward the "common good" by the state, at the expense of individual interest. One of the most important scholars in the "cutting edge" of this philosophy was J. G. A. Pocock, with his *The Machiavelian Moment: Florentine Political Thought and the Atlantic Republican Tradition*.

The revisionists, however, have not been without critics who question their assumptions. In our research we found convincing evidence that the thought of the Founders concerning human nature is more sophisticated and cosmopolitan than the narrow view of the revisionists reflected in the perspectives underlying their philosophy. They have failed to appreciate the essential evolution of the concept of virtue and its multiple relationships to self-interest, the complexity of modern human existence, and the potential ramifications of their concept of the "common good," with its acceptance of classical public-spiritedness severed from respect for moral or religious restraints.

Yet, for an extended period it seemed that what had become the ideology of revisionism would reign supreme in the disciplines of history and political science, especially when it found affinity with the counter-culture of the sixties and the seventies. But these decades carried a two-edged sword.

While revisionism gained momentum, there began to appear at the same time a general popular swell of frustration that was soon reflected in the media, the halls of government, and even in academia. At first primarily engendered by the war in Vietnam, the concern grew with continued manifestations that the country was in serious moral decline. Frightening statistics concerning illigitimacy, narcotics use, sexually transmitted diseases, the many threats to the traditional family, crime rates, poverty in the cities, the tragic failure of the welfare system, the separation of rights from responsibility—these and many more concerns became public issues.

Gradually, the concept of virtue was disinterred. Books, articles, and statements appeared from various prominent sources, including former Secretary of Education William Bennett's *Book of Virtues,* an overnight best seller, and Senator Daniel Patrick Moynihan's *Family and Nation,* a stirring account of the American family under siege. Mario Cuomo began to promote fundamental or "core values" for the public schools on the basis that, after all, there is at least some national understanding of what is right and what is wrong. Barbara Dafoe Whitehead's "Dan Quayle Was Right" in the *Atlantic Monthly* challenged members of "the policy and research communities [who had] backed away from the entire issue" concerning the tragic dissolution of two-parent families. And *U.S. News and World Report* dedicated an entire issue to the discussion of virtue.

Even articles in scholarly academic journals such as the *American Political Science Review* reflected the renewed interest in the concept of virtue. A thought-provoking piece by James Q. Wilson, one of America's premier political scientists and former president of the American Political Science Association, resurrected Jefferson's and the Scots' concept of "The Moral Sense"; Davis C. Paris's inclusive study entitled "Moral Education and the Tie that Binds in Liberal Political Theory," and Shelley Burtt's "The Politics of Virtue Today: A Critique and a Proposal," suggested the possibility of a judicious balance between private and public virtue, "without falling victim to [the] democratic romanticism" of the revisionists.

Some writers and scholars have issued warnings that corruption in America was at a crisis stage. According to Robert Bellah in his widely discussed *Habits of the Heart*, "The time may be approaching when we will either reform our republic or fall into the hands of despotism." "The barbarians," writes Alisdair McIntyre in his *After Virtue*, "are not waiting beyond the frontiers, they have already been governing us for quite some time. And it is our lack of consciousness of this that constitutes part of our predicament." McIntyre warns that "the new dark ages . . . are already upon us." And national journalist George F. Will, in his *Statecraft and Soulcraft*, laments what he believes to be the hedonistic ethic, the loss of the higher spiritual values of Western civilization, the subversion of civility, the plethora of self-seeking interest groups, and a "fat and flabby government, capable of giving but not leading."

Many now realize the general character of the problem of moral decline and disorientation, but solutions remain elusive. The strength of academic-espoused relativism is but one of the barriers facing the revitalization of a widely accepted concept of virtue. Jeffrey Stout, in his provocative study *Ethics After Babel*, reviews the frequently expressed concerns of a number of scholars that American pluralism has been carried to such extremes that it may be difficult to moderate philosophical and even religious differences, making a unified effort difficult.

Others claim that the contemporary proliferation of moral "languages" may now preclude concerted efforts at moral recovery. According to MacIntyre, our moral tradition has fragmented into lost "languages." Bellah contends that America's "primary language," which is traditional liberalism, is too individualistic and ill-suited for general discourse on the "common good" (a term often used, but with few attempts at analyzing or defining it) and that our "secondary languages" of morals are products of tradition—biblical and civic republicanism, which, according to Bellah, are fading in influence.

Suggestions range from a return to classical moral philosophy, to the revival and rejuvenation of the traditional "secondary languages," to the regeneration of churches nationwide with a view to a common commitment, to claims that the cultivation of virtue is the responsibility of government, to the development of a moral "Esperanto"—that is, create an *ersatz* moral language and then attempt to get the public to accept it.

Still others believe that traditional religious and communitarian values must be restored and made operable. In *Empower the People*, Peter L. Berger and Richard John Neuhaus emphasize the key importance of the neighborhood, the family, the church, and the voluntary associations in social life—"those institutions standing between the individual in his private life and the large institutions of public life." This issue is kept alive through the ongoing debate between communitarians and their modern liberal critics.

In writing *In Search of the Republic,* we have examined in some detail the currently ignored moral horizon that we believe clearly operated in the hearts and minds of the Founders and that was accepted by both those who promoted and those who opposed the Constitution. During the Founding period the people were bound together by a common moral language. Furthermore, the values on which the "language" was based had a core, indeed a transcendent core, which meant these values were universal, timeless, and absolute to them.

If there is to be a widespread return to virtue, it must result from deep personal motivation, widely felt. The legitimacy of the concept must be accepted. In order to be an effective moral teaching virtue must bring with it an aura of transcendence. It must have a time-honored core. If there is a necessary link between the proper functioning of public institutions and virtue, then it might well be time to reconsider the roots of our moral foundations.

1

Introduction:
Public Virtue and the Roots
of Republican Government

Men are qualified for civil liberty in exact proportion to their disposition to put moral chains on their own appetites; in proportion as their love of justice is above their rapacity; in proportion as their soundness and sobriety of understanding is above their vanity and presumption; in proportion as they are more disposed to listen to the councils of the wise and good, in preference to the flattery of knaves. Society cannot exist unless a controlling power upon the will and appetite be placed somewhere, and the less of it there is within, the more there must be without. It is ordained in the eternal constitution of things, that men of intemperate minds cannot be free. Their passions forge their fetters.[1]

Edmund Burke

VIRTUE AND THE MODERN REPUBLIC

THE IDEA OF VIRTUE was central to the political thought of the Founders of the American republic. Every body of thought they encountered, every intellectual tradition they consulted, every major theory of republican government by which they were influenced emphasized the importance of personal and public virtue. It was understood by the Founders to be the *precondition* for republican government, the base upon which the structure of government would be built. Virtue was the common bond that tied together the Greek, Roman, Christian, British, and European ideas of government and politics to which the Founders responded.

Despite its central role in the political theory of republicanism, the concept of virtue has not been well understood. It is an idea that has

1

not been static, but has undergone an important metamorphosis that has not been clearly recognized. The purpose of this book is to consider the evolution of the idea of public virtue, to discuss its central role in the political thought of the founding of the United States and the framing of its Constitution, and to describe its relationship with the other political and cultural elements of the American republic.

Preconditions of Republican Government

How did the Framers of the Constitution view republican government? There were, of course, a variety of views among the Framers, yet there was general agreement over two critical elements of republican government: first, that there were essential preconditions that must exist before republican government is a possibility and that those preconditions must be continually fostered and maintained; second, that the elements of republican government included public and private institutions, governing structures and procedures, popular beliefs, character, and commitments.

As the leaders of the new American states considered the viability of a republic, the fundamental question they asked was whether Americans had sufficient virtue to make self-government work—to soften the sharpest edges of self-interest, to temper the most disruptive personal and social passions, and to ensure sentiments of support and patriotism for the polity. Given the nature of man as they understood it, they were not at all confident that self-government over time was even a possibility. But of one thing they appear to have been certain: a citizenry lacking in virtue was not capable of sustaining a democratic republic, whatever its structure. According to Thomas Jefferson, "It is in the manners and spirit of a people which preserve a republic in vigour." Furthermore, "degeneracy in these is a canker which soon eats into the heart of its laws and constitution."[2]

The Founders repeatedly emphasized the importance of the character of the people and their political culture as the precondition for republican government. George Mason argued that the "genius of the people must be consulted" in the structuring of the Constitution.[3] Madison emphasized the importance of the "genius of the people of America, [which is] the spirit which activates the State legislatures, and the principles which are incorporated with the political character of every class of citizens."[4] For Madison, republican government was the only form of government "reconcilable with the genius of the people of America [and] with the fundamental principles of the revolution."[5]

In his important discussion of the structure of government in *The Federalist* No. 51, Madison wrote that a "dependence on the people is, no doubt, the primary control on the government; but experience has taught mankind the necessity of auxiliary precautions." The structure of government, the separation of powers and checks and balances, the scheme of representation, all were auxiliary to the primary protection against the excesses of governmental power. Alexander Hamilton, in *The Federalist* No. 84, argued that guarantees of individual liberties such as freedom of the press "must altogether depend on public opinion, and on the general spirit of the people and of the government."

Constitutional structures and procedures were designed to filter out corrupt leaders and promote virtuous officials to exercise political power. While the Federalists and anti-Federalists disagreed over how to assure virtuous government, they agreed on its importance and argued together that a virtuous people were essential for republican government. Government itself was necessary because of a lack of virtue, because men were not "angels," as Madison put it. The less virtue was possessed by the people, the more government they needed. The less able they were to exercise their rights and liberties in moderation, the greater need there would be for government coercion and limitations on individual actions.

The Evolution of Modern Virtue

Unlike the classical idea of virtue, where the organized development of civic virtue in the citizenry was the prime objective of government, the Founders saw virtue as a means to assure individual liberty and self-government. The concept of virtue had evolved considerably from the Greek understanding of it. In part, however, virtue was still equated with "public regardedness," a willingness to sacrifice individual concerns for the benefit of society as a whole; but this was seen as a concern for the common well-being, not an all-consuming and unqualified acquiesence to the political regime. It was expected that people would voluntarily temper their demands and pursuits enough so that liberty could flourish. The ideal of virtue was an important source of personal restraint and willingness to contribute to the common good. Colonial Americans claimed that they possessed these qualities necessary for self-government.[6] And, in part, virtue was equated with wisdom and foresight, with enlightened leadership and statesmanship. The cardinal virtues dating from classical times—wisdom, courage, discipline, and justice—were still considered important, although to a certain degree with an altered connotation. An appeal to virtue in elected officials meant that their pride and desire for a positive reputation, as well as the pride of the people in being represented by virtuous men, would cause them to rise above selfish, narrow concerns.[7]

Virtue was also associated with the Judeo-Christian virtues of faith, hope, and charity or love and benevolence. People were to be motivated by a sincere interest in and love for others, so that the freedom and pursuit of their own self-interest would be voluntarily channeled and constrained. Social peace and harmony could not proceed from governmental direction alone; there must be popular commitment to those values as well.[8] Religion caused a fusion of *personal* and *public* virtue—a modern *republican* virtue—that represented an amalgam of some elements of traditional civic virtue and of personal virtue, which was impregnated with biblical moral theology.

The Founders believed that virtue was a practical necessity for a people determined to govern themselves. More than the classical notions that emphasized such ideas as patriotism and willingness to fight and die for the state, public virtue represented voluntary self-restraint, a commitment to a moral social order, honesty and obedience to law, benevolence, and a willingness to respect the unwritten rules and norms of social life. Whether this was a result of fear of God's wrath and judgment, or a pure love of others did not particularly matter to the polity as a whole. It was *assumed* that there was sufficient virtue to make a system based on individual liberty work. If there was insufficient virtue, then order would have to be imposed by force and coercion, by pervasive governmental intervention in individuals' lives. The Founders clearly recognized that contradiction and their whole effort in forming a government assumed it could be avoided.

From the beginning, American colonists considered themselves a virtuous people "in the double sense of possessing superior moral qualities (in the Christian sense) and in the sense of possessing, to a greater extent, those qualities for self-government (the Greek notion of virtue)." According to Donald Lutz, "European commentators merely reinforced American beliefs when they spoke of the 'natural man' living on American shores in possession of the manly virtues found in the state of nature. The flight from European decadence had been prominent among the motivations for religious emigration to America during the 1600s."[9] Significantly, more than one foreign observer commented upon the "virtue," or the "manners," or the "character," or the "morals," or the "genius" of the American people, and found them extraordinary. And more than one suggested that these characteristics made the American republican system possible.

During the same period that de Tocqueville's *Democracy in America* was being published in Paris (1835), an Austrian immigrant named Francis Grund published two commentaries in the United States (1837 and 1839), which were similar in observation to de Tocqueville's work. Grund was singularly impressed with the domestic virtue he perceived among the American people in his day, and suggested that there was a relationship between the "domestic habits" of Americans and their beliefs. In all the world, he commented, "few people have so great respect for the law and are so well able to govern themselves." Perhaps, he surmised, they were "the only people capable of enjoying so large a portion of liberty without abusing it." "I consider the domestic virtue of the Americans as the principle source of all their other qualities. It acts as a promoter of industry, as a stimulus to enterprise and as the most powerful restraint of public vice. . . . No government could be established on the same principle as that of the United States with a different code of morals. The American Constitution is remarkable for its simplicity; but it can only suffice a people habitually correct in their actions, and would be utterly inadequate to the wants of a different nation. Change the domestic habits of the Americans, their religious devotion, and their high respect for morality, and it will not be necessary to change a single letter in the Constitution in order to vary the whole form of their government."[10]

The idea of the necessity of virtue—developed as a "modern" doctrine and practice from an amalgam of classical, medieval, Renaissance, Reformation and biblical concepts—was commonplace. Out of this metamorphosis came the belief that virtue and morality—specifically biblical *morality*—were synonymous, although they were sometimes referred to as separate concepts. Moral theology had pushed the stark differences in behavior expectation between the clergy and the masses, once typical in Europe, into the background. Modern casuistry, using a scriptural base, presented to the common man—as well as to the "elites"—a code of moral or virtuous behavior to which he too was expected to adhere. The growth of sentiments of human dignity were fertilized by the belief of a direct relationship between man and his Creator. This belief, in turn, stimulated the growth of theology, and together they enhanced a vital, revolutionary sense of individualism and individual worth.

Virtue was seen as a form of restraint against corruption and, at the same time, as a stimulator of positive moral action. Virtuous restraint applied to governments, to sovereigns, and to individuals. On the other hand, virtuous obligation to purposeful moral behavior as expounded by the Bible became encumbent on all men. The Bible was a guide that left little doubt about what individual virtuous or moral behavior was. Indeed, the Ten Commandments, the Sermon on the Mount, and a variety of other biblical exhortations provided a yardstick, an expected norm, with which to measure not only the actions of men, but the relative "justice" of government. Virtue played both a social and a political role for society. "Individualism" was expected to lead not to anarchy but to personal energy and creativity, held in

bounds by responsible behavior. Together, these beliefs helped energize a common system of symbols and values that contributed to the
unity of society.

Recent scholarship on the American founding has often failed to
give sufficient attention to the *evolutionary* character of the concept of
virtue. When historians refer to virtue, they are often drawn back to
classical antiquity, narrowing their definition of the term to its ancient
expression, and confusing it with the "modern" concept of virtue.
Centuries before the Constitution was written, the concept of virtue
had begun its metamorphosis. It had, over time, become infused with
biblical Christianity, which had become a kind of "general Christianity," even within medieval Christendom, and had emerged as a body
of moral precepts. The gradual emergence of ideas of freedom and
human dignity, the growth of the modern state, and the utopian ideal
of a holy commonwealth proved catalysts to the metamorphosis of
the meaning of virtue. With the advent of societal complexity and
increased pluralism in nearly every phase of life, the concept of virtue
continued its metamorphosis, always being adapted and molded to
some extent to fit the circumstances, yet never ceasing to remain an
ideal that people took seriously.

The American Founders were aware of the problems of "democracy" that had plagued the ancient Greeks and had resigned themselves to the reality that they could learn little of positive value from
them. They had come to the conclusion that classical philosophy had
relied too heavily on the expectation of the consistency of stringent
virtuous behavior, devoid of any self-interest. Their understanding of
the nature of man reflected a profound awareness of his selfishness
and aggressiveness. Nevertheless, they believed that man had certain
redeeming qualities, that he had the potential for self-government.
The Founders believed that the "auxiliary precautions" they had
devised, *combined* with, rather than replacing, individual virtue,
might just make it all possible. They also believed that no structure of
government in a republic would long survive the absence of virtue in
the people. They believed that their efforts might decide once and for
all if self-government was even possible.

While some of the colonial thinkers apparently believed that virtue
could be inculcated through reason, most thought its primary source
to be in religion. Yet, the Founders were vigorously opposed to
establishing a state church; their concern was with freedom of conscience and religion as a fundamental right for all Americans to enjoy.
To a substantial degree, they saw virtue as a product of the general
Judeo-Christian beliefs that permeated the colonies, and of organized
religion and family life.[11] Virtue was to be privately developed and

nurtured, the state itself was not to be responsible for it. Since general Christianity and the different churches were already viewed as a primary source of virtue, government need only keep from interfering in these areas. There was a clear and fundamental recognition of the importance of religion and its relationship with republican government, as reflected in legislation enacted by the first congresses. The Northwest Ordinance of 1787, which was re-enacted by the first Congress, declared that "religion, morality and knowledge, being necessary to good government and the happiness of mankind, schools and the means of education shall be forever encouraged." As Clinton Rossiter has noted, schools in America had long since been actively involved in promoting virtue, "whether designed to reinforce true religion or 'to form the Minds of the Youth to virtue.' " Primary education had been devoted to what Rossiter called the five Rs— "Reading, Riting, Rithmatic, Rules of virtuous conduct, and Religion."[12]

State constitutions and declarations reinforce the idea of the importance of religion in making self-government possible. The final clause in the Virginia Declaration of Rights, for example, states that "it is the mutual duty of all to practice Christian forebearance, love, and charity, towards each other."[13] A religious oath was often required of candidates running for elected office. In Pennsylvania, each member of the legislature was required to make the following declaration: "I do believe in one God, the creator and governor of the universe, the rewarder of the good and the punisher of the wicked. And I do acknowledge the Scriptures of the Old and the New Testament to be given by Divine inspiration."[14] There would be no specific religious orthodoxy, and the idea of an ecclesiastical policy or theocracy was clearly rejected. Freedom of belief and conscience were to be assured. But the assumption was that there would be a moral foundation for republican government and that private religion and general Christian beliefs would serve as an important source of that foundation.

The failure to recognize the evolution in the meaning of public virtue has led some scholars to argue that the framing of the Constitution did not presuppose the continued existence of public virtue, that the idea of public virtue was central to the Revolution but lost its significance by 1787. Madison and others are described as accepting the decline in virtue and embracing the belief that the common good was but the outcome of the mediation of individual conflict and competition. Gordon S. Wood has argued that the Founders abandoned the idea of public virtue because Americans as a people failed to satisfy the classical expectations essential to virtue. The lack of a natural aristocracy, the absence of class differentiations, he suggests, caused Madison and others to abandon the idea of public virtue and resign themselves to facilitating the pursuit of self-interest and hoping that the ensuing conflict would produce the public interest. Wood acknowledged that the Founders continued to champion virtue even as he argues that they saw its demise. He concluded that the lack of the necessary cultural preconditions meant that virtue would not be part of the new American Republic, and that, indeed, the Constitution had provided a new revolutionary republic "which did not require a virtuous people for its sustenance."[15] John Diggins argued in his study of American political thought that "the Classical idea of virtue . . . was an idea whose time had come and gone by 1787."[16] And similarly, J. G. A. Pocock has written that the "decline of virtue had as its logical corollary the use of interest," that the idea of classical virtue gave way to the belief that individuals would only pursue their own desires. Interests and factions were to function in an atmosphere not constrained by notions of virtue, but the inevitable restraints as individual interests collided.[17]

These interpretations among scholars can be traced, at least in part, to the belief that virtue and self-interest are incompatible; that the Founders recognized the pervasiveness of self-interest and simply concluded that virtue was not possible; that their attention shifted to structural and procedural devices to check the effects of the pursuit of unbridled self-interest; and that they became convinced that pluralistic competition would produce the public, collective good they sought.

Conflicting interpretations are further rooted in efforts to place the Founders in one of two basic schools of political thought. For some, the Founders were champions of liberalism, of a Lockean economic, materialistic individualism that sought to maximize opportunities for the pursuit of self-interest. For others, the Founders were republicans, following Montesquieu, the English Commonwealthmen, and Machiavelli in the "tradition of republican humanism" that "called upon the citizen to control his passions and subordinate his interests to the common good." Liberalism and republicanism are offered as contradictory explanations of the intellectual roots of the American founding.[18]

In contrast to this debate, we argue that the Founders attempted to, and were ultimately successful, in responding to both traditions. They believed that republican virtue and liberal individualism—*self-interest, properly understood*—are compatible and interdependent. Liberty requires individual restraint. If those restraints are to a substantial degree developed voluntarily, then external, governmental coercion may be minimal. If voluntary constraints are lacking, if the people are not able to limit their own interests when necessary to accomplish public purposes or to protect the rights of others, then government intervention becomes increasingly pervasive, and the purposes of liberalism are not achieved.

The tensions between liberal and republican ideas are greatly reduced as the evolutionary nature of virtue is recognized. Actually, the kind of stringent classical virtue that Wood, Diggins, Pocock, and others were discussing clearly *was*, to a significant degree, rejected by the Founders as inconsistent with the "genius" or spirit of the American people. They clearly believed that some of the more severe classical notions of virtue were inappropriate for modern republics, and especially the American. But they also recognized that a *modern* virtue was very much a part of the American political culture of the eighteenth century. Thus, while rejecting the extremes of one meaning of virtue, they built their scheme of government upon a substantially modified conception of virtue, while not entirely rejecting the former.

The Constitution itself makes no mention of public virtue. For the Framers, personal and public virtue were a *precondition* for the kind of government embodied in the Constitution. Public virtue, general religious beliefs, personal restraint and concern for others, were not to be provided for through national governmental institutions and efforts in the classical tradition, but through private efforts and primary institutions, supported by local government. The idea of religious freedom precluded constitutional provisions establishing an arbitrary national orthodoxy. State governments could encourage and support religious activity, but the political culture of civic virtue was to be produced primarily by the individual churches, family life, local education, and by a general commitment to Christian principles of personal restraint and benevolence. Joseph Story's *Commentaries on the Constitution* well summarized the intent of the Framers concerning religion:

> In some of the states, Episcopalians constituted the predominant sect; in others, Quakers; and in others again, there was a close numerical rivalry among contending sects. It was impossible that there should not arise perpetual strife and perpetual jealousy on the subject of ecclesiastical ascendancy, if the national government were left free to create a religous establishment. The only security was in extirpating the power. But this alone would have been an imperfect security, if it had not been followed up by a declaration of the right of the free exercise of religion, and a prohibition . . . of all religious tests. Thus, the whole power over the subject of religion is left exclusively to the state governments, to be acted upon according to their own sense of justice, and the State constitutions.[19]

SOURCES OF THE FOUNDERS' POLITICAL THEORY

The Framers of the Constitution, and particularly its most articulate proponents, grounded their ideas and actions on a careful balancing of concerns and values. They assumed the existence of public and personal virtue, but did not rely on them alone. They gave great attention to the structure and process of government. The system they devised was a creative synthesis of ideas from their own fertile minds, the political theories of others, and the clear lessons of history and personal experience, all of which were brilliantly adapted to the American people. The Framers of the Constitution sought guidance and direction from virtually all of the sources of political thought available to them in the late eighteenth century.

Modern research has demonstrated the variety of sources which apparently influenced the thought of the American Founders. One of the most important and pioneering contributions in identifying these sources has come from Bernard Bailyn. After analyzing the literature—from pamphlets, books, and other publications—prominent during the Revolutionary period, he suggested at least five major sources—the classical, the Enlightenment, English common law, New England Puritanism, and the radical English Whigs.[20]

As to the classical, Bailyn contended that although the Founders repeatedly used terms and quotes from that ancient period, their impact was minor. According to Bailyn, "Knowledge of classical authors was universal among the colonists with any degree of education, and references to them abounded in the literature." Some of the most quoted Greek philosophers were Homer, Plato, Herodotus, Aristotle, Polybius, and Plutarch; among the Romans, Cicero, Tacitus, Seneca, Livy, Cato, and Justinian.[21] However, these citations were but "window dressing with which to ornament a page or a speech and to increase the weight of an argument. . . . [T]hey were everywhere illustrative, not determinative of thought."[22] The American spokesmen made classical terms "analogous to their times," to "their own provincial virtues."[23] As far as the Founders were concerned, classical history provided a source of "warning of the course to be shunned, without pointing out that which ought to be pursued."[24]

According to Bailyn, Enlightenment rationalism was composed of a combination of "liberal reform" and "enlightened conservatism." Frequently cited in American prints and discourses were "Montesquieu and later Delolme on the character of British liberty and on the institutional requirements for its attainment; Voltaire on the evils of clerical oppression, Beccaria on the reform of criminal law, Grotius, Pufendorf and Vatel on the laws of nature and of nations, and

Burlamagui on the limitations of public authority necessary for a free society." And, of course, John Locke was universally cited on natural rights and the contract. Bailyn makes a point that although the citations expressed from the writings of the above are "plentiful . . . the knowledge they reflect, like that of the ancient classics, is at times superficial."[25] "Except for Locke's, their influence . . . was neither clearly dominant nor wholly determinative."[26]

The American spokesmen were also apparently well acquainted with the English common law tradition. They frequently cited the great figures of England's legal history, such as Sir Edward Coke, Bracton, Bacon, and Blackstone, who was second only to Montesquieu as the most widely quoted authority in writings on the Constitution during the 1770s and 1780s.[27] There was also reference to such seventeenth-century scholars as Henry Spelman, Thomas Madox, Robert Brady, and William Petyt. "The common law," writes Bailyn, "was manifestly influential in shaping the awareness of the Revolutionary generation. But, again, it did not in itself determine the kinds of conclusions men would draw in the crises of the time."[28]

Bailyn did not ignore the religious influences on the thinking of the American spokesmen. He was impressed by what seemed to be the impact of Puritanism on New England—"especially . . . the political and social ideas associated with convenant theology." This "elaborate system of thought . . . had been consolidated and amplified by a succession of writers in the course of the seventeenth century, channeled into the main stream of eighteenth-century political and social thinking by a generation of enlightened preachers, and softened in its denominational rigor by many hands until it could be received, with minor variations, by almost the entire spectrum of American Protestantism." And according to Bailyn, this heritage "offered a context for everyday events nothing less than cosmic in its dimensions. It carried on into the eighteenth century and into the minds of the Revolutionaries the idea, originally worked out in the sermons and tracts of the settlement period, that the colonization of British America had been an event designed by the hand of God to satisfy his ultimate aims."[29]

However, it was to a multiple "generation" of what came to be known as "Commonwealthmen," that Bailyn believed to have found the Revolutionary and Republican "synthesis." Their thought "overlapped with that of those already mentioned but . . . was yet distinct in its essential characteristics and unique in its determinative power. The origins of this tradition," writes Bailyn, "lay in the radical social and political thought of the English Civil War and of the Commonwealth period, and it had developed in the early eighteenth century through a succession of writers associated with religious dissent and opposition politics . . ."[30] Among these late seventeenth century and early eighteenth century "theorists, 'country' politicians, and publicists,"[31] were Milton, Harrington, Molesworth, Bolingbroke, Henry Nevel, Benjamin Hoadly, Algernon Sidney, John Trenchard, and Thomas Gordon.

Bailyn believes that the most important eighteenth-century transmitters of this tradition were the libertarian writers Trenchard and Gordon. Their weekly "Independent Whig" and "Cato's Letters," while published in England, were reprinted frequently in colonial newspapers and prints. "Trenchard and Gordon ranked in the minds of Americans with the treatises of Locke as the most authoritative statement of the nature of political liberty."[32]

Then there were Richard Price, Joseph Priestly, John Cartwright, and James Burgh, a generation of English Reformers who were contemporary to the revolutionary period. According to Isaac Kramnick, these writers "were staple reading of Americans in the revolutionary era."[33] "Burgh, through his *Political Disquisitions*" (published in 1774), he points out, "was literally the schoolmaster for a whole generation of middle-class radicals in England and America."[34] These reformers were also prominent in the development of the concept of virtue and its relationship to the marketplace. "Priestly," continues Kramnick, "schooled England's new men of business in the series of dissenting academies at which he taught."[35]

Caroline Robbins and Gordon S. Wood have been among the most prominent writers to emphasize with Bailyn the importance of the English libertarian heritage, including English Whig political theory, which was rooted in the sixteenth-century commonwealth experience. Although they are not without their critics, their research has served to remind us of the importance of the heritage of English radical thought to America. They have been in the forefront of the revival of interest in republicanism as an integrating theme, and the importance of ideology.[36]

Still, the search for sources goes on. Garry Wills, for example, has reduced from Bailyn's more general use of the Enlightenment a thesis demonstrating the vital importance of the Scottish Enlightenment in particular. In so doing, he underlines the impact of, among others, David Hume, Adam Smith, Francis Hutcheson, Henry Home Kames, and Thomas Reid, particularly on Jefferson's philosophy in the Declaration of Independence, and on the political thought of James Madison.[37]

J. G. A. Pocock is another important contributor whose writings have caused comment. He emphasizes the impact of the classical, the Machiavellian, and the Florentine Renaissance in the development of eighteenth-century radical thought.[38]

Finally, an example may be taken from the research of Donald S. Lutz and Charles S. Hyneman. These scholars conducted a lengthy and comprehensive study of the political writings published in America during the "Founding Era,"—the years 1760 to 1805.[39] They found that the book most frequently cited by Americans during this period was the Bible. And while reprinted sermons accounted for nearly three-fourths of the biblical citations, their nonsermon sources were substantial. "It is relevant . . . to note the prominence of biblical sources for American political thought, since it was highly influential in our political tradition, and is not always given the attention it deserves."[40]

Hyneman and Lutz found Locke and Montesquieu to be prominent in the political writings during the 1760s and 1770s, with Locke emphasized more during the revolutionary period, and Montesquieu increasing in importance during that of Constitutional consideration and construction. They also confirmed that numerous English Whigs were prominent during this "Founding Era." On the other hand, they concluded, that with the exception of Hume, citations among those associated with the Scottish Enlightenment were not very prominent. And, in the case of Hume, "we may today read him as a member of such a category, but Bailyn and others are probably correct when they say that Americans during the founding era often saw him as an exponent of Whig republicanism, or else as a covert Tory."[41]

Lutz emphasizes the need for continued research on the founding period. He suggests that "we need to consider the extent to which the debate surrounding the adoption of the U.S. Constitution reflected different patterns of influence than did the debates surrounding the writing and adoption of the state constitutions, or the revolutionary writing surrounding the Declaration of Independence."[42] Furthermore, he contends that there is a need to "move beyond a Whig-Enlightenment dichotomy as the basis for debate on this issue. Debate in the future should include biblical and common law sources as well . . . ,"[43] and "there is a richness in the early state constitutions and the debates surrounding them that remains yet to be seriously studied in terms of American political theory."[44]

Virtue: A Consistent Ideal

While we have some sense of the range of political theorists and writers who influenced the Framers of the U.S. Constitution, we are not certain of the relative influence of the different theorists and the ideas they championed. There is, of course, a voluminous literature on the ideological influences on the founding of the American republic. In this book, we draw upon some of these works, *while focusing on the idea of virtue*, both public and personal, and its relationship to the basic elements of modern republican government; *for that idea and ideal is critical to every source drawn upon by the American Founders. And what is more, this ideal is a fusing link that connects the thought of the Revolutionary period with that of the Constitutional.* Christianity and its emphasis on virtue was a central component of the intellectual environment in which the founders matured and acted. The role of Judeo-Christian principles and ideas are only part of the story of the Founding of the American republic, but are a part that deserves much more attention and study. Outstanding and innovative scholars such as Bailyn, Robbins, Wood, and Pocock have provided persuasive evidence of the overwhelming influence of America's English heritage, as well as that of the tradition of the Renaissance. Still, there needs to be more understanding and synthesis with regard to the impact of the religious factor in the heritage of Western civilization and its influence in the development of the American republic. In fact, the Renaissance provides not only an enlightened secular heritage, but a substantial and vitally important religious one as well, and one which affected political as well as religious thought both in England and in America. Specifically, unless an attempt at greater synthesis is made, the critical importance of a "modern" republican virtue will be overlooked, as will be a full understanding of the evolution of "modern" republicanism as a whole. Although Pocock recognizes that the American Revolution "employed—and in some measure was occasioned by—an oppositional ideology that had been nurtured in British politics for nearly a century;" and while he points out that recent research has demonstrated that "the American Revolution was less . . . the first political act of revolutionary enlightenment as the last great act of the Renaissance;" and while he suggests a Renaissance influence on English "country ideology;" and while he recognizes a "Renaissance ideology within whose confines the Americans had begun their revolution," there must be a greater synthesis of this scholarly information with, for instance, the development of Puritan thought and the profound influence on the West of the Renaissance religious tradition. When the American founding fathers are described as "civic humanists,"[45] only part of the story has been told, and one that may be somewhat distorted as well. We need to be concerned, for example, with the substantial *religious* influence of the Renaissance humanists on England and then on the Americans of the Revolutionary and Constitution-building era—a vital influence that deeply affected the evolution of religion in the Western world and contributed significantly to the evolution of doctrines of moral virtue, freedom, resistance to tyranny, religious toleration, human dignity, natural rights, and benevolence—all of which helped form the warp and the woof of modern republicanism. Indeed, these influences on social, economic, and political theory were ubiquitous. Even the more "secular" ideas were often influenced by them. The attitudes, beliefs, the very character of the American Founders could not help but have been deeply affected by them, for these influences permeated the culture which spawned them and nurtured them. Thus, the American founders were more than "civic humanists." And while their vocabulary included terms that indicated a classical origin, these came to be transformed, in their thinking at least, to describe and justify a decidedly "modern" republican ideal.

In examining the ideas underlying the founding of the American republic, we have attempted to identify some of the conduits, by no means all of them, through which certain concepts, primarily that of "virtue," passed in metamorphosis and influenced the thinking and motivation of the American founders, and thus, modern republican ideology. Among the sources contemporary to the Founders that we cite, we place some emphasis on *The Federalist Papers. The Federalist Papers* are, of course, an indispensible source in understanding the ideas of the Framers. *The Federalist Papers*, however, were not a complete and comprehensive explanation of the theory of the Founding. They were, rather, short political essays, published in newspapers, that sought to convince the public that the Constitution should be ratified. Thus, Hamilton, Madison, and Jay, in writing the essays, did not describe in great detail what they meant by virtue or how it was to be provided. Their understanding of this central concept can be seen in other of their writings; *the idea of virtue was commonly understood and was not controversial.* Their essays concentrated on addressing concerns of excessive power of the central government, the protection of individual rights, the representation of states, and other aspects of the framing that were being criticized and challenged.

We also refer frequently to the writings of Alexis de Tocqueville, a French aristocrat who came to America in 1831 and for nine months investigated the beliefs and institutions of the American people and interviewed hundreds of them, including President Andrew Jackson. His interpretation of democracy in America was published in Paris in early 1835. In an amazingly short period of time, *Democracy in America* came to be acclaimed a masterpiece in France, England, and the United States. "Now, 150 years later, it still lays fair claim to being considered the most insightful book ever written about American society and politics."[46]

De Tocqueville wrote *Democracy in America* a generation after the ratification of the Constitution, yet he was as concerned with those historical events and ideas, which predated and influenced the basic concepts of the American republican democracy, as he was with current beliefs and institutions. He gives us a scholarly interpretation of forces in being during the time of his visit to the United States, yet with historical perspective. He is important to this volume since he deals with the beliefs and values of the American people over their history to and including his time. Their beliefs and values, their social and primary institutions, as well as their political institutions, are considered in some detail.

De Tocqueville believed that the religious beliefs that the Pilgrims and Puritans brought with them to the New World contributed significantly to the development and growth of democratic institutions. He found a working compatibility in much of modern Christian beliefs and modern republicanism and perceived the importance of "general" Christianity that mightily influenced the thinking and action of Americans. In contrast to some modern writers, de Tocqueville did not believe that public and private virtue ended with the establishment of the republic. His writings reflect the influence of the concepts of modern republicanism that had developed in the American system. Unlike *The Federalist Papers,* written in defense of the specific provisions of the Constitution, *Democracy in America* brought together the political thought of the founders into a coherent theory of what de Tocqueville believed they intended, along with how their system had functioned during its first few decades. De Tocqueville fills in the gaps of the *The Federalist Papers* and other writings and thereby provides a most useful analysis of the ideas underlying American republican government.

NOTES

1. Edmund Burke, *The Works of Edmund Burke,* Vol. 4 (Waltham, Mass.: Little, Brown, 1866), pp. 51–52.
2. Thomas Jefferson, *Notes on the State of Virginia,* ed., William Peden (Chapel Hill, N.C.: University of North Carolina Press, 1955), pp. 164–65.
3. Max Farrand, *Records of the Federal Convention of 1787* (New Haven, Conn.: Yale University Press, 1927), Vol. 1, p. 101.
4. *The Federalist,* No. 55.
5. *The Federalist,* No. 39.
6. Gordon S. Wood, *The Creation of the American Republic, 1776–1787* (Chapel Hill, N.C.: University of North Carolina Press, 1969), Chapter 3.
7. Garry Wills, *Explaining America: The Federalist* (Garden City, N.J.: Doubleday, 1981), Chapter 27.
8. Donald S. Lutz, "Bailyn, Wood, and Whig Political Theory," *The Political Science Reviewer,* Vol. 8 (Fall 1977), pp. 118–19.
9. *Ibid.,* pp. 188–89. Here Lutz refers to Wood's discussion in pp. 18–28, 53–65, and 70–75, of his *The Creation of the American Republic.*

10. Francis Grund, *Aristocracy in America* (reprinted in New York: Harper, 1959), pp. 212–13. We appreciate being introduced to Francis Grund's writing in Sydney Ahlstrom, "The Puritan Ethic and American Democracy," in George L. Hunt, ed., *Calvinism and the Political Order* (Philadelphia: Westminster, 1965). See also "The Americans in Their Moral, Social, and Political Relations," in Henry S. Commanger, ed., *America in Perspective* (New York: Random House, 1948).

11. See, generally, Dante Germino, "Carl J. Friedrich on Constitutionalism and the 'Great Tradition' of Political Theory," in J. Roland Pennock and John M. Chapman, *Constitutionalism* (New York: New York University Press, 1979), pp. 19–31; Paul Sigmund, "Carl Friedrich's Contribution to the Theory of Constitutionalism-Comparative Government," in Pennock and Chapman, pp. 32–46.

12. Clinton Rossiter, *The First American Revolution* (New York: Harcourt, Brace, 1956), p. 193; *The Political Thought of the American Revolution* (New York: Harcourt Brace, 1956), p. 195.

13. Cecilia M. Kenyon, "Constitutionalism in Revolutionary America," in Pennock and Chapman, *Constitutionalism*, p. 97.

14. *Ibid.*, p. 101.

15. Wood, *The Creation of the American Republic*, p. 52. See also pp. 474–75, 507–8, 543–45, 562–63, 606–15.

16. John Diggins, *The Lost Soul of American Politics* (New York: Basic, 1984), p. 12; "Republicanism and Progressionism," *American Quarterly*, Vol. 37 (Fall 1985), pp. 572–48.

17. J. G. A. Pocock, *The Machiavellian Moment* (Princeton, N.J.: Princeton University Press, 1975), pp. 520–26; "*The Machiavellian Moment* Revisted: A Study in History," *Journal of Modern History*, Vol. 53 (1981); pp. 49–72. "Virtue, Rights, and Manners: A Model for Historians of Political Thought," *Political Theory*, Vol. 9 (1981); pp. 353–68. See also J. H. Hexter, "Republic, Virtue, Liberty, and the Political Universe of J. G. A. Pocock," in J. H. Hexter, *On Historians* (Cambridge: Harvard University Press, 1979), pp. 252–303.

18. Diggins, *Lost Soul of American Politics*, p. 16. For a more in-depth study of this debate, see Isaac Kramnick, "Republican Revisionism Revisited," *American Historical Review*, Vol. 87 (June, 1982); Pocock, *The Machiavellian Moment*; Forest McDonald, *Novus Ordo Seclorum* (Lawrence, Kans: University Press of Kansas State, 1985); the essays in Robert Goldwin and William Schambra, *How Democratic is the Constitution?* (Washington, D.C.: American Enterprise Institute, 1980); and Robert H. Horwitz, ed., *The Moral Foundations of the American Republic* (Charlottesville: University Press of Virginia, 1986). Important essays on this subject may be found in Lance Banning, "Jeffersonian Ideology Revisited: Liberal and Classical Ideas in the New American Republic," and Joyce Appleby, "Republicanism in Old and New Contexts," *The William and Mary Quarterly*, Vol. XLIII (January 1986). Appleby also edited an informative special issue on "Republicanism in the History and Historiography of the United States in *American Quarterly*, Vol. 37 (Fall 1985).

19. Joseph Story, *Commentaries on the Constitution of the United States*, Vol. 2 (Boston: Little, Brown, 1858), pp. 666–67.

20. Bernard Bailyn, *The Ideological Origins of the American Revolution* (Cambridge, Mass.: Belknap, 1967); *Pamphlets of the American Revolution* (Cambridge, Mass.: Belknap, 1965); *The Origins of American Politics* (New York: Knopf, 1968). See analysis by Donald S. Lutz, "The Relative Influence of European Writers on Late Eighteenth-Century American Political Thought," *The American Political Science Review*, Vol. 78 (March, 1984); and Robert E. Shalhope, "Toward a Republican Synthesis: The Emergence of an Understanding of Republicanism in American Historigraphy," *William and Mary Quarterly*, Vol. 29 (January, 1972).

21. Bailyn, *Pamphlets of the American Revolution*, pp. 20–21.

22. Bailyn, *Ideological Origins of the American Revolution*, pp. 24, 26.

23. Bailyn, *Pamphlets of the American Revolution*, p. 22.
24. *The Federalist*, No. 37.
25. Bailyn, *Pamphlets of the American Revolution*, pp. 23–24.
26. *Ibid.*, p. 25.
27. Lutz, "Influence of European Writers," p. 193.
28. *Ibid.*, p. 26.
29. *Ibid.*, p. 27.
30. *Ibid.*
31. Bailyn, *Ideological Origins*, p. 34.
32. Bailyn, *Pamphlets of the American Revolution*, p. 30.
33. Kramnick, "Republican Revisionism Revisited," pp. 635–36.
34. *Ibid.*, p. 640.
35. *Ibid.*, pp. 644–46.
36. Caroline Robbins, *The Eighteenth Century Commonwealthman* (Cambridge: Harvard University Press, 1959). An analysis of the "Court" Whigs may be found in Reed Browning, *Political and Constitutional Ideas of the Court Whigs* (Baton Rouge: Louisiana State University Press, 1982). Browning's book demonstrates the differences between Whigs and Tories and the differences between Whig factions. See also Isaac Kramnick, *Bolingbroke and his Circle: The Politics of Nostalgia in the Age of Walpole* (Cambridge: Harvard University Press, 1968). Concerning the importance of new scholarship on republicanism, see Joyce Appleby, "Republicanism and Ideology," *American Quarterly*, pp. 461–73; "Republicanism in Old and New Contexts," pp. 20–34; Lance Banning, "Republican Ideology and the Triumph of the Constitution," *The William and Mary Quarterly*, Vol. 31 (1974); "Jeffersonian Ideology Revisited: Liberal and Classical Ideas in the New American Republic," pp. 3–19.
37. Gary Wills, *Inventing America* (New York: Vintage, 1979), and *Explaining America*. See also Douglass Adair, "That Politics May be Reduced to a Science: David Hume, James Madison, and the Tenth Federalist," *Huntington Library Quarterly*, Vol. 20 (1965–1967).
38. Pocock, *The Machiavellian Moment*.
39. Charles S. Hyneman and Donals S. Lutz, *American Political Writing During the Founding Era*, Volumes I and II (Indianapolis: Liberty, 1983).
40. Lutz, "European Writers and 18th Century American Political Thought," p. 192.
41. *Ibid.*, p. 196.
42. *Ibid.*, p. 196.
43. *Ibid.*, p. 190.
44. Lutz, "Bailyn, Wood, and Whig Political Theory," p. 135.
45. J. G. A. Pocock, "Virtue and Commerce in the Eighteenth Century," *Journal of Interdisciplinary History*, Vol. 3 (Summer, 1972), pp. 119–21.
46. Everett Carll Ladd, *The American Polity: The People and Their Government* (New York: Norton, 1985), see summary on p. 3–7.

2

The Metamorphosis of the Idea of Virtue

VIRTUE: AN ANCIENT CONCEPT

AT LEAST AS FAR BACK as the classical Greek and Roman philosophers, the relationship between republics and the ideal of *virtue* had been discussed, with the inference that some degree of civic virtue—that is, the sacrifice of self-interest for the good of the whole—was necessary for the health of the *polis*. The concept reemerged with some emphasis during the Middle Ages and in the period of the Renaissance and the Reformation, where it became the daily fare of both philosophers and revolutionaries, men of religion as well as spokesmen of the Enlightenment. During this period, virtue was infused with Christianity and began to emerge as integral to biblical moral theology.

The idea of covenant and personal calling, the acceptance of free will, and the gradual rejection of determinism, the acceptance of biblical ideals of faith, charity, benevolence, and a variety of other influences all helped shape ideas of private and public virtue and gave them a primary role as the precondition for popular government.

The Classical Concept of Virtue

In classical philosophy man was a *polis* animal. His virtue was acquired only within the confines of the well-ordered city. The "ancient moral virtue [was], at least in part, the *end* of the *polis*."[1] Plato saw the *polis* as, in effect, closed, because human and material resources were affected by a rationally determined hierarchy of values. State and society were viewed as one, and, hence, virtue was intimately related to government. Inherent in the classical philosophy was the assumption that either virtue or corruption was within the purview of public control. The republic made the virtuous individual and the virtuous individual made the republic. The citizen was taught to serve the state and to be a citizen of the state as determined by the character of the state. In a very real sense, man was seen as the creature of the state. Here the state could demand exclusive proprietorship on the energies and affections of its citizens. The individual citizen was to subliminate his self-interest to that of the state. There was little practical concern for individual rights or liberties; liberty was viewed as an opportunity for virtuous activity.[2] According to Professor Herbert J. Muller, "The Greeks never made a clear distinction between the state and society, or drew up bills of rights protecting 'the people' against the state, because the *polis* was virtually indistinguishable from society or the people, embracing all their major interests and constituting their highest interest. They were not so much citizens with abstract rights as members of a community with status, as in a family. . . . They made no clear distinction either between the ethical and the political, still less between things that are Caesar's and things that are God's."[3] This merging of the individual with the state removed him from what the late Professor Hannah Arendt called "some of the most essential characteristics of human life."[4] In referring to the Greek concept of man and the state, Franz Neumann adds: "It may be assumed that man, outside his sociopolitical existence, does not exist or is, at least, not considered relevant. Man has rights and duties not as an isolated individual, not prior to civil society, but only in and through it. . . . The power of the *Polis* is no external one confronting individual rights of the citizen. The rights of the citizens are rather rights of the *status activus*, expressing the identity between man and the State of which he is a member."[5]

Classical civic virtue, then, meant the patriotic subordination of one's personal interests to the common welfare. The public good was to transcend particular advantage. Inherent was a fear of self-interest, materialism, and corruption. "Discipline," "duty," "courage," "honor," and "manliness" were common expressions relating to civic virtue. Among the ancient "cardinal virtues" to which even the magistrates were encouraged to adhere, were "justice," "fortitude," "temperance," and "wisdom." Courage on the battlefield, moderation in physical appetites, reverence for law, and care for those who could not care for themselves were manifestations of civic virtue.

The Greek tradition, however, also included a concern for "moral virtue," which was to include, yet surpass, civic virtue. Aristotle's discussion of the man imbued with "greatness of soul" describes a personal virtue, one that extends beyond courage and duty to more private characteristics of artistic taste, conversation, and friendship. Ultimately, a life of virtue produces a life that subordinates human concerns to the divine. Thomas Pangle argues that this element of the Greek understanding of virtue has often been ignored, yet it was of primary importance for the assimilation of classical ideas by Christian political philosophers.[6]

VIRTUE AND RENAISSANCE HUMANISM

The idea of "virtue" was emphasized in earnest during the Renaissance, particularly among a priestly and scholarly group called the "Renaissance humanists." This is not to suggest that the concept of virtue was of no concern before or between the classical and the Renaissance periods. Thomas Aquinas, for example, the greatest of the Scholastics, wrote in the thirteenth Century of virtue and the common good. For him, governmental authority was limited to assuring peace and order so that human happiness could flourish. His *Summa Theologica* was an examination of Christian theological principles such as love and their importance for politics and government.

The Renaissance humanists, as Paul Oskar Kristeller has stated, were "the professional heirs and successors of the medieval rhetoricians, the so-called *dictatores*."[7] They are emphasized here because they became one of the main conduits through which the idea of virtue was passed on to continental Europe, England, and finally to America. And "Renaissance humanism" was not the only conduit through which classical virtue passed in metamorphosis to its modern republican connotation. There were many tributaries along the way. This particular channel, however, provides an important example of how "virtue" came to be transformed from its classical meaning to the interpretation that was espoused by Americans in search of a republic. This period is important to the study of virtue, for it was a time when the concept became particularly infused with biblical moral theology, thereby causing it to become an important ingredient in the development of modern republican thought. And, significantly, it was also used for some time, on the other hand, as a philosophical and theological resource to reinforce state absolutism in the West.[8]

Many humanists were so enamored with the concept that they looked primarily on the virtues of civic pride and patriotism to reinforce society rather than laws or effective institutions. These other props, they generally reasoned, would not be sufficient by themselves to maintain the necessary unity without civic virtue, which included a wide allegiance to the public weal. Patrizi, for example, in Book IV of his *The Founding of the Republic*, wrote that the foundation of stability and endurance in a political society was virtue.[9] By this he meant the absence of private ambition, the subservience of individual interest to those of the republic. He defined corruption as the failure to support the common good. He was endorsed by Machiavelli in his *The Discourses*. Here, the author of *The Prince*, who had concentrated on the qualities of leadership, now turned as well to common public spirit. In the preface to *The Discourses*, he discussed service to one's country in behalf of the public good, the *res publica*. Both Patrizi and Machiavelli looked to forms of political socialization to indoctrinate the people in civic virtue, such as education, parental guidance, and political participation.

Machiavelli rejected the incorporation of Christian virtues into the classical concept of virtue. He suggested that love and kindness, and honesty and justice might at times well conflict with the pursuit of the public common good. He reasoned that political affairs cannot be judged by Christian values.[10] Machiavelli, concluded Quentin Skinner, "sought to undermine the prevailing pieties" by "discussing the connections between the pursuit of *virtù* and the requirements of the Christian faith. This relationship was scarcely seen as problematic by the more orthodox defenders of republican liberty. While they agreed that any citizen who possesses the quality of *virtù* will be distinguished by his willingness to place the interests of his community above all other concerns, they never implied that this might lead to any conflicts with the requirements of virtue in the conventional Christian sense."[11]

Virtue and "Reason of State"

Other humanists, who, with Machiavelli, saw a possible conflict between *virtù* and biblical virtues, but who did not wish to give up what they believed to be the salutary effects of Christianity on the stability of society, tried to assuage the problem by seeking to legitimate state actions based on utilitarian considerations, as long as the "end" it sought was deemed virtuous. Under the concept of "reason of state" for example, the belief in the superiority of the state over all private rights was retained.[12] It was first widely used in the sixteenth and seventeenth centuries in order to rationalize the employment of ruthless political power. "'Reason of state' furnished a principle of action, a law of motion, to the state, based upon the rational faith that the state is the highest of all goods." This concept was combined with the term "policy," in its Machiavellian usage, to infer an expedient or a utilitarian action in behalf of the preservation of the state. This double standard of morals even infiltrated the religious conflicts of the time, including Calvin's political thought, where it was accepted that "policy," or "state prudence" in a good cause such as promoting the "true" religion, was permissible. Both leaders of the Reformation and the Counter-Reformation used this reasoning to bolster their legitimacy. And throughout, an integral part of "civil virtue" was the assumed unqualified support of the common good and the sacrifice of self-interest by the individual. It meant the triumph of utilitarian reason of the state over Christian morality.

For some time it was also assumed that the magistrates should be supported because they expressed the will of the state, which was the same as the will of God, thereby adding force to the "virtue" of "obedience." Here was a continued expression of the age-old obsession to preserve the community and provide for public order at all costs, which lasted well into the American colonial period. As John Winthrop insisted, "The care of the publique must oversway all private respects."[13]

In the sixteenth and seventeenth centuries there was an attempt to establish a marriage of Christian moral theology and the "reason of state," in effect, as Spengler put it, to unite Christ "the man of truth," with Pilate, "the man of reality."[14] In a somewhat modified form, it was used by constitutional theorists in an attempt to preserve the state. And certain divines taught the doctrine that "reason of state" was acceptable if "policy" was geared to righteous ends. Catholic Casuists, according to George Mosse, "attempted to put politics and morality into a positive relationship to Christianity"; and Protestant divines such as Perkins, Ames, and Winthrop attempted to harmonize the word of God with the idea of "reason of state." This all had the result of modifying the perceived limits of state power over the individual and worked to assuage and reduce the most extreme ideas of civic virtue concerning the obligation of the individual toward the state. At the same time, even when making expedient decisions—to be sure for a "righteous" reason—the expectation was that the magistrate would act virtuously.[15]

Virtue and the Legacy of Christian Humanism

During the Renaissance and prior to the Reformation, there had been a revival in the centers of learning and, among lay and priests alike in Italy, in the study of classical thought. New translations of the ancient Greek philosophers appeared and there was renewed interest in writings from the original Greek and a passion for Platonism and Neo-Platonism. This literary movement—*studia humanitatis*—ranged from rhetoric to moral philosophy.

During this period there was a renewed interest in the Scriptures, especially in their translation from the original Greek. More than one

scholar became convinced that mistranslations and misinterpreta-
tions of the Scriptures made from Latin were the cause of much
confusion and the prostitution of religious doctrine. There developed
a substantial feeling that the Scholastics had been frustrated in their
search for truth because of this, and there was a growing restlessness
to get back to original sources, both philosophical and religious, to
replace Scholastic dialectic disputations with simple truths. The metamorphosis of the concept of virtue was directly related to the increased interest in and the availability of translations, printings, and
commentaries of Greek philosophy and the Bible. It was not at all
uncommon, for instance, to compare Plato's ideal of the "soul"
favorably with that of the Scriptures. And, it became commonplace to
embellish the ideal of classical virtue with deep spiritual overtones
and merge it with biblical concepts of virtue.

Furthermore, it was but natural that these Humanists would deal
with the term "virtue," since they were reformers. They emphasized
a mission of practical activity not only to revivify individual existence,
but to reform the Christian community as well. To these reformers
their task, while spiritual, was related to practical life, where, as
Martin Fleisher points out, "the new man and the new society are
inextricably interwoven." Their "Christian vocation called all men to
dedicate themselves to reform and perfection of the Christian community." During the period that immediately preceded the virtual
breakdown of Christian concord in Western Europe, they "were
actively engaged in challenging many of the existing beliefs and
actual practices of their civilization as they sought to reform and
revitalize the Christian commonwealth. They shared with many a
fellow Christian humanist a reasonable hope that such a campaign
might very well succeed in bringing the life of the community closer
to the teachings of Christ."[16]

The metamorphosis of the concept of virtue among the Renaissance humanists merged certain aspects of classical thought with
what had become almost a "new" Christianity, produced from newly
translated copies of, and commentaries on, the Bible. An important
ingredient in this metamorphosis was the development of a "moral
theology" that further impregnated virtue with spiritual and moral
overtones while superimposing God as the ultimate entity to which
man was responsible. The advocates of this blending of philosophy
with theology are sometimes called "Christian humanists," a term
which Skinner finds peculiar, since "all the humanists were of course
Christian, with the possible exception of Machiavelli."[17] Differentiation
among the Renaissance humanists in this regard was, perhaps,
simply a matter of the degree to which they emphasized the "Christian virtues." Robert L. Cord, in historical perspective, refers to those

of the humanist tradition down through the ages as "theistic" humanists on the one hand, and "secular" humanists on the other.[18]

The Italian Connection

The marriage of the classical and the biblical can clearly be seen in the writings of Francesco Petrarch (1304–1374), who, according to Kristeller, was the "first great representative" of Renaissance humanism, and "probably the earliest humanist who had significant impact on the thought of his time."[19] In his writings, one finds reference to and the influence of Seneca, Cicero, and especially Plato. At the same time, however, Petrarch, typical of the Renaissance humanists, was a devout Christian, and there was little doubt where his primary allegiance rested. "I do not adore Aristotle," he remarked, "but I have another whom to adore. He does not promise me empty and frivolous conjectures of deceitful things which are of use for nothing and not supported by any foundation. He promises me the knowledge of Himself. . . . It is He in whom I can trust, whom I must adore."[20] Petrarch insisted that the "highest part" of his "heart" was "with Christ."[21] He agreed, however, with Augustine in his *City of God* that Plato was the premier of the ancient philosophers, that if he had been a contemporary of Christianity he would have become a Christian. What is more, "Cicero himself would have been a Christian if he had been able to see Christ and to comprehend His doctrine."[22]

In Petrarch can be seen an example of the metamorphosis in the philosophy of virtue, a concept that was seen—at least as early as the Greek philosophers—as fundamental to a healthy community. In theory, virtue restrained men's passions, on the one hand, so that peace and cooperation might preserve the community. On the other hand, virtue promoted the sacrifice of self-interest for that of the community, thus sparing it from ruinous factious conflicts and class antagonism. The Renaissance humanists emphasized a vital yet often overlooked factor (except by a few others such as Locke and de Tocqueville) that the mere philosophical instruction in virtue as vital to the public good was not sufficiently motivating to men generally over time. Nor did appeal to reason, by itself, move men, in the face of moral conflict or adversity, to persevere in virtuous behavior. The ideal of virtue, to be effective over time, must be *internalized*. It is not enough to understand virtue; it must also be *loved*. A primary motivation for virtue, then, was *spiritual* as well as intellectual, sponsored by faith as well as by philosophical reasonableness or dialectic disputation. And, these early humanists conceded, the foremost key to unlocking the door leading to this spiritual reaffirmation of virtue was Christian faith.

While Petrarch acknowledged that Aristotle, for instance, had written well of virtue, he contended that the Greek philosopher's treatises on the subject lacked the authority to inspire. "I see virtue, and all that is peculiar to vice as well as to virtue, egregiously defined and distinguished by him and treated with penetrating insight. When I learn all this, I know a little bit more than I knew before, *but mind and will remain the same as they were, and I myself remain the same. It is one thing to know, another to love; one thing to understand, another to will. He teaches what virtue is, I do not deny that; but his lesson lacks the words that sting and set afire and urge toward love of virtue and hatred of vice or, at any rate, does not have enough of such power.*"[23] According to Petrarch, the love of virtue stems primarily from the love of God, and is expressed in its primary form through virtuous behavior: "What is the use of knowing what virtue is if it is not loved . . . this cannot be achieved outside the doctrine of Christ and without His help." The "true and unique source" of goodness and wisdom "has its origin in heaven, the source of the water that springs up in eternal life . . . for those to whom more is not granted, it is sufficient to know God and virtue so far as to know that He is the most lucid, the most fragrant, the most delectable, the inexhaustible source of all that is good, from which, through which, and in which we are as good as we are, and to know that virtue is the best thing next to God Himself. When we know this, we shall love Him for His sake with our heart and marrows, and virtue we shall love for His sake too. We shall revere Him as the unique author of life; virtue we shall cultivate as its foremost adornment."[24] Here was suggested a personal and powerful motivation to practice virtue that transcended the idea of political socialization.

Another Renaissance humanist who made an impact on the metamorphosis of virtue was the celebrated Marsilio Ficino (1433–1499).[25] Ficino emphasized the immortality of the soul[26] and imposed on the classical concept of virtue the ideal of Christian morality as gleaned from the Scriptures. He became an important proponent of what became known as biblical "moral theology." Integral to his philosophy of virtue, was love—love of God and one's fellow man.

Ficino's concern with the concept of virtue in terms of a deep spiritual and emotive experience, combined with secular learning, was typical of his time. "There is nothing more wonderful nor more lovely," he wrote to the orator Marco Aurelio, "than learning united with virtue. . . . When singular . . . learning is united with surpassing virtue, from this conjunction, as if of the Sun and Jupiter, such splendour bursts forth from the learning and such fire from the virtue that, by these rays and flames which spread from the rising to the setting sun, the minds of even the most distant peoples are aroused and kindled, gently enticed and violently seized."[27]

To Ficino, in his amalgamation of classical and biblical thought, virtue was "a quality of the soul." Among its expressions were "wisdom," "contemplation of the divine," "justice," "courage," "temperance," and "prudence." These are virtues, according to Ficino, "to the extent they are practiced by us for the sake of worshipping, imitating, and realizing God. The worship of God is therefore the virtue of virtues. But the reward of the virtues is the realization of God."[28]

Virtue, according to Ficino, was gained as a result of searching for God. "Those men seek God the most direct way," he wrote, "who first of all cut back the immoderate desires of the soul through the civil virtues. They then cut them back to the quick by the purgatorial virtues. Thus cleansed, in the third stage they root them out with all their might through the virtues that belong to the purified soul. When these desires have been rooted out, as far as is humanly possible, such men finally are formed by the model virtues which are in God."[29] Ficino did not relate "humanitas" merely to the studies of Greek and Latin, but, like other humanists of the time, included as well "humaneness." To him a primary "virtue" was "kindness."[30] "Individual men, formed by one idea in the same image," he continued, "are one man. It is for this reason, I think, that of all the virtues, wise men named only one after man himself: that is humanity, which loves and cares for all men as though they were brothers, born in a long succession of one father." The "humane man," according to Ficino, is one who will "persevere in the service of humanity."[31] Here was a philosophy of unity among men and civic virtue fully impregnated with biblical moral theology.

Ficino's definition of virtue included charity and divine love, not only as a universal doctrine, but as the crucial link to bind men in social union; a union of spiritual brotherhood and friendship made possible by the love of God, "kindled by the breath of divine spirit."[32] Here, he believed, was the answer to unity and cooperation among men. According to Kristeller, this theology had an unmeasurable impact on the philosophy of human dignity and "led to the conscious awareness of a solidarity of all men which imposed definite moral and intellectual obligations upon each individual."[33] As with the ancient philosophers, Ficino was concerned with the means of promoting unity in society through a virtuous citizenry and virtuous leaders: "It is the duty of the citizen to consider the state as a single being formed of its citizens who are the parts; and that the parts should serve the whole, not the whole the parts. For when the profit of the part alone is sought, there is no profit at all for either part or whole. When, however, the good of the whole is sought, the good of both is assured. . . . Let each man love and reverence his country as he would the founder of his family. Let the ordinary citizen obey the ancient, well-tried laws, just as he would obey God, for such laws are not established without God."[34]

Within this admonition, however, is the warning that the magistrate, too, has responsibilities to act virtuously. If he does not, God will hold him accountable: "Let the magistrate remember that he is subject to the laws in just the same way as the ordinary citizen is subject to the magistrate. Let him understand that when he is passing judgment he is himself being judged by God. . . . [H]e should know that Heaven's highest place is reserved for the man who has done his best to model his earthly country on the heavenly one. For nothing pleases the universal ruler of the world more than the universal good."[35]

Thus, Ficino, in his interpretation of virtue, contributed to the idea that there were certain expectations that one could reasonably assume from magistrates and rulers. It would not be long before the idea would inspire the passion of modern revolutionary idealists and some of the advocates of moral theology and philosophy that rulers who prostituted their lawmaking powers could be deposed, even destroyed.

The Oxford Circle

One of the most important factors relating to the metamorphosis of the concept of virtue was the transference of Renaissance humanist thought from Italy to other countries of Europe, particularly to England. During the fifteenth and sixteenth centuries, numerous Oxford students, along with many of their counterparts on the Continent, went to Italy to study. A large number of Englishmen received their degrees in canon law in Italy, especially at Bologna, Padua, and Florence. Others came to Italy to partake of the "new learning" offered in Ficino's "Platonic Academy" and elsewhere. An important group of Oxford scholars who were to be singularly influenced by Renaissance humanism were John Colet (ca. 1466–1519), Thomas Linacre (ca. 1460–1545), William Grocyn (ca. 1466–1519), and Thomas More (1487–1535). Colet, Linacre, and Grocyn had studied in Italy and were significantly responsible for bringing the "new learning" to Oxford.[36] These scholars, together with the celebrated Thomas More and William Lily (Grocyn's godson, who had also studied Latin and Greek in Italy), formed a brilliant philosophical school, the "Oxford Circle," its members known as the "Oxford Reformers."[37] The Oxford Circle was joined by Desiderius Erasmus who later became an important conduit through which the "new learning" and the spirit of reform gained wide recognition, not only at Oxford, but at Cambridge and throughout Western Europe.[38] They were in the vanguard of the English Renaissance.

The scholars of the Oxford Circle, like their humanist forebears, were enamored with Greek theory and theology, especially Platonism, while reserving their primary theological devotion to Christianity. They were concerned with the "soul," with moral theology, and with virtue. "Platonism," Sears Jayne insists, "was only a tributary to the main stream of Colet's thought."[39] His interpretation of virtue advocated the rejection of all "ungodliness" and "unrighteousness," and was amply enriched with moral theology, including abstinence from "dishonesty," "lust," "robbery," "envy," "deceit," "maliciousness," "covetousness," "gluttony," "fornication," "perverseness;" men were encouraged to cease being "proud," "boasters," "covenant-breakers," "unmerciful," and "backbiters."[40] Typical of the Renaissance humanists, Colet taught that men should become an imitation of Christ and should love one another. True works were demonstrated by "steadfast goodness," where one "acts well to the utmost of his power, everywhere and at all times, with all and towards all."[41] As far as Colet was concerned, righteousness and brotherly love were vital political as well as moral principles, since their adherence purified the nature of man from "multiplicity" to "simplicity," unity, and peace.[42] To the "cardinal virtues," Colet added the Pauline trilogy of "Hope, Faith, and Charity," or Love.[43] To these humanists, wrote Skinner, "no one can be counted a man of true *virtùs* unless he displays all the leading Christian virtues as well as the 'cardinal' virtues singled out by the moralists of antiquity."[44]

Colet's moral theology of virtue dealt not only with the renovation of men's souls but with that of society in general. As Harbison put it, "John Colet was able to travel to the New Athens (in Italy) and returned fired with the call to build the New Jerusalem in England."[45] He dealt with a timeless problem—that of the conflict between private interest and communal order. Indeed, the problem of maintaining order in the nation or the community over time had been the *bête noire* of the early republics. Interest and faction had time and again broken the tender strands of unity, leading to class conflict, civil war, and dissolution. Even the apparently wisest laws seemed impotent to cement different classes or interests in united effort over time. The story of the Italian republics portrays a similar sequence.

Colet was convinced that since people did not possess, "of their own proper nature," a "means" to "hold together in firm and lasting union," it followed that "they must be made to approximate by some power external to, and higher than, themselves; in which, as in a bond that holds the whole body together, the members of the society may make common confederation." The only alternative to order established by incessant force and coercion becomes spiritual—*the uniting of souls*. The uniting power of which Colet spoke to his Oxford audiences "will bear the same relation to the human commonwealth, that the soul does to the body. If, then, mankind are to be arranged together in order, and keep their places in the beauty of regularity, there must needs be some power at work among them, transcending the nature of man; a power which unites, stays, and holds together. It must unite their division; stay their drifting nature, and rapid propensity to evil; and, by its simple harmony, hold together the discordant minds and wills of men."[46]

Colet's response to the problem directly and indirectly inspired revolutionaries both in England and America, and which Commonwealthmen and Republicans, and philosophers such as de Tocqueville, declared emphatically was the foundation of a happy society. "Now what is this power that compels men thus to assemble and confederate together, but the Spirit that is above them? It is this which gathers them together, that by its inspiration they may draw breath again, and be united in the bond of common aspirations: the Spirit of God accomplishing, what human nature failed to do, the arranging of men in fair order in a commonwealth." This "Holy Spirit" among men is a "life-giving, uniting," and "connecting power . . . whose property it is to bind together, in one framework of citizenship, different men and opposite minds."[47] In effect, Colet believed that this power, operational among believing men, was the only true and lasting source of unity in freedom.

Sir Thomas More, along with Colet and others, represented a continuing emphasis on the idea of a Christian commonwealth. Like the Greeks of old, they believed that the foundation of a commonwealth or a republic was civic virtue (now reinforced with biblical virtue). Without the undercarriage of religion forwarding a universal and cementing belief—a civil religion—unity within the political and social order would naturally decay, since each part would then go its own way.[48] They had come to the conclusion that the "city upon a hill" required a certain kind of people—a virtuous people—and that the moral theology of Christianity best provided the fodder to create such exceptional and virtuous citizens. Generations later, James Madison and Alexis de Tocqueville were to come to the same conclusion. And, while not the first, More, in his mythical *Utopia*, also advocated, as Madison was later to do in a different manner, that in order to preserve virtue, certain institutional arrangements were also essential.

Both More and Machiavelli, each in his own way and interpretation, noted virtue as essential to the perpetuation of a commonwealth. J. H. Hexter's analysis of the two works is interesting. According to Hexter, when Machiavelli uses the term in relation to what the prince needs to acquire or hold on to *lo stato*,[49] he was not contemplating moral virtues or goodness. "The impulsions to which *virtù* respond in *Il Principe* emanate from *lo stato* and the military and political means necessary to its appropriation and exploitation."[50] To Machiavelli, rule and order were paramount, and virtue, or civic virtue, a tool to be used in whatever manner necessary to legitimate *lo stato*. However, as Hexter maintains, Machiavelli had dislocated virtue, and reason, and nature from any relation to each other.[51] In the final analysis, *The Prince* "has nothing whatever to do with justice but only with what 'it is necessary for a prince wanting to maintain himself' to do."[52] "*Stato* has here altered the orbit of the most ordinary of all words used for discriminating between right and wrong."[53]

More, on the other hand, believed that virtues, such as justice, had been perverted as a mask to protect the self-interest of the rich and powerful; and that majesty, splendor, and glory were expropriated terms. As far as More was concerned, the greatest sin of the English aristocracy was pride—the desire to rise above and dominate others. "Pride," he warned, "becomes a nursing mother of ambition, avarice, faction and discord."[54] Thus, both More and Machiavelli saw a society without justice, and from that basis followed divergent paths—More in his *Utopia* rejecting the situation as fraudulent, and Machiavelli in his *The Prince* advocating the use of the hierarchy and prerogatives by the prince to gain and/or to maintain rulership over the commonwealth.

More believed that man's highest good, individually and collectively, was attainable only through the practice of virtue. To him the model of virtue was Christ, and men became virtuous to the extent that they followed his example. Typical of Christian Humanists, More added faith, hope, and charity, or love, to the cardinal virtues of temperance, courage, wisdom, and justice. He made clear in the *Utopia* that he interpreted humanism to mean humane.

Though More believed that virtuous behavior was an expression of reason, that reason was tied to two important beliefs that energized the doctrine of virtue: the immortal soul, and judgment.[55] These beliefs made virtue something more than reasonable behavior dictated by the nature of things. Virtue's source was God, the creator of nature and man. Man's behavior, then, carried with it a heavier meaning and motivation—eternal reward and punishment. More's Utopians, as had Plato, refuted men who advocated that the gods did not exist; they believed that divine retribution was essential to assure appropriate human deportment. On the other hand, the greatest pleasure comes from the "recollection of a well-spent life and the sure hope of happiness to come."[56] "Mental pleasures" for the most part "arise from the practice of the virtues and the consciousness of a good life."[57] And according to More, "religion easily brings this home to a mind which really asserts—God repays, in place of a brief and tiny pleasure, immense and never-ending gladness." More's Utopians "maintain, having carefully considered and weighed the matter, that all our actions, and even the very virtues exercised in them, look at last to pleasure as their end and happiness."[58]

Generations after More, John Adams and others saw the desire to be respected as a restraint on man's corrupt behavior as well as a motivation to act nobly and virtuously.[59] In *Utopia*, Thomas More wrote of the same phenomenon: "Remembrance of the love and good will of those whom you have benefited gives the mind a greater amount of pleasure than the bodily pleasure which you have foregone would have afforded."[60] The people of More's fictional *Utopia* not only attempt to "discourage crime by punishment," but "offer honors to invite men to virtue. Hence, to great men who have done conspicuous service to their country they set up in the marketplace statues to stand as a record of noble exploits and, at the same time, to have the glory of their forefathers serve their descendants as a spur and stimulus to virtue."[61] Honor was to be paid to the virtuous dead. There is significant stress on honor in Book II of Utopia. Here it is defined and expressed as the reward of virtue rather than in terms of high birth and wealth or military exploits which was common in Europe.[62]

From Colet, More, Erasmus, and others, the "Christianized" concept of virtue made its way as the companion to the struggle for reform in England.[63] Its impact germinated from many sources. Oxford, and especially Cambridge, produced scholars who were concerned with what they felt to be a lack of virtue in society and were much taken with the idea of a republic—a virtuous commonwealth. During the reign of Edward VI, there arose a radical group of "Commonwealthmen," who were characterized by angry criticism of existing society. Their views paralleled the sermons of an equal number of radical divines. One of the foremost of these social critics was Hugh Latimer (ca. 1485–1555), who was one of the primary inspirations behind the Commonwealth movement as a whole. Some of the most influential of his younger disciples were Thomas Bacon (1512–1567) and Thomas Lever (1521–1577), who joined Latimer while they were students at St. John's College, Cambridge. Other scholars who were influenced by humanism were John Fisher, Robert Crowley, and Sir Thomas Smith, who was Professor of Greek at Cambridge. These men sought social harmony in the tradition of Plato with the moral theology of Christianity. Their great concern, stated Skinner, was "for the protection of the common good against the encroachments of an uncaring [unvirtuous] individualism."[64] They denounced covetousness and selfishness in terms reminiscent of More's *Utopia*.

Like More, some of the prominent humanists became advisors to princes, where they advocated the cardinal virtues and such "princely virtues" as liberality, clemency, and honesty. A number of printed works appeared that encouraged virtue in the princes.[65] Budé, in his *Education of the Prince*, associated honor with morality,[66] and Erasmus, in his *The Education of a Christian Prince*, wrote that the true Christian is "the man who has embraced Christ in the innermost feelings of his heart, and who emulates Him by his pious deeds." This admonition to piety was directed toward both the ruler and those "[c]losest to him, . . . the magistrates, who obey in part and rule in part." These advisors should be "men of the best character and with the greatest interest in the public welfare." Erasmus sought a pattern of government taken from the "one Master of Christian men. . . . who alone is in all ways to be imitated. It is proper enough to gather from others whatever virtues they have; but in Him is the perfect example of all virtue and wisdom."[67] According to Professor Skinner, "Whether or not they couched their advice in the form of answers to specific social and political grievances, there was widespread agreement amongst the northern humanists about the nature of the advice to be given to their rulers and magistrates. They almost invariably focused on the claim that the key to political success lies in the promotion of the virtues. As with their *quattrocento* predecessors, their basic demand was not so much for a reformation of institutions, but rather for a change of heart. However, among the most radical of these theorists, especially in England," were those who "insisted on the need for the whole body of the citizens to acquire and practice the virtues as a precondition of attaining a 'well-ordered' commonwealth."[68]

In these years, pregnant with the growth of both intellectual and spiritual discovery, the idea of an ordered commonwealth was an important subject upon which men debated. While some advocated, as had some Scholastics, that the primary element in an ordered community was the proper institutions, others claimed that the most important factor was virtue in the magistrates, other than the virtue required of the citizens. In his search for a republic, James Madison incorporated all three ideas.[69]

In a very real sense, humanists such as Colet, Erasmus, More, and Latimer proved to be among the forerunners of the Reformation and the Commonwealth movement in England, even though More, in his support of a unified "Christendom" in Europe, may have been opposed to the results. They contributed, both directly and indirectly, to the "Christenized" concept of virtue which, with the help of the science of printing, spread throughout England, to its institutions of learning, to its clergy, and to its people; where, along with the growth of moral theology, it was caught up with such concepts as "covenant," "commonwealth," and "calling," concepts that were so vital to English colonization in America.

VIRTUE, FREEDOM, AND COVENANT

Important to the evolution of the idea of virtue was acceptance in Christianity of the free will of the individual and the rejection of determinism. Individuals could covenant with god, thus exercising their own free will as well as binding God to an agreement they voluntarily initiated. Such freedom was constrained by the notion of the calling, and moral theology provided guidelines for individual behavior that encouraged individual growth and self-betterment and recognized the role of self-interest in human life. Personal virtue, in all aspects of life was a fundamental expectation.

At least since the English priest Pelagias challenged St. Augustine's doctrine of predestination with his doctrine of freedom of will, which portrayed man as an autonomous human being with a substantial portion of freedom of choice and action, men have sought to reconcile what appeared to be fundamental contradictions in beliefs concerning God and the world about them.[70] Some claimed that the concept of an omnipotent, omniscient God and that of man's free agency were contradictory. Others held that faith in the "mechanistic" view of science, precluded the idea of men as self-determining organisms able to influence their environments. Still others claimed the irreconcilability of philosophical liberty and necessity, or political liberty and order—philosophical concepts that engendered conflicting views on man and government between Locke and Hobbes.

The debate over determinism and freedom of the will continued for centuries within the Church, and must be seen as contributory to the modern development of the ideology of freedom. While Luther and Calvin adopted Augustinian predestination, more than a few Scholastics and priests moved steadily toward a more pronounced doctrine of freedom of the will. From Holland, Remonstrants, under the influence of the Dutch theologican Arminius (1560–1609),[71] were planting seeds for freedom of the will in Protestantism, while momentarily failing to alter strict Calvinism. Nevertheless, what came to be known as "Latitudinarians" in Holland and England, carried the banner future generations would mold into freedom of choice and conscience—free will and toleration. Before religious establishments in America had eschewed determinism, or had allowed the doctrine to die a silent death; before religious pluralism and toleration there had become the final stepping-stones to separation of church and state, Latitudinarianism was leading the Anglican Church toward increased toleration and amenability with the doctrine of free will. More than once, though it may have been primarily to promote peace and progress in the American colonies, England reprimanded certain of her colonies in America for their lack of toleration. Usually, though not always in individual cases, the Latitudinarian attitude was accompanied by strong beliefs in freedom of will.

One of the most important concepts to come from the Judeo-Christian tradition was the covenant. According to Milton R. Konvitz, "It is one of the most pervasive ideas of the Bible, and is one that has cut deeply into American political thought and institutions."[72] The ideal of the conditional covenant performed a number of valuable services for modern Christianity. One of the most important of these was its use as a vehicle to bury or mute the doctrine of determinism. For if man could freely covenant with God and gain blessings conditioned upon his obedience and good behavior, then the existence of free will was clearly implied. To be sure, while a number of the great Protestant spokesmen attempted to rationalize the incongruity between determinism and the covenant, the conditional covenant based on man's free agency was destined to triumph. And the concept of modern virtue, coalescing with moral theology, gave the ideal support. The indication became unmistakable that man was clearly involved in the process of his own salvation. He had freedom to choose the moral path or travel the dark road of depravity. Of his own free will, he could covenant with God, as the people of the Old Testament, and serve him, or he could reject God, and therefore forfeit the gift. But the reception or the forfeiture of the gift was not completely out of his hands. He was not unalterably at the mercy of the Fates. The doctrine of freedom of the will, combined with biblical moral theology and the concept of covenant, implied that man was *capable* of choosing to be virtuous, and what is more, that he *ought* to do so.

Both the Pilgrims and the Puritans placed great emphasis on the concept of the covenant. Catalysts to the development of covenant or federal theology were highly respected theologians such as Richard Baxter, William Perkins, John Preston, and William Ames, some of whom were more widely quoted and read in the American colonies than were either Luther or Calvin. According to Konvitz, "the word 'federal' comes from the latin word foedus, which means covenant or compact—from which we get the word 'federal,' meaning a league or an association, an organization that flows out of a covenant."[73]

Federal theology taught that man, by the use of his free will, was capable of both freedom and self-restraint, and that without sacrificing his rights or personhood, could covenant to practice civic and personal virtue, the adherence to which would insure not only his salvation, but make community and self-government possible. As Konvitz puts it, "Covenant or federal theology was based on an effort to establish a ground for the moral and the political obedience of citizens, as well as the basis for the possibility of salvation. The Puritan theologians found the essence of covenant in the idea of a voluntary engagement, such as an engagement made between businessmen, like a bond or a mortgage, an agreement binding two parties. The covenant, in the Bible, brought God and man together within a single order." Perry Miller concurs. "The covenant was a gift from God, yet it entailed responsibility on Him as well as upon men. . . . In the Covenant, He is ruled by a law, constrained to be moral, committed to sweet reasonableness."[74]

There is no doubt that this combined metamorphosis of covenant theology and virtue contributed meaningfully to the growth of freedom and free institutions in America especially. "Now, this daring idea of a covenant between a deity and a people," adds Konvitz, "is unknown in other religions and cultures; it is a special aspect of the religion of Israel. It was taken over by Christianity and adapted to its own theological needs, and it became especially prominent as a feature of Protestant thought, for the Reformation placed the bible at the center of Christian theology."[75] Too, the Mosaic covenant, which has been so important to the Hebraic-Christian tradition, implied obligations and restraints upon the leadership of the people. It is significant that the Law of Moses obliges local judges to administer their function with justice, but specifies no other requirements. However, there are included a great number of obligations and restraints applicable to the national rulers.

In the sphere of the religious, the ideal of covenant led to Congregationalism. Therefore, churches in New England became voluntary Christian societies made up of people who shared common beliefs as covenanting congregants. "What held them together," writes Dâniel Boorstin, "was no unified administrative structure, but a common quest, a common way of living."[76] On the other hand, Konvitz insists that an "even more important consequence of the idea of covenant was its obvious relevance to political life. Just as the church is created by covenanters, so, too, the political order comes into existence as the voluntary creation of covenanting members of society. Thus, in 1620, the Pilgrims aboard their sailing vessel on their way to America entered into a covenant, known as the Mayflower Compact, in which they stated: 'We whose names are underwritten . . . Do by these Presents, solemnly and mutually in the presence of God and one another, covenant and combine ourselves together into a civil Body Politick." Konvitz calls this preamble "an extraordinary statement . . . but it was the most natural thing for the Pilgrims to do, for it was a direct and an unavoidable consequence of their invincible belief in their covenant theology." Then he asks, "how else can human beings limit their own freedom of action but by freely entering into a covenant among themselves?"[77]

After having been banished from Massachusetts, Roger Williams and his followers established the *Providence Agreement,* a form of covenant that also covered civil government. In 1639, the *Fundamental Orders of Connecticut* established a "Public State or Commonwealth." From there, charters and compacts and later constitutions became commonplace.

It should not be supposed, however, that the direct impact of the Judeo-Christian concept of covenant was the only influence on the penchant for Americans to make political and economic relationships contractual. Written and unwritten contracts and agreements had been used in commerce in southern Europe at least since the fourteenth century, and became an integral part of the growth of commerce. In the Middle Ages, examples can be found of covenantial agreements between members in communal or military groups, as well as in feudal arrangements. When the English separatists put into effect the Mayflower Compact, and when England used corporate charters to establish colonies in America, their methods were not without precedence. There was, for example, "a precedence for them which goes back to the Mediterranean colonies at the end of the Middle Ages, long before the appearance of Protestantism."[78] In contemplating the impact of contracts and covenants on the Western world, however, the vital influence of the biblical covenant should not be overlooked.

The Evolution of Puritanism

The seventeenth century in England has been called a "spiritual infatuated age,"[79] a crucial age which set in motion forces that were to profoundly affect events in the coming generations, both in England and in the New World. During this period the church and the university, Christianity and humanism, influenced, stimulated, and engendered great changes in government and society. The metamorphosis of Puritanism was to lead a peculiar form of nation-building based on the dream of a Christian commonwealth in the memory of ancient Israel, a commonwealth based upon covenant, the virtue of its citizens, and the directing hand of God. Therefore, the events of the seventeenth century, which were related to this Puritan metamorphosis, become important to our understanding of what happened both in England and America in that century, and in the following century.

Puritanism had grown steadily in both size and influence during the Elizabethan reign as religious unity and expression crumbled during the Reformation. By the seventeenth century in England, several divergent strains had become predominant. While the strict Anglicans sought to preserve forms and rituals and the Episcopal form of government, the Puritans placed the authority of religion in the Scriptures and supported the Presbyterian form of church organization as the more democratic.[80] Some Anglicans, characterized by such as Launcelot Andrews, Richard Hooker, and John Cosins, shared a fundamental difference with the Puritans—the doctrine of divine grace. While the Puritans at first preached irresistable grace and predestination, most Anglican divines sooner or later came to believe that man could participate in his own salvation, an important prerequisite for republican government, and an ideal which would penetrate Puritanism as well.

A strong intellectual, as well as a spiritual, strain of Puritanism became connected with the Cambridge Colleges, so much so that Cambridge became singularly important in the movement and metamorphosis of Puritanism. From there, both in terms of doctrine and personnel, Cambridge contributed, to a significant degree, to the religious, the moral, and eventually the political and economic thought of the Puritan movement in the American colonies. In the early years of the colonies, it was primarily outstanding divines and intellects from Cambridge who were most read and whose precepts were most advocated and repeated. The Cambridge scholars, influenced by John Fisher, Erasmus (who taught there from 1511 to 1514), and others of the tradition of "Christian humanism," turned more to the spiritual content of religion than to its formalism, and pursued a broad study of history and other disciplines.[81]

By the time of Elizabeth, not only was the Reformation tradition well established at Cambridge, the Puritan spirit there was vital and evangelical. "If to the Cambridge of Cranmer, Latimer, Ridgley, and Tyndale belongs the high honor of having first recognized and promulgated in England the doctrines of the Reformation, to the Cambridge of the Pilkingtons, Beaumont, and Cartwright belongs the more equivocal distinction of having educated our earlier Puritanism and given shelter to the principle of dissent."[82]

An important milestone in the growing Puritan trend at Cambridge was the foundation of Emmanuel College in 1584. Sir William Mildmay, who founded the college, remarked that he had but "set an acorn," and that "God alone knew what would be the fruit thereof when it became an oak."[83] He had been educated at Christ's College at Cambridge when it had been a Puritan stronghold. The first master of Emmanuel was Lawrence Chaderton, to be followed by John Preston, "one of the moving spirits of the time," who "thundered out his Calvinist message to king, common lawyer, student, parliamentarian, and whoever would harken." He also helped nudge John Cotton into the ministry, "a happening of considerable importance for the intellectual history of colonial America."[84] Chaderton was the tutor of William Perkins, "who became one of the leading lights among Puritan divines, and whose evangelical fervor is said to have been responsible for the notable crop of excellent preachers at Cambridge. This was 'Painful' Perkins, whose works were more highly esteemed by the New England Puritans than those of any other modern theologian, excepting Perkins' pupil, William Ames."[85] Perkins, Ames, and Richard Sibbes were foremost among those who promoted a full-blown moral theology by their Protestant casuistry. They helped in a significant way to assure that the emphases on biblical virtues in human conduct was a main theme in Puritan doctrine.

Indeed, Emmanuel College, through its alumni and its doctrinal impact, was to be of no small import to the New England colonies in America. Thomas Ball, in his "Life of Preston," depicted New England as a "new plantation" emerging from the Emmanuel oak. And Cotton Mather wrote that "If New-England hath been in some respect *Immanuel's Land*, it is well; but this I am sure of, *Immanuel College* contributed more than a little to make it so."[86] Morison's research indicates that in those early years no less than thirty-three of the university immigrants to New England were connected with Emmanuel and, according to Morison, the first governing body of the Bay Colony included two Emmanuel men, Isaac Johnson and Simon Bradstreet.[87]

Three of Emmanuel's own—John Cotton, Thomas Hooker, and Thomas Shepard—were to make outstanding contributions to early New England Puritanism. These Emmanuel graduates, writes Professor Morison, printed their stamp "indelibly upon New England."[88] "Through the pulpit and the press," concurs J. Rodney Fulcher, "they expounded the tenets of the 'covenant theology,' which gave systematic expression to their religious faith, and the points of the Congregational polity, which provided the basis for the organization and government of their churches. . . . They preached to awaken the slumbering spirits of the unregenerate in the meeting houses and to straighten the ethical paths of their converted membership. Equipped with the learning of Cambridge scholars, fired with the zeal of religious converts, and chastened by the persecution of Laudian Anglicanism, these three Puritan divines of the immigrant generation set themselves to their providential mission of establishing a purified church in the wilderness."[89]

The Cambridge Platonists

It was also from Emmanuel and Christ's Colleges that a significant and extraordinary group of faculty and scholars in the mold of the Christian humanists emerged who came to be called the "Cambridge Platonists," covering a period roughly between 1633 and 1688. "With scarcely an exception, [they] came out of a Puritan background,"[90] and some of them had evidently become sympathetic to the substance of Pelagian-Arminian doctrine after the Synod of Dort, and were often called "Remonstrants." They rejected the Calvinistic doctrine of irresistible grace and predestination, as they did all forms of determinism, advocating instead the doctrine of free will, a universal atonement through Christ, and conditional grace through virtue and morality.

Among the most prominent of the early Cambridge Platonists were Benjamin Whichcote (1609–1683), John Smith (1618–1652), Henry More (1614–1687), Ralph Cudworth (1617–1688), and John Wilkins (1614–1672).[91]

The Cambridge Platonists were also identified with the Latitudinarians as "Latitude men," since they reacted against what they believed to be an undue emphasis on religious "enthusiasme," or fanaticism, formalism, ritual, and sectarianism. They would give wide range or "latitude" to religious belief. They emphasized rather prayer and godly living, moderation, religious toleration and the real possibility of a spiritual relationship with Christ and God. According to their contemporary and advocate, Gilbert Burnet, "They wished things might be carried on with more moderation; and they continued to keep a good correspondence with those who differed from them in opinion, and allowed a great freedom both in philosophy and in divinity: from whence they were called men of Latitude."[92]

Their strong belief in freedom and freedom of the will, and a loving Creator-God marked them as opponents of all forms of determinism, whether it be that fatalism which claims that all things derive from material elements, or theological doctrines of fatalism such as predestination and irresistible grace.[93] Throughout their philosophy one encounters reverence for God, the dignity of man, the importance of moral virtue and freedom of will.

Since the Cambridge Platonists viewed man as made in the image of God, they opposed strict Calvinism as well as Hobbesianism because they believed these doctrines degenerated man. They saw man inherently possessing dignity and reason. To them, reason and religion need not be enemies. In fact, they assumed that moral behavior enhanced man's reason to recognize truth. The light of reason, they maintained, was the criterion of men's action and belief. Rational man, made in the image of a rational God, was created to think for himself. Above reason was "divine sagacity," which energized the reason of the righteous. Reason, then, according to the Cambridge Platonists, does not replace Scripture, but collects, interprets, and supplements it. Scripture, they believed, was uniquely suited to reason, and God was the true object of reason. They were *rational theologians.* They sought to bring every truth or doctrine to the test of Christian reason, and to estimate it by a moral standard—in other words, by its tendency to exalt or degrade our conceptions of the divine.

Although these "Latitude men" from Cambridge are called "Cambridge Platonists," their primary allegiance was to their belief in God, the principle foundation of their philosophy was Christianity, and their primary text was the Bible. As one reads through their works it becomes obvious, that while the influence of Platonism is there, the fundamental theses are biblical. Platonism is brought in to assist, not to establish basic principles. It should be remembered that the Cambridge Platonists were university teachers in an age when a parade of classical learning was part of the idiom of scholarly discussion.[94] They offer another example of the scholars and divines in the generations before the American Revolution who, by their influence and the force of their moral casuistry, contributed to the growth of modern ideals of virtue and concomitant moral theology; ideals which influenced the course of political ideology as well.

NOTES

1. Edmund D. Carlson, *"Democracy in America* and de Tocqueville's New Science: Civic Virtue in a Commercial Republic," in Sidney A. Pearson, Jr., *The Constitutional Polity: Essays on the Founding Principles of American Politics* (Washington, D.C., University Press of America, 1983), p. 93.

2. Thomas Pangle, "Civic Virtue: The Founders' Conception and the Classical Conception," in Gary Bryner and Noel Reynolds, eds., *Constitutionalism and Rights* (Provo, Utah: Brigham Young University Press, 1986).

3. Herbert J. Muller, *Freedom and the Ancient World* (New York: Harper, 1963), p. 169.

4. Hannah Arendt, *The Origins of Totalitarianism* (New York: Meridian, 1963), p. 297.

5. Franz Neumann, *The Democratic and the Authoritarian State: Essays in Political and Legal Theory* (Glencoe, Ill.: Free Press, 1957), pp. 73–74.

6. Pangle, "Civic Virtue."

7. Paul Oskar Kristeller, *Studies in Renaissance Thought and Letters* (Rome: Edizioni di Storia e Letteratura, 1956), p. 564. It should be noted here that the Renaissance humanists are often considered the forebears of the philosophs in

France, the Saint-Simonians, and eventually socialists and communists. Their history, however, is a "two-edged sword." Their part in the influence on Puritanism, on such concepts as freedom, covenant, and virtue, indeed, their impact on the whole of modern Christianity and republican philosophy is often overlooked.

8. Volumes could be written on the events and ways of thought that had a direct and an indirect impact on the nature of the concept of "virtue." To mention but a few: the breakdown of authority of the Holy Roman Empire; the emergence of the Renaissance and Reformation; new translations and commentaries on the Bible for popular consumption; the enactment of the Law Codes of 1641 and 1648; the growth of the philosophy of resistance to tyranny; ideas of freedom that energized the Puritan Revolution and bolstered the new and growing sense of human dignity and worth; the search for a "New Jerusalem in America."

9. Francesco Patrizi, *The Founding of a Republic* (Paris, 1585), of. 196b; Quentin Skinner, *The Foundations of Modern Political Thought* (New York: Cambridge University Press, 1978), Vol. 1, p. 175.

10. Niccolo Machiavelli, *The Discourses*, translated by Leslie J. Walker and edited by Bernard Crick (Harmondsworth, England: Penguin, 1970), pp. 176–77, 515. Skinner, *Foundations of Modern Political Thought*, pp. 182–83.

11. Skinner, *Foundations of Modern Political Thought*, p. 182–83.

12. See George L. Mosse, *The Holy Pretence: A Study in Christianity and Reason of State from William Perkins to John Winthrop* (Oxford: B. Blackwell, 1957).

13. Quoted in Perry Miller, *The New England Mind: The Seventeenth Century* (New York: Macmillan, 1939), p. 416.

14. Oswald Spengler, *Untergang des Abendlandes* (Munich: Beck, 1959) Vol. 2, p. 262; Mosse, *The Holy Pretense*, p. 44.

15. Mosse, *The Holy Pretense*, Chapters 3–6, pp. 34–87.

16. Martin Fleisher, *Radical Reform and Political Persuasion in the Life and Writings of Thomas More* (Geneva: Droz, 1973), pp. 3, 5–6.

17. Skinner, *Foundations of Modern Political Thought*, p. 232. (Italics added).

18. Robert L. Cord, *Separation of Church and State* (New York: Lambeth, 1982).

19. Paul Oskar Kristeller, *Eight Philosophers of the Italian Renaissance* (Stanford, Calif.: Stanford University Press, 1964), p. 5.

20. Francesco Petrarch, *Le traité De sui e multorum ignorantia*, L. M. Capelli, ed. (Paris: H. Champion, 1906), p. 66; and Ernst Cassirer et al., eds., *The Renaissance Philosophy of Man* (Chicago: University of Chicago Press, 1963), p. 101.

21. Petrarch, *Le traité De sui*, p. 77; and Cassirer, et al., *The Renaissance Philosophy of Man*, p. 113.

22. Cassirer, et al., *The Renaissance Philosophy of Man*, p. 115.

23. *Ibid.*, p. 103. (italics added)

24. *Ibid.*, pp. 104–6.

25. Professor Kristeller claims Ficino "was the greatest Florentine philosopher and metaphysician in the proper sense of the word. He and his circle gave their imprint to a whole period of Florentine culture, and added an element to it that had been absent before, and that was to stay for generations." Kristeller, *Eight Philosophers*, p. 50.

26. *Ibid.*, p. 46. "Ficino's doctrine of immortality, and his arguments for it, made a profound impression on many thinkers of the sixteenth century, and it may well be due to his indirect influence that the immortality of the soul was formally pronounced a dogma of the Catholic Church at the Lateran Council of 1512." *Ibid.*, p. 47.

27. "Letter of Marsilio Ficino to Lotterio Neroni," in *The Letters of Marsilio Ficino* (London: Shepheard-Walwyn, 1975), Vol. 3, pp. 18–19.

28. "Letter of Marsilio Ficino to Antonio Calderini," *ibid.*, Vol. 1, pp. 159–

60. It can be expected that "justice" in this case takes a more theoretical/Christian than classical meaning since the Greek notion of justice countenanced many and severe social and economic inequalities between different classes, and slave population without any rights. Even Aristotle's ideal constitution included similar inequities.

29. "Letter of Marsilio Ficino to Francesco Lapaccini and Migliore Cresci," *ibid.*, Vol. 1, pp. 57–58.

30. "Letter of Marsilio Ficino to Tommaso Minerbetti," *ibid.*, Vol. 1, p. 101.

31. *Ibid.*

32. "Letter of Marsilio Ficino to Bernardo Bembo," *ibid.*, Vol. 3, p. 50.

33. Kristeller, *Studies in Renaissance Thought,*, p. 271.

34. "Letter of Marsilio Ficino to Piero del Nero," in *The Letters of Marsilio Ficino*, Vol. 1, p. 124.

35. *Ibid.*

36. It should not be overlooked, however, that a number of Italian scholars came to Oxford and Cambridge. Among these were Stefano Surigone, Cornelio Vitelli, Lorenzo da Savona, and Caio Auberino. See Skinner, *Foundations of Modern Political Thought*, p. 195.

37. Frederic Seebohm, *The Oxford Reformers* (London: Longmans, Green, 1887).

38. Beatus Rhenanus, *Christian Humanism and the Reformation: Selected Writings of Erasmus; With the Life of Erasmus*, 2nd rev. ed. (New York: Fordham University Press, 1975). Skinner argued that that there was a "new and self-confident humanist culture in France, England, and Germany by the beginning of the sixteenth century." Skinner, *Foundations of Modern Political Thought*, p. 198.

39. Sears Jayne, *John Colet and Marsilio Ficino* (Oxford University Press, 1963), p. 39. "He was, of course, influenced by humanism, as he was influenced by Florentine Neo-Platonism; but the influence was superficial. . . . [H]e was profoundly Christian. Eugene F. Rice, Jr., "John Colet and the Annihilation of the Natural," *Harvard Theological Review*, Vol. 45 (July 1952), p. 142. Leland Miles, in his *John Colet and the Platonic Tradition* (La Salle, Ill.: Open Court, 1961), on the other hand, warns the reader not to underestimate the influence of Platonism on Colet.

40. John Colet, "Exposition of St. Paul's Epistle to the Romans," in his *Opuscula Quaedam Theologica*, Vol. 4, with translation, introduction and notes by J. H. Lupton (London, 1867), republished in Westmead, England: Gregg International, 1966, pp. 62–67.

41. *Ibid.*, p. 108.

42. John Colet, *De Sacramentis Ecclesiae Super Opera Dionysii*, "Synopsis," with translation, introduction, and notes by J. H. Lupton (London, 1867), republished in Westmead, England: Gregg, 1966, p. 33; and "Exposition of St. Paul's Epistle to the Romans," p. 74.

43. John Colet, *Lectures on Romans*, with translation, introduction and notes by J. H. Lupton (London, 1874), republished in Ridgewood, N.J.: Gregg, 1965, p. 23.

44. Skinner, *Foundations of Modern Political Thought*, p. 126.

45. E. Harris Harbison, *The Christian Scholar in the Age of the Reformation* (New York: Scribner, 1956), p. 69.

46. Colet, "Exposition of St. Paul's Epistle to the Romans," pp. 35–36.

47. *Ibid.*, pp. 35–36.

48. Franklin Le Van Baumer, "The Conception of Christendom in Renaissance England," *Journal of the History of Ideas*, Vol. 6 (April 1945), p. 132.

49. "*Lo stato* is no body politic; it is not the people politically organized, the political expression of their nature and character and aspirations, their virtues and their defects. Rather it is an inert lump, and whatever vicarious vitality it displays

is fused into it not by the people, but by the prince who gets it, holds it, keeps it, and aims not to lose it or have it taken away." J. H. Hexter, *The Vision of Politics on the Eve of the Reformation* (New York, 1973), pp. 182, 188.

50. *Ibid.*, pp. 190–92.

51. *Ibid.*, p. 210.

52. *Ibid.*, p. 209. Here Hexter quotes from *The Prince*, Chapter 15.

53. *Ibid.*, p. 192.

54. Sir Thomas More, *Utopia* in Edward Surtz and J. H. Hexter, eds., *The Complete Works of St. Thomas More* (New Haven: Yale University Press, 1965), p. 138.

55. *Ibid.*, p. 161.

56. *Ibid.*, p. 173.

57. *Ibid.*, p. 175.

58. *Ibid.*, p. 167.

59. See Gordon S. Wood, *The Creation of the American Republic, 1776–1787*, Chap. 14.

60. Sir Thomas More, *Utopia*, pp. 165–67.

61. *Ibid.*, p. 193.

62. *Ibid.*, pp. 157, 167–69.

63. For a discussion of the spread of humanism in northern Europe, consult Skinner, *Foundations of Modern Political Thought*, Chapter 7, "The Diffusion of Humanist Scholarship," pp. 193–212.

64. Skinner, *Foundations of Modern Political Thought*, p. 226. See commentary on the above, pp. 224–28. We appreciate consulting Skinner on this era.

65. According to DeLamar Jensen, these "Mirror of Prince" books "of advice to rulers usually [contained] long lists of attributes and characteristics that rulers should exhibit in their personal and public lives. . . . *The Book of the Courtier* by Baldassare Castiglione is a good example. . . . Literature was not an autonomous cultural entity during the Renaissance, but was woven into the broader fabric of cultural and political life. The introduction of paper into the West and the invention of printing had a profound effect on the interplay of literature and politics." "Humanism and the Renaissance Prince," unpublished manuscript prepared for delivery at Brigham Young University, February 19, 1986.

66. Guillaume Budé, *Education of the Prince* (Paris, 1547, reprinted in Farnborough, England: Gregg, 1966), pp. 87, 169, 187, 189, 192. Skinner, *Foundations of Modern Political Thought*, p. 234.

67. Desiderius Erasmus, *The Education of a Christian Prince*, translated and edited by Lester K. Born (New York: Columbia University Press, 1965), pp. 156, 237, 177. "Early in the year 1515 proposals had been made to Erasmus to join the court of Prince Charles (the future Charles V), and his actual appointment and assumption of office probably took place at the end of that year or on the first day of January, 1516." *The Education of a Christian Prince*, which eventually went into some forty editions, "was prepared during this period and was intended from the first for the young prince (then only fifteen years old)." Lester K. Born, "Erasmus on Political Ethics: the *Institutio Principis Christiani*," *Political Science Quarterly*, Vol. 43 (1928), p. 520. See also Erasmus, *The Praise of Folly*, trans., John Wilson, 1688; reprinted (London: Clarendon, 1913).

68. Skinner, *Foundations of Modern Political Thought*, pp. 228–29.

69. See Chapter 6 of this book for an explanation of Madison's ideas.

70. A more ancient concern over free will can be seen in Arthur W. H. Adkins, *Merit and Responsibility: A Study in Greek Values* (Oxford: Clarendon, 1960), especially Chapters 1 and 2, pp. 1–29.

71. James Nichols and W. R. Bagnall, eds., *Writings of Jacobus Arminius*, (Grand Rapids, Mich., 1956), Vol. 1, p. 217; Jacobi Arminii, *Opera Theologica* (Frankfurt, 1631), 6 vols., First English translation in London, 1825–1828, and

again at Auburn in 1853; John Gill, *The Cause of God and Truth: Being an Examination of the Principle Passages of Scripture Made Use of by the Arminians, in Favor of Their Scheme* (London, 1735); Piere du Moulin, *Anatome Arminianisme,* translated in London from original Latin copy in 1620; published in the United States as *The Anatomy of Arminianism* (Norwood, N.J.: Walter J. Johnson, 1967).

72. Milton R. Konvitz, "The Confluence of Torah and the Constitution," *Jews, Judaism, and the American Constitution* (American Jewish Archives, 1982), p. 14. "In the Bible, the word for covenant is *berit,* which is probably derived from the word meaning binding. Various types of covenant can be found in the Bible. There is, for instance, the unilateral covenant that the Creator made immediately after the Flood, symbolized by the rainbow." The covenant of Sinai, however, was "bilateral and conditional." If the Hebrew nation would but keep the covenant with God and obey his voice, they would become a holy nation. (Genesis 9:11; Exodus 19:5–8; Deuteronomy chaps. 29–31). *Ibid.* See also John von Rohr "Covenant and Assurances in Early English Puritanism," *Church History,* Vol. 65 (June, 1965).

73. *Ibid.,* pp. 15–16.

74. Perry Miller, *The New England Mind: The Seventeenth Century,* pp. 378–379. Konvitz, "The Confluence of the Torah and the Constitution," p. 14. See also Champlin Burrage, *The Church Covenant Idealists Origin and Development* (Philadelphia: American Baptist Publication Society, 1904).

75. Konvitz, "The Confluence of the Torah and the Constitution," p. 15.

76. Daniel Boorstin, *The Americans: The Colonial Experience* (New York: Vintage, 1958), p. 17; Konvitz; "The Confluence of the Torah and the Constitution," p. 16.

77. Konvitz, "The Confluence of Torah and the Constitution," p. 16.

78. Charles Verlinden, *The Beginnings of Modern Colonization* (Ithaca, N.Y.: Cornell University Press, 1970), p. 10. "The constitutions of some of these communes served as models in certain colonial areas. Genoa, for example, used its own communal constitution in the colonies of Pera on the Bosporus and Caffa in the Crimea. So-called free companies fought in nearly all the European wars in the later Middle Ages, and their members were bound together by an agreement. In some cases these companies were transplanted overseas, and a new agreement was established with the object of regulating not only their internal government but also control of the conquered country. This was done by the Catalan and Navarrese companies in their colonies in Greece in the fourteenth century." *Ibid.,* p. 9.

79. William Chappell, *The Preacher, or the Art and Method of Preaching* (London, 1656), publisher's preface.

80. Paul Russell Anderson, *Science in Defense of Liberal Religion: A Study in Henry More's Attempt to Link Seventeenth-Century Religion with Science* (New York: G. P. Putnam, 1933), p. 19.

81. *Ibid.,* pp. 20–21.

82. James Bass Mullinger, *History of the University of Cambridge* (Cambridge: Cambridge University Press, 1873–1911), Vol. 2, p. 208.

83. John Dykstra Eusden, *Puritans, Lawyers, and Politics in Early Seventeenth-Century England* (New Haven: Yale University Press, 1958), p. 35.

84. Thomas Fuller, *History of the University of Cambridge* (London, 1655), Vol. 2, p. 147.

85. Samuel Eliot Morison, *The Founding of Harvard College* (Cambridge: Harvard University Press, 1935), p. 95.

86. Cotton Mather, *Magnalia Christi Americana* (London, 1702), Vol. 2, Bk. 3, p. 216.

87. Morison, *The Founding of Harvard College,* p. 92. John Harvard, benefactor of Harvard College, also attended Emmanuel.

88. *Ibid.*, p. 94.

89. J. Rodney Fulcher, *Puritan Piety in Early New England: A Study in Spiritual Regeneration from the Antinomian Controversy to the Cambridge Synod of 1648 in the Massachusetts Bay Colony*, Dissertation (Princeton, N.J.: Princeton University, 1963), pp. 15–16.

90. Gerald R. Cragg, ed., *The Cambridge Platonists* (New York: Oxford University Press, 1968), p. 8. John Tulloch, *Rational Theology and Christian Philosophy in England in the Seventeenth Century*: Vol. 2, *The Cambridge Platonists* (London, 1874).

91. Rosalie L. Colie, *Light and Enlightenment: A Study of the Cambridge Platonists and the Dutch Arminians* (Cambridge: Cambridge University Press, 1957). Most historians do not mention Wilkins as a "primary" Cambridge Platonist. His primary activities were with Oxford, but his allegiance to the ideals of his colleagues at Cambridge, plus his contribution to the development of experimental science, attach to him some importance.

92. Gilbert Burnet, *History of His Own Time*, with historical and biographical notes (reprinted in London, 1875), pp. 128–29. See also Alexander Nairne, "The Cambridge Platonists," *The Church Quarterly Review*, Vol. 61 (January 1926), p. 221 and Gerald R. Cragg, *From Puritanism to the Age of Reason: A Study of Changes in Religious Thought Within the Church of England, 1660–1700* (Oxford: Oxford University Press, 1980),; *The Church and the Age of Reason, 1648–1789*, (New York: Athenium, 1961).

93. They rejected the philosophy of Hobbes as deterministic and ethically relativistic. See Samuel I. Mintz, *The Hunting of Leviathan: Seventeenth-Century Reactions to the Materialism and Moral Philosophy of Thomas Hobbes* (Cambridge: Cambridge University Press. 1962).

94. John Alexander Stewart, "Cambridge Platonists," in *Encyclopedia of Religion and Ethics*, Vol. 3, pp. 168–69.

3

Virtue Comes to America

As the revolutionary era approached, events both in America and England served as catalysts to the development of American "republicanism." The concept of virtue, as it had evolved through the generations, was republicanism's integrating force. There were, of course, other influences such as the lessons of experience, the resort to history, and the philosophy of the British libertarians, as well as the language of the classical philosophers. But the driving emotional force, without which all the other influences combined may have fallen short of what eventually was achieved, stemmed from America's religious foundations, identified as the Protestant or Judeo-Christian ethic and, more directly, the Puritan ethic. Whatever the contribution of other intellectual, economic, and social phenomena—and it was substantial—here was the electricity that energized the republic.

RELIGION AND THE MISSION OF AMERICA

In the American colonies, the idea of historical progress was very much alive as they moved toward independence. There were strong religious sentiments that America had been set apart in history and preserved for a chosen people who would bring about great things for the glory of God. Not a few believed that Providence had guarded America and had selected it to be a "New Jerusalem." They believed, writes Robert Nisbet, "that America was not only a destined nation, but a redeeming nation."[1] Many would have agreed with de Tocqueville's vision that North America had been discovered "as if it had been kept in reserve by the Deity, and had just risen from beneath the waters of the Deluge,"[2] and that the colonists were "not a mere party of adventurers gone forth to seek their fortune beyond

[the] seas, but the germ of a great nation wafted by Providence to a predestined shore."[3] "I think I see," he continued, "the destiny of America embodied in the first Puritan who landed on those shores, just as the whole human race was represented by the first man."[4] To de Tocqueville, the "newness" of America, the isolation from other powers, the heritage the colonists had brought with them, combined with "[a] thousand circumstances independent of the will of man [to] facilitate the maintenance of a democratic republic in the United States."[5]

From the 1520s onward, the Puritans had been characterized by a more radical break with the Holy Roman Empire than most other "reformed" churches and even Luther were willing to go, and by their decidedly British experience. The Puritans were also attached to the concept of the *covenant* to a greater degree than the other Bible-reading Christian communities. The Christianity that emerged from the Reformation had carried with it a sense of mission, which, prostituted by fanatical zeal, led to wars and crusades. On the other hand, this same sense of participation in the unfolding of momentous historical events for the glory of God contributed to the founding of nations and the emergence of modern self-government. The British Puritans, having arisen out of the Church of England, sought to carry the Reformation to its logical conclusion, that is, to return the mother church to the purity of sacred scripture. Thus, as Perry Miller writes, the Puritan immigrants came to America with the belief that "their errand was not a mere scouting expedition: it was an essential maneuver in the drama of Christendom. . . .These Puritans did not flee to America; they went in order to work out that complete reformation which was not yet accomplished in England and Europe."[6]

The colonial Puritans had a sense of mission that emerged naturally with the integrating of their religious philosophy with the new land of America; and in the wilderness of America it was not difficult for them to find a striking resemblance between themselves and ancient Israel. According to Sydney Ahlstrom, "That many Puritan Christians would consider themselves a 'people of the Covenant' was almost inevitable. Persecuted, ridiculed, and abused during their formative period, and driven to the Old Testament by their need for historical precedents and specific legal guidance, they ineluctably came to identify their situation and their goals with those of the Chosen People, God's Israel. . . . In the American wilderness, the Puritan's situation and its parallel with Israel's role in history became even more striking. . . . And finally, given their concern for moral order, civic duty, and the general welfare, they sometimes envisaged the body politic or commonwealth as being collectively in covenant with the Lord for a special corporate task in the world."[7]

They came to see America as a new promised land set apart by Providence for a new people, a new church, a new state, a new Jerusalem, in the vision of John Winthrop writing in 1630, "We must consider that wee shall be as a Citty upon a Hill, the eies of all people are upon us."[8] "God sifted a Whole Nation," cried William Stoughton, "that he might send Choice Grain over into this Wilderness."[9] It was the first-generation Puritan layman Edward Johnson who praised the colonial adventure as the settlement of a new Mt. Zion in the American wilderness, and as the Revolution began, many of the clergy used the pulpit openly and brazenly for a call to arms, typically referring to the revolutionary troops as the "Armies of Israel." "The finger of God," spoke clergyman Phillip Payson in 1782, "has indeed been so conspicious in every stage of our glorious struggle, that it seems as if the wonders and miracles performed for Israel of old were repeated over anew for the American Israel, in our day."[10]

This idea of a special people in a special land remained part of the American religious philosophy down through the Revolution and the Founding, and saturated the election sermons,[11] which were delivered by the New England clergy. Throughout these incredible years, countless referrals to "Providence" and the "Finger of God" merged with the sense of mission and national deliverance.[12] The great American adventure not only carried with it the blessings of God, the whole affair, it was reasoned, had been directed by God as a vital historical sequence in the last days. And if Providence had placed such great opportunities and blessings at their disposal, then the Americans also faced an ominous responsibility as instruments in the hand of God. Provost Smith, among others, called upon his countrymen to think solemnly of the future: "Look forward also to distant posterity. Figure to yourselves millions and millions to spring from your loins, who may be born freemen or slaves, as Heaven shall now approve or reject your councils. Think, that on you it may depend, whether this great country, in ages hence, shall be filled and adorned with a virtuous and enlightened people; enjoying Liberty and all its concomitant blessings, together with the Religion of Jesus, as it flows uncorrupted from his holy oracles; or covered with a race of men more contemptible than the savages that roam the wilderness."[13]

Samuel West's acknowledgement in 1776 of "the dispensations of Providence toward this land ever since our fathers first settled in Plymouth," and his insistence that "Providence has designed this continent for to be the asylum of liberty and true religion,"[14] were certainly not uncommon texts for the speeches and sermons of the day. In that same year, Charles Chauncy preached that it was under God's "all-wise overruling influence that a spirit was raised up in all the colonies nobly to assert their freedom as men and English-born subjects."[15] "In the rise and in the whole progress of the unnatural controversy between Great Britain and the now United Independent American States," spoke the Reverend Chauncey Whittelsey in 1778, "the hand of God has been, I must think, very conspicuous." To the New England ministry, Providence had been manifest throughout not only the colonization efforts, and the Revolution, but the coming forth of the Constitution as well. Clergyman William Rodgers was far from alone among his colleagues, nor was he speaking to uninitiated ears when he preached that the Constitution had emerged under the guidance of Providence. And when, on the fourth of July 1789, the Reverend Ashbel Green publicly gave thanks to God for the divine guidance to those who founded the Republic and sealed its glory with the Constitution, his declaration was not a revelation to his audience, but another confirmation of consensus. "All the forms of civil polity have been tried by mankind, except one," offered the celebrated Ezra Stiles in his Election Sermon of 1783, "and that seems to have been reserved in Providence to be realized in America. . . . How wonderful the . . . events of Providence! We live in an age of wonders; we have lived an age in a few years; we have seen more wonders accomplished in eight years than are usually unfolded in a century."[16]

It was the New England ministry, not the Founders, who first announced America had been set apart by God, and that this people had been chosen to create a new and higher community for the example and edification of mankind. This belief had become so established by the Revolution that it was in fact part of the existing political or civil orthodoxy. This sense of a "new way of life" was poignantly expressed by Crevecoeur's praise of "This New Man, the American," which was written some time before the Revolution.

VIRTUE AND RELIGION

For Americans, the Bible was the primary source of the idea of virtue, as the principles, thought, and doctrine of that volume were brought forth and established for common consumption by the Renaissance, the Reformation, and the Puritan movement in England. The most immediate motivating force for public virtue was the biblical and Christian doctrines of benevolence or the Golden Rule and service and the spiritual transformation that the Puritan movement produced in England—the requirement to live outside one's self in genuine love and interest toward others. More than "public regardedness," public virtue was the application of these principles by a Christian people to the society in which they lived; here may be seen the religious basis upon which American society was built. Puritan philosophy permeated the colonies, and most of the American Founders and spokesmen, to say nothing of the clergy whose moral and intellectual reach was far and wide, were raised under the omnipresent influence of the Protestant/Puritan ethic, which, when combined with the lessons of the Old Testament, formed a potent influence.

Classical ideas and language were, of course, characteristic of colonial political thought. While many of the terms were drawn from secular antiquity, they were often infused with a new depth of meaning, which drew a moral or an emotional response that reflected their application to the religious beliefs in colonial society. More often than not, if the specific terms were drawn from the ancient philosophers, they were interpreted under the influence of the biblical prophets. If the "containers" came from Greece or Rome, the "wine" within was nurtured, and gained its savor from Israel.

Puritanism incorporated the use of reason and moral theology in calling for involvement in good works and strenuous daily effort in behalf of God, man, and self. The idea of virtuous participation in church and state became particularly pronounced. The advocacy of Puritan spokesman Richard Steele, as early as 1668, was that "every man should be of some use in the *Body Politick* as well as in the Body Mistical, or else he is but an Artificial Member, a mere wooden leg," and that "when a man brings no good or profit to the Church or Common-wealth, that's one of *no* calling," and that men in their daily activities ought to "make a suitable return of honor and service unto God" by being involved with "The Public Good," and service to "his generation."[17] Professor Ernest Tuveson in his *Redeemer Nation*, concluded that the dominant philosophy in early American Christianity was the idea that God was "redeeming both individual souls and society in parallel course."[18] And Perry Miller, in his *The Life of the Mind in America*, pointed out that the religious revivals that from time to time enlivened religious expression in America were stimulated by the proposition that both men's souls and the physical aspects of the community were in the need of redemption.[19] This dual obligation as perpetuated by colonial Christianity, especially through Puritanism, was generally referred to as "virtue," carrying with it the connotation of relating to both the person and the community, to individual and civic moral responsibility.

Puritan America went beyond the philosophy of the ancients, incorporating the influences of biblical scholarship as well as the lessons of the Puritan Revolution and that of New World colonization. The mixture was to engender a "virtue" that became increasingly more inclusive and expansive in scope. Furthermore, the idea came to be accepted that *private* virtue must precede *public* virtue. Public virtue was simply the extension of private virtue into public affairs. The core of man's willingness to sacrifice his immediate self-interest on behalf of the community, his willingness to serve the public and to participate in its activities, indeed, even that revolutionary spirit, necessary to bring a concerted and militant defense of the colonies, had its origin in private virtue.

Virtue and the Private Realm

Among colonial Americans, it was generally believed that the major source of virtue and morality was religion, although there were some who believed that virtue and morality could be learned by reason. A number of modern writers have tended to separate the "general," "civil" religion of the times from the influence of the established sects. This is a mistake, however, for the strength of the general civil religion was not generated primarily by the state, or through philosophy or reason, but by the primary institutions of society. These institutions—family, school, churches, neighborhood, and other local institutions, were, in fact, the *primary feeders* and *stimulators* of the general civil religion. Institutions such as the family inculcated and nurtured values of concern for others, respect for law and social order. They assumed a primary role in influencing and shaping values and beliefs essential to social life. Without these mediating socializing agents, the general civil religion would have lost its necessary constant nurturing and would have become anemic. To suppose that the "civil religion" was or is entirely self-generating, is to project extreme naîveté. It was to be fostered and nourished from the hearth, the classroom, and the pulpit.

Thus, the development of virtue, to a great extent, had been removed from the political realm to these other institutions of society as a separation between society and government had evolved. Modern republicans were apparently conscious of the fact that, with this separation, the primary institutions of society inherited a responsibility to be the foundation of the nation's "civil religion." These mediating primary institutions gave foundation, legitimacy, and strength to the symbols and rituals of the state in a way that the state in itself could not have done. The primary institutions, not the state, made the community; they, not the political institutions, gave the people the allegiance and the positive emotional response to coalesce the Republic. More than anything else, the nation's great leaders, such as Washington, maintained their prestige by their example of virtue. It was the primary institutions that provided the new generations with the political socialization that gave patriotism its viability. The more the state assumes the primary directive role of political socialization through indoctrination and propaganda, the more it will be unable to count upon the genuine spontaneous response of its people over time. It will eventually be forced, in order to perpetuate the regime, to resort to a high level of administrative direction of society and greater degrees of force and coercion or at least the threat of force and coercion.

The single most important ingredient in virtue as it developed into New World republican philosophy was the biblical concept of charity or love, benevolence and its corollary, brotherhood and brotherly love. It assumed that men had an obligation to one another; and that obligation extended to the obligation of the individual to the commonwealth, and the obligation of the magistrate to the people.

At the core of this moral behavior was a belief in God, reinforced by *both* an "organized" *and* a "general" religious establishment. Without this *de facto* "establishment," morality simply would not have survived in America. "Morals and religion are inextricably joined," insists Sir Patrick Devlin. "No Society has yet solved the problem of how to teach morality without religion."[20] "There is no significant example in history before our time," concur the historians Will and Ariel Durant, "of a society successfully maintaining moral life without the aid of religion."[21] De Tocqueville saw this in relation to America. "It must never be forgotten," he wrote, "that religion gave birth to Anglo-American society. In the United States, religion is therefore mingled with all the habits of the nation and all the feelings of patriotism, whence it derives a peculiar force."[22]

One of the most vital factors by which religion energized and directed the merging of classical and biblical virtue was to infuse certain ideals, symbols, concepts, documents, and institutions, with a sense of the "sacred" in the sentiments of Americans. There was a "sacred" aura to the Declaration of Independence and later to the Constitution.[23] Samuel Adams, in signing the Declaration, could say without fear of ridicule that God had been reenthroned. During the Revolution, ministers and governors alike called Americans to arms as "the armies of Israel" and in the name of God. Deep in the emotional content of the American tradition was the idea that the colonization and development of the country carried with it a "sacred" mission. According to Ralph Ketcham, "The last step in the path marked out by moral awareness, taken often in New England pulpits and elsewhere in America, was to insist that *nations* likewise will be held accountable in the final judgment. The American colonies especially, in a common figure of speech, were conceived as a city set upon a hill to shine for all the world to see. An incalculable dynamism and sense of purpose is imparted to a people which so sees itself."[24]

Long before the Revolution ever took place, the term "liberty" had taken a "sacred" connotation, and had become part of the idea of virtue. The seeds of freedom, which had been fertilized with the Reformation, united with the Saxon tradition in England and blossomed in the Puritan revolution. "The most powerful single force for freedom in early America," argued Rossiter, "was the devotion to liberty in the colonial mind."[25] That force was based on the ultimate value of the individuality of each human being. The philosophy of the Declaration, the basic concepts and unique features undergirding the revolution—covenant or contract, higher law, unalienable rights, human dignity, virtue—were all *primarily* the product of the evolution of American Christianity, particularly Puritanism. American Christianity, with its Judaic influence, was not just *compatible* with the philosophy that energized men to love freedom, that made them see themselves as heirs of human dignity, subject to law higher than the state; *it was primarily responsible for the philosophy.* Its strength and force of motivation came from the general belief in its "sacredness," its divine nature. It gave man an orientation toward something higher than himself. Human dignity gained its primary force in America from the belief that man was made for eternity, that he had some share in an essence more than human, and that his freedom was divinely ordained.

PURITANISM, VIRTUE, AND REVOLUTIONARY AMERICA

The history of the early American colonies is replete with periodic "declensions" from what the clergy and others believed to be the solid virtues of early Puritan history. There was a tendency to glorify the past or a period of the past, with a desire to restore that which was supposedly lost. Sermons or "Jeremiads," calling for a renewal of the faith, typically invoking the Prophet Jeremiah, were common in colonial America.[26] The Jeremiad served to renew the Puritan sense of mission, to redefine it, and to inspire religious revival and national rejuvanation, expressed in the desire to renew old covenants and to rededicate to the life of virtue.[27]

A religious revival, to become known as "The Great Awakening," swept through the colonies between 1739 and 1742, and continued until approximately 1750. Beginning in Georgia, it soon spread throughout New England. Heimert and Miller suggest that this "awakening" "marked America's final break with the Middle Ages and her entry into a new intellectual age in the church and society."[28] A new vocabulary, a new thought, a new ideology, linking freedom with personal and civic virtue, indeed, a "republican" ideology was being forged from American religion bolstered by the ideas of the British dissenters and libertarians, and in the experience of the colonial setting of the New World. There was also a renewed reference to the Puritan past. The Great Awakening was a call for freedom, virtue and spiritual rejuvenation. It proved to be a catalyst to the growth of both "democratic" and "revolutionary" sentiments in the colonies.

A catalyst of the Great Awakening was George Whitefield, an Episcopal minister who called for a return to a "vital religion" and a repudiation of the corrupt and decadent establishment. The Awakening helped spread republican and revolutionary vocabulary to the masses, particularly through the assemblies addressed by preachers like Whitefield. "Looking to the New Testament as their model," wrote Harry S. Stout, "the revivalists rediscovered the effectiveness of extemporaneous address in their struggle against the Standing Order."[29] Armed with scriptures and charisma, revivalists such as Jonathan Edwards helped provide "pre-Revolutionary America with a radical, even democratic, social and political ideology, and evangelical religion [which] embodied, and inspired, a thrust toward American nationalism."[30]

Among the far-reaching results of the Great Awakening was a renewal in the emphasis of virtue, both individual and civic. By the 1730s, the clergy began to speak of *social redemption* as well as *individual salvation*. Edwards, Gilbert Tennant, and others talked about the establishment of the kingdom of God in America.[31] They opposed what they believed to have been the widespread "rationalism" that had been popularized in the colonies and called for an outpouring of the Spirit. In Edwards' *Thoughts on the Revival*, he advocated the redemption of American society through "affectionate" religion. Edwards believed that "In the Awakening . . . God had called on his American people to will a reorganized society into being. For Edwards, the ultimate test of sainthood was whether a man was so acting as to 'promote' God's historical program."[32] Sainthood was to be expressed in virtuous action, a total commitment of love to the redemption of society, a "great and universal benevolence." "Evangelical religion . . . considered virtue possible only after justification, and virtuous acts as flowing spontaneously. . . . A regenerate heart made it possible for man to choose the good, and to pursue it, 'without being at the trouble of a train of reasoning.' Calvinism's vision of the social good flowed into political protest, into challenges to the 'rulers' of colonial society, and eventually, into the discussion and the activity that preceded and accompanied the American Revolution."[33]

The Spread of Republican Language

Revivalistic oratory and technique, as developed by Whitefield and others, was different from sermons spoken in the individual churches. The revivalists were independent of local ministerial rule, and their "mass address to a voluntary audience," who were generally not their parishioners, "forced a dialogue between speaker and hearer that disregarded social position and local setting. . . . In gathering their large and unfamiliar audiences, the revivalists utilized the only form of address that could be sure to impress all hearers: the spoken word proclaimed extemporaneously in everyday language. . . . Evangelical rhetoric performed a dual function: it proclaimed the power of the spoken word directly to every individual who would hear, and it confirmed a shift in authority by organizing voluntary popular meetings and justifying them in the religious vocabulary of the day."[34]

Thus, the revivalistic technique brought the revolutionary rhetoric of the informed publications into the popular assemblies with the emotional force of the spoken word. There emerged a noticeable relationship between the revivals and the dissenter movements. As the revolution approached there had developed a common revolutionary vocabulary, and a common ideology. According to Stout, "Despite the differences in intellectual substance between the revivals and the rebellion, those movements exhibited a close rhetorical affinity that infused religion and political ideas with powerful social significance and ideological urgency."[35]

Symbolic communal activities were also means by which colonists of all stations became acquainted with the prevailing thought of the times and the "language" that expressed that thought. During the French and Indian Wars colonial consensus seemed to cling to the power of and the emotional and sanguine ties to the mother country. But British actions of the 1760s began to systematically sever those ties; and the Americans had already developed a "language" replete with terms related to and calling upon the concept of virtue that vitalized republicanism. Clergy and revolutionary spokesmen related to the colonial populace not only their interpretation of events but a common rhetoric that stimulated a response and evaluation of those events. The patriot leaders combined the spoken word with such communal rituals as "voting, militia musters and economic associations." This combination tended to create a "collective conscience," in Virginia for example, between the gentry and the evangelicals, that fostered unity in a virtuous community through an appeal to a common defense of its cherished rights.[36]

Another means by which republican ideology was developed and communicated to the body of colonists, especially the "humbler ranks" to whom, according to Rhys Isaac, "the pamphlets were rarely addressed," were the events at "court-day." These monthly meetings brought people from far and wide for what turned out to be lessons in civic virtue—legal instruction, participation, and social interaction. Isaac writes that in Virginia, for example, "It was in its monthly concourse at the courthouse that [the] Virginia community was most fully embodied and represented, in ranked order, to itself."[37] It was at these community meetings with their ceremonial forms that the people became acquainted and involved with the local legal functioning of their community, and the dispensation of justice. The renewal of the county's *commission of the peace* was feted with an elaborate round of oath-taking by the public officials, and there was the swearing in of juries and the participation of witnesses; and participation in the elections by the voting freemen. "Written instruments and records (commissions, writs, indentures, and so forth) were of course a central part of the proceedings, but they could not be valid as social facts or serve as a basis for action until they had been incorporated into the oral-aural information system by being read aloud, by the emphatic forms of oath-taking, and by a dramatic 'subscribing' in the presence of the community."[38]

After the court proceedings, there were festivities on the grounds of the court that usually lasted far into the afternoon. Here congenial conversation, the exchange of news and opinions, and an occasional discourse on a subject by a prominent member of the community were heard. According to Isaac this form of information exchange was so effective that the "press served, especially in connection with local news, rather to authenticate reports passing by word of mouth than to carry news in its fullness. The newspapers of that time, with their fine print, their long reports from the courts of Europe, and their polemical exchanges in learned literary style, replete with Latin quotations, were not directed to the general populace. Persons of this rank were expected to receive the more important messages contained in the fine print through reading aloud and through conversation at courthouses, ordinaries, and other places of assembly as news became part of the common stock of knowledge."[39]

Within this verbal interaction there developed a "republican language" that was widely understood. According to Isaac, "Such customary dramatic means for the reinforcement of values and forms of authority, combined with the range of activities that took place at the court-day fair, shaped social identity and communal experience. That was why the concourse of people at such centers as the courthouse was so important; and it is against this background that we must view the remarkable phenomenon of Virginia's almost dissent-free mobilization for rebellion and revolution."[40]

It should be remembered, however, that the American colonists also enjoyed a relatively high level of literacy. Puritan Massachusetts witnessed early the first public elementary and grammar schools in America, and their maintenance was assigned to the town governments: "There was an enormous emphasis placed upon education, not simply in terms of literacy—which was high—nor even practical education—which was necessary—but good old-fashioned classical learning, broad and all-encompassing. People needed to be able to read the scriptures for themselves, it was believed, and they needed to be able to comprehend the human experience described in them. Hard work, individual ownership, and basic education were all a part of the dissenter's ethic of standing on one's own feet before God."[41] When the Reverend Samuel Webster delivered his Massachusetts Election Sermon in 1777, he pled, "Let the people by all means encourage schools and colleges, and all the means of learning and knowledge, if they would guard against slavery. For a wise, a knowing and a learned people, are the least likely of any in the world to be enslaved." "Man must have something more than a fortuitous complex of virtue and vices," confirmed Rossiter in his analysis of colonial thought. "He was *educable*—he could learn why to cherish virtue and shun vice, how to serve the community and defend liberty. Free government rested on virtue, virtue on knowledge, knowledge on regular technique of education."[42]

Many colonists read and were influenced *directly* by the tracts, pamphlets, editorials, books, and printed sermons during the revolutionary period, which served greatly to spread and confirm the Puritan-libertarian doctrines of virtue, dissent and liberty. "The reading of those colonists who were inclined to books, generally favoured the cause of liberty. . . . Their books were generally small in size and few in number: A great part of them consisted of those fashionable authors, who have defended the cause of liberty. *Cato's Letters*, the *Independent Whig*, and such productions were common in one extreme of the colonies, while in the other, histories of the Puritans kept alive the remembrance of the sufferings of their forefathers, and inspired a warm attachment, both to the civil and the religious rights of human nature."[43]

Bailyn was struck in his study of colonial political literature by the "undeniable evidence of the seriousness with which colonial and revolutionary leaders took ideas, and the deliberateness of their efforts." He concluded that the "American Provincials" were "remarkably well informed students of contemporary social and political theory."[44] John Adams agreed in no uncertain terms. "A native American who cannot read or write is as rare as a camel or an earthquake. It has been observed that we are all of lawyers, divines, politicians, and philosophers. And I have good authorities to say, that all candid foreigners who have passed through this country, and conversed freely with all sorts of people here, will allow that they have never seen so much knowledge and civility among a common people in any part of the world."[45]

In Virginia and throughout the colonies, it was the impact of the "republican language" that dramatized events and solidified thought that forged the forces of revolution. And it was the concept of virtue that laced the republican language with emotional content, ideological zeal and near-universal meaning. " 'Virtue,' at the heart of patriot aspirations," wrote Isaac, "was not just a moral quality or disposition; it was a program for the preservation and regeneration of society. By the operation of virtue, the necessary ranking of society could be rendered compatible with the dignity and worth of free men. It was to this vision that the patriot leadership thrilled," and it was the spiritual impact of the ideal of virtue that was communicated in various ways throughout the colonial communities that engendered a "basis for popular action."[46] "Virtue" became more than a series of personal responsibilities interpolated from the Scriptures and other moral discourse; it became more than self-sacrifice for the good of Church and commonwealth. As the marriage between modern "virtue" and "republicanism" developed, the concept went beyond "the ability to comprehend" universal moral values; it absorbed as well belief in "the capacity to direct and control one's own actions," and "independence from the control of others."[47]

THE RELIGIOUS BACKGROUND OF THE FOUNDERS

The Founders, as a whole, were deeply religious men. Religion played a vital role in most of their lives; and their beliefs, activities, their ideals and hopes were influenced both directly and indirectly by the religious culture in which they were reared. The foundation of their modern republican philosophy was based on a belief in God. Whatever the concepts that merged to form this republican doctrine—the dignity of man, natural law, natural rights, the right of resistance—all were superimposed with an aura of the sacred. Many of the Founders were Christian in their persuasion; others remained in various degrees skeptical of the divinity of Christ, though seldom so of the utilitarian nature of his doctrine for republicanism. Others believed in "one God," as creator of the universe, a God whose providence remained a real force in history. Unfortunately, many of the Founders who believed in this "activist" God are summarily and incorrectly lumped under the general category of "Deists." For to the Deist, God was a Creator of *first instance*, and did not now function as an "activist" force in history. Nevertheless, Deists did generally believe in the immortality of the soul and a judgment by a just God for actions committed in this life. "The probability that we may be called to account hereafter," wrote Thomas Paine, the self-styled Deist, "will, to reflecting minds, have the influence of belief; for it is not our belief or disbelief that can make or unmake the fact. As this is the state we are in, and which it is proper that we should be in, as free agents, it is a fool only, and not the philospher, nor even the prudent man, that will live as if there was no God. . . . Were a man impressed as fully and strongly as he ought to be with the belief of a God, his moral life would be regulated by the force of belief; he would stand in awe of God and of himself, and would not do the thing that could not be concealed from either."[48]

While some of the Founders did not actively participate in church rites, they believed in a God that had immediate relevance to their lives. Christians, believers in "one God," *and Deists* all believed that man had a soul and was destined for life beyond his earthly habitation, that there had been established by their Creator certain natural laws among which were those relating to man's relationship to his fellowmen, and that man would be judged at last for that responsibility. This foundation provided a base upon which these men were able to build their modern republican philosophy.

The Founders launched themselves on their great experiment with the harmonizing foundation common to nearly all of them—a belief in God as the Creator of the universe and as the endower of men's basic rights. It was this faith that sustained them both in what they believed to be the righteousness of their endeavor and in the energy required to carry it through. It carried them through the dark hours of the Revolution, and bound them together amid the inevitable disagreements at the Philadelphia Convention where the Constitution was born. To be sure, numbers of the Founders may have differed in their interpretation of God and some were critical of practices in the religious organizations of their time. But these qualifications had little effect on their personal allegiance to God as it did so many of the Philosophes in Europe. "I was never without some religious principles. I never doubted . . . the existence of the Deity," wrote Franklin.[49] Said Adams, "I have been a church-going animal for seventy-six years."[50] Narrating an occasion when he was asked if he believed in

God, John Jay responded, "I answered that I did, and that I thanked God I did."[51]

Benevolence and The Founders

A fundamental aspect of the religious philosophy of the Founders was its view of the human personality, including the doctrine of the immortal soul and the concept of human dignity. This energized and legitimized the nature of rights and duties, the insistence upon individual worth and responsibility, brotherhood, and charity or love. It is significant how often reference to benevolence or the Golden Rule appears in the words of the American Founders and spokesmen, accompanied by expressions of their belief in God. This concept was the cornerstone in their ideal of virtue. Thus, they sound very much like the Renaissance humanists, the Latitude men, and the Cambridge Platonists of previous generations. Typical are Madison's statement that "[W]hat is here a right towards men is a duty towards the Creator,"[52] and his prayer that over the Republic would be erected "one Empire of Reason, benevolence and brotherly affection."[53] Jefferson insisted that "there is only one God, and He all perfect; . . . to love God with all thy heart and thy neighbor as thyself is the sum of religion,"[54] that "nature hath implanted in our breasts a love of others, a sense of duty to them, a moral instinct, in short, which prompts us irresistibly to feel and to succor their distresses."[55] Thomas Paine affirmed in *The Age of Reason* that "I consider myself in the hands of my Creator. . . . To do good is my religion. . . . I believe that religious duties consist in doing justice, loving mercy, and endeavoring to make our fellow creatures happy."[56] Franklin admonished that the most "acceptable service" one can "render to" God "is in doing good to his other children,"[57] that "the Scripture assures me that at the last Day, we shall not be examin'd what we *thought*, but what we *did*; and our Recommendation will not be that we said *Lord, Lord*, but that we did GOOD to our Fellow Creatures."[58] John Adams' belief was that the concept of "love your neighbor as yourself, and do to others as you would that others should do to you," was "a great principle of the law of nature."[59] "My religion," he emphasized, "is founded on the love of God, and my neighbor." While natural law assumed the right of self-preservation, it also obligated men to be benevolent, that is, to have "affection for the good of others."[60] And George Washington, in his farewell address to his revolutionary troops stated: "I now make it my earnest prayer that God . . . would incline the hearts of the citizens . . . to entertain a brotherly affection for one another, for their fellow citizens of the United States at large, and particularly for their brethren who have served in the field. And finally that He would most graciously be pleased to dispose us all to do justice, to love mercy, and to demean ourselves, with that charity, humility and pacific temper of mind, which were the characteristics of the Divine Author of our religion, and without an humble imitation of whose example in these things, we can never hope to be a happy nation."[61] These statements and numerous like them give examples of the extent to which the Judeo-Christian ethic had penetrated the modern American concept of virtue and was embraced by the Founders.

There was a general admonition in colonial America to express brotherly affection. "At the community level," wrote Madison's biographer Ralph Ketcham, "the compulsion to make life count for good expressed itself in numerous humanitarian enterprises, of which the Quakers furnish the most notable examples. Significantly, Benjamin Franklin's career in Philadelphia, the best individual expression of this impulse, had its origin . . . in the clubs organized in Boston by Cotton Mather to encourage a brotherly concern among Christians. Though this outreach could and did have its less commendable watch-and-ward aspects, a citizenry conditioned to attitudes of concern for fellow citizens and experienced in the methods of humanitarianism nevertheless would have priceless habits and skills for the tasks of revolution and nation building."[62]

The Religious Culture of James Madison

According to Ketcham, the importance of the religious culture of the Framers can be traced in the writings of Madison throughout his lifetime. Madison's Judeo-Christian background, wrote Ketcham, "united him with nearly all the leaders in revolution and nation building, including the heterodox Franklin and Jefferson, in commitment to certain moral standards. To them all, the Ten Commandments, the Sermon on the Mount, and the twelfth chapter of Paul's Epistle to the Romans were canonical. . . . It is not possible to understand the purpose and earnestness of Madison's public life without sensing its connection with the Christian atmosphere in which he was raised."[63]

If one considers Madison as an example of the educated young men of his time, the influence of religious culture is clear. According to Professor Ketcham: "Certain elements of Christian thought had almost universal acceptance in colonial America and are important to an understanding of Madison's intellectual growth. The Christian affirmation, for example, that each human soul has infinite worth, and the emphasis in the Protestant tradition that the essence of this worth is the relationship of each individual to the Almighty, were of vast significance. There were, therefore, limits to the claim the state could make upon the individual. Whatever Christians disagreed about and however their conduct might fall short, they all affirmed that in any ultimate confrontation between mere human dictates and the law of God, the former must give way. In accepting this view, Madison acknowledged that there is a nontemporal source of values; he insisted that the state live up to them, and he affirmed that individuals in a society were bound by more-than-earthly obligations."[64] It was from this Christian tradition that Madison "inherited a sense of the prime importance of conscience, a strict personal morality, and understanding of human dignity as well as depravity, and a conviction that vital religion could contribute importantly to the general welfare."[65]

Every one of Madison's teachers, as far as we know, continued Professor Ketcham, "was either a clergyman or a devoutly orthodox Christian layman. In fact, so pervasive was Christian influence, especially in rearing children, that an education under other than Christian auspices was virtually unknown. Even the technically non-sectarian College of Philadelphia founded by Franklin gave its students the usual training in Christian morality and was presided over by a zealous Anglican minister."[66] Madison studied for five years under the Scottish minister-educator Donald Robertson where he appears to have been schooled in English, Greek, Latin, and the works of such philosophers as Aristotle, Plato, Montesquieu, and Locke. He enjoyed the tutelage of the Anglican minister Thomas Martin for two years. And although his studies branched far afield from religion, even to geography and mathematics, the religious element remained fundamental. Madison was an astute pupil of theology. William Rives, who reviewed Madison's copious notes taken from the New Testament called them profound.[67] He was later retained by the newly established University of Virginia to develop a catalogue of ancient and modern theologians for the university library. One of the most prolific writers on James Madison, Gaillard Hunt, has suggested that Madison, upon completing his college education, could have contemplated entering the ministry.[68]

Madison's experience as a student at Princeton (then College of New Jersey), according to Professor Ketcham, represented some of the most important factors and influences that shaped the man who would come to be known as "The Father of the Constitution." Apparently, Madison's parents were so impressed with Reverend Martin, a graduate of the College of New Jersey, that the decision was made to send their son there rather than to William and Mary.

At the time of Madison's matriculation, in 1769, two lively and intense dissenting traditions claimed preeminence there—those of the colonial Great Awakening, and the dissenting-libertarian movement from England. "Founded by Presbyterians anxious to assure that educated ministers would fill the pulpits of their rapidly increasing churches, it was strongly influenced by the 'New Lights,' who, following Jonathan Edwards, the Tennants, and Samuel Davies, sought to make Presbyterianism a vital, personally-felt force in the lives of increasing numbers of laymen."[69] Furthermore, from the beginning (1746), the College had been in close contact with and displayed sympathy toward the English dissenting academies. When the authorities at the College of New Jersey sought advice and precedent from Great Britain, they turned to these dissenting academies rather than to Oxford or Cambridge."[70]

"When Madison went to the middle colonies and to the Presbyterian stronghold at Princeton," wrote Ketcham, "he placed himself at the center of the English dissenting tradition in North America. He found there that enlightened men took for granted the pattern of thought which, from Cromwell's day, had opposed religious establishment, ecclesiastical hierarchy, courtly influence, and every other manifestation of privileged and therefore easily and inevitably corruptible power. The heroes of this tradition were Milton, Algernon Sidney, Locke, and, most widely read of all in the American colonies, the authors of *Cato's Letters*, John Trenchard and Thomas Gordon. Obsessed with an almost paranoid suspicion that all power in human hands would be abused, and on guard against exaggerated pretensions to authority, those who read the dissenting writers were ready to enlist, as Witherspoon had done in Scotland and would do again when he signed the Declaration of Independence, in any campaign to resist 'domination and tyranny.' In the presence of this eternal vigilance, James Madison undertook his college studies."[71]

John Witherspoon had arrived from Scotland in 1768 to become the President of the College of New Jersey. He was a Presbyterian Minister who had been educated at Edinburgh University. He was to have substantial influence on his new country as the only clergyman to sign the Declaration of Independence and as a member of the Continental Congress from 1776 to 1779, and again from 1780 to 1782. Although Madison's religious and political beliefs developed from many sources and experiences, the influence of Witherspoon on him must have been considerable. According to Richard B. Morris, Witherspoon, "whose expositions of the doctrines of resistance and liberty quickly established him throughout the Continent as an imposing . . . intellectual," was "most influential in shaping Madison's . . . outlook."[72] Madison, upon graduation, had remained at Princeton for six months to read under his tutelage and, according to Ketcham, "the impression is inescapable that Madison had in Witherspoon a remarkably able, learned, and eloquent teacher."[73]

The venerable Witherspoon brought to his students at Princeton a great intellectual heritage from both England and Scotland. The Scottish Revolution, it should be noted, was a companion to the Puritan Revolution. Some of the most important Reformation literature was written by Scottish scholars and ministers. Rutherford's *Lex Rex or the Law and the Prince* (1644), for example, challenged the divine right of kings with the premise that biblical or God's law stood above that of the king rather than being coterminous with it. The book was banned in Scotland and later publicly burned. It is likely that, to a greater or lesser extent, the doctrine of *Lex Rex* was brought to America through the influence of Scottish immigrants such as John Witherspoon. Furthermore, "we know from Witherspoon's reading lists that Robertson, Smollett, Hume, Hutcheson, Kames, Adam Smith, Ferguson, and others were familiar to him, and that he brought their books to America."[74] And among the multitude of other writings assigned to his students were Grotius, Pufendorf, Barbeyrac, Cumberland, Selden, Burlamaqui and Locke.[75]

Perhaps one of the most important influences on Witherspoon was Francis Hutcheson. He was, writes Professor Robbins, "both subject to and part of the common influences and enthusiasms of the first half of the eighteenth century."[76] According to Ralph Hamoway, Hutcheson was closely "acquainted with Locke's political writings," and was "early exposed to whig revolutionary doctrine as expounded in the theories of James Harrington, [and] Algernon Sidney."[77] He was influenced by his close friendship with Robert Molesworth, who was a friend of Trenchard and a supporter of the Revolution of 1688, who served in both the Irish and British parliaments for nearly 30 years, and who Caroline Robbins describes as the premier liberal Whig of his time. In his *System of Moral Philosophy* (published posthumously in 1775), Hutcheson placed great emphasis on the principle that virtue and happiness were closely related. To him, virtue was the bedrock of a happy society. He emphasized as well benevolence and man's moral sense. He also advocated liberty and the right of resistence against corruption and tyranny.

So it was that Witherspoon brought to Princeton a great heritage of political thought. He was especially concerned that his Princeton students be "well instructed on the major concern of eighteenth-century moral philosophers: the proper relation between religion and ethics, between faith and being a good person." In Witherspoon's philosophy, "the basic inquiry was 'what *Honesty* or virtue is, consider'd by itself; and in what manner it is influenc'd by Religion: How far *Religion* necessarily implies virtue; and whether it be a true saying, that it is impossible for an Atheist to be Virtuous, or share any real degree of Honesty, or Merit.'" And, as far as Witherspoon was concerned, the answer rested "unequivocally on the side of religion. He told his classes that 'the whole Scripture is agreeable to sound philosophy,' meaning that he rejected rationalist insinuations that the Bible contained passages absurd to reasonable men and therefore best denied or at least passed over. . . . Throughout, Witherspoon insisted on the orthodox Christian view that life was real and earnest and that the only salvation for sinful men was a devout Biblical faith."[78]

Thus, while the "college of New Jersey in Madison's day *was* the seedbed of sedition and nursery of rebels . . . , it was as well a school for statesmen trained to seek freedom and ordered government through the pursuit of virtue."[79] As he "came to accept as well the Lockean concepts of representation and government by consent, he *added* them to his earlier education in the politics of virtue. A great gulf, therefore, separates the thought of Madison (and the other Founding Fathers)," suggests Ketcham, "from that of believers in such later concepts as Benthamite utilitarianism and simple majoritarian democracy, who denied that principles of justice and virtue can be identified and made the foundation of government, and therefore have a higher sanction than the will of the majority."[80]

Providence and the Founders

Since the American Founders were products of the religious environment into which they were born, nurtured, and attained manhood, they were certainly not immune from the religious concepts of the Covenant, a Chosen People, and a New Israel; for these ideas permeated the thinking of the colonies. It appears that, as events transpired leading to the Revolution, the Declaration, and the Constitution, the Founders spoke more and more in terms of a mission for the new land they occupied, and referral to an intervening Providence appeared increasingly in their writings and their spoken word. Their sense of history and belief in God combined to engender a cautious hypothesis that Providence had placed them in this place and at this time with opportunities that had great import for mankind. Rossiter reminds us that "American statesmen and writers were to assert that God had singled out this country for peculiar blessings, but in bestowing His grace had also bestowed a particular responsibility for the success of free government."[81]

Robert A. Rutland, editor of *The Papers of James Madison*, insists that Madison's chief interest in life was to prove that America had been chosen by Providence for an experiment to test man's capacity for self-government. "The free system of government we have established," stated Madison, "is so congenial with reason, with common sense, and with a universal feeling, that it must produce approbation and a desire of imitation, as avenues may be found for truth to the knowledge of nations. Our country, if it does justice to itself, will be the workshop of liberty to the Civilized World, and do more than any other for the uncivilized."[82]

"I always consider the settlement of America with reverence and wonder," wrote John Adams in his *A Dissertation on the Canon and the Feudal Law*, "as the opening of a grand scene and design in Providence for the illumination of the ignorant, and the emancipation of the slavish part of mankind all over the earth."[83] Hamilton wrote in the first *Federalist*, "It has been frequently remarked that it seems to have been reserved to the people of this country, by their conduct and example, to decide the important question, whether societies of men are really capable or not of establishing good government from reflection and choice, or whether they are forever destined to depend for their political constitutions on accident and force." "The last hope of human liberty," confirmed Jefferson, "rests on us."[84] And Paine wrote in *Common Sense*, "The cause of America is in great measure the cause of all mankind."[85] Both Jefferson and Adams had seen universal significance in the principles of the Declaration of Independence that went beyond the confines of the United States. "May it be to the world what I believe it will be (to some parts sooner, to others later, but finally to all)," wrote Jefferson, "the signal of arousing men to burst the chains under which monkish ignorance and superstition had persuaded them to bind themselves, and to assume the blessings of security and self-government."[86] To his wife, Adams prophesied that the day of the signing would become "the most memorable . . . in the history of America." Through the gloom of the trying days ahead, he saw "rays of ravishing light and glory." He warned that if America failed in her divinely appointed mission, it would be "treason against the hopes of the world."[87]

Time and again the leaders among the Founders referred to what they believed to be an intervening Providence in their behalf. In the second *Federalist*, John Jay expressed his pleasure that "Providence" had "in a particular manner blessed" America in its natural attributes, and had "been pleased to give this one connected country to one united people descended from the same ancestors, speaking the same language, professing the same religion, attached to the same principles of government, very similar in their manners and customs and who, by their joint counsels, arms, and efforts fighting side by side throughout a long and bloody war, have nobly established general liberty and independence." "It is impossible for the man of pious reflection," wrote Madison in *The Federalist* concerning the founding of the nation, "not to perceive in it a finger of that Almighty hand which has been so frequently and signally extended to our relief in the critical stages of the Revolution. The real wonder," he offered, "is

that so many difficulties should have been surmounted with a unanimity almost as unprecedented as it must have been unexpected. It
is impossible for any man of candor to reflect on this circumstance
without partaking of the astonishment."[88] On the same subject Hamilton was to write in the "Letters of Caesar and Cato" in October of
1787, "for my own part, I sincerely esteem it a system, which,
without the finger of God, never could have been suggested and
agreed upon by such a diversity of interests."[89] "Let us pause, my
fellow citizens," wrote Madison and Hamilton concerning past political failures, "for one moment over this melancholy and monitory
lesson of history; and with the tear that drops for the calamities
brought on mankind by their adverse opinions and selfish passions;
let our gratitude mingle an ejaculation to Heaven, for the propitious
concord which has distinguished the consultations for our political
happiness."[90] And Washington insisted that the "Supreme Being"
had protected "the liberty and happiness of these United States."[91]
He frequently referred to "the interposition of Providence," or "the
interposing Hand of Heaven," or "the Supreme Ruler of the Universe." In discussing the trials which had been weathered by the new
nation, he stated emphatically: "The Hand of Providence has been so
conspicuous in all this, that he must be worse than an infidel that lacks
faith, and more than wicked, that has not gratitude enough to
acknowledge his obligations."[92] In his *Inaugural Address* President
Washington submitted: "No people can be found to acknowledge and
adore the Invisible Hand which conducts the affairs of men more than
the people of the United States. Every step by which they have
advanced to the character of an independent nation seems to have
been distinguished by some token of Providential agency." In his
Second Inaugural Address, Thomas Jefferson acknowledged "that Being
in whose hands we are, who led our Forefathers as Israel of old, from
their native land and planted them in a country flowing with all the
necessaries and comforts of life, who has covered our infancy with
His providence and our ripe years with his wisdom and power." "In
the beginning of the Contest with G[reat] Britain," Franklin had
reaffirmed to the Philadelphia Convention, "when we were sensible
of danger we had daily prayer in this room for the divine protection.
Our prayers . . . were heard, and they were graciously answered. All
of us who were engaged in the struggle must have observed frequent
instances of a Superintending providence in our favor. To that kind
providence we owe this happy opportunity of consulting in peace on
the means of establishing our future national felicity . . . the longer I
live, the more convincing proofs I see of this truth—*that God governs in
the affairs of men* . . . I also believe that without his concurring aid we

shall succeed in this political building no better than the Builders of Babel."[93]

The Importance of Religion for Public Virtue

Not only did the American Founders, in general, express a belief in God, they often expressed the idea that virtue or morality needed the fostering care of religion to keep it energized. Religion and belief in God were viewed as essential to the promotion and longevity of virtue and morality, and hence the perpetuation of Republican government. "Few men who cherished virtue as the foundation of liberty," argued Rossiter, "ever doubted that religion was in turn the foundation of virtue."[94] Perhaps Franklin has best expressed the importance of religion as a primary force in the indoctrination and reinforcement of virtue in society. "You yourself may find it easy to live a virtuous Life without the Assistance afforded by Religion," Franklin responded to a critic, "you having a clear Perception of the Advantages of Virtue, and the Disadvantages of Vice, and possessing a Strength of Resolution sufficient to enable you to resist common Temptations. But think how great a Proportion of Mankind consists of weak and ignorant Men and Women, and of inexperienc'd and inconsiderate Youth of both Sexes, who have need of the Motives of Religion to restrain them from Vice, to support their Virtue and retain them in the Practice of it until it becomes *habitual*, which is the great Point for its Security. . . . If men are so wicked as we now see them *with religion*, what would they be if *without it*."[95]

Madison, in *The Federalist* No. 39, warned that the future of constitutional institutions would be based, not upon the power of the government, but upon the ability of the people to govern themselves. He was convinced that a "belief in a God all Powerful wise and good is so essential to the moral order of the world and to the happiness of man, that arguments which enforce it cannot be drawn from too many sources."[96] "Of all the dispositions and habits, which lead to political prosperity," concurred George Washington in his *Farewell Address*, "religion and morality are indispensable supports. In vain would that man claim the tribute of Patriotism, who should labor to subvert these great pillars of human happiness, these firmest props of the duties of Men and Citizens. The mere politician, equally with the pious man, ought to respect and to cherish them. A volume could not trace all their connections with private and public felicity. . . . And let us with caution indulge the supposition, that morality can be maintained without religion. Whatever may be conceded to the influence of refined education on minds of peculiar structure—reason and experience both forbid us to expect, that national morality can prevail in exclusion of religious principles. It is substantially true, that virtue or morality is a necessary spring of popular government."[97] "Our Constitution," reaffirmed Adams in no uncertain terms, "was made only for a moral and religious people. It is wholly inadequate to the government of any other." "We have no government armed with power capable of contending with human passions unbridled by morality and religion," he stated in October of 1798.[98] And Samuel Adams added, "Revelation assures us that 'righteousness exalteth a nation.' Communities are dealt with in this world by the wise and just Ruler of the Universe. He rewards or punishes them according to their general character. The diminution of public virtue is usually attended with that of public happiness, and the public liberty will not long survive the total extinction of morals."[99] Chief Justice Joseph Story, whose distinguished career on the Supreme Court coincided with the presidency of Madison, wrote in his commentaries that religion with its sponsorship of morality and virtue was essential to political freedom: "Piety, religion and morality are intimately connected with the well-being of the state, and indispensable to the administration of civil justice," he declared. "The Promulgation of the great doctrines of religion, the being, and attributes, and providence of one Almighty God, the responsibility to him for all our actions, founded upon moral freedom and accountability; a future state of rewards and punishments, the cultivation of all the personal, social and benevolent virtues—these never can be a matter of indifference in any well-ordered community." In conclusion, he stressed, "It is indeed, difficult to conceive how any civilized society can well exist without them."[100]

Alexis de Tocqueville argued that religious belief in America was closely allied to other elements of the American polity. "Liberty regards religion as its companion in all its battles and its triumphs," he wrote, "as the cradle of its infancy, and the divine source of its claims. It considers religion as the safeguard of morality, and morality as the best security of law and the surest pledge of the duration of freedom."[101] He emphasized that "it must never be forgotten that religion gave birth to Anglo-American society. In the United States, religion is therefore mingled with all the habits of the nation and all the feelings of patriotism."[102]

These "habits," "feelings," "manners" or "ethics," whose importance for the American experience so impressed de Tocqueville and others, were manifestations of a sense of personal and civic responsibility which gained their most immediate influence primarily from the Christian or Puritan ethic and spirit that were developed in England and were extended to America. The idea of virtue became an integral part of American religious thought and practice applied to the public attitude and philosophy of the time.

VIRTUE AND THE REVOLUTION

As the period immediately preceding the Revolution grew more volatile with each passing event, the concept of virtue ignited an increasing emotional response from the American colonists. This emotional response was partly a cause and a result of growing feelings of alienation from England. In the past, sermons had given homage to the British Constitution and the Crown; now there was expressed increasing dissent and estrangement from the mother country and her leadership. The emotional attachment that remained was related to Britain's past and the principles of the British Revolution. Modern England came to be seen as a prostitution of its glorious heritage. A king without "kingly virtues," it was oft-expressed, was only a man. In effect, what was happening in America was a rebirth of the Puritan revolutionary spirit. A second Puritan revolution—or the New World continuation of the original Puritan revolution and the "glorious Revolution"—was taking place.

"The colonial opposition," wrote Christopher Dawson, "felt that it represented not only local interests but Whig constitutional principles and the traditions of the English Revolution. The political philosophy of Sidney and Locke provided a common platform on which the representatives of the American Enlightenment . . . could unite with the leaders of the Puritan democracy of New England . . . in the same way as the Whig aristocrats had combined with the Protestant bourgeoisie in 1688."[103] James Burgh's condemnation of British corruption was widely read in the colonies. Thomas Jefferson was particularly drawn to Whig history. In his *Summary View of the Rights of British America*, he likened colonial resistance against British tyranny with that of the British radicals. Inasmuch as Americans were heirs of English liberty, wrote Morison, "they would not, could not accept any second-rate status in the English Empire—and they had read in their well-thumbed Algernon Sidney and John Locke, that if a Prince breaks his implied compact with his people, it is their right, their duty, to resist."[104]

The messages of British radicals, such as Sidney, which proclaimed the right of resistance to the abuse of power, were turned into moral mandates. England had become corrupted by violating her constitution, corrupted by allowing the continuation of an unrepresentative Parliament, and corrupted by a conspiracy to envelop her American colonies in tyranny. American spokesmen and their iisteners spoke often of the "corrupting manners of England." "[C]ontemporary England," observed Colbourn, "was frequently shown racing toward economic, moral, and political collapse, ridden with corruption, and afflicted with an unrepresentative Parliament."[105] Certain segments of colonial society were particularly concerned with what they considered to be the evil influences of "patronage." According to Frank Fox, patronage "was the oil that lubricated not only English society but English politics, English arts, even English science. . . . In Walpole's England it figured into everything."

> Under a patronage system every man was dependent on some higher person in society—his 'patron'—for many of the important opportunities of life. In order to get an education, in order to marry the right kind of wife, in order to find gainful and dignified employment, a person depended not upon his own intelligence or resources but upon his patron, someone higher in the socio-economic scale. . . .
>
> Patronage had two critical drawbacks. In the first place, it spelled a marked loss of individual independence. Everyone was obliged to be obsequious and servile. No one could be proud and self-reliant. . . . In the second place, patronage spelled corruption, especially in politics. The constant trading of favors back and forth is the very definition of corruption . . . [W]ith the machinery of patronage in motion, any constitutional separation of powers wholly ceased to exist—for the king was effectively buying off Parliament.[106]

Even though patronage had also infected colonial society, Americans were never comfortable with it. "[The] children of the founding Puritans and Quakers never could bring themselves to countenance patronage's bad features. Corruption and the loss of personal independence had a special meaning in America; these were the things that the Jeremiad sermons denounced most vehemently." As of "1767, the last year of Wentworth's rule, the world of patronage that England had so carefully transplanted was already in the twilight of its years. . . . Americans . . . came to see personal dependency as a corrupting influence—*the* corrupting influence—in English politics."[107] According to Pocock, they believed that the crown's patronage power multiplied "the incidence in society of individuals whose modes of social and political existence entailed a dependence upon government that made them a menace to their neighbors." Virtue, continues Pocock, "required an individual so independent of other men and their social structures that his dedication to the *res publica* could be wholly autonomous."[108]

Such issues as the attempt of the British to cajole Americans into paying for part of the costs of the French and Indian War, the Stamp Act, the Townshend Act (both taxes, which the colonists argued Parliament had no legal right to levy), "virtual" rather than direct representation (the idea that each member of Parliament "virtually" represented all the members of the Empire), and further abuses considered in violation of the colonists' Natural Rights by Crown and Parliament, were seen as both constitutional *and moral* issues. These, combined with the rumor that an Anglican bishop was to be foisted upon the colonies, stimulated the belief that a conspiracy of corrupt power was directed against colonial freedoms and institutions. This led Morison to conclude that (in Virginia at least), the question of resistance and finally independence was made "entirely on political, philosophical and emotional grounds."[109] And Professor Stout reminds us that although the republican *vocabulary* "was largely provided . . . through the Commonwealth tradition . . . the ethos and ideological fervor of republicanism did not derive so much from the injection of Commonwealth vocabulary into colonial pamphlets as from the translation of the evangelical experience into secular theoretical vocabulary that more adequately embodied, for some, the revolutionary thrust first widely experienced in the revivals."[110]

As the philosophy of Republicanism came to be more discussed and developed, the ideal of civic virtue grew as an indispensable part of the doctrine. Virtue made a "republican people," and only a "republican people" could support a popular republic. Virtue, then, becomes a utilitarian necessity to popular government. Gordon S. Wood has narrated well both the remarkable resilience of classical and medieval concepts and the transformation of civic virtue in the eighteenth century to complement a modern, Christian community.

> That the greatness, indeed the very existence of a republic depended upon the people's virtue was "a maxim" established by the "universal consent" and the "experience of all ages." All these notions of liberty, equality, and public virtue were indelible sentiments "already graven upon the hearts" of Americans, who realized fully the fragility of the republican polity.
>
> In a monarchy each man's desire to do what was right in his own eyes could be restrained by fear or force. In a republic, however, each man must somehow be persuaded to submerge his personal wants into the greater good of the whole. This willingness of the individual to sacrifice his private interests for the good of the community—such patriotism or love of country—the eighteenth century termed "public virtue." A republic was such a delicate polity precisely because it demanded an extraordinary moral character in the people. Every state in which the people participated needed a degree of virtue; but a republic which rested solely on the people absolutely required it. Although a particular structural arrangement of the government in a republic might temper the necessity for public virtue, ultimately "no model of government whatever can equal the importance of this principle, nor afford proper safety and security without it." Without

some portion of this generous principle, anarchy and confusion would immediately ensue, the jarring interests of individuals, regarding themselves only, and indifferent to the welfare of others, would still further heighten the distressing scene, and with the assistance of the selfish passions, it would end in the ruin and subversion of the state. The eighteenth-century mind was thoroughly convinced that a popularly based government "cannot be supported without Virtue." Only with a public-spirited, self-sacrificing people could the authority of a popularly elected ruler be obeyed, but "more by virtue of the people, than by the terror of his power." Because virtue was truly the lifeblood of the republic, the thoughts and hopes surrounding this concept of public spirit gave the Revolution its socially radical character—an expected alteration in the very behavior of the people, "laying the foundation in a constitution, not without or over, but within the subjects."[111]

Virtue, as Rossiter has pointed out, was made "the essence of liberty." With Montesquieu, Americans of the Revolutionary era concluded: "Fear is the principle of a despotic, honour of a kingly, and virtue is the principle of a republican government."[112] Writing in 1775, Samuel Williams concurred. "In a *despotic government*, the only principle by which the Tyrant who is to move the whole machine, means to regulate and manage the people, is Fear; by the servile dread of his power. But a *free government*, which of all others is far the most preferable, cannot be supported without virtue."[113]

Nevertheless, it should not be supposed that the ideal of virtue in the Revolutionary period was a classical carbon copy. Modern virtue had become something more—and as well something less—than classical virtue. The ideal of freedom, for instance, had become to a great extent a spiritual one, the concept of human dignity fairly a religious sacrament.

On the other hand, civic virtue had lost its classical severity and had come to mean an almost spontaneous loyalty freely and individually expressed by moral individuals. The colonists not only recoiled from English political corruption, they feared moral corruption as well, and in terms of moral theology. The public vernacular was expressed not merely in terms of virtue against corruption, but good against evil, virtue against vice and righteousness against sin. "In both England and America," writes Pocock, "there existed an ideology which presented governmental 'corruption' as a nearly total threat to society and personality."[114] And while this observation certainly has merit, it does not tell the full story without an acknowledgment that the threat to "society" was seen by Americans at least to include primary institutions such as family and religion; and that the threat to "personality" included connotations of biblical morality.

Most certainly the use of terms such as corruption, virtue, natural rights, human dignity, freedom, and a host of others carried with them to a greater or lesser extent the penetrating heritage of biblical religion. To suggest, for instance, that "the predominant language in which [the idea of power reverting to the people] was expressed by eighteenth-century radicals was one of virtue, corruption, and re-form, which is Machiavellian, classical and Aristotelian,"[115] is to depreciate not only the substantial influence of philosophers such as Locke, but the penetrating influence of the religious environment as well. It must be remembered that many terms attributed to philosophy past and present had by the eighteenth century and before assumed the mantle of the "sacred;" that is, their meaning, and hence their impact was significantly influenced by a profound religious heritage. One wonders whether these terms would have incited the emotion and carried the force of authority they did had they remained solely philosophical in meaning.

If the conflict with Britain was increasingly seen as a moral battle between virtue and corruption, the same concept caused Americans to look inward to their own worthiness. According to Stout, "The dynamic for revolution issued from a deep sense of moral corruption and degradation that found a target in English oppression but, more important, spoke to the sins of colonial society itself. For generations of colonists schooled in the language of the covenant, judgment, and collective accountability, the Jeremiad functioned as the 'form of discourse' capable of driving them to a moral revolution. Considered as an intellectual movement, the Revolution represented a spiritual purge administered to a corrupt established order in the interest of restoring a pure order that would both free the colonists from a decadent oppressor and cleanse their own society. The Revolution was inspired by this highly unstable compound of pious contrition and political rebellion, moral reformation and patriotic resistance."[116]

Virtue became the unifying theme that sublimated many of the strains that had divided or threatened to divide the people of the colonies. Many began to question whether enough republican virtue was extant in the colonies to complement the righteousness of their cause. There was a nagging source of anxiety among Americans: "How could they denounce British corruption if their own virtue was questionable?"[117]

The transformation of Americans into a "republican" people was not institutionally created; it was the result of a faith, an ideology, a creed. As Professor Fox puts it, "Institutions might curtail the fallen and perverse in man's nature, but institutions could not alter that nature itself. For that task there had to be some sort of redemptive, regenerating experience, something the political philosophers could not easily define or comprehend. The American Founders may not have been able to define or comprehend it either, but they knew it when they saw it, and as the American Revolution drew upon them they referred to it with ever greater insistence. It was the cement of republican society, the thing that, beyond institutions, held that society together and made it work. Without it, clearly, there could be no American republic, just as in Nathaniel Bacon's day there was no Virginian republic. The Founders called it 'public virtue.' "[118] As Heimert and Miller have argued, *this phenomenon brought an affinity, a brotherhood, between the ideas of Puritanism and republicanism.*

For the Americans, religion and republicanism "would work hand in hand to create frugality, honesty, self-denial, and benevolence among the people."[119] This was the essence of John Winthrop's "City Upon a Hill," and it influenced all aspects of Puritan life—not that they always achieved it against the corruption of man's "fallen nature," but that they sought for it, often with great diligence. As Wood explained: "The Americans would then 'shew to the nations of the earth (what will be a most singular phenomenon) amidst all the jarring interests, subtlety, and rage of politics' that they 'had virtue enough to think of, and to practice these things.'" Thus, the view of America as a city upon a hill "assumed a new republican character."[120] Sermons and histories tended to glorify America's past in superlatives that exaggerated earlier virtues, bringing a connecting link through Jeremiads and other means of communication, filling "believers" with a resolve to "return to first principles." "Virtue" and "first principles" were seen as the keys to both the attainment and the preservation of liberty and free government. The Virginia Declaration of Rights of 1776 stated that "no free government, or the blessings of liberty, can be preserved to any people, but by a firm adherence to justice, moderation, temperance, frugality and virtue, and by frequent recurrence to fundamental principles." Four years later the new Massachusetts Bill of Rights reaffirmed that "a frequent recurrence to the fundamental principles of the constitution, and a constant adherence to those of piety, justice, moderation, temperance, industry and frugality, are absolutely necessary to preserve the advantages of liberty, and to maintain free government."

The rising sense of crisis that culminated in the issuing of the Declaration of Independence produced a groundswell of concern for virtue. "The decade of crisis brought new popularity to the cult of virtue that had long held sway in the colonies," Rossiter observed. "All the familiar techniques that earlier colonists had borrowed from England and converted to their purposes were revived for the emergency."[121] Having wrestled with the issue of independence, John Adams noted that "the Furnace of Affliction produces Refinement in

States as well as Individuals." If America was required to "suffer Calamities" in the effort to win her independence, "it will have this good Effect, at least," he reasoned in a letter to his wife, July 3, 1776: "it will inspire Us with many Virtues, which We have not, and correct many Errors, Follies, and Vices, which threaten to disturb, dishonour, and destroy Us."[122]

Virtue and Liberty

The ideal of "liberty" assumed greater importance with each act of Britain that appeared to be part of a growing conspiracy to "enslave" the colonies. Britain came to be increasingly seen as both corrupt and determined to spread that corruption to America. As such, the conflict could not help but take on religious overtones. Time and again the clergy and the spokesmen of dissent referred to the American Colonies as a troubled Israel facing a corrupting force, which sought to destroy their freedom and virtue. This oratory rose in crescendo far into the Revolution itself. *"The sermons of American ministers,"* concluded Royster, *"repeatedly linked the fight against Britain with the fight against sin. Engagement and zeal in both struggles offered the hope of a dual salvation: the soul of the Christian and the liberty of America."*[123] The importance of guarding one's liberties as advocated in Molesworth's *An Account of Denmark,* and Trenchard and Gordon's warnings against the corrupting influence of power in their *Cato's Letters* and *The Independent Whig,* were also discussed in terms of virtue versus corruption, freedom versus slavery. John Dickinson lamented that England had defaulted on her Saxon heritage, and charged the Americans with the task of preserving Saxon liberties.

"Patriotism and the Puritan Ethic," Edmund Morgan has written, *"marched hand in hand from 1764 to 1789."*[124] "I have long been convinced," Samuel Adams wrote to John Scollary, in 1776, "that our Enemies have made it an Object, to eradicate from the Minds of the People in general a Sense of true Religion and Virtue, in hopes thereby the more easily to carry their point of enslaving them. Indeed, my friend, this is a subject so important on my Mind, that I know not how to leave it."[125] And John Adams warned that "Liberty can no more exist without virtue and independence than the body can live and move without a soul."[126]

The concept of virtue, ever widening in scope and inclusiveness, ever drawing men back to look deeply into their own thoughts and motivations, became a regenerating force that led to a moral "revolution" of thought and action within the Colonies—an "awakening and revival of American principles"[127]—before a shot was ever fired against Britain. Virtue had founded concepts of republicanism upon a moral dimension that spoke with a single voice: only a virtuous people could enjoy the luxury of prolonged freedom. Only a nation whose citizens and leaders were virtuous could maintain the proper unity and patriotism necessary for republican government. "This virtue is love of our country," wrote Samuel Williams, echoing many of his fellow clergy, "This is the most efficacious principle to hold the different parts of the empire together, and to make men good members of the society to which they belong. . . . Virtue, like gravitation, will ever draw towards the center. And so long as this can be kept up, the rulers and the people, by its influence, will be kept in that place, and move in that course, which the laws of their country have assigned them. And this is the only way to have the state prosperous, and the members good subjects of it."[128]

During the revolutionary period there was a clear consensus that a republic, to stand, must house a virtuous, republican people; and that wholesale corruption was the death-knell of republicanism. As Shalhope has put it, "Americans, drawing heavily upon English libertarian thought, created a unique attitude toward government and society that literally permeated their culture." This attitude, however, caused "anxiety for eighteenth-century Americans and bafflement for twentieth-century historians because it placed so much stress upon intangibles such as 'virtue' and 'character.' Republicanism meant maintaining public and private virtue, internal unity, social solidarity, and it meant constantly struggling against 'threats' to the 'republican character' of the nation."[129] This consensus, Wood argued, gave a "moral dimension, a utopian depth, to the political separation from England. . . . Americans had come to believe that the Revolution would mean nothing less than a reordering of eighteenth-century society and politics as they had known and despised them—a reordering that was summed up by the conception of Republicanism."[130] The quest for virtue, then, was more than a general undertaking applied to the individual and the operations of society. It was also a basis of an effort to purify the principles and forms of society. "The leaders of the American Revolution," wrote Bailyn, "were . . . concerned, like the eighteenth-century English radicals . . . with the need to purify a corrupt constitution and fight off the apparent growth of prerogative power."[131]

It was this consensus that provided the cooperation and support essential for a society, a cooperation that is not enforced by political power, but *freely and spontaneously created*. It was not just fear of England's military and political aggressiveness that motivated them; there was a moral crusade with deep spiritual overtones.

Virtue, according to Clinton Rossiter, was one of the "three grand supports in colonial as well as in English political thought. There can be no doubt," he wrote, that in this emphasis on virtue "was a practical philosophy of huge consequences for the American future."[132] "Few people in history have been more given to public moralizing, to proclaiming a catalogue of virtues and exhorting one another to exhibit them, than the American colonists," Rossiter declared. "Practical morality was an important by-product of Puritanism and rationalism as well as the actual experiences of the colonists. Yet so prevalent was this pattern of thought, so universal and self-generating was the urge to preach the solid virtues, that we may consider it an independent working philosophy to which thousands of colonists subscribed directly."[133]

The emphasis upon public virtue was not a stress upon collective philosophy—that the individual should be subordinate to the state—but the Christian view that by purity of soul man ought voluntarily to live outside himself in genuine interest for the welfare of others and, if the occasion requires, sacrifice his own interests and desires for the welfare of others. This submission to authority was not tantamount to merging the individual personality into the system, nor did it threaten the loss of identity. Individualism was at the core of the American concept of virtue. Here political thought viewed the individual as protected by natural and civil rights. If he was prone to sacrifice his self-interest from time to time, this did not involve the sacrificing of his personhood to the state. He was prior to, antecedent to the state. Virtue was, for colonial Puritans, a broad, all-encompassing guide to behavior. According to Rossiter, "A thorough check of newspapers and magazines, the chief purveyors of this morality, shows these virtues to have been the most repeatedly discussed: wisdom, justice, temperance, fortitude, industry, frugality, piety, charity, sobriety, sincerity, honesty, simplicity, humility, contentment, love, benevolence, humanity, mercy, patriotism, modesty, patience, and good manners." Newspapers throughout the colonies teemed with "original essays, letters, and London reprints" eulogizing these virtues and stressing their role as the basis of republican government.[134]

Revolutionary leaders were hailed as examples of virtue. Washington was renowned not only for his military prowess, but Commager observed that he was "revered like no other man of his time, in the Old World and the New, as a symbol of nobility and virtue."[135] This was also true of men like Adams, Jefferson, and Madison. They became "living legends to their countrymen, not only for the stature of their accomplishments but also for the quality of their virtue."[136] The adoration extended to Europe: "When Benjamin Franklin strolled the streets of Paris during the peace negotiations, he was held in awe. Here, said the jaded Parisians, was the very model of regenerate man. A self-made businessman, a self-taught scholar, a canny inventor, a cunning diplomat, a boldly imaginative scientist, a statesman wise beyond his years, and withal, a humble and sober patriot, Franklin was the epitome of public virtue—and was perceived so unspotted by the world that he wore his coonskin cap to those dazzling affairs of the French court, delighting the ladies and disarming his diplomatic adversaries. Small wonder that for the French philosophers of the Enlightenment, America was the place to try the Grand Republican Experiment."[137]

The symbol that Adams proposed to place on the Great Seal of the United States of America revealed his predilection. He suggested the engraving of Hercules (by Gribelin) "resting on his club with Virtue pointing to her rugged mountain on one hand, persuading him to ascend, and Sloth glancing at her flowery paths of pleasure, wantonly reclining on the ground to seduce him into vice."[138] (And, interestingly enough, Jefferson proposed a scene of the Children of Israel directed by Moses with a "cloud by day and a pillar of fire by night"; and Franklin's design proposed Moses extending his hand over the sea, the waters overwhelming Pharaoh, and divine rays extending from heaven. The motto: "Rebellion to tyrants is obedience to God.")[139]

Jefferson's Puritan disposition was revealed when he came to see, by direct contact, the corrupt state of European society. "Europe swelled Jefferson's pride in the simple virtue of American life and the superiority of American character," Merrill D. Peterson wrote of his years abroad, between 1785 and 1790. "At first dazzled by the splendor of the Old World, he soon concluded 'that the game was not worth the candle.' In letters to American friends, he warned against the aesthetic temptations of Europe; and he denounced the moral corruptions of European civilization, Chinard said 'as vehemently as any Puritan preacher and with the same frankness of expression.'"[140]

In Patrick Henry's "Liberty or Death" speech, he accused the British of corruption and conspiracy to subvert American liberties; and significantly, these charges are embellished with various and repeated references to the *Book of Jeremiah* and other biblical notations. Charles L. Cohen, in his analysis of the speech, suggested that its significance "lies in the way it instances the importance of religious as well as political currents in the colonial Revolutionary thought. The Bible could teach Virginians a provocative lesson: Jeremiah could unmask a devious conspiracy as effectively as 'Cato' in the *Independent Whig*."[141]

The Revolution and the Decline of Virtue

The thrust of virtue as a philosophy and a conditioner of action, which had grown with such intensity in the few years before the revolution, seemed to lose its influence, to some extent, as the war progressed. When the war with England finally began, explained Wood, "the self-sacrifice and patriotism of 1774–75 soon seemed to give way to greed and profiteering at the expense of the public good." This was not necessarily true of the general masses who had little to do with the actual business of war. Still, the more intense emphasis upon virtue in the years before independence may have been in some measure a "consequence of a momentary sense of danger."[142] And with this "declension," as the clergy called it, the corrupt concomitants of war emerged—inflation, the lust for luxury goods, privateering, black marketeering, and, trafficking with the enemy. "Much evidence suggests that graft and fraud pervaded the supply of the army throughout the war."[143] The once enthusiastic support of non-importation from England, the wearing of homespun, and the abstinence from tea also began to give way. "Many Revolutionaries," observes Royster, "neither volunteered to fight for liberty nor sacrificed enough to properly sustain those who fought." They "seemed to be losing the virtue on which independence was supposed to rest."[144] Wood observed that the people of Boston "never seemed capable of recapturing the patriotism of those wonderful years of 1774 and 1775."[145]

As the revolution dragged on, there appeared a certain retrenchment in zeal, both in the military and in the civilian population—amply identified by Patrick Henry's oft-quoted "Sunshine Patriot" speech. General Nathanael Greene warned that a people who knew freedom but would not defend it, committed, in effect, "spiritual suicide."[146] This appearance of corruption combined with the illusiveness of early victory over England, the treason of Benedict Arnold, and other indications that all was not well with the "spirit" of America, caused great concern among the revolutionary leaders. As far as Samuel Adams was concerned, the only alternatives were victory through the armor of virtue, or defeat insured by corruption. "But let us depend," he urged "not upon the Arm of Flesh but on the God of Armies. We shall be free if we deserve it. We must succeed in a cause so manifestly just, if we are virtuous."[147]

So, the illusion was shattered. Jefferson's contention that virtue was not hereditary proved to be accurate indeed. The Americans came to recognize more clearly the nature of man—that nature with which Madison and others would struggle in designing the republic. "The Revolutionaries knew," Royster contended, "that the most common and most important decisions of the later war years dealt not with allegiance to independence but with the character of independence. They did not so much fear losing the war as losing the virtue that gave the war its purpose. . . . Almost everyone who talked about the beginning of the war contrasted Americans' early ardor and unselfishness with the meanness of later years."[148] Man's faith and virtue, it was seen now with great clarity, were always at war with his basest nature—just as the early Puritan ministers claimed it was—and if the former proved victorious at one time it did not follow that the predominance would necessarily last indefinitely.

Nevertheless, in spite of the difficulties, victory was won. There had been enough virtue—perhaps barely enough, but enough. "The wonder is," wrote Carl Van Doren, "not that some [patriots] were false, but that most of them were true to the ragged colours of a perilous cause."[149] Perhaps the perceived decline of virtue even spurred the more valiant to dedicate themselves more strenuously than ever to the cause of the Revolution. "If the defense of liberty relied on public virtue," suggested Royster, "signs of weakness endangered both the movement for independence and the nation's hope for survival. . . . [Yet,] Americans could acknowledge lapses of zeal from which virtue could still revive." One must now look to the future. The real question remained: Did enough virtue survive in the new community of States to constitute a "republican people?" "The future of American political ideology lay not only in appealing to a Union, a Constitution, a group of proven leaders, or other visible tokens of victory. The future would also depend on the appeal to public virtue. The Revolutionary War's legacy claimed such virtue for Americans but left them open to doubt that they were still achieving it."[150]

NOTES

1. Robert Nisbet, *History of the Idea of Progress* (New York: Basic Books, 1980), p. 197.

2. Alexis de Tocqueville, *Democracy in America,* trans. Henry Reeve (New York: Knopf, 1945), Vol. 1, p. 302.

3. *Ibid.*, p. 34.

4. *Ibid.*, p. 301.

5. *Ibid.*, p. 299.

6. Perry Miller, *Errand into the Wilderness* (Cambridge: Harvard University Press, 1956), p. 11.

7. Sydney E. Ahlstrom, *Theology in America: The Major Protestant Voices From Puritanism to Neo-Orthodoxy* (Indianapolis: Bobbs-Merrill, 1967), pp. 28–29.

8. John Winthrop, "A Modell of Christian Charity," in Perry Miller and Thomas H. Johnson, *The Puritans* Vol. 1 (New York: Harper and Row, 1963), p. 199. See Sacvan Bercovitch, *The Puritan Origins of the American Self* (New Haven: Yale University Press, 1975).

9. Quoted in Clinton Rossiter, *Six Characters in Search of a Republic* (New York: Harcourt, Brace, and World, 1960), p. 101.

10. Cited in James Hitchinson Smylie's "American Clergymen and the Constitution of the United States of America, 1781–1796," (Ph.D. dissertation, Princeton Theological Seminary, Princeton, New Jersey), and quoted in Michael Chadwick, *God's Hand in the Founding of America, As Acknowledged by the Early Clergymen of the United States* (Salt Lake City: Deseret Book Co., 1980), p. 3.

11. See Franklin P. Cole, *They Preached Liberty* (Indianapolis: Liberty Press, 1979), p. 18.

12. See Sidney E. Mead, *The Old Religion in the Brave New World* (Berkeley: University of California Press, 1977), pp. 123–24.

13. Quoted in Clinton Rossiter, "The American Consensus, 1765–1776," in John C. Wahlke, *The Causes of the American Revolution* (Lexington, Mass.: D. C. Heath, 1973), p. 161.

14. Cole, *They Preached Liberty*, p. 53.

15. *Ibid.*, p. 48.

16. *Ibid.*, p. 54.

17. Richard Steele, *The Husbandman's Calling* (London, 1668), pp. 7–8, 15, 234 (italics added). We appreciate Professor Hyrum Andrus drawing our attention to the writings of Steele, and for our many hours of discussion concerning the Puritan ideal of "living outside oneself" in service to others.

18. Ernest Tuveson, *Redeemer Nation: The Idea of America's Millenial Role* (Chicago: University of Chicago Press, 1974), p. 12; Nathan O. Hatch, *The Sacred Cause of Liberty: Republican Thought and the Millennium in Revolutionary England* (New Haven: Yale University Press, 1977) builds upon Tuveson's work; see also Conrad Cherry, ed., *God's New Israel: Religious Interpretations of American Destiny* (Englewood Cliffs, N.J.: Prentice-Hall, 1971); and William A. Clebsch, *From Sacred To Profane America: The Role of Religion in American History* (New York: Harper and Row, 1968).

19. Perry Miller, *The Life of the Mind in America: From the Revolution to the Civil War* (New York: Harcourt, Brace, and World, 1965), p. 10.

20. Sir Patrick Devlin, *The Enforcement of Morals* (Oxford: Oxford University Press, 1965), p. 25.

21. Will and Ariel Durant, *Lessons of History* (New York: Simon and Schuster, 1968), p. 51.

22. de Tocqueville, *Democracy in America*, Vol. 2, p. 6.

23. Catherine L. Albanese, *Sons of the Fathers: The Civil Religion of the American Revolution* (Philadelphia: Temple University Press, 1976).

24. Ralph Ketcham, *James Madison: A Biography* (New York: Macmillan, 1971), pp. 47–48.

25. Clinton Rossiter, *The First American Revolution*, p. 191.

26. "This genre of public address rested on the foundation of a covenant between God and His chosen people wherein He promises to be their God if they obey His commandments. Unfortunately, the members of the elect nation seldom live up to their responsibilities. As they turn away from God, He berates and punishes them for their misdeeds. Nevertheless, prophetic rehearsal of the people's sins reaffirms God's gracious providence and love. While announcing immediate disaster, it anticipates future reformation. In the final analysis, affliction makes eventual fulfillment of God's promises surer." Charles L. Cohen, "The 'Liberty or Death' Speech: A Note on Religion and Revolutionary Rhetoric," *The William and Mary Quarterly*, Vol. 38 (October 1981), p. 708. See also Sacvan Bercovitch, *The American Jeremiad* (Madison: Univerity of Wisconsin Press, 1978) and "How the Puritans Won the American Revolution," *Massachusetts Review* Vol. 17 (1976).

27. Norman Pettit, "The Puritan Legacy," *The New England Quarterly*, Vol. 48 (June 1975), pp. 286–87.

28. Alan Heimert and Perry Miller, eds., *The Great Awakening: Documents*

Illustrating the Crisis and its Consequences (Indianapolis: Bobbs-Merrill, 1967), pp. xiv–xv. See also Perry Miller, "The Great Awakening from 1740 to 1750," *Encounter* (1956).

29. Harry S. Stout, "Religion, Communications, and the Ideological Origins of the American Revolution," *The William and Mary Quarterly*, Vol. 34 (October 1977), pp. 528–29. "The foundation of both the religious and the literary culture of Puritan New England was the English Bible, which was read in the Geneva version until about 1680 and thereafter in the King James. . . . Next in importance to the Bible in the reading of the Puritans were biblical commentaries and theological treatises." Randall Stewart, "Puritan Literature and the Flowering of New England," *The William and Mary Quarterly*, Vol. III (July 1946), p. 320.

30. Alan E. Heimert, *Religion and the American Mind* (Cambridge: Harvard University Press, 1966), p. viii.

31. Perry Miller, *Jonathan Edwards* (New York: W. Sloane, 1949).

32. Heimert and Miller, eds., *The Great Awakening*, p. l.

33. *Ibid.*, pp. lvii–lviii.

34. Stout, "Religion, Communications, and the Ideological Origins of the American Revolution," pp. 527, 528, 530.

35. *Ibid.*, p. 521.

36. See Rhys Isaac's "Preachers and Patriots: Popular Culture and the Revolution in Virginia," in Alfred Young, ed., *American Revolution* (Dekalb: Northern Illinois University Press, 1976), pp. 125–156.

37. Rhys Isaac, "Dramatizing the Ideology of Revolution: Popular Mobilization in Virginia 1774–1776," *The William and Mary Quarterly*, Vol. 33 (July 1976), pp. 364–65.

38. *Ibid.*, p. 366.

39. *Ibid.*, p. 369.

40. *Ibid.*, pp. 366–67. "The Revolution began in Virginia with two solemn rituals enacted by the county representatives gathered at Williamsburg—the 'courthouse' of the province. On May 24, 1774, the House of Burgesses resolved to keep the first day of June (the date for the enforcement of the act of Parliament closing the Port of Boston) as a day of fasting and prayer for 'divine Interposition that the Minds of his Majesty and his Parliament . . . may be inspired from above with Wisdom, Moderation, and Justice.' "

41. Frank W. Fox, Clayne L. Pope, and Larry T. Wimmer, "American Heritage: An Interdisciplinary Approach," unpublished manuscript (Provo, Utah: Brigham Young University, 1983), pp. 63–64. A revised 3rd edition of this manuscript was published under the same title in Dubuque, Iowa (Kendall/Hunt, 1986) before this book went to the press.

42. Clinton Rossiter, *The Political Thought of the American Revolution* (New York: Harcourt, Brace, and World, 1963), p. 100.

43. David Ramsay, *History of the American Revolution* (Philadelphia, 1789), pp. 29–30 (italics added).

44. Bernard Bailyn, "Political Experience and Enlightenment Ideas," in John C. Wahlke, *The Causes of the American Revolution*, pp. 186–187. See also Bailyn, ed., *Pamphlets of the American Revolution, 1750–1776*; and *Education in the Forming of American Society* (Chapel Hill: University of North Carolina Press, 1960).

45. C. F. Adams, ed., *The Works of John Adams* (Boston: Little, Brown, 1856), Vol. 4, p. 359.

46. Issac, "Dramatizing the Idealogy of Revolution," p. 368.

47. Fox *et al.*, "American Heritage," p. 62.

48. Thomas Paine, *The Age of Reason* (London: Watts, 1938), pp. 106–9.

49. L. Jesse Lemisch, ed., *Benjamin Franklin: The Autobiography and other Writings* (New York: New American Library, 1961), pp. 92–93.

50. Adams, ed., *The Works of John Adams*, Vol. 19, p. 637.

51. Henry P. Johnson, ed., *The Correspondence and Public Papers of John Jay, 1763–1826,* Vol. 4 (New York: Da Capo, 1971), p. 357.

52. James Madison, "Remonstrance," in Saul K. Padover, *The Complete Madison: His Basic Writings* (New York: Harper, 1953), p. 300.

53. Gaillard Hunt, ed., *The Writings of James Madison* (New York: G. P. Putnam, 1902), Vol. 6, p. 69.

54. A. A. Lipscomb and A. E. Bergh, eds., *The Writings of Thomas Jefferson* (Washington, D.C.: Jefferson Memorial Association, 1903–04), Vol. 15, p. 384.

55. *Ibid.,* Vol. 14, pp. 139–43.

56. Paine, *The Age of Reason,* p. 1.

57. Jared Sparks, ed., *The Works of Benjamin Franklin* (Boston: Hilliard, Gray, 1840), Vol. 10, p. 423.

58. Lemisch, *Benjamin Franklin: Autobiography,* p. 320. See also Andrew M. Allison, *The Real Benjamin Franklin* (Salt Lake City: Freemen, 1982). An extended subject index of exerpts from the writings of Franklin make this book especially valuable.

59. L. H. Butterfield, ed., *The Adams Papers: Diary and Autobiography of John Adams,* Vol. 13 (Cambridge: Harvard University Press, 1961), pp. 240–41.

60. Adams, ed., *The Works of John Adams,* Vol. 6, p. 234.

61. Saul K. Padover, *George Washington, President of the United States, 1732– 1789: The Washington Papers* (New York: Harper, 1955), pp. 257–62.

62. Ketcham, *James Madison: A Biography,* p. 47.

63. *Ibid.,* p. 48.

64. *Ibid.,* p. 47.

65. *Ibid.,* p. 50.

66. *Ibid.,* p. 46. All the essential requirements for a virtuous community were imparted in the institutions of education: "proper (personal) beliefs, correct (personal) day-to-day habits, charitable (personal) relationships, and all the rest. And individual moral accountability filled every waking moment, making each Christian conscious that every step he took might be right or wrong. Akin to this concern for eternal salvation and moral awareness was an insistence that life count for something, that a wasted life was a sinful life." p. 47.

67. William C. Rives, *Life and Times of James Madison* (Boston: Little, Brown, 1859), Vol. 1, pp. 33–35.

68. Gaillard Hunt, *The Life of James Madison* (New York: Russell and Russell, 1968), p. 16. "No evidence exists that he ever planned to make either divinity or the law his means of livelihood, but physical unfitness may have been the factor that kept him from making such plans. He studied them both for the advantages that resided in a knowledge of them." Irving Brant, *James Madison: The Virginia Revolutionist* (Indianapolis: Bobbs-Merrill, 1941), Vol. 1, p. 111.

69. Ketcham, *James Madison: A Biography,* p. 29.

70. *Ibid.*

71. *Ibid.,* pp. 38–39.

72. Richard B. Morris, *Seven Who Shaped Our Destiny* (New York: Harper and Row, 1973), p. 192.

73. Ketcham, *James Madison: A Biography,* p. 44.

74. *Ibid.,* p. 45.

75. *Ibid.,* p. 43. In much of their doctrine the Scots and the Americans drew from the same fountain. A lack of understanding of important factors has caused some writers to see the influence of the "Scottish School" as being singularly important in the philosophy of the American founders, as if the basic concepts of the American revolution and republic originated in first instance with them, or as if the "Scottish Enlightenment" was *the* singular conduit through which these ideas came to America. See Isaac Kramnick, "Republican Revisionism Revisited." In his *Inventing America: Jefferson's Declaration of Independence,* Garry Wills makes

this mistake of emphasis. Following other historians who have emphasized the idea that Locke was rather peripheral in his influence on the American founding, he stopped in midstream in his analysis of who influenced the ideas that appeared in the Declaration of Independence. See Ralph Hamoway, "Jefferson and the Scottish Enlightenment: A Critique of Garry Wills's *Inventing America: Jefferson's Declaration of Independence*," *The William and Mary Quarterly*, Vol. 36 (October 1979), pp. 508–9.

76. Caroline Robbins, "When It Is that Colonies May Turn Independent: An Analysis of the Environment and Politics of Francis Hutcheson (1694–1746)," *The William and Mary Quarterly*, Vol II (April, 1954), p. 225.

77. Hamoway, "Jefferson and the Scottish Enlightenment," p. 509; Kramnick, "Republican Revisionism Revisited."

78. Ketcham, *James Madison: A Biography*, p. 42.

79. *Ibid.*, p. 44.

80. *Ibid.*, p. 48.

81. Rossiter, *Six Characters In Search of a Republic*, p. 101.

82. Adrienne Koch, *Power, Morals, and the Founding Fathers* (Ithaca, N.Y.: Cornell University Press, 1961), p. 105.

83. Adams, ed., *The Works of John Adams*, Vol. 3, p. 452. The "Dissertation" was first published in August of 1765. It was later reprinted in London in 1782 and Philadelphia in 1783.

84. John Dewey, *The Living Thoughts of Thomas Jefferson* (New York: Longman's, Green, 1940), p. 56.

85. "There is an exaltation, an excitement, about *Common Sense* that conveys the very uncommon sense of adventure Americans felt as they moved toward independence. With it would come new perils, but also new opportunities, new freedoms. They knew they were on the threshold of a great experience not only for themselves but perhaps for the whole world." Edmund S. Morgan, *The Birth of the Republic* (Chicago: University of Chicago Press, 1956), p. 75.

86. Paul Leicester Ford, ed., *The Works of Thomas Jefferson* (New York: G. P. Putnam, 1904–5), Vol. 12, p. 477.

87. L. H. Butterfield, ed., *Adams Family Correspondence* (Cambridge: Harvard University Press, 1963), pp. 30–31.

88. *The Federalist*, No. 37.

89. Paul Leicester Ford, *Essays on the Constitution of the United States* (Brooklyn, N.Y.: Historical Printing Club, 1892), pp. 251–52.

90. *The Federalist*, No. 20.

91. John C. Fitzpatrick, ed., *The Writings of George Washington 1745–1799* (George Washington Bicentennial Commission, 1931; reprinted at Westport, Connecticut, 1970), Vol. 27, pp. 116, 249, 281.

92. *Ibid.*, Vol. 12, p. 343.

93. Max Farrand, ed., *The Records of the Federal Convention of 1787*, Vol. 1, p. 451.

94. Clinton Rossiter, *The Political Thought of the American Revolution*, pp. 220–21.

95. Albert Henry Smyth, ed., *The Writings of Benjamin Franklin* (New York: Haskell, 1970), Vol. 9, pp. 521–22 (italics in the original).

96. Hunt, *The Writings of James Madison*, Vol. 9, p. 230. See also Brant, *James Madison: The Virginia Revolutionist*, pp. 118–20.

97. George de Huszar, et al., *Basic American Documents* (Ames, Iowa: Littlefield, Adams, 1953), Vol. 2, pp. 108–9.

98. Adams, ed., *The Works of John Adams*, Vol. 9, p. 229.

99. Letter from John Adams to John Scollary of Boston, April 30, 1776; from the *Samuel Adams Papers*, Bancroft Transcripts, New York Public Library.

100. Joseph Story, *Commentaries*, p. 661.

101. Tocqueville, *Democracy in America*, Vol. 1, p. 46.

102. *Ibid.*, Vol. 2, pp. 144–45.

103. Christopher Dawson, "The Birth of Democracy," *The Review of Politics*, Vol. 19 (January 1957), p. 57.

104. Samuel Eliot Morison, "Prelude to Independence: The Virginia Resolutions of May 15, 1776," *The William and Mary Quarterly* Vol. 8 (July 1951), p. 485. See also Pauline Maier, "John Wilkes and American Disillusionment with Britain," *The William and Mary Quarterly*, Vol. 20 (July 1963), pp. 373–76.

105. H. Trevor Colbourn, "John Dickinson, Historical Revolutionary," *Pennsylvania Magazine of History and Biography* Vol. 83 (1959), p. 283. Shalhope discusses John Dickinson and quotes Colbourn in his "Toward a Republican Synthesis," pp. 59–60.

106. Fox *et al.*, "American Heritage," pp. 66–67.

107. *Ibid.*, pp. 67–69.

108. Pocock, "Virtue and Commerce," pp. 120, 129.

109. *Ibid.*

110. Stout, "Religion, Communications, and the Ideological Origins," p. 541.

111. Gordon S. Wood, *The Creation of the American Republic 1776–1787*, pp. 92 and 68. Here Wood quoted sermons and other patriotic prints.

112. Rossiter, *The Political Thought of the American Revolution*, pp. 199–200.

113. Samuel Williams, *A Discourse on the Love of Our Country* (Salem, 1775), pp. 13–14.

114. Pocock, "Virtue and Commerce," p. 123.

115. *Ibid.*, p. 124.

116. Stout, "Religion, Communications, and the Ideological Origins," p. 523. See Page Smith, ed., *Religious Origins of the American Revolution* (Missoula: University of Montana, 1976), an anthology of documents (such as excerpts from Calvin's *Institutes*) with Smith's running commentary on how historians have too often missed religious influences on American revolutionary ideology.

117. Isaac, "Preachers and Patriots," p. 145.

118. Fox *et al.*, "American Heritage," p. 56.

119. Wood, *Creation of the American Republic*, p. 118.

120. *Ibid.*

121. Rossiter, *The Political Thought Of The American Revolution*, p. 200.

122. Letter to Abigail Adams, written from Philadelphia, in L. H. Butterfield, Marc Friedlaender, and Mary-Jo Kline, eds., *The Book of Abigail and John: Selected Letters of the Adams Family, 1762–1784* (Cambridge: Harvard University Press, 1975), p. 140.

123. Charles Royster, "The Nature of Treason: Revolutionary Virtue and American Reactions to Benedict Arnold, in *The William and Mary Quarterly* Vol. 36 (April 1979), p. 165 (italics added).

124. Edmund Morgan, "The Puritan Ethic and the American Revolution," *The William and Mary Quarterly*, Vol. 24 (January 1967), p. 42 (italics added).

125. H. A. Cushing, ed., *The Writings of Samuel Adams* (New York: G. P. Putnam, 1904), p. 286. See also F. Nwabueze Okoye "Chattel Slavery as the Nightmare of the American Revolutionaries," *The William and Mary Quarterly*, Vol. 37 (January 1980), and David S. Lovejoy, "Samuel Hopkins: Religion, Slavery, and the Revolution," *The New England Quarterly*, Vol. 40 (June 1967), p. 227.

126. Bernard Bailyn, "A Fear of Conspiracy against Liberty," in Robert F. Berkhofer, Jr., *The American Revolution* (Boston: Little, Brown, 1971), p. 101.

127. Adams, *The Works of John Adams*, Vol. 10, p. 284.

128. Williams, *Discourse on Love of Our Country*, pp. 13–14.

129. Shalhope, "Toward a Republican Synthesis," pp. 71–72.

130. Wood, *Creation of the American Republic*, pp. 47–48.

131. Bailyn, *Idealogical Origins*, p. 283.

132. Rossiter, *The First American Revolution*, pp. 226, 221. The other two pillars were Natural Law and Natural Rights, and Whig Constitutionalism.

133. *Ibid.*, p. 219.

134. *Ibid.*, pp. 219–20. See also Richard L. Bushman, ed., *The Great Awakening* (New York: Atheneum, 1969).

135. Henry Steele Commager, "Brilliant Originals. Whatever happened to the political genius that founded America?" *The Washington Post Magazine*, October 10, 1982, p. 33.

136. Fox *et al.*, "American Heritage," p. 73.

137. *Ibid.*, pp. 73–74.

138. Charles Francis Adams, *Familiar Letters of John Adams and His Wife, Abigail Adams, During the Revolution* (Boston: Ayer, 1875), pp. 210–11.

139. Richard S. Patterson and Richardson Dougall, *The Eagle and the Shield: A History of the Great Shield of the United States* (The United States Department of State, 1978); Gaillard Hunt, "The Seal of the United States: How it was Developed and Adopted," The United States Department of State (1892); reprinted with additions, 1909.

140. Merrill D. Peterson, *The Jefferson Image in the American Mind* (New York: Oxford University Press, 1960), p. 416.

141. Cohen, "Liberty or Death," pp. 704–5, 717. See also William Wirt Henry, *Patrick Henry: Life Correspondence and Speeches* (New York: Scribner's, 1891). Henry warned his fellow compatriots not "to be betrayed with a kiss" (Jeremiah 18:22); expressed frustration with those "who having eyes, see not, and having ears, hear not" (Jeremiah 5:21); and insisted that "Gentlemen may cry, peace, peace—but there is no peace" (Jeremiah 6:14). See Henry, pp. 138, 139, 141; and Cohen, p. 706.

142. Wood, *Creation of the American Republic*, p. 415.

143. Royster, "Nature of Treason," p. 176.

144. *Ibid.*, pp. 175, 179.

145. Wood, *Creation of the American Republic*, p. 421.

146. Richard K. Showman et al., eds., *The Papers of General Nathanael Greene* (Chapel Hill: University of North Carolina Press, 1976), Vol. 1, p. 83. Royster, "Nature of Treason," p. 166.

147. *Warren-Adams Letters, Being Chiefly a Correspondence Among John Adams, Samuel Adams, and James Warren* (Massachusetts Historical Society, 1917–1923), Vol. 1, pp. 369–70.

148. Royster, "Nature of Treason," p. 181.

149. Carl Van Doren, *Secret History of the American Revolution* (New York: Viking, 1941), p. 435.

150. Royster, "Nature of Treason," pp. 191, 193.

4

Civil Religion and Republican Government

A PUBLIC PHILOSOPHY or religion generally carries with it the legitimacy of transcendence; that is, its general impact will be conditioned by the extent to which it is deemed to carry a supernatural, sacred, or pseudo-sacred authority. In America, the public philosophy or the general religion reflects to a significant extent the Judeo-Christian influence characteristic of Western civilization. According to Walter Lippmann, "The concepts and principles of the public philosophy have their being in the realm of the immaterial entities. They cannot be experienced by our sense organs or even, strictly speaking, imagined in visual or tangible terms. Yet these essences, these abstractions, which are out of sight and out of touch, are to have and to hold men's highest loyalties."[1] In the American experience, what LaPiere came to call the Judeo-Christian ethic not only served to legitimize the nation as an independent entity, but to attribute to its political philosophy basic content and a kind of spiritual confirmation that strengthened national purpose and solemnized political and social values and ideals, rituals and practices.[2]

This phenomenon, in turn, contributed enormously to the mores and expectations of civility. As Lippmann put it, "The defenders of civility . . . cannot do without the signs and seals of legitimacy, of righteousenss and truth. For it is a practical rule, well known to experienced men, that the relation is very close between our capacity to act at all and the conviction that the action we are taking is right."[3] One of the most important ingredients of what became the American public religion or philosophy was tied to a general belief or acceptance that America had been singled out to perform a great mission and that the nation rested, as it were, in the bosom of Providence.

The ideal of a New Israel, a "city upon a hill," a sacred common-wealth, was ubiquitous to the Puritan movement and heavily pro-moted by the Protestant sects.

The direction given to the contemplation of history provided by the Judeo-Christian belief in an omnipotent, omniscient God, who was in command of events, and whose will had rational purpose, lent itself to the belief that America had been shielded from mankind until its rightful heirs had been led out of Babylon, that Providence had protected the fledgling nation and led it successfully through the battle for freedom, and that, if worthy, it was destined to be a beacon of righteousness and good government for the world. Significantly, this belief in Providential direction of history seems to have been generally accepted not only by the clergy and the masses, but by many of the political leaders as well. As Robert Nisbet has noted, Christian philosphers have had before them "the image of progress as the unfolding through long ages of a design present from the very beginning of man's history," and have emphasized the "gradual, cumulative, *spiritual* perfection of mankind, an imminent process that would in time culminate in a golden age of happiness on earth."[4]

The concept of civil religion helps explain one of the paradoxes of colonial America: while some citizens were uninterested and even hostile to the specific denominations and criticized sectarianism, they were still a deeply religious people. They accepted a general civil religion that provided unenforced and sometimes unwritten norms and values that were absolutely essential for liberty to flourish. Biblical, Judeo-Christian teachings were at the heart of their public philosophy.

THE IDEA OF CIVIL RELIGION

Since time immemorial people have wrestled with the functional relationship between society and order. Societies cannot survive without order. Indeed, as Simone Weil has postulated, it is primary to even food and shelter: "Order is the first need of all."[5] "Civil order" has been described in many ways, usually to include laws or general rules and expectations, beliefs and customs, duties and rights, and a generally accepted means of conducting and regulating cooperative effort. There must exist minimum faith in, and a sense of legitimacy toward, the form and functioning of the community by the members of the community, or social order will sooner or later disintegrate. Neither the model republic nor the centralized dictatorship will long endure unless something energizes that legitimacy on a more or less continual basis. The subject of religion and its relationship to order and stability has preoccupied theorists of government from Plato to Machiavelli, from Rousseau to Madison. Anne M. Cohler has argued, referring to the classical polities, that "the differences between Athens, Sparta, and republican Rome are reduced to a question of the amount and kinds of self-control required to maintain the rule of those citizenries."[6] Before Plato, the great Solon had warned that *doxa*, the passion of life, must be disciplined if *eunomia*, order, was to exist. For, to the degree that self-control is diminished, to the degree that certain societal functions cease to be carried out in a more or less spontaneous manner, to that degree the coercive power of the state must be expanded to protect the community from disorientation, disorder, disintegration, or perhaps even revolution.

The lessons from the Greek experience and the disorder that plagued the Roman republic clearly demonstrate that stable government could not be provided for without public order. One sees, for example, in the life of Cicero, both the emphasis on the utilitarian nature of religion or the "sacred," and the deep fear of societal disruption that preoccupied the classical culture. As Gibbon pointed out in his *Decline and Fall of the Roman Empire*, the practice of politics in the classical world was virtually synonymous with the practice of religion. Roman rulers, even such great statesmen as Cicero, were particularly energetic in assigning religion a part in keeping the masses docile. Philosophers were often willing actors in this charade. "The various modes of worship which prevailed in the Roman world were all considered by the people as equally true, by the philosopher as equally false, and by the magistrate as equally useful."[7] The Roman state, adds Durant, "seduously exploited the piety of the people to promote the stability of society and government. It adapted the rural divinities to urban life, built a national hearth for the goddess Vesta, and appointed a college of Vestal Virgins to serve the city's sacred fire. Out of the Gods of the family, the farm, and the village it developed the *di indigentes*—or native gods—of the state, and arranged for these a solemn and picturesque worship in the name of all the citizens."[8]

In spite of his love of justice and natural law, Cicero was nevertheless primarily concerned with the preservation of public orthodoxy so that Rome might remain the Eternal City. In Cicero's time that orthodoxy was the Roman cult of the gods. There is little doubt that Cicero believed that without such public beliefs the state would eventually unravel. He promoted the Roman "civil religion" and belief in the official gods for utilitarian reasons. While he may not have believed in the religion of the Romans privately, he still contended "these matters ought not to be discussed in public, lest much discussion destroy the established religion of the nation."[9] In his *De Officiis*, Cicero argued that the community's system of justice and the fabric of its social life depended upon the citizen's belief in the gods. If reverence toward the gods atrophied, he warned in *De Natura*

Deorum, then such virtues as good faith, brotherhood and justice would atrophy with it. He was so vitally concerned with the maintenance of social equilibrium that he feared the radical infusion of foreign eastern cults and religions into Roman society, lest they disturb the public orthodoxy, weaken the civil religion and perhaps break the tender bond of order in the Republic. According to Professor Peter Gay, Cicero "disclosed by his conduct the gulf between a few philosophers and the mass of believers, private disenchantment and public observance."[10] The inability of the Roman system to maintain social, political, and moral "cement" as society decayed from within left Cicero, as others before him, with little alternative— in his mind at least—but to support the existing incorporated system of the gods and the tyranny of the state.

Kings and pharoahs have claimed legitimacy by divine appointment or confirmation; some national leaders have even been transposed into deity. Kings have ruled by "divine right," and prophets and popes have been invested with civil power as "God's spokesmen on earth." In the opening of Augustine's *City of God,* Roman theology is denounced as the worship of false gods, plunging Rome into corruption and vice. Augustine insisted that eternal life was not to be obtained by worshipping the gods of civil theology, as he sought to refute those who attributed the decline of Rome, particularly the sack of Rome by the Goths, to the Christian civil religion and its prohibition of the worship of the ancient Roman gods.[11]

John Locke saw Christianity as a "general" civil religion. While he lamented the contention within the Christian establishment, he nevertheless insisted that pristine Christianity was true as a doctrine, and was both reasonable and "civil."[12] As far as he was concerned, the requirements for civil life coincided with both reason and the teachings of Christianity. Like the Remonstrants and the Christian Humanists, he rejected predestination and taught salvation by works. "Repentance," he charged, "is as absolute a condition of the covenant of grace as faith . . ."[13] The Christian doctrine of eternal life and judgment, together with the process of repentance, through which man "is really sorry for his sins and abhors them [and] will turn from them and forsake them," and do "works meet for repentance," helps make him a good citizen.[14] On the other hand, to disobey God "is direct rebellion," and "government and order are at an end, and there can be no bounds set for the lawless exorbitancy of unconfined man."[15] Christian morality, which compliments both the law of nature and of reason, places right and wrong on true foundations, and forms "the bonds of society, and of common life, and laudable practices," and offers "such a complete rule of life as the wisest man must acknowledge tends entirely to the good of mankind, and . . . all would be happy, if all would practice it."[16]

On the other hand, Rousseau, in his *Social Contract*, argued from a much different perspective, claiming that the terms "Christian" and "republic" were "mutually exclusive," that "Christianity preaches only servitude and dependence. Its spirit is so favorable to tyranny that it always profits by such a regime."[17] Too, Christianity was charged with diverting the attention and the allegiance of the people from the *polis* to more remote entities, and hence, with being an enemy of civic virtue.

There is, in this debate over the character of the relationship between religion and the community, the recurring idea that some kind of generally accepted dogmatic belief, which has the character of the transcendent or the "sacred," is salutary, perhaps even essential to the republic or, for that matter, any society. Nations have created and nurtured symbols, histories, saints, martyrs, anthems, ideologies, and civil religions that have both spiritual and secular roots, in an attempt to secure the legitimacy of their governments and regimes. Significant public resources have been invested in propaganda and efforts to indoctrinate citizens and gain their support and allegiance.

The importance of some form of unifying dogma or orthodoxy, some form of "sacred" or transcendent belief and means of indoctrination has not been made obsolete by time. Even the modern state, some have argued, needs some form of general emotional support from the people in order to assure legitimacy and avoid disintegration. David Easton, for instance, calls this phenomenon "diffuse support," which he sees engendered primarily through the various forms of socialization. This support thus generated on behalf of the political community or the regime, he suggests, is particularly necessary during periods of severe stress; if "such support threatens to fall below a minimal level, regardless of the cause, the system must either provide mechanisms to revive the flagging support or its days will be numbered." Among these "mechanisms," Professor Easton indicated, is the "structural regulation of support," which "requires the system to transform its goods and structures as a means of maintaining at least some kind of system for making authoritative allocations." In contrast, he observed, "A system may seek to instill in its members a high level of *diffuse support* in order that regardless of what happens the members will continue to be bound to it by strong ties of loyalty and affection. This is a type of support that continues independently of the specific rewards which the member may feel he obtains from belonging to the system." The means for "generating this diffuse and generalized support may entail the positive encouragement of sentiments of legitimacy and compliance, the acceptance of a notion of the existence of the common good transcending the particular good of any particular individuals or groups, or the kindling of deep feelings of community. Thereby, sentiments of legitimacy, recognition of the general welfare, and a sense of political community are bred deeply into the maturing members of a system through the usual processes of political socialization and through the various special measures a system may adopt if it sees such support as declining." Easton is certain "that no system could endure for very long if it did not seek to build up a reservoir of support—frequently described as patriotism, love of country, loyalty, and the like—upon which it could count regardless of the particular trials and tribulations or frustration of desires that the members might experience at the moment."[18]

The concept of "diffuse support" within a community drawing its strength from sources other than force and coercion has occurred frequently in modern political research. Much has been written, for example, on the use of "indoctrination" in which ideology plays a primary role in political socialization, joined by primary institutions such as family, school, and church on the political socialization of the young.[19] However often regimes throughout history have attempted to establish and maintain order by force and coercion, there has remained the expectation that support for the regime or the community as a whole cannot be totally dependent upon this means, and that some other emotive force and influence must be generated somewhere within the system that will embellish the regime or the community with legitimacy and generate support and obedience by the citizens. This concept has been variously designated "civil religion," "common religion," "public theology," "public philosphy" or "public orthodoxy." Michael Novak, who uses the term "civil religion," summarizes it as "a public perception of . . . national experience, in the light of universal and transcendent claims upon human beings; a set of values, symbols, and rituals institutionalized as the cohesive force and center of meaning uniting . . . people."[20] Richard J. Bishirjian, in contrast, differentiates "civil religion," from "public philosophy," contending that writers on the subject often confuse the two.[21] The terms used are closely connected, often overlap, and are subject to various interpretations, yet the underlying concept is central to the idea of republican goverment.

Civil Religion, the State, and Society

The term *civil religion* has been used to describe the *official* religion of a given state or political regime. Most frequently, the term is used to describe those nations of antiquity—including ancient Greece and Rome, the Holy Roman Empire, and the unified national church-state systems that emerged out of the Renaissance and Reformation. The term has also been used to describe the system of "established" churches during the American colonial period. Civil religion is also used to describe, in the broadest sense, a people's or a nation's "official" or generally accepted dogmas, symbols, traditions, rituals, and practices, inherited and reinforced by various forms and methods of indoctrination and socialization. Some writers have suggested that the concept might be too inclusive and amorphous to warrant reference as "civil religion," and too vague to permit the identification of parameters necessary for thorough study and explanation.

Still others refer to civil religion to describe a nation's or a community's "common," or "general," or "unofficial" religion or theology or philosophy. In this frame of reference, it is argued that even though the "religion" is neither specifically organized nor officially established, the generally held beliefs and values that are its expression are integral to the society's culture; therefore, its impact on other groups and formal institutions of society entitle it to reference as "civil religion." (It is here most often referred to simply as "religion," without reference to a particular religious sect or creed.) In a system with multiple sectarian religions, this "general religion" will express principles that are either promoted by, sanctioned by, or at least amenable to the collectivity of the particularist sects that make up the body of *organized*, though not official or state, churches. Although this genre of "civil religion" is unofficial, certain aspects of it may become institutionalized in national rituals, shrines, or symbols. An example of this type of "civil" religion or theology is the "general," or "common" religion or theology or philosophy of the United States, but it is sometimes difficult to know which form or mixture of the concept of "civil religion" a particular writer is referring to when the term is used.

Donald G. Jones and Russell E. Richey have divided the idea of civil religion into five manifestations: *"folk religion,"* a "common religion . . . emerging out of the life of the folk," their "actual life, ideas, values, ceremonies, and loyalties"; *"transcendent universal religion of the nation,"* rendering "prophetic judgment on the nation," functioning "as a source of meaning and social solidarity for the nation"; *"religious nationalism,"* where the "nation takes on a sovereign and self-transcendent character," sometimes called "the religion of patriotism"; *"democratic faith,"* the "human values and ideals of equality, freedom, and justice without necessary dependence on a transcendent deity or a spiritualized nation"; and *"Protestant civic piety,"* reflected in "the fusion of Protestantism and nationalism and the pervading Protestant coloring in the American ethos."[22]

It is difficult to identify a clear, widely acceptable definition of civil religion. There is, however, common expectation that the official or the unofficial "civil religion," or public orthodoxy, or civil theology will be a force for order and continuity in society. If a society does not possess one form of "civil religion," it must, for the sake of unity, order, and permanence, possess another. Sociologist Robin W. Williams's contention that "every functioning society has, to an important degree, a 'common religion'";[23] Sidney E. Mead's statement that "religion is the mainspring of any integrated society";[24] and Richard T. Hughes's warning that "to wish to be rid of civil religion is to wish to be rid of life in society altogether,"[25] are representative of this idea of the importance of civil religion.

"Religion," in its various forms, has throughout history contributed much to the "diffuse support" of the nation or the regime in which it has functioned. According to Paul Tillich, religion's strength stems from its commanding position as "the substance of culture." For Tillich, "Religion as ultimate concern is the meaning-giving substance of culture, and culture is the totality of forms in which the basic concern of religion expresses itself. In abbreviation: religion is the substance of culture, culture is the form of religion. Such a consideration definitely prevents the establishment of a dualism of religion and culture."[26] Similarly, anthropologist Ruth Benedict, in her *Patterns of Culture*, claims that "what really binds men together" in communities "is their culture—the ideas and the standards they have in common."[27]

Religion may engender a sense of the transcendent, which, when incorporated into the symbolism of the state, tends to infuse the state or regime with a kind of "sacred" legitimacy. When stimulated, this can bring highly emotive responses from the community and can influence the behavior of the citizens independent of, yet supportive of, the political instruments of coercion. The generally accepted belief in things "sacred" will serve to restrain actions considered by the community to be profane, corrupt, disuniting, or disfunctional, while setting "acceptable" behavior expectations with reference to them. As Stephen J. Tonsor points out, "One of the most important functions of the *sacred* is to set limits, to define boundaries."[28]

The phenomenon of religion or the "sacred" has helped provide the substance by which congregations of people have become or remained communities, and the requisite support by which regimes have ruled with at least some measure of legitimacy. The unity of ancient communities, for instance, appears to have depended to a significant degree upon myths that explained the origin of the world, the gods, society, men, and community life and responsibility, all in terms of the actions of the gods. The daily existence of the people was dominated by a belief in intracosmic gods who were thought to be responsible for all that happened.[29] The fusion of societal mores and law with the "sacred" was an extremely important consideration in strengthening the community, since, as it has often been suggested, without placing law or custom in the realm of the "sacred," men will sooner or later lose allegiance to their authority. According to Heinrich A. Rommen, "In the early periods of all peoples, the mores and laws, undifferentiated from the norms of religion, were looked upon as being exclusively of divine origin."[30] William A. Robson has argued that "since the law in early society is generally believed to have come directly from God, it would seem likely that we should find no clear dividing line between law and religion. This is indeed the case in almost all the great systems of law known to us. In the early ages of mankind, law and religion were often so closely interwoven that it is scarcely possible to say where one begins and the other leaves off."[31]

A sense of things "sacred" in a culture may protect the individual citizen from feelings of anomie and provide for him certain structures, mores and beliefs that give him meaning and place in his environment. In effect, this can serve to stimulate "order" in the individual personality and hence the community. According to Mircea Eliade, "'the sacred' is an element of the structure of consciousness, and not a moment in the history of consciousness. The experience of the sacred is indissolubly linked to the effort made by man to construct a meaningful world."[32] "Life is not possible," he wrote, "without an opening toward the transcendent; in other words, human beings cannot live in chaos. Once contact with the transcendent is lost, existence in the world ceases to be possible."[33] The loss of the "sacred," Robert Nisbet argues, is tantamount to the loss of "community." Although the formation of human aggregates is possible without a sense of the "sacred," "community" is not. It is the sense of the "sacred," offers Professor Nisbet, that establishes the cement that protects the community in its existence as the foundation of society and culture, "for to endow anything with sacred signficance—human life, birth, marriage, death, the community or nation—is to remove it from the sphere of things which must be justified by expediency or pragmatic consideration."[34]

According to the distinguished economist Frank Knight, unity in society is dependent on both the rule of law and religion. Together they form the sacred, or in his words, the "mystical" uniting force of society. It is "unreal," he writes, "to conceive a society without a moral attitude, which means a religion of some kind, enforced by approval and disapproval, and without an organized mechanism of sanctions. The two . . . must work together effectively to keep infractions at a low level."[35] This unity may thus operate to limit the "evils of *stunted lives* on the one hand and *excess* on the other."[36] And although there must be the fact of the force of law, men must also have "some prior fundamental principles in common, principles accepted and supported with substantial unanimity and with intense emotional fervor, a mystical ineffable sense of one-ness. . . . The basis of unity must be mystical, religious."[37] Professor Knight insists that "the sociological and historical role of religion, morals and legal formalism is precisely to furnish this mystical basis for unity, which not only enables societies to stand up against conflicts when conflicts come, but more important, enables men to accept the degree of rule of force of traditional law which is necessary for peace in any group."[38] And beyond this there are the unwritten "rules of the game," "sportsmanship," and other expressions of character found in moral theology that are not enforced by law nor heavily influenced by free discussion. These depend primarily on the influence of religion. "In a word," concludes Knight, "the basis of the social order is religion."[39]

There is often the element of fear of the wrath of god or the gods implicit in certain forms of "civil religion." This, too, may place the regime, which in times past has played the role of intermediary between the citizenry and the gods (and in modern times between the citizens and the unfolding of history), in a favorable position as legitimate authority. Machiavelli, who lauded religion among the Romans as a source of stability, was convinced that order in society was, to a great extent, dependent upon fear of the gods and the belief by the people that their laws and political structure carried sacred or divine sanction. He thus advocated "civil religion" for purely utilitarian purposes. "In truth," he proclaimed, "there never was any remarkable lawgiver amongst any people who did not resort to divine authority, as otherwise his laws would not have been accepted by the people; for there are many good laws, the importance of which is known to the sagacious lawgiver, but the reasons for which are not sufficiently evident to enable him to persuade others to submit to them; and therefore do wise men, for the purpose of removing this difficulty, resort to divine authority."[40] Tyrants have typically promoted "sacred" or "pseudo-sacred" devices in an attempt to keep the allegiance or acquiescence of the masses towards the regime. Both democracies and dictatorships attempt to imbue national symbols and rituals with some form of "sacred" legitimacy.[41]

Much has been written by theorists on "civil religion" or "civil theology" in America. According to Daniel F. Rice, "Since the appearance of Will Herberg's *Protestant, Catholic, Jew* in 1955—there has been an explicit and sometimes frenetic concern among theologians, church historians, and sociologists of religion with the thesis that there has emerged out of the American experience a phenomenon sociologist Robert N. Bellah chose to call 'civil religion.'"[42]

Professor Herberg's thesis of "civil religion" has been a sort of launching pad from which many modern writers have posited their own ideas concerning the subject. He defined civil religion as a common or general religion that exists "over and above conventional religion," and in which "there is to be found among Americans some sort of faith or belief or set of convictions, not generally designated as religion but definitely operative as such in their lives in the sense of providing them with some fundamental concept of normativity and meaning."[43] Herberg called this common religion "the American Way of Life," which, he believed, had emerged as "distinct from the conventional religion of the denominations," and had actually worked to sustain "the society in which the denominations find their place in mutual legitimation."[44] His conclusion was that "we have in America an invisible, formally unacknowledged, but very potent religion—the religion of democracy, the religion of the American Way of Life—of which the conventional religions are felt to be more or less adequate expressions."[45]

While not denominational in itself, the religion of America, according to Herberg, expresses certain beliefs that are generally accepted and promoted. "Most emphatically," he wrote, Americans "believe in God," "hold the Bible to be an inspired book" indeed "the Word of God," believe "children should be given religious instruction and raised as church members," and "hold religion to be of very great importance."[46] They believe in "life after death," and tend to place a high valuation "on their own virtue."[47] They "feel they *ought* to love their fellow men."[48] Thus, according to Herberg, this "American Way of Life is, at bottom, a spiritual structure, a structure of ideas and ideals, of aspirations and values, of beliefs and standards; it synthesizes all that commends itself to the American as the right, the good, and the true in actual life. It embraces such seemingly incongruous elements as sanitary plumbing and freedom of opportunity, Coca-Cola and an intense faith in education—all felt as moral questions relating to the proper way of life. The very expression 'way of life' points to its religious essence, for one's ultimate, overall way of life is one's religion."[49] It is, continues Herberg, "an organic structure of ideas, values, and beliefs that constitutes a faith common to Americans and genuinely operative in their lives, a faith that markedly influences, and is influenced by, the 'official' religions of American society. Sociologically, anthropologically, if one pleases, it is the characteristic American religion, undergirding American life and overreaching American society despite all indubitable differences of region, section, culture, class."[50]

According to Professor Herberg, if the American Way of Life is to be described in one word, that word is "democracy." However, that word or term would have to be described in its peculiar "American sense. On its political side it means the Constitution; on its economic side, 'free enterprise'; on its social side an equalitarianism which is not only compatible but indeed actually implies vigorous economic competition and high mobility. Spiritually, the American Way of Life is best expressed in a certain kind of 'idealism' which has come to be recognized as characteristically American."[51]

Robert N. Bellah has suggested that "there actually exists alongside of and rather clearly differentiated from the churches an elaborate and well-institutionalized civil religion in America."[52] It acknowledges a higher law than the state or even the people, and encapsulates belief in a body of natural rights that emanate not from the beneficence of the state but from God's dispensation. It charges the political process with the responsibility of contributing to the unfolding of God's purposes on earth. Inherent in this doctrine is what Professor Rice refers to as "a point of revolutionary leverage."[53] This civil religion, in the words of Bellah, was not simply "religion in general," rather, "while generality was undoubtedly seen as a virtue by some . . . the civil religion was specific enough when it came to the topic of America. Precisely because of this specificity, the civil religion was saved from empty formalism and served as a genuine vehicle of national religious understanding."[54] Although Bellah believes the American civil religion to be both formal and institutionalized, "it has no official support in the legal and constitutional order. . . . Belief in the tenets of the civil religion are legally incumbent on no one and there are no official interpreters of civil theology."[55]

The idea of civil religion, then, incorporates a number of elements that must be clearly understood, yet they cannot be clearly separated. Organized religions, in addition to purely spiritual functions, help provide the motivation for social order, restraint, and charitable interaction. General religious beliefs that are not sectarian, but enjoy wide social consensus, contribute much to a nation's political culture. Political symbols, traditions, and other elements of the political culture may be grounded in religious beliefs, but may also have secular roots. Religion, then, is not the only source of political culture and nonbelievers can accept the role of symbols and traditions without embracing religion itself. The American Founders, however, saw religion as the primary source of and motivation for public spiritedness and political culture.

THE AMERICAN FOUNDERS AND CIVIL RELIGION

From the beginning of the American colonization there has existed some form of civil religion, a phenomenon that has exerted a profound effect on the development of American republicanism. The existence of a civil religion is not remarkable. The essential point to be developed here is the way in which the Framers integrated their idea of civil religion with the structure of government they created.

Some of the American Founders avoided affiliation with the organized religions of their day. They almost universally—even those who claimed membership in individual faiths—subscribed to what John Locke had inferred was the general religion of Western civilization, applied particularly to the emerging American culture. They tended to support a "general" religion in much the same way that de Tocqueville later did; and, just as he, they recognized its importance to the health of the Republic.

Whatever their religious beliefs—whether they were by philosophy or conversion Christians, whether they believed in but one Supreme Creator whose power and presence were universal (as did early "Unitarians" such as Jefferson), or whether they accepted the God of "first instance" as in Deism[56]—there was in evidence a *general religion* that permeated the thought of these early Americans and the communities that spawned them. It superimposed over the nation a sort of harmony that superseded the conflict between the sects, between the "churched" and the "unchurched," and the sects and the revivals. Generally, both the "churched" and the "unchurched," Christian and Deist, accepted certain fundamental norms about God and morality that had become deeply ingrained in their general culture over the years. This "general" philosophy or theology countenanced a belief in God, obligations to one's fellow men, and acceptance of that doctrine de Tocqueville was later to emphasize as so critical for citizens of a democratic republic—immortality and a final judgment. It was Franklin who perhaps best outlined the basic aspects of this general "theology" or "philosophy." "Here is my creed," he wrote, "I believe in one God, Creator of the universe. That he governs it by his providence. That he ought to be worshipped. That the most acceptable service we render to him is in doing good to his other children. That the soul of man is immortal, and will be treated with justice in another life respecting its conduct in this. These I take to be the fundamental points of all sound religion."[57]

Jefferson's creed is similar: "1. That there is one only God, and He all perfect. 2. That there is a future state of rewards and punishments. 3. That to love God with all thy heart and thy neighbor as thyself, is the sum of religion."[58] These, suggested Jefferson, were principles in which "God has united us all."[59] "Reading, reflection and time," continued Jefferson, "have convinced me that the interests of society require the observation of those moral precepts only in which all religions agree (for all forbid us to murder, steal, plunder, or bear false witness), and that we should not intermeddle with the particular dogmas in which all religions differ, and which are totally unconnected with morality."[60] In his first inaugural address, he extended his hope that "the United States will be enlightened by a benign religion, professed, indeed, and practiced in various forms, yet all of them including honesty, truth, temperance, gratitude, and the love of man; acknowledging and adoring an overruling Providence which by all its dispensations proves that it delights in the happiness of man here and his greater happiness thereafter."[61] So, too, did Thomas Paine express his devotion to God and his "hope for happiness beyond this life,"[62] that the purpose of life was "for our own happiness and His glory," and that he relied upon "His protection both here and hereafter."[63] Samuel Adams referred to these basic concepts as "the religion of America," indeed, "the religion of all mankind."[64]

It was this general form of religious "feeling" or faith—developed from the Hebraic-Christian-Puritan ethic—which, as de Tocqueville later perceived, was the primary ingredient in developing and sustaining that morality which promoted unity, harmony and cooperation in the American community. It was the basic influence in keeping society from bursting its seams. Its emphasis on moral behavior as a guide for interaction with others allowed social, economic and political exchange to a degree unknown in other countries. The infusion of benevolence or the Golden Rule into the American concept of virtue tended to mute the natural savagery of man and to influence the expression of self-interest so that it was not all-pervasive. It developed generally expected modes of behavior which, in turn, put social pressure, if not the pangs of conscience, on erratic, corrupt or selfish behavior. It tended to stimulate that kind of responsible behavior that keeps the heady mixture of freedom and democracy within certain bounds so that it does not run away with itself. In short, it helped create a people who could be self-governing.

As de Tocqueville later pointed out, these principles and concepts became the cement for the new adventure in constitution-making. They were not only generally believed, but venerated. They provided a basis for community and for cooperative endeavor. They gave both the moral legitimacy and the stubborn determination that was needed to complete the bloody separation from England as well as providing the values upon which their political doctrines would be founded. They provided a general feeling of hope and positive anticipation for the future, and gave the individual and the collective psychological strength to bear the frustrations and setbacks involved in the development of the nation. They provided the moral restraints on behavior without which self-government would have been impossible under any conditions. Finally, it was the "given" nature of this general religion that augmented its strength: the Founders assumed its existence and created the Constitution upon the base provided by the general religion.

Although some of the American spokesmen questioned the divinity of Christ or held anti-clerical attitudes in various degrees, most of them saw Christianity, especially with its advocacy of benevolence, as a body of thought and as a motivator of the kind of individual and collective behavior necessary for self-government. Even some "nonbelievers" were convinced of the utility of Christianity as a moderating force on the democratic "mob." Few could contemplate a more perfect doctrine by which to unify free men on a foundation of liberty and justice.

Religion, Law, and Civic Responsibility

Religion in America also played an important role in the development of the rule of law and freedom. Both the organized religions and the general religious atmosphere combined to give sanctity to legitimate law and to enshrine the ideal of responsible freedom. Not only the ministry, but government leaders and other citizens as well, incorporated God into the public philosophy along with other civil values and rituals. Sydney E. Ahlstrom informs us that "it is upon the spirit of American democracy that Puritanism worked its most direct and powerful effects; and if we look to the center of the Puritan faith, we may perceive the springs of its peculiar power to mold personal values, to gird the citizen or magistrate for his work, to arouse and maintain his sense of civic duty, to intensify his determination to live responsibly before and under the law, and to make him aware that neither individual men, or groups of men or even nations were above the law or were laws unto themselves." And these ideals continued after Puritanism became a more general religious philosophy than institutionalized churches. "In these areas, moreover, Puritan nurture continued to have a powerful shaping effect on succeeding generations even after the original standards were relaxed."[65]

According to Professor Ahlstrom, "The proper starting place for an understanding of this dynamic act in American history is the cardinal doctrine of Judeo-Christian tradition: divine sovereignty." The founders of New England's Holy Commonwealths "had a rigorous, awe-filled concern for God's almighty will as [it] was revealed in the Scripture. This legalism [inspired the] conviction that the Bible, through command, counsel, and historical example, provided precise divine guidance for church, state and personal life. . . . Ancient Israel, moreover, became for them a veritable model in both civil and ecclesiastical matters and in the interrelation of the two."[66] Law permeated their activities. They considered themselves bound to the law even when they were selecting ministers to be over them. Both Thomas Hooker and Governor John Winthrop taught that the governors as well as the people were under God's rule. Here was acknowledged the ideal of a "rule of law," a sanctioned "higher law," which later became such an important part of the ideological concepts championed by the American Founders, coupled with the added legitimacy and authority engendered by the Puritan belief that America had been set apart as a new "land of promise" for the modern "children of Israel."

"The reform and purification of church discipline and doctrine through a return to the principles of the primitive apostolic church," writes legal historian George Lee Haskins, "was not only the deliberate and unswerving aim of the early Puritans in England but the primary purpose of the founding of the Bay Colony. To God's word as declared in Scripture, the colonists consistently turned for guidance and justification, both in the matter of church polity and in the framing and the administration of their laws. The decisions of the courts were expected to conform to that Word, and an order of the General Court in 1636 had expressly so provided in situations for which no positive law had been established." It was not uncommon to incorporate "literal biblical phraseology into the body of statutory law."[67]

The Puritan ideal of covenant proved to be a catalyst to the growth of the idea of the rule of law. The covenant was the Puritans' central affirmation of participation in God's purposes in ordering a corrupt world. It was not just an agreement; it was a legal and binding contract. It was to be a judge and a teacher. And, as the years went by, the idea of civic virtue and "law-abidingness" began to merge with the doctrine of regeneration. According to Ahlstrom, "as the accent on law-abidingness grew, so did the optimistic conviction that even unregenerate human nature could aspire to moral perfection. This movement culminates in both the vision and the sense of civic duty exhibited in the Revolutionary epoch by many of the new nation's founding fathers."[68]

The experience and practice with the covenant and direct representation in both church congregations and town governments naturally contributed to the eventual republican system of elected representatives who serve at the behest of their constituents. And no doubt, the practice of colonial charters and church covenants led to the expectation that constitutions would be written documents, outlining the purposes and powers of government as well as restrictions of particular powers, including the inference that acts of government that violated the terms of the constitution were null and void.

The commonplace infusion of God and the "sacred" into American public symbols and celebrations—from the Fourth of July to Presidential proclamations—needs little elaboration, although the salutary impact of this practice may not always be perceived. It was but a natural tendency for the American founders and spokesmen to imbue certain civic symbols, concepts, documents and institutions with the aura of the "sacred." This proclivity no doubt developed from both religious belief and common sense notions of utility. An example can be taken from the sacralizing of freedom and natural rights in the American tradition. As far as Jefferson was concerned, the ideal of individual freedom was not an accident of nature, but a gift from God. "Can the liberties of a nation be thought secure," he asked, "when we have removed their only firm basis, a conviction in the minds of the people that these liberties are the gift of God? That they are not to be violated but with His wrath?"[69]

And Alexander Hamilton spoke for many of his countrymen when he stated: "The sacred rights of mankind are not to be rummaged for among old parchments and musty records. They are written as with a sunbeam in the whole volume of human nature, by the hand of the Divinity itself, and can never be erased by mortal power. . . . Upon this law depend the natural rights of man: the Supreme Being gave existence to man, together with the means of preserving and beautifying that existence. He endowed him with rational faculties, by the help of which to discern and pursue such things as were consistent with his duty and interest; and invested him with an inviolable right to personal liberty and personal safety."[70]

The Founders: Religious, But Not Always Sectarian

While John Adams, for example, believed there had been a certain corruption of Christianity, he accepted the Christian ethic as indispensable to a free and stable society. He, like Jefferson, revered Christianity in its pristine purity as expressed in the New Testament. "The substance of Christianity as I understand it," he wrote, "is eternal and unchangeable and will bear examination forever." He lamented, however, that Christianity had "been mixed with extraneous ingredients which I think will not bear examination and they ought to be separated."[71] Yet, even in its present form, Adams marveled at Christianity's character and salubrious influence. In his diary dated July 26, 1796, he wrote, "The Christian religion is, above all the religions that ever prevailed or existed in ancient or modern times, the religion of wisdom, virtue, equity, and humanity."[72] Again, under the date of August 14, 1796, he wrote of Christianity as a leavening, morally restraining force, while emphasizing the Golden Rule and the doctrine of immortality. In his words one can perceive the importance he placed on Christianity as a means of political socialization:

> One great advantage of the Christian religion is that it brings the great principle of the law of nature and nations—Love your neighbor as yourself, and do to others as you would that others should do to you— to the knowledge, belief, and veneration of the whole people. Children, servants, women, and men, are all professors in the science of public and private morality. No other institution for public and private morality, no other institution for education, no kind of political discipline, could diffuse this necessary kind of information so universally among all ranks and descriptions of citizens. The duties and rights of the man and the citizen are thus taught from early infancy to every creature. The sanctions of a future life are thus added to the observance of civil and political, as well as domestic and private duties. Prudence, justice, temperance, and fortitude, are thus taught to be the means and conditions of future as well as present happiness.[73]

Although he, too, was sometimes frustrated with the sectarian dogma of his time, Benjamin Franklin still contended that the Christian system of religion and morality was "the best the world ever saw or is likely to see;"[74] and he subscribed personally to its basic "essentials" which were "to be found in all the religions we had in our country." He "respected them all, tho' with different degrees of respect." He regularly paid his "annual subscription for the support of the only Presbyterian minister or meeting we had," contributed his "mite" to the construction of new churches in Philadelphia, "whatever might be their sect,"[75] and urged his daughters to attend "church whoever preaches."[76] From his own observations it seems that, in spite of certain reservations, he saw both denominational religion and "general" religion as salutary for the Republic. In his "Proposals Relating to the Education of Youth in Pennsylvania"(1749) he advocated the study of history that would "afford frequent opportunities of showing the Necessity of a *Public Religion*, from its Usefulness to the Public, the Advantage of a Religious Character Among private Persons; the Mischiefs of Superstition, etc., and the Excellency of the *CHRISTIAN RELIGION* above all others Ancient and Modern." According to Franklin, "The general natural tendency of reading good history must be to fix in the minds of youth deep impressions of the beauty and usefulness of virtue of all kinds, public spirit, fortitude, etc."[77]

James Madison described Christianity in 1832 as "the best and purest religion;"[78] and in 1833, his contemporary, Justice Joseph Story, called Christianity "the religion of liberty." "In a Republic," he wrote, "there would seem to be a peculiar propriety in viewing the Christian religion as the great basis on which it [republican liberty] must rest for its support and permanence, if it be what it has ever been deemed by its truest friends to be, the religion of liberty. Montesquieu has remarked that the Christian religion is a stranger to mere despotic power."[79]

Thomas Jefferson and General Christianity

For many years, Christianity had been in metamorphosis; stimulated by the influence of widespread scripture reading, it had been slowly exorcising some of the classical Greco-Roman influences that had penetrated its doctrine throughout the centuries. It was these remaining vestiges of Greco-Roman thought that caused Jefferson— the most misunderstood of the Founders with regard to religion—and others to lash out against certain elements of *organized* religion in the United States. Yet, if Jefferson was "unchurched" because of his philosophical and theological quarrel with some of the clergy, he remained devout in his belief in God, unmoving in his admiration for the "pure" doctrines of Christ as moral guidelines. He was far more impressed with the founder of Christianity than he was with many of His modern followers: "Of the systems of morality ancient or modern, which have come under my observation," he wrote, "none appear to me so pure as that of Jesus. He who follows this steadily need not, I think, be uneasy, although he cannot comprehend the subtleties and mysteries erected in His doctrine by those who, calling themselves His special followers and favorites, would make Him come into the world to lay snares for all understanding but theirs."[80] He was convinced that the system of morality as advocated by Christ was "more perfect than those of any of the ancient philosophers. The morality of Jesus, as taught by himself, and freed from the corruptions of latter times, is far superior."[81] Jefferson preferred to return in doctrine to the "unlettered Apostles, the Apostolic Fathers, and the Christians of the first century."[82] In a letter to Dr. Joseph Priestly, Jefferson called Christian philosophy "the most sublime and benevolent but the most perverted system that ever shone on man."[83] And to his friend and clergyman, Dr. Benjamin Rush, he wrote: "Notwithstanding these disadvantages, a system of morals is presented to us, which, if filled up in the style and spirit of the rich fragments he left us, would be the most perfect and sublime that has ever been taught by man."[84]

Jefferson saw the doctrines of Christianity as being utilitarian and universal in application, having the potential of uniting all mankind in "one family in the bonds of love, peace, common wants, and common aids."[85] Jefferson, who had questions concerning the divinity of Christ, still contended that, "had the doctrines of Jesus been preached always as pure as they came from his lips, the whole civilized world would now have been Christian."[86]

While Jefferson firmly believed in Christianity as an unequalled moral doctrine, his concern for individual liberty led him to champion religious freedom. Freedom of belief was bound up with other personal freedoms, and while a commitment to Christian beliefs was part of his political culture, he championed efforts such as the Virginia Statute of Religious Freedom as essential in assuring individual liberty. "I have sworn upon the altar of God," he wrote, "eternal hostility against every form of tyranny over the mind of man."[87] Pure Christianity, for Jefferson, posed no such threat.

Jefferson was not alone in these sentiments. Anti-clericism in America usually did not carry with it a repudiation of religion or of Christianity as it did in France. Being "unreligious" and "unchurched" were often two different situations. The influence of Christianity in America was widespread. According to Franklin, "Atheism is unknown there so that persons may live to a great age . . . without having their piety shocked by meeting either an atheist or an infidel."[88] Franklin saw in this general Christianity a highly utilitarian doctrine for individual happiness and the peaceful functioning of a democratic republic. "As to Jesus of Nazareth," pondered Franklin, "I think the system of morals and his religion, as he left them to us, the best the world ever saw or is likely to see; but I apprehend it has received various corrupting changes, and I have . . . some doubts as to his divinity; though, it is a question I do not dogmatize upon, having never studied it, and think it needless to busy myself with it now, when I expect soon an opportunity of knowing the truth with less trouble."[89]

ALEXIS DE TOCQUEVILLE AND AMERICAN "GENERAL" RELIGION

When the French philosopher Alexis de Tocqueville visited America not long after the establishment of the United States Constitution, he claimed to have found there a "general Christianity" which, far from having lost its import with the coming of the

Constitutional Republic, was more essential than ever before. In his view, a modern democratic republic needed a "civil religion"; indeed, needed it more than any other kind of government.

De Tocqueville's concern with the phenomenon of democracy in his time led him to contemplate the importance of culture and the cultural attributes that he came to perceive as necessary for the birth or survival of democracy. De Tocqueville was particularly interested in the utilitarian impact of religion on modern democracy. He leaves the truth or falsity of religious belief to another realm, yet he does not undercut religion nor does he attack its spiritual doctrines. His point is that religion is important in utilitarian ways. He suggests that people can be motivated by the mind as well as the heart, that moral concepts advocated by religion may be promoted because they are practical and salutary; though by no means would he deny the necessity of belief. "I have neither the right nor the intention," he confessed, "of examining the supernatural means that God employs to infuse religious belief into the heart of man. I am at this moment considering religions in a purely human point of view; my object is to inquire by what means they may most easily retain their sway in the democratic ages upon which we are entering."[90]

The Importance of the "Sacred"

De Tocqueville emphasized the importance of "dogmatic belief" and its relationship to religion. "It arises in different ways, and it may change its object and its form; but under no circumstances will dogmatic belief cease to exist, or, in other words, men will never cease to entertain some opinions on trust and without discussion." Without this common belief, he insisted, "no society can prosper; say, rather, no society can exist; for without ideas held in common there is no common action, and without common action there may still be men, but there is no social body."[91] De Tocqueville was convinced that men simply could not do "without dogmatic belief," and that "it is much to be desired that such belief should exist among them." He believed that among the various kinds of dogmatic belief, "the most desirable appears . . . to be dogmatic belief in matters of religion; and this is a clear inference, even from no higher consideration than the interests of this world. There is hardly any human action, however particular it may be, that does not originate in some very general idea men have conceived of the Deity, of his relation to mankind, of the nature of their own souls, and of their duties to their fellow creatures. Nor can anything prevent these ideas from being the common spring from which all the rest emanates."[92] Without such beliefs, de Tocqueville believed that "men lose the objects of their fondest hopes as if through forgetfulness. They are carried away by an imperceptible current, which they have not the courage to stem, but which they follow with regret, since it bears them away from a faith they love to a skepticism that plunges them into despair."[93]

De Tocqueville believed that men naturally yearn for the "sacred": "Men are therefore immeasurably interested in acquiring fixed ideas of God, of the soul, and of their general duties to their Creator and their fellow men; for doubt on these first principles would abandon all their actions to chance and would condemn them in some way to disorder and impotence."[94] De Tocqueville reasoned that the emotionally sustaining influence of religion was essential for freedom since, without faith, men lose their assurity, judgment, and confidence, which then causes them to seek some other dogmatic belief or direction to take its place:

> When the religion of a people is destroyed, doubt gets hold of the higher powers of the intellect and half paralyzes all the others. Every man accustoms himself to having only confused and changing notions on the subjects most interesting to his fellow creatures and himself. His opinions are ill-defended and easily abandoned; and, in despair of ever solving by himself the hard problems respecting the destiny of man, he ignobly submits to think no more about them.
>
> Such a condition cannot but enervate the soul, relax the springs of the will, and prepare a people for servitude. Not only does it happen in such a case that they allow their freedom to be taken from them; they frequently surrender it themselves. When there is no longer any principle [sic] of authority in religion any more than in politics, men are speedily frightened at the aspect of this unbounded independence. The constant agitation of all surrounding things alarms and exhausts them. As everything is at sea in the sphere of the mind, they determine at least that the mechanism of society shall be firm and fixed; and as they cannot resume their ancient belief, they assume a master. . . . *If faith be wanting in [man], he must be subject; and if he be free, he must believe.*"[95]

Manners, Morals, and The Democratic Republic

De Tocqueville's central concern in studying modern democracies was the cultural attributes, the manners, the customs and the character of the people in a given polity—which he identified as "the whole moral and intellectual condition of a people"[96]—for, as far as he was concerned, this revealed more about the character of the system than any other single factor. Like the American Founders before him, he came to believe that a democratic republic required a special kind of people. "The importance of manners," he concluded, "is a common truth to which study and experience incessantly direct our attention. It may be regarded as a central point in the range of human observation, and the common termination of all inquiry. So seriously do I insist upon this ground [point] that if I have hitherto failed in making the reader feel the important influence of the practical experience, the habits, the opinions, in short, of the customs of the Americans upon the maintenance of their institutions, I have failed in the principle [sic] object of my work."[97] The "manners" or "customs"—"the moral and intellectual condition"—of the people, emphasized de Tocqueville, are more important than their "physical circumstances," even their "laws." "I am convinced," he wrote, "that the most advantageous situation and the best possible laws cannot maintain a constitution in spite of the manners of a country; whilst the latter may turn the most unfavorable positions and the worst laws to some advantage."[98]

In applying this formula to his observations of *Democracy in America*, the French philosopher claimed to see the main difference between the United States and other nations on the American continent. "The customs of the Americans of the United States are, then, the peculiar cause which renders that people the only one of the American nations that is able to support a democratic government; and it is the influence of customs that produces the different degrees of order and prosperity which may be distinguished in the several Anglo-American democracies."[99]

In America the faith was Christianity; the dogmatic belief, of course, was Christian; and the "customs" of the people were permeated with Christian influences. One major reason why de Tocqueville felt that "fixed" or "dogmatic" ideas accepted by faith were so vital, was the fact that men simply could not, by themselves, reason out these first principles. "Religion" not only consigned these "ideas," but endowed them with the "sacred," thereby settling the problem of truth and falsity—at least as far as those who "believed" were concerned. Religion then, according to de Tocqueville, "is the subject on which it is most important for each of us to have fixed ideas; and unhappily it is also the subject on which it is most difficult for each of us, left to himself, to settle his opinions by the sole force of his reason."[100]

Nevertheless, insisted de Tocqueville, it was these "fixed ideas" "respecting God and human nature," that were "above all others . . . most suitable to withdraw from the habitual action of private judgment and in which there is most to gain and least to lose by recognizing a principle of [sic] authority. The first object and one of the principal advantages of religion is to furnish to each of these fundamental questions a solution that is at once clear, precise, intelligible, and lasting, to the mass of mankind." This "imposes a salutary restraint on the intellect; and it must be admitted that, if it does not save men in another world, it is at least very conducive to their happiness and their greatness in this."[101]

Religion and The Democratic Republic

De Tocqueville came to see an inseparable relationship between the American democratic republic and the body of those universal principles that, having emerged from the evolution of modern Christianity, had permeated American society and had become a moral structure of generally accepted beliefs. The only alternative to the tyranny of the state in the preservation of order is some public philosophy or theology that is so generally accepted as legitimate among the people that order becomes more or less spontaneous; that is, the people restrain themselves, on the one hand, and, on the other, perform certain duties on behalf of the state or community and to their fellow men. "These habits of restraint," reasoned de Tocqueville, "recur in political society and are singularly favorable both to the tranquility of the people and to the durability of the institutions they have cherished."[102]

Without restraints, freedom is likely to degenerate into chaos and disorder. De Tocqueville emphasized the importance of religion and its salutary effects on a system of freedom. "Liberty regards religion as its companion in all its battles and its triumphs, as the cradle of its infancy and the divine source of its claims. It considers religion as the safeguard of morality, and morality as the best security of law and the surest pledge of the duration of freedom."[103] Religion, he believed, was essential so that popular government might be tempered and moderated. Religion promotes and legitimates self-restraint, both in the rulers and the ruled, mitigates those individualist tendencies that destroy compassion and philanthrophy and that tend to atomize society, and at the same time supports the maintenance of responsible freedom. This allows moral suasion, the influence of faith and common sense, to become forces of human motivation. Without this well from which democracies must drink to perpetuate themselves, societal rules and regulations will eventually become relative and confusing. The loss of religion and a moral structure in a democratic society is tantamount to the loss of balance, measurement, and stability. "I doubt," surmised de Tocqueville, "whether man can ever support at the same time complete religious independence [absence] and entire political freedom."[104]

Therefore, a democratic republic was in need of *greater*, not *lesser*, influence of a "civil religion" or theology than a tyranny. "Despotism may govern without faith but liberty cannot. Religion is much more necessary in the republic . . . than in the monarchy. *It is more needed in democratic republics than in any others. How is it possible that society should escape destruction if the moral tie is not strengthened in proportion as the political tie is relaxed? And what can be done with a people who are their own masters if they are not submissive to the Deity?*"[105]

In spite of the numerous religious sects de Tocqueville found in America, he perceived there to be a "general" Christianity, a commonly accepted public philosophy, one which he found highly salutary for the republic. He believed that some form of public philosophy was necessary for any degree of unity and cooperation in a democracy, and that this general public philosophy with its Christian foundation formed the peculiar character of democracy in America. "Christianity," he wrote, "has retained a strong hold on the public mind in America; and I would more particularly remark that its sway is not only that of a philosophic doctrine which has been adopted on inquiry, but of a religion which is believed without discussion. In the United States, Christian sects are infinitely diversified and perpetually modified; but Christianity itself is an established and irresistible fact, which no one undertakes either to attack or to defend."[106] Although the "sects in the United States" were "innumerable," de Tocqueville saw them all resting on the moral foundation that ancient Christianity had bequeathed them. "They all differ in respect to the worship which is due the Creator; but they all agree in respect to the duties which are due from man to man. Each sect adores the Deity in its own peculiar manner, but all sects preach the same moral law in the name of God." They were "comprised within the great unity of Christianity, and Christian morality is everywhere the same." Therefore, de Tocqueville spoke of the "Gospel" in terms of the "general relations of men to God and each other, beyond which it imposes no point of faith."[107]

De Tocqueville returned time and again to a contemplation of the relationship between the nature of man, religion, and political institutions. "On my arrival [in America]," he wrote, "the religious aspect of the country was the first thing that struck my attention, and the longer I stayed there, the more I perceived the great political consequences resulting from this new state of things."[108] In a nutshell, the colonists had "brought with them into the New World a form of Christianity which I cannot better describe than by styling it a democratic and republican religion. This contributed powerfully to the establishment of a republic and a democracy in public affairs."[109] In Americans, this philosopher believed he had found a "republican" people who could coalesce "the spirit of religion and the spirit of freedom. . . . In America religion is the road to knowledge, and the observance of the divine laws leads man to civil freedom."[110] Not only did de Tocqueville see religion as "one of the most prominent . . . causes to which the maintenance of the political institutions of the

Americans is attributable," he also observed that "religion is not less useful to each citizen than to the whole state. The Americans show by their practice that they feel the high necessity of imparting morality to democratic communities by means of religion."[111] "The Americans," he explained, "combine the notions of Christianity and of liberty so intimately in their minds that it is impossible to make them conceive the one without the other. . . . I have known of societies formed by Americans to send out ministers of the Gospel into the new Western states, to found schools and churches there, lest religion should be allowed to die away in those remote settlements, and the rising states be less fitted to enjoy free institutions than the people from whom they came."[112] While all Americans might not be devotees of religion, they nevertheless, he believed, "hold it to be indispensable to the maintenance of republican institutions."[113]

Undoubtedly, de Tocqueville's amazement with the Christian religion in America was due to the fact that it presented a picture so startlingly different from religion in his own country of France. "In France," he observed, "I had almost always seen the spirit of religion and the spirit of freedom marching in opposite directions. But in America I found they were intimately united."[114]

De Tocqueville believed that "common" or "general" Christianity served to "instill morality into democracy," and thus to moderate some of the destructive passions unleased by the dynamics of democracy, and to assuage the excesses of the new freedom inherent in it. He was *convinced that Christianity must be maintained at any cost in the bosom of modern democracies.*"[115] Therefore, government magistrates, he reasoned, should offer a show of belief in Christian doctrines, and support this "civil theology"—even if they, themselves, are concerned but with its practical, utiltarian application; even if their own faith be wanting. He argued that "the legislators of democracy and all of the virtuous and enlightened men" therein should have as their "unceasing object . . . to raise the souls of their fellow citizens and keep them lifted up towards heaven. It is necessary that all who feel an interest in the future destinies of democratic society should unite, and that all should make joint and continual efforts to diffuse the love of the infinite, lofty aspirations, and a love of pleasures not of the earth."[116]

De Tocqueville concluded that the most important component of this "civil theology" was the doctrine of the immortality of the soul. This belief, encapsulating as it did a Creator, an immortal soul and a judgment, above all, served as a sedative to man's natural unruliness and selfishness. De Tocqueville was certain that men who believed that there was nothing beyond this life could not make good democrats, for the restraint, engendered by a fear of, or reverence for, a just

God and a final judgment, would not be activated in their lives and influence their behavior. America's "general" religion and the religions of America were "simple, and practical means of teaching men the doctrine of the immortality of the soul." And, according to the philosopher, *"that is the greatest benefit which a democratic people derives from its belief, and hence its belief is more necessary to such a people than to all others."* Therefore, he warned, if such a religion "has struck its roots deep into democracy, beware that you do not disturb it; but rather watch it carefully as the most precious bequest of aristocratic ages."[117] He went so far as to advocate that "if among the opinions of a democratic people any of those pernicious theories exist which tend to inculcate that all perishes with the body, let men by whom such theories are professed be marked as the natural foes of the whole people. . . . I should not hesitate to decide," he continued, "that the community would run less risk of being brutalized by believing that the soul of man will pass into the carcass of a hog than by believing that the soul of man is nothing."[118]

He was not hesitant to remind the democratic government of its responsibility in this regard. "The sole effectual means which governments can employ in order to have the doctrine of the immortal soul duly respected is always to act as if they believed in it themselves; and I think that it is only by scrupulous conformity to religious morality in great affairs that they can hope to teach the community at large to know, to love, and to observe it in the lesser concerns of life."

By the time he had finished his sojourn in this unique Republic, de Tocqueville had become convinced that there existed no country "where the Christian religion retains a greater influence over the souls of men than in America; and there can be no greater proof of its utility and of its conformity to human nature than that its influence is powerfully felt over the most enlightened and free nation of the earth."[119]

NOTES

1. Walter Lippmann, *Essays in The Public Philosophy* (Boston: Little, Brown, 1955), p. 162.

2. See Richard LaPiere, *The Freudian Ethic* (London: Allen and Unwin, 1959).

3. Lippmann, *Essays in The Public Philosophy*, p. 180.

4. Robert Nisbet, *History of the Idea of Progress*, p. 47.

5. Simone Weil, *The Need for Roots: Prelude to a Declaration of Duties Toward Mankind*, translated by Arthur Wills (Boston: Beacon, 1952), p. 11.

6. Anne M. Cohler, "Christian Opinion and Montesquieu's Rhetoric," paper delivered at the Annual Meeting of the American Political Science Association, August 31, 1978.

7. Edward Gibbon, *The Decline and Fall of the Roman Empire* Vol. 1 (New York: Modern Library, 1932), p. 25.

8. Will Durant, *Caesar and Christ* (New York: Simon and Schuster, 1944), p. 61.

9. Cicero, *De Natura Deorum*, trans. and ed. Austin Stickney (Boston: Ginn, 1892), Book 3, Chapter 40.

10. Peter Gay, *The Enlightenment: The Rise of Modern Paganism* (New York: Norton, 1977), p. 155; Frederick Wilhelmsen and Willmore Kendall, "Cicero and the Politics of Public Orthodoxy," in Richard J. Bishirjian, *A Public Philosophy Reader* (New Rochelle, N.Y.: Arlington House, 1978), p. 136.

11. Saint Augustine, *The City of God*, translated by Marcus Dods, with an Introduction by Thomas Merton (New York: Modern Library, 1950), Books 1, 2, 7.

12. We appreciate having consulted Michael P. Zuckett's excellent article, "Locke and the Problem of Civil Religion," in Robert H. Horwitz, *The Moral Foundations of the American Republic* (Charlottesville: University Press of Virginia, 1986), pp. 181–203, for both content and source. See also Horwitz, "John Locke and the Preservation of Liberty: A Perennial Problem of Civic Education," same volume, pp. 136–64.

13. John Locke, *On the Reasonableness of Christianity* (Chicago: Henry Regnery 1965), Section 167. Zuckett, "Locke and the Problem of Civil Religion," p. 188.

14. *Ibid.*, Section 171. Zuckett, "Locke and the Problem of Civil Religion," p. 188.

15. *Ibid.*, Section 14. Zuckett, "Locke and the Problem of Civil Religion," p. 188.

16. *Ibid.*, Section 243. Zuckett, "Locke and the Problem of Civil Religion," pp. 188–89.

17. Jean Jacques Rousseau, *The Social Contract*, translated by Willmoore Kendall (Chicago: Regnery, 1954), Bk. 4, Chap. 8, pp. 204–23.

18. David Easton, *A Framework for Political Analysis* (Englewood Cliffs, N.J.: Prentice-Hall, 1965), pp. 124–25.

19. See generally David Easton and R. D. Hess, "The Child's Changing Image of the President," *Public Opinion Quarterly*, Vol. 24 (1960); "Youth and the Political System," in Seymore Martin Lipset and L. Lowenthal, eds., *Culture and Social Character* (New York: Free Press of Glencoe, 1961), "The Child's Political World," *Midwest Journal of Political Science*, Vol. 6 (1962); Frances Fitzgerald, *America Revisited—History School Books in the Twentieth Century* (Boston: Random, 1980); Kenneth Langton and M. Kent Jennings, "Political Socialization in the High School Civics Curriculum in the U.S.," *American Political Science Review*, Vol. 62 (1968), p. 866.

20. Michael Novak, *Choosing our King: Powerful Symbols in Presidential Politics* (New York: Macmillan, 1974), p. 44.

21. Bishirjian, *Public Philosophy Reader*, pp. 24, 92. To John Dewey it is "the common faith"; to John E. Smylie, "the nation itself"; to Sidney E. Mead "the religion of the Republic"; to Robert N. Bellah and Michael Novak, the "civil religion"; to Martin Marty and Walter Lippmann, the "public philosophy"; to Daniel Boorstin, the "American Creed"; and to Conrad Cherry, it is reflected in the nation's basic documents.

22. Russell E. Richey and Donald G. Jones, *American Civil Religion* (New York: Harper and Row, 1974), pp. 15–18.

23. Robin M. Williams, Jr., *American Society: A Sociological Interpretation* (New York: Knopf, 1951), p. 312.

24. Sidney E. Mead, "The Nation With the Soul of a Church," *Church History*, Vol. 36 (September 1967), p. 41.

25. Richard T. Hughes, "Civil Religion, the Theology of the Republic, and the Free Church Tradition," *Journal of Church and State*, Vol. 22 (Winter 1980), p. 77.

26. Paul Tillich, *The Theology of Culture* (Oxford: Oxford University Press, 1959), p. 42. Edward Shills, "The Intellectuals and the Powers: Some Perspectives for Comparative Analysis," in Philip Rieff, ed., *On Intellectuals* (Garden City, N.Y.: Doubleday, 1970).

27. Ruth Benedict, *Patterns of Culture* (Boston: Houghton Mifflin, 1961), p. 16.

28. Stephen J. Tonsor, "Political Religion," *Modern Age* (Winter 1979), p. 88.

29. See discussion by Bishirjian, *Public Philosophy Reader*, pp. 17–74.

30. Heinrich A. Rommen, *The Natural Law: A Study in Legal and Social History and Philosophy* (St. Louis: B. Herder, 1949), p. 3.

31. William A. Robson, *Civilization and The Growth of Law* (New York: Macmillan, 1935), p. 38.

32. Mircea Eliade, *No Souvenirs: Journal 1957–1969* (London: Routledge, Kegan, Paul, 1978), p. 237.

33. Mircea Eliade, *The Sacred and the Profane: The Nature of Religion* (New York: Harcourt, Brace, 1959), pp. 33–34.

34. Robert Nisbet, *Twilight of Authority* (New York: Oxford University Press, 1975), p. 87. See also Daniel Bell, *The Cultural Contradictions of Capitalism* (New York: Basic, 1976), p. 62.

35. "Economic Theory and Nationalism," in Frank Knight, *The Ethics of Competition and Other Essays* (New York: Harper, 1935), p. 302.

36. *Ibid.*, p. 303.

37. Frank Knight, "The Case for Communism from the Standpoint of an Ex-Liberal," unpublished lecture, p. 25.

38. *Ibid.*, p. 26.

39. *Ibid.*, p. 18. It should be noted that Professor Knight expresses the above opinions in spite of his well-known rejection of the claims of churches generally. We appreciate Professor Louis Midgley's detailed study of the writings of Frank Knight in his unpublished manuscript, "Frank Knight and the Morality of Competition: A Radical Criticism of Economic and Political Liberalism," prepared for delivery at the 1978 Annual meeting of the American Political Science Association, New York, New York, on August 31–September 3, 1978. See also, Knight, *On The History and Method of Economics* (Chicago: The University of Chicago Press, 1956).

40. Machiavelli, *The Discourses* (New York, 1940), I, 18, pp. 148, 168.

41. It is not uncommon to suggest that totalitarian ideologies are, in effect, expressions of "secular religions" in which concern for life in this world has replaced the transcendent God of philosophy and religion. In Norman Cohn's *The Pursuit of the Millenium* (Fair Lawn, N.J.: Essential Books, 1957), he sees the prototype of modern totalitarianism in revolutionary millennial movements of the late medieval and early modern periods. According to Bishirjian, "The chief modern political ideology, Marxism, is very much a civil religion and the religious judgments to be found in it are representative of the species. They are: (a) Reality is defective. . . . (b) Paradise is to be in this world. . . . (c) Revolution is redemptive." Bishirjian, *Public Philosophy Reader*, p. 25. Henri de Lubac, in his *The Drama of Atheist Humanism* (New York: Sheed and Ward, 1950), depicts the compulsion of such as Feuerbach, Marx and Nietzsche to replace God with man as a self-creating being, in effect, his own creator. See analysis by Bishirjian, *Public Philosophy Reader*, pp. 25–30.

42. Daniel F. Rice, "Sidney F. Mead and the Problem of 'Civil Religion,' " *Journal of Church and State* (Winter 1980), p. 53. See Will Herberg, *Protestant,*

Catholic, Jew: An Essay in American Religious Sociology (Garden City, N.Y.: Double-
day, 1955); Robert N. Bellah, "Civil Religion in America," *Daedalus,* Vol. 96
(Winter 1967); "America's Civil Religion in the 1970's," *Anglican Theological Review,*
Supplementary Series, Vol. 1 (July 1973); "Religion and Polity in America,"
Andover Newton Quarterly, Vol. 15 (November 1974); *The Broken Covenant: American
Civil Religion in Time of Trial* (New York, 1975); *Habits of the Heart: Individualism and
Commitment in American Life* (Los Angeles: University of California Press, 1986).

43. Herberg, *Protestant, Catholic, Jew,* p. 87.

44. Will Herberg, "Religion in Secularized Society: The New Shape of
Religion in America," *Review of Religious Research,* Vol. 3 (Spring 1962), pp. 145–47.

45. Will Herberg, "Religion and Culture in Present Day America," in
Thomas T. McAvoy, *Roman Catholicism and the American Way of Life* (Indiana:
University of Notre Dame Press, 1960), pp. 4–9.

46. Herberg, *Protestant, Catholic, Jew,* p. 72.

47. *Ibid.,* p. 73.

48. *Ibid.,* p. 76

49. *Ibid.,* p. 75.

50. *Ibid.,* p. 77.

51. *Ibid.,* p. 78. "But above all, the American is idealistic. Americans cannot
go on making money or achieving worldly success simply on its own merits; such
'materialistic' things must, in the American mind, be justified in 'higher' terms, in
terms of 'service' or 'stewardship' or 'general welfare.' Because Americans are so
idealistic, they tend to confuse espousing an ideal with fulfilling it and are always
tempted to regard themselves as as good as the ideals they entertain: hence the
amazingly high valuation most Americans quite sincerely place on their own
virtue. And because they are so idealistic, Americans tend to be moralistic: they
are inclined to see all issues as plain and simple, black and white, issues of
morality. Every struggle in which they are seriously engaged becomes a crusade."
Ibid., p. 79.

52. Bellah, "Civil Religion in America," p. 1.

53. Daniel F. Rice, "Mead and the Problem of 'Civil Religion,'" p. 60.

54. Bellah, "Civil Religion in America," p. 4.

55. *Ibid.,* p. 12.

56. "Every person of whatever religious denomination," insisted Paine, "is
a *Deist* in the first article of his Creed. Deism, from the Latin work *Deus,* God, is
the belief of a God, and this belief is the first article of every man's Creed."
Thomas Paine, "Of the Religion of Deism Compared with the Christian Religion,
and the Superiority of the Former Over the Latter," published in *Prospect* (February 18, 1804), in Philip S. Foner, ed., *The Complete Writings of Thomas Paine* (New
York: Citadel, 1945), Vol. 2, pp. 796–802.

57. Smyth, ed., *The Writings of Benjamin Franklin,* Vol. 10, p. 84.

58. Lipscomb and Bergh, eds., *The Writings of Thomas Jefferson,* Vol. 15, pp.
384–85.

59. *Ibid.,* Vol. 14, p. 293.

60. John Dewey, *The Living Thoughts of Thomas Jefferson,* p. 102.

61. Saul K. Padover, ed., *The Complete Jefferson,* (Freeport, N.Y.: Books For
Libraries, 1969), pp. 385–87.

62. Thomas Paine, *The Age of Reason,* (New York: G. P. Putnam, 1890),
p. 21.

63. Paine, "Of the Religion of Deism," in Foner, *Complete Writings of Thomas
Paine,* Vol. 2, p. 798.

64. William V. Wells, *The Life of Samuel Adams,* 2d. ed. (Freeport, N.Y.:
Books For Libraries, 1969), Vol. 3, p. 23.

65. Sydney E. Ahlstrom, "The Puritan Ethic and the Spirit of American
Democracy," in George L. Hunt, ed., *Calvinism and the Political Order* pp. 97–98.

66. *Ibid.*, pp. 101–2.

67. George Lee Haskins, "The Sources of Law in Massachusetts," in David D. Hall, ed., *Puritanism in Seventeenth-Century Massachusetts* pp. 61–62.

68. Ahlstrom, "The Puritan Ethic and the Spirit of American Democracy," p. 106.

69. Padover, *Works of Thomas Jefferson*, p. 83.

70. Alexander Hamilton, "The Farmer Refuted," (February, 1775); John C. Hamilton, ed., *The Works of Alexander Hamilton*, Vol. 2 (New York: Charles S. Francis, 1851), p. 80.

71. Lester J. Cappon, ed., *The Adams-Jefferson Letters, 1812–1826* (Chapel Hill: University of North Carolina Press, 1959), Vol. 2, p. 608.

72. C. F. Adams, *The Works of John Adams*, Vol. 3, p. 421.

73. *Ibid.*, pp. 423–24. Norman Cousins, *In God We Trust* (New York: Harper, 1958), pp. 199–200. Cousins's book is a pioneering study on the religious sentiments of the American Founders.

74. Smyth, ed., *Writings of Benjamin Franklin*, Vol. 15, p. 324.

75. *Ibid.*, Vol. 1, p. 324.

76. Nathan G. Goodman, ed., *A Benjamin Franklin Reader* (New York: Thomas Y. Crowell, 1945), p. 237.

77. Smyth, ed., *Writings of Benjamin Franklin*, Vol. 2, p. 392–93.

78. Hunt, ed., *The Writings of James Madison*, Vol. 1, p. 21.

79. Story, *Commentaries*, Vol. 1, p. 319.

80. Dewey, *Living Thoughts of Thomas Jefferson*, p. 103. Lipscomb and Bergh, *Writings of Thomas Jefferson*, Vol. 12, pp. 345–46. See also Adrienne Koch, *The Philosophy of Thomas Jefferson* (New York: Columbia University Press, 1943), p. 26. In his *Notes on Religion*, which were compiled in 1776, Jefferson's opposition to the clergy was expressed in terms of their alleged encroachment on the civil rights of others. He communicated this concern again in his *Notes on the State of Virginia* in 1785. From at least 1800 on he became especially indignant and vociferous with what he believed to be the shortcomings of the clergy; and he appears to have become increasingly enamored with Christianity as a moral system. It was during this period that Jefferson's religious beliefs began to come under severe attack by his political opponents, who demonstrated the same lack of understanding concerning his religious beliefs as do many modern writers. See Charles O. Lerche, Sr., "Jefferson and the Election of 1800: A Case Study in the Political Smear," *The William and Mary Quarterly*, Vol. 5 (October 1948), pp. 467–91.

81. Dewey, *Living Thoughts of Thomas Jefferson*, p. 108. See also Letter to John Adams, July 5, 1814, in Lipscomb and Bergh, *Writings of Thomas Jefferson*, Vol. 14, pp. 147–51; and Letter to Charles Thompson, January 9, 1816, in Paul Leicester Ford, ed., *The Writings of Thomas Jefferson*, Vol. 10, pp. 5–6 (italics in the original).

82. Letter to John Adams, October 13, 1813, in Lipscomb and Bergh, *Writings of Thomas Jefferson*, Vol. 13, p. 390.

83. *Ibid.*, Letter to Dr. Joseph Priestly, March 21, 1801, Vol. 10, pp. 228–29. Vol. 15, p. 323.

84. *Ibid.*, Letter to Dr. Benjamin Rush, April 21, 1803, Vol. 10, pp. 379–85.

85. Paul L. Ford, ed., *The Works of Thomas Jefferson*, Vol. 9 (G. P. Putnam's: New York, 1905), p. 463; Cousins, ed., *In God We Trust*, p. 17.

86. Letter to Dr. Benjamin Waterhouse, June 26, 1822, in Lipscomb and Bergh, *Writings of Thomas Jefferson*, Vol. 15, pp. 383–85. In other writings, Jefferson takes the position against the divinity of Christ. He rejected such doctrines as "immaculate conception" and "His corporal presence in the Eucharist." Cappon, ed., *Adams-Jefferson Letters*, p. 384. His emphasis was on the moral teachings and doctrine of Christ. "I am a Christian," he wrote, "in the only sense in which I believe Jesus wished everyone to be, sincerely attached to His doctrine in preference to all others; ascribing to him all human excellence, and believing that

he never claims any other." Ford, *The Works of Thomas Jefferson*, Vol. 9, p. 457; Cousins, ed., *In God We Trust*, p. 117.

87. Lipscomb and Bergh, *Writings of Thomas Jefferson*, Vol. 15, p. 323.
88. Smyth, ed., *Writings of Benjamin Franklin*, Vol. 8, p. 613.
89. *Ibid.*, Vol. 10, p. 84.
90. Tocqueville, *Democracy in America*, Vol. 2, pp. 23–24.
91. *Ibid.*, p. 9.
92. *Ibid.*, p. 21.
93. *Ibid.*, Vol. 1, p. 324.
94. *Ibid.*, Vol. 2, p. 21.
95. *Ibid.*, pp. 22–23 (italics added).
96. *Ibid.*, Vol. 1, p. 310. "I remind the reader of the general significance which I give to the word *customs:* namely the moral and intellectual characteristics of men in society." *Ibid.*, p. 331.
97. *Ibid.*, p. 334.
98. *Ibid.*
99. *Ibid.*, p. 334.
100. *Ibid.*, Vol. 2, p. 21.
101. *Ibid.*, p. 22.
102. *Ibid.*, Vol. 1, p. 316.
103. *Ibid.*, p. 46.
104. *Ibid.*, Vol. 2, p. 23.
105. *Ibid.*, Vol. 1, p. 318 (italics added).
106. *Ibid.*, Vol. 2, pp. 6–7.
107. *Ibid.*, Vol. 1, pp. 314–15.
108. *Ibid.*, p. 319.
109. *Ibid.*, p. 311.
110. *Ibid.*, p. 43.
111. *Ibid.*, Vol. 2, pp. 152–53.
112. *Ibid.*, Vol. 1, p. 317.
113. *Ibid.*, p. 316.
114. *Ibid.*, p. 319.
115. *Ibid.*, Vol. 2, p. 156 (italics added).
116. *Ibid.*, p. 154.
117. *Ibid.*, pp. 154–55 (italics added).
118. *Ibid.*, p. 155.
119. *Ibid.*, Vol. 1, p. 314, 319.

5

The Separation of Church and State

ONE OF THE MOST RADICAL INNOVATIONS in the founding of America was the formal, constitutional separation of church and state. It was radical in two senses: first, it signaled a clear break with tradition and practice that had carried up to the writing of some of the state constitutions, emphasizing the establishment of state religion. Second, it seemed incongruous that the Framers relied so greatly on civic virtue and its religious underpinnings yet rejected the idea that the state should take responsibility for assuring civic virtue. The constitutional separation of church and state, like the other elements of the American Republic, was the result of an evolution of ideas. It brought together the Founders' commitment to freedom of conscience with the concern that religion be a healthy and vibrant force in society.

Much of the writing on religious toleration has argued that the growth of toleration was a result of the growing plurality of denominations in Western Europe and, eventually, in the American colonies. Toleration was inevitable as each church wanted "freedom for itself" and concluded that "the only way to get it for themselves was to grant it to all others."[1] Nonreligious influences and concerns also contributed to the rise of toleration and, eventually, the separation of church and state. There is also, however, a long history of the fight for freedom and human dignity within the religious tradition, which had its influence on Enlightenment thinking and the ideas of the "churched" and "unchurched" alike. According to A. James Reichley, "for the mass of Americans, Puritanism . . . was . . . a stronger source . . . than the Enlightenment in shaping American

beliefs in progress and individual rights. . . . In any case the
Enlightenment itself, in its Scottish and English embodiments, was in
part derived from Puritanism."[2] While we do not discount the multiple forces that led to freedom and toleration, the emphasis here is on
how these ideals were developed and nurtured over the centuries by
men of faith.

Religious tolerance and concern for freedom of conscience and
belief were viewed as consistent with the vitality of religion and its
contribution to the political culture of public virtue. The idea of a
general civil religion of Christianity sought to curb the conflict from
the direct political activity of churches while maintaining a firm
commitment to the principles of freedom of conscience, self-restraint,
and concern for others that were essential to social order and came
substantially from religious belief.

THE RELATIONSHIP BETWEEN RELIGION
AND THE STATE

For over a thousand years prior to the settlement of America,
the Old World had lived under the belief that the unity of church and
state was necessary for the maintenance of civil order. It was Con-
stantine, in 313 A.D., who saw the possibility of using the Christian
sect to benefit his empire; and in 383 Theodosius I made Christianity
its official religion. The great fear of the state had always been
disorder and disunion, and religion was seen as a unifying, legitimizing force to perpetuate civil life. In medieval Europe, the Catholic
Church formed the foundation, the "common corps" of "Christendom," upon which government rested. When that "common corps"
had been disrupted by the Reformation, the individual European
states emerged as miniature realms, each with its own state religion.
The church remained the mentor of the state, and the state the
protector and promoter of the church. As Sidney Mead has argued,
"[e]ach Established church that resulted made for its place in its
nation the same sort of claims that the universal Catholic Church had
made for its ubiquitous transnational authority. . . . In this situation
no substantive difference was made between church and commonwealth. Both were merely ways of looking at the same body of
people. This was evidenced in the legal structure by the merging of
monarch into God, legitimated by some forms of the doctrine of the
divine right of kings."[3] Uniformity was still revered as essential to
national unity and internal peace. Yet, in attempting to enforce this
uniformity, sixteenth- and seventeenth-century Europe was engulfed
in religious wars and persecutions.

Religion and the Colonization of America

Although there were various reasons behind the colonization of America, religion played a conspicuous role, not only among those groups seeking escape from religious persecution or those seeking to develop a Christian commonwealth in the New World, but also among those who came for primarily economic reasons. In their charters, too, the importance of religion was manifested.[4] The new immigrants tended to resort to some of the practices that had been commonplace in their homelands. As Edmund S. Morgan put it, the founders of New England "knew, from the works of theologians, what principles they must embody in their new institutions."[5] Winthrop's "city upon a hill" and the Puritan idea of a Christian commonwealth carried with them the shadow of the Old Testament kingdom. Just as some had labeled Old England the "New Jerusalem," where the complete Reformation and true form of Christianity would be brought forth, the inhabitants of "New England" looked upon themselves as having fled the corruptions and persecutions of Egypt—their term for England—and having inherited a new Canaan.

According to Richard Reinitz, this idea of a civil polity patterned after Old Testament kingdoms was used by the New England Puritans "to infuse the Old Testament with Christian meaning and to link the dispensations. . . . [I]t served further to place their venture within the framework of the history of mankind and the eschatological future. It also helped individual Puritans to understand their relationship to Christ. It was a means of connecting the present with the past and the future, the unique with the universal, the human with the divine."[6]

The Massachusetts Bay Colony was organized under many of the old traditions that had been part of the civil order down through the centuries. There was, of course, the age-old fear of the breakdown of order in the community. Tradition spoke with a loud voice that a civil religion, with the state as its protector and viceregent of the diety, was a primary means to insure the unity and stability of society. Therefore, heresy meant more than a mere affront to the ecclesiastical authorities; it was seen as a threat to the very order of society. To John Cotton and others, Roger Williams, with his insistence on freedom of conscience from both civil and ecclesiastical interference, and his perception of society where church and state remained in separate spheres of authority, presented a threat to the very fabric of New England society—and challenged God's purposes in the New Jerusalem. To the New Englander—and many previous generations—the idea that the state could be sustained without a civil religion and a ruling orthodoxy, or that an independent ecclesiastical system could sustain its authority without the fostering care and protection of the state, was unreasonable. Freedom of conscience, which would give free rein to the heretics, the papists, the anti-Christians, indeed all of the unregenerate, was a frightening prospect. One can understand why Roger Williams's orthodox contemporaries in New England saw him as, in Perry Miller's words, "a demon of discord and subversion."[7] "Williams," continued Miller, "was hacking savagely at the root of every ecclesiastical organization through which Western civilization had striven to confine the anarchical impulses of humanity."[8] Even in the times of Madison, there were many people—usually associated with the anti-Federalists—who were concerned lest the discontinuity of the close relationship between church and state through disestablishment might mean the demise of religion and the consequent destruction of the morality which undergirded the community. Indeed, this issue was central to the split between the Federalists and anti-Federalists. The anti-Federalists were fearful that the separation of church and state would mean the end of Christianity, while the Federalists believed that such a separation would cause Christianity to thrive and prosper. The hope that a plurality of free and independent religions, reinforced by an emotional attachment by the populace to a "general" Christianity, would sustain the unity of a commonwealth, was a perilous one. The faith of Williams, Penn, Madison and Jefferson that virtue and religion would flourish in an ecology of freedom of conscience was the foundation of a dramatic revolution in political thought.

Puritanism and the Separation of Church and State

Among the many important ideas that flowered in the Puritan revolution was the claim of independence from established secular and ecclesiastical control. The growing availability of the printed scriptures and religious commentaries for common consumption deprived the establishment clergy of their once-favored position of being the sole source of the people's religious information, interpretation, and consultation. The Puritans were joined by various separatist sects and spokesmen such as the Latitudinarians who criticized the reigning orthodoxy and advocated religious tolerance.

The Elizabethan Settlement of 1559 had attempted to bring the various religious sects into the fold of the Anglican Church, but neither the doctrinaire Catholics nor the radical Protestants were satisfied with the arrangement. The Separatists began to organize their own congregations. John Robinson, a Cambridge graduate, and the progenitor of the Plymouth Colony, perhaps best expressed the reasoning of the Separatists. Having become a Separatist in 1604, Robinson penned A Justification of Separation from the Church of England where he repeated the Puritan criticism of the influence of "popery" and the speciousness of the pomp and ritual of the established religion. Robinson described the "true church" as a congregation of God's elect, "the orderly collection and conjunction of the Saints into and in the covenant of the New Testament: wherein the Saints, are the matter; the covenant the form, from which two concurring, the church ariseth, and is by them constituted."[9]

George Selement, in his study of some of the prominent Separatists, suggests that it was their particular concept of the covenant that bore the seeds of a revolutionary concept of religion. According to Selement, the "Separatists took the covenant interpretation of the Bible in a direction that implicitly and eventually explicitly had revolutionary implications, regarding not only the nature of the church but the relationship of church and state."[10] For the Separatists, a great division existed between the Abramic covenant and the covenant of the New Testament. In the third century, St. Cyprian, Bishop of Carthage, had advocated that under the New Testament religious violations ought to be punished by spiritual rather than physical means as under the Old Testament. And a similar argument was offered by Origin during the same period. Later, pre-Reformation reformers such as Sebastian Frank (1499–1542), Italian Protestant Sebastian Costillio (1509/1515–1563), Dutch Anabaptist Dietrich Phillips (1504–1568) and others, argued against the use of the Old Testament model to justify coerced Christian conformity.[11]

These and similar arguments were used by the Separatists during the English Commonwealth period. The covenant of the Old Testament no longer applied to Christians. Christ had fulfilled the ancient law; the ancient system of theocracy was now obsolete. "Such an interpretation of the Scriptures led Separatists to the repudiation of national covenants, their own peculiar typological interpretation of Israel, and eventually to a denial of the magistrates' right to interfere in religious matters."[12]

Robert Harrison, who with Robert Browne probably formed the first "visible" separated church, led out in what was to become a common Separatist rejection of the idea that England was the New Jerusalem, the successor of Israel, an elect nation, and that the English magistrates had inherited the mantle of the prophets and kings of ancient Israel.[13] Other prominent Separatists, such as Henry Ainsworth, Francis Johnson and John Robinson, echoed the contention of Harrison and Browne. Under the new covenant, they reasoned, Christ had established a new church of the apostolic model that was different from that under the Abramic covenant where the kings of Israel were simultaneously God's appointed custodians of the church. Those who maintained the efficacy of the "old" covenant, they argued, exalted the magistrate above Christ. Ainsworth and Johnson claimed that while Israel was indeed a national church, Christ's New Testament Church was a "spiritual Kingdom."[14] Ainsworth (1571–1622), like Browne and Robinson a Cambridge graduate, was a major Separatist leader (along with Henry Barrow and John Greenwood) in the next generation after Harrison and Browne. His writings, among which was *Annotations on Five Books of Moses*, were apparently read by Roger Williams.[15]

Robinson was particularly adamant in his contention that the Abramic covenant had been abrogated. Since the new covenant with Christ was demonstrated by the elect and since a national church must include regenerates and even papists, it could not be a true church. If Israel had been a nation of the elect of God, England, he reasoned, was not. Under the modern covenant, loyalty to Christ was to supercede allegiance to the magistrate.

This argument, extended to its full potential, engendered the conclusion that magistrates had no right to meddle or interfere in religious matters. Robinson advocated that the Christian religion be left to the conscience of the individual. Here was an ecclesiastical argument for separation of church and state. However, as George Selement points out, the "English Separatists, although often portrayed as the most logical of Puritans, never made such a conclusion."[16] Even though they contended that there should be no king but Christ, they did not argue for "the separation of church and state or the total elimination of the secular arm from religious affairs. . . . Separatist thinking was obviously contradictory. On the one hand, they denied the existence of a national covenant and the king's right to govern the church, insisting that the new covenant made Christ's rule supreme over the saints. On the other, they acknowledged the magistrates right to enforce true religion. . . . Separatists, like most sixteenth and seventeenth century Puritans . . . refused to let their dissent lead to such dangerous notions as democracy or toleration."[17] Separatists generally agreed that the magistrate could not force church membership on the citizen; yet the magistrate could subdue idolatry and false worship in the tradition of the Old Testament among the church membership. In other words, the tenets of the true church could be enforced upon those who had voluntarily joined, but men could not be compelled to join. While they feared the encroachment of the English government to force them into the Anglican Church, they also, typically, were concerned with the possibility of the creation of disorder due to the proliferation of sects.[18]

Still, the various Separatist groups contributed to arguments for religious toleration and freedom that had been and were being advanced by the "Latitude Men" of Europe, including many scholars from Oxford and Cambridge. The development of ideals of religious toleration, then religious freedom, and finally the separation of church and state, stemmed not only from secular opposition, but from within religion itself. During these years of revolutionary change, Christianity was undergoing a metamorphosis, one which had an astounding impact not only in Europe but in America as well. Neither the Renaissance humanists from Italy, nor the Oxford Christian humanists, nor the Latitude Men from Holland and England, nor the Cambridge Platonists, ever sought the demise of religion. They all supported Christianity, and most of them wished to see the Church reformed from within if possible. They turned to the Bible as a source of strength and direction that superseded even their great love of philosophy. They all contributed not only to the development of a philosophy of religious toleration and freedom, but, in concert, a general philosophy of freedom and the dignity of man. The main source of legitimation in these scholars' love of freedom was gained from the New Testament. The battle for political and individual liberty was inextricably intertwined with the struggle for religious liberty.

THE RISE OF RELIGIOUS TOLERATION

Religious as well as secular influences led to the development of religious tolerance that was ultimately expressed as the separation of church and state. The Reformation and its shattering of the Catholic Church produced a plurality of religions that, by the nature of their growing numbers, eventually contributed to religious toleration as well. Encouraged by ministers of religion as well as by philosophers, toleration became part of the intellectual climate in which the Founding unfolded. John Locke's writings on toleration were influential there as were those of a variety of other thinkers. The Cambridge Platonists were also contributors to the development of the idea of toleration, but have been given too little attention in this context. A broad overview of their ideas, and those of Locke, are provided below as further examples of the kinds of concepts that contributed to the Founders' understanding of religious toleration and the relationship between religion and the state.

The Cambridge Platonists as "Keepers of the Flame"

In a very real sense, the Cambridge Platonists must be seen as "keepers of the flame" of that doctrine of love, grace, freedom, and moral force that had been part of Christianity from the very beginning, and had been so often distorted by ecclesiastic organization and religious imperialism. They were, writes Rosalie Colie, "as they have so often been called, the heirs of Erasmus. . . . Like Erasmus, like Chillingworth, like Jeremy Taylor and Lord Falkland, the Cambridge Platonists sought religious and civil peace in a world torn apart by physical and spiritual war."[19] Cambridge Platonism, adds Ernst Cassirer, was bound "to the past in the whole philosophical movement of the Italian and the English Renaissance, and to the future in the general history of thought in the eighteenth century." Their thought was "an integrating factor, an important and necessary stage in the growth of the modern mind."[20]

It seems that time and again down through the centuries, reformists within the Christian establishment revived an almost desperate determination to return Christianity to what they believed to be its pristine glory, and to fight against those doctrines that they were certain were an apostasy from true principles. It was as if an inherent power or "spirit" in Christianity was waging a constant battle to break forth from that prostitution that men inevitably made of it once they organized it into churches and sects. From Paul, through Pelagius, and even to such as Whichcote, Smith and More at Cambridge, came the indictment that men, through the espousal of false doctrines, overemphasis on ritual and sectarianism, had replaced the vitality and moral strength of biblical Christianity with forms, intolerance, even tyranny, and doctrinal absurdities. Significantly, the words of the Cambridge Platonists as "Latitude Men," with regard to religious toleration and freedom of conscience, and the emphasis on moral action rather than ritual, bear not only a close resemblance to the thought of John Locke, but to that form of "general Christianity" with its emphasis on individual and collective virtue and morality rather than ritual, which appears to have helped form the viable religious beliefs of some of the American Founders, particularly Jefferson, Madison, and Franklin.

"As theologians," confirms Samuel I. Mintz, "the Cambridge Platonists sought a *modus vivendi* between the extremes of sectarian controversy on the one hand and the dangers of atheism on the other. Although the majority of the Platonists had been trained in Puritan Emmanuel College, they reacted against dogmatic Calvinist theology, especially against the insistence on man's original sin and predestination. What they sought was a view of salvation which depended neither on arbitrary election into a state of grace, nor upon man's mere passive acceptance of so many articles of belief, but upon the probity and uprightness of man's moral life."[21]

Typical of other Latitude Men, the Cambridge Platonists advocated religious toleration. All Christians, they believed, were united with basic moral doctrines that were more important than particular rituals or dogmatic creeds. Their thought precedes and is similar to Locke's theory of toleration. In each case, divergencies in Christianity were to be "tolerated." The concept of true religious freedom and separation of church and state was yet to reach fruition, but surely "toleration" was their forerunner.

Henry More was among those few who would take toleration a step further, to include non-Christians. "There is a right in every Nation and Person to examine their Religion, to hear the Religion of Strangers, and to change their own, if they be convinced."[22] According to More, the "Christian Prince or the Supreme Magistracy" ought to "contribute to the advancement of the Gospel of Christ," and was charged with "defending and promoting of our religion," but only to that extent that "is plainly discoverable in the written word of God in the *Literal* and *Historical* meaning thereof." He should extend "liberty of conscience to all such have not forfeited it;" that is, when "nothing moves them but conviction of conscience [rather than] some treasonable and treacherous design against the religion and government under which they live." By granting liberty of conscience to such a "serious people," the Chief Magistrate "will avoid the justifying of iniquity of other religions [which function] not by power of Reason and Conscience, but by outward force," and check an undue exertion of power by "the Priesthood," and assure that they be "more cautious in how they clogge the Gospel with unwarrantable trumperies." More, in language remarkably similar to that which was to distinguish the philosophy of Locke, made a point that "these serious people shall not be deprived of their *Liberty, Lives,* or *Estates,* nor any way impaired in their private fortunes."[23] It is the "common Right of Mankinde, that no man is to be persecuted for Religion, if he have not forfeited that Right by taking upon him the liberty of persecuting others."[24] Therefore, according to More, true Christians "are . . . to permit Full Liberty of Conscience to all those that do not forfeit it by mixing with their religion such Principles as are contrary to good manners and Civil Right, or repugnant to . . . [the] Principle of Liberty."[25] Religion as well as the State must not be prejudicial to man "in his Civil Rights, in his Liberty, Estate, or life." "Agents of Religion" must not deprive "anyone of their Civil Rights," for this would be a transgression "against the Law of Nations, and the common Right of all Mankind."[26] The only restriction More would place on the non-conspiratorial, non-Christians was that "they shall be disabled from bearing any Office of trust in the Commonwealth."[27]

More based his idea of free will on the presumption that man had been endowed by God with an immortal soul and that "Man's soul is a rational Being."[28] Furthermore, he described the *"Boniform Faculty of the Soul"* as "a Faculty of that divine Composition, and supernatural Texture, as enables us to distinguish not only what is simply and absolutely the best, but to relish it, and to have pleasure in that alone. . . . He therefore who acts according to this Faculty, conforms to the best and *divinest* in us."[29] In short, within man's eternal soul, at least "the *intellectual* part of the Soul,"[30] is the power of action, or "Motions made by the Soul upon deliberation."[31] To More, *right reason* "which is in man, is a sort of Copy or Transcript of that Reason of Law eternal which is registered in the Mind Divine."[32] Man's soul, then, provides him with not only free will and choice, but stimulates that will with "right reason," so that it may freely reach conformity with the will of the Creator. Men are not helpless pawns of Fate or capricious gods, but are the creatures of will and choice. By that endowed will man may free himself from "the prejudices that attend passion,"[33] or decide not to do so; though "'Tis better to obey God than Men, or even our own apetites."[34] By choosing the "Moral good," which is "Intellectual and Divine," and above "animal apetite,"[35] "we are lifted up and cleave unto God."[36]

The Cambridge Platonists believed that Christ's sacrifice was for all mankind, conditioned upon repentance. Therefore, they interpreted "grace" in a different way from the Calvinists. Whichcote describes "the Grace of the Gospel" as the "Remission of Sins [through] Repentance,"[37] a process by which Christ assists man in his "Reconciliation with the Rule of Righteousness."[38] To these Men of Latitude, the Augustinian-Calvinistic doctrine of irresistible grace, whereby some men are arbitrarily selected and led to salvation, while the rest remained damned, was a pernicious doctrine of fate and determinism, which rejected man's free will. "We are able through Grace," Whichcote wrote, "to avoid evil and do good."[39]

Locke and Toleration

Arminianism also provided an important contribution to toleration in both Holland and in England. Arminianism was, in effect, formally recognized in Holland and in 1630 a Remonstrant Church and school were erected in Amsterdam. According to Rosalie Colie, "The free city of Amsterdam, a miracle of practical toleration compared to the other cities and states of the seventeenth century, took pride in the civic and spiritual virtues of the Remonstrant communion in their city; in the years that followed, more than one important civic official worshipped in the Remonstrant church. In Rotterdam a group set up a church contemporaneously with their fellows in Amsterdam, connected with which was an "Illustre School"; of great importance to the city. Although the University of Leyden attempted to exclude Remonstrants from its doors, they were shortly readmitted—the toleration they had been denied so short a time before was granted them after 1630 almost without question."[40] This was the Holland to which Locke came in his exile from his mother country.

One of the great characters in the genealogy of Arminianism was the Dutch divine Phillippus van Limborch (1633–1712), a Remonstrant pastor and Professor of theology at Leyden. He was the grandnephew of Episcopius, and like Episcopius and Arminius, opposed the determinism of strict Calvinism. He took his place with the Latitudinarians with his promotion of freedom of the will and in his belief that the Church should be broad enough to accept freedom of conscience. Limborch was one of the most celebrated theologians in Holland and was known throughout Western Europe, including England. It is not surprising then that when John Locke came to Holland as an exile, he became acquainted with Limborch's thought to a significant degree. According to H. R. Fox Bourne, one of Locke's most distinguished biographers, Limborch's mind was the most stimulating to operate on Locke's during this period.[41] "The longer Locke was in his company," wrote Richard Aaron, "the deeper grew the friendship between them, and it was kept alive by frequent correspondence until Locke himself died. Of all the good things that Holland gave him, the best was the companionship of Limborch."[42]

Locke, whose thought was to become so critical to the tradition of freedom both in England and America, came in *direct* contact with the tradition of Arminianism, and no doubt the genealogy of that tradition as it stretched back through history. However, it should not be assumed that Locke arrived in Holland "empty-headed" with regard to either the excitement of science or philosophical leanings toward freedom and religious toleration. He had been in contact with both before. According to Patrick Romanell in his "Introduction" to Locke's *A Letter Concerning Toleration,* "Reflecting a timorous and taciturn soul, Locke's thoughts concerning toleration, like his ideas on everything else, took a long time to gestate and reach the public's attention. All of his religious writings carry the Latitudinarian stamp of his student days at Oxford, where he came under the influence of the English Theologian, John Owen, one of the earliest pioneers in the struggle for freedom of worship. Our author's very first work (1660), an unpublished essay entitled 'Whether the Civil Magistrate May Lawfully Impose and Determine the Use of Indifferent Things in Reference to Religious Worship,' the substance of which is incorporated in the *Letter,* anticipates his constant plea for 'mutual toleration' throughout his life."[43]

Locke perceived human institutions in a religious setting. His contract theory for the origin of civil society assumed a transcendent design, that the "works of nature sufficiently evidence a Deity."

Locke contended that the world was in a "state of darkness and error, in reference to the 'true God,' " until "our Savior found the world." The "clear revelation he brought with him, dissipated this darkness; made the one invisible true God known to the world."[44] In this connection Locke, in his *Letter*, reaffirmed the idea that the ancient Law of Moses had been fulfilled by Christ, and that a new covenant was born with Christianity.[45] A new relationship between church and state and religious tolerance was the outcome. According to Locke, if a man possesses great civil or religious power, "but lacks charity, meekness, and good will in general towards all mankind, even towards those who do not profess the Christian faith, he falls short of being a Christian himself. *The kings of the Gentiles exercise lordship over them*, said our Savior to his disciples, *but ye shall not be so* (Luke XXii. 25)." In Locke's theory, "The business of true religion . . . is not made for outward pomp, nor for ecclesiastical dominion, let alone for force; but for regulating men's lives in accordance with virtue and piety. He who wishes to enlist under the banner of Christ must first of all declare war upon his own vices, his own pride and lusts; otherwise, without holiness of life, purity of manners, benignity and meekness of spirit, it is in vain for him to seek the name of Christian."[46] The true Christian will be characterized by "benevolence and charity."[47]

In the tone of the Cambridge Platonists, Locke reasoned that "if the Gospel and the Apostles are to be believed, no man can be a Christian without charity, and without the faith which worketh, not by force, but by love."[48] Men should "tread in his steps and follow the perfect example of the Prince of peace, who sent out his disciples to subdue nations and gather them into his church, not armed with the sword, or with force, but furnished with the Gospel, the message of peace, and the examplary holiness of their conduct."[49]

Locke believed it "necessary above all to distinguish between the business of civil government and that of religion, and to mark the true bonds between the church and the commonwealth."[50] Locke stated emphatically that "the care of souls is not committed to the civil magistrate, any more than to other men. It is not committed to him by God; because it does not appear that God ever gave any such authority to one man over another as to compel other men to embrace his religion. Nor can any such power be vested in the magistrate by men, because no man can so far abandon the care of his own eternal salvation as to embrace under compulsion a worship or faith pre-scribed by someone else, be he prince or subject. For no man, even if he would, can believe at another's dictation. It is faith that gives force and efficacy to the true religion that brings salvation."[51] Therefore, "the care of souls cannot belong to the civil magistrate, because his power consists wholly in compulsion," while "true and saving religion consists in the inward persuasion of the mind, without which nothing has any value with God." Thus, "the civil power ought not to prescribe articles of faith, or doctrines, or forms of worshipping God, by civil law."[52]

With regard to the power of religion, on the other hand, Locke was concerned lest religion usurp the civil authority. He believed "the end of a religious society" to be "the public worship of God, and, by that means, the gaining of eternal life. All discipline ought therefore to aim at this end, and all ecclesiastical laws to be confined within these limits. In this society nothing is or can be done that relates to the possession of civil or earthly goods; no force is to be employed here for any reason whatever. For force belongs wholly to the civil magistrate, and the possession and use of outward goods is subject to his jurisdiction."[53] According to Locke, the only legitimate authority the church had over the individual was related to excommunication, for "no church is bound in the name of toleration to cherish in her bosom a man who, after admonition, continues obstinately to offend against the laws established in that society." However, "care must be taken that the sentence of excommunication carry with it no insulting words or rough treatment, whereby the ejected person may be injured in any way, in body or estate. For all force . . . belongs to the magistrate, and no private person is allowed to use it, except only in self-defence. Excommunication neither does nor can deprive the excommunicated person of any of his civil goods or private possessions."[54]

Finally, Locke offered that "no private person ought in any way to attack or damage another person's civil goods because he professes another religion or form of worship. All the rights that belong to him as a man, or as a citizen, are inviolably to be preserved to him. These are not the business of religion."[55] The only exceptions Locke would concede in his theory of toleration were religions that required all who took membership therein to grant their "allegiance and service" to a foreign prince or power; and athiests, since "[p]romises, covenants, and oaths, which are the bonds of human society, can have no hold upon or sanctity for an athiest; for the taking away of God, even only in thought, dissolves all."[56]

The Roots of Religious Freedom

In England, Arminianism began to penetrate the religious and political fabric, with the exception of the Presbyterians with their staunch adherence to Calvin. In the generation between the Synod of Dort and the death of Laud, there was a doctrinal transition in the Church of England. By 1688, Arminianism had technically triumphed in England. According to Geoffrey F. Nuttall, "The influence of Arminianism in England, is vast. If at all adequately dealt with, it would include, besides the gradual, and eventually almost insensible, adoption of the doctrine of general redemption, the consideration of the increasingly large place allowed to reason in religion as over against superstition; also it would show the growth in mutual tolerance among Christians and the toleration of multiformity in religion by the State, which came to accompany this. All these phenomena undoubtedly had other theological, and also other more secular, contributory causes besides what may, broadly speaking, be called Arminianism; but Arminianism played no small part."[57] And these ideas contributed significantly to the intellectual atmosphere that gave root to American republicanism and the critical question of the interaction of religious and secular ideas and institutions.

In America, the imported ideals of the Renaissance humanists, the Cambridge Platonists, including the multitude of Arminian-Latitudinarians, and Separatists born of revolution, along with other domestic influences, were to have their impact on the growth of religious toleration. So too did the Puritan doctrine of the church as a voluntary congregation of believers, joined by mutual covenant. This belief eventually led to a major contribution to the developing climate of religious freedom, and, according to Reichley, "would profoundly influence both the development of individualism in the United States and American constitutional theory on the proper relationship between church and state."[58] Experiments in religious freedom sponsored by William Penn in Pennsylvania and Roger Williams in Providence were also contributory factors to what would eventually become separation of church and state in America. Both contributed to religious pluralism, religious toleration, and freedom of conscience. Both contributed to the belief that America had been chosen by Providence for a special purpose. Both provided stepping-stones to the First Amendment of the Constitution. Some scholars have failed to recognize the extent to which religious leaders actually embraced Christian values of love and toleration. Many European divines had been transformed by the Christian message and did not simply accept toleration as an inevitable consequence of the rise of religious pluralism. Many of their early American counterparts also championed religious toleration as a result of their spiritual conversion, and not simply from selfish necessity or a concern for survival.

It is difficult to pinpoint an exact genealogy of influence of any one of the above sources. It would be difficult, for instance, to demonstrate a person-by-person influence through the generations of the Oxford humanists, or the Cambridge Platonists; yet their influential positions, their writings, and their zeal, to say nothing of the perpetuation of their ideals over the years, would suggest that their influence on new generations was substantial. If one accepts that there had developed a movement or spirit within Christianity on behalf of love, toleration and freedom, and that this phenomenon was born out of something different from (although contributory to) the appearance of religious pluralism, then the idea of a religious "climate," increasingly amenable to the ideals inherent in modern Christianity as a moral force, must be taken into consideration. Ideals and ideas *do* influence the socio-political environment, and *vice versa.* It can be argued, for instance, that the Great Awakening did not happen in a social vacuum; nor was it merely the reflection of religious pluralism. Its popularity must be seen to some degree as another contribution—and an important one at that—to the metamorphosis of religious thought that had been ongoing for some time.

When Perry Miller wrote: "[A]lthough [Roger] Williams is celebrated as the prophet of religious freedom, he actually exerted little or no influence in institutional developments in America, . . . only after the conception of liberty for all denominations had triumphed on wholly other grounds did Americans look back on Williams and invest him with his ill-fitting halo,"[59] he appeared not to have considered the possibility of a real contribution of Williams's doctrine and experience as inputs to the "general" and accumulative development of freedom of conscience that spanned the generations and finally came to magnificent fruition in the Declaration of Independence and the Constitution of the United States. While it is impossible to measure the exactness of the influence of the Rhode Island experience on succeeding generations, that contribution surely played a role in the development of political and religious sentiments and philosophy in America. Reichley is correct in arguing that "the availability of Williams as a culture hero . . . at least reinforced support for religious liberty among later generations of Americans. And the theology of continuing revelation, which both the Pilgrims and Williams in different ways represented, provided an ideological foundation on which future attempts at pluralism might grow."[60] Furthermore, Reichley suggests that "the founders held the belief, inherited in various forms from the Pilgrims, Roger Williams, John Locke, the Baptists, and William Penn, that religious liberty is itself a primary *religious* value within the theist-humanist tradition from which the United States had grown. Coerced religion, they were persuaded, was an impediment rather than an aid to genuine faith."[61]

However, Miller is right in pointing out that there were other, institutional forces that were leaning toward a truly functional separation of church and state. Aaron Seidman, in his study of the early Massachusetts Bay Colony, reports that emphasis on the specific civil "calling" forged, even in the beginning, a kind of technical separation of church and state. "In the documents of the colony and in the writings of its leading men, separation was constantly implied and expressed."[62] One document, for example, stated that: "As it is unlawful for church-officers to meddle with the sword of the Magistrate, so it is unlawful for the Magistrate to meddle with the work proper to church officers."[63] Though practice varied from time to time, and from issue to issue, and "despite a certain amount of interaction between church and state in the Puritan Commonwealth of early Massachusetts, the essential boundaries of the two organizations were kept well defined." So it was "from the start," writes Seidman, that "incipient seeds of the latter complete division between church and state were already active."[64] Nevertheless, one should not overlook the powerful influence of the ideal of benevolence and toleration as incorporated in the modern concept of virtue, or their relative expression in such experiments as Rhode Island and Pennsylvania.

The Legacy of Roger Williams

Roger Williams (1603–1683) played a pivotal role in transplanting the idea of freedom of conscience from European Latitudinarian philosophy to American political practice. Born in London and reared an Anglican, Williams rejected the pope and the Roman Church.[65] Later, however, he also came to oppose the Episcopal form of church government and repudiated the Presbyterian belief that true religious liberty came from the suppression of what were considered to be false doctrines. He saw little difference between the priestcraft of the Catholics and the Anglicans, and the Presbyterian ministry. He criticized the idea of a professional ministry, contending that the clergy should work by their own hands for their sustenance. He was educated at Cambridge when Puritanism was gaining strength there and would very likely have come into contact there with scholars who believed in religious reform and toleration and the greater importance of the Christlike life over ritual and sacraments. Undoubtedly, Roger Williams came to America in 1630 influenced by the Oxford and Cambridge advocates of toleration and freedom of conscience and with his own commitment to religious liberty.

Cambridge produced many scholars who championed freedom of religious thought. It produced groups of stalwarts who pressured the Anglican establishment for religious toleration and nurtured the ancient concept of freedom of the will over the idea of predestination, a concept crucial for the American Revolution and the Constitution. For these scholars, the Bible created a sense of human dignity, which, in turn, fostered a sense of individual worth and a spiritual feeling of closeness to God. This permitted individuals to bypass religious organizations set up as intermediaries. The established clergy and many secular sovereigns believed that the Bible was a revolutionary document. Many of them fought desperately to keep it out of the hands of the masses, and to punish those who had the temerity to offer new translations or to print copies and commentaries. The idea of religious freedom had begun in Europe before a Pilgrim was ever to set foot in America.

Once in New England, Williams repudiated the idea of Abramic covenant and developed his own theory of church and state. Concurring with the Separatists, he asserted that the advent of Christ had inaugurated a new covenant that replaced the Jewish theocracy of the Old Testament. Christ had united each believer in a spiritual union, and therefore there was no longer a need for a national covenant. Christ was the king of the new spiritual Israel. In his *Queries of Highest Consideration*, Williams instructed Parliament that the new covenant of Christ did not countenance a new land of Canaan. The new covenant had, he insisted in his debate with Cotton, voided the example of Israel. While Cotton used as his reference point the Old Testament law and the practice of Israel in his justification of civil action against heretics, Williams embraced the Separatist reliance on the New Testament, which brought a new covenant and a new church, made up of the elect of Christ, rather than a nation. Israel was a unique situation, not a precedent. Now, under Christ, "all nations" were "merely civil," quite different from Israel which was a "national Church."[66]

Incorporated into Williams's thought was the ideal of love that the Christian humanists had associated with Christ. Christ's example indicated that conversion should be encouraged by persuasion rather than force, and that great "latitude" should be tolerated in matters of religion. Williams, however, citing Christ's mercy and love for mankind, would take toleration even further than most humanists, who, when they spoke of toleration, kept their frame of reference generally within the boundaries of "the common corps of Christendom." Williams would offer the gift in the name of Christ to all men. "It is the will and command of God," he wrote in *The Bloudy Tenent,* that, "since the coming of His Son, the Lord Jesus, a permission of the most paganish, Jewish, Turkish, or anti-Christian consciences and worships be granted to all men in all nations and countries; and they are only to be fought against with that sword which is only, in soul matters, able to conquer—to wit, the sword of God's Spirit, the Word of God."[67]

Compulsion in matters of religion were anathema to the spirit of Christianity: "An enforced uniformity of religion throughout a nation or civil state confounds the civil and religious, denies the principles of Christianity and civility, and that Jesus Christ has come in the flesh."[68] Persecution, he continued, was contrary to "the most holy Spirit of God, persuading and compelling the Spirits and souls of man."[69] False teachings were to be confronted only through spiritual refutation.

Most importantly, Williams extended his concept of freedom of religion to where even the Seekers dared not go—to the separation of church and state. Williams developed his concept of a new covenant into support for the complete separation of church and state and religious liberty. As far as he was concerned, civil authority had no responsibility over religious matters. The magistrate, even the king, had no divine powers in this new dispensation. Rather than being the viceregent of the established church, the magistrate ought to protect all religious groups from religious persecution. Church and state had separate responsibilities. The state was entrusted with the obligation to protect the civil peace and punish crimes against the civil state. The clergy was responsible for a man's soul. They wielded only the spiritual sword; their most severe punishment for disobedience to church doctrine should be excommunication. All men, regardless of religious opinions, were eligible to hold political office. Magistrates were selected by majority vote and not by religious ordination.

Williams's advocacy of separation of established church and state was consistent with his commitment to individual conscience, and he accepted a plurality of religious adherence—however reluctantly in the case of Quakers. He advocated a general religious belief as important to both individuals and to community order. A general religious belief, he suggested, was essential for "government and order in families, towns, etc." As did the Christian humanists and the Latitude Men, Williams believed this general Christianity encompassed certain basic beliefs that were inherent in, and could be accepted by, all men, regardless of the differences in their religious sacraments, for it was "written in the hearts of all mankind, yea, even in pagans." Its primary tenets consisted of a belief in God, in life after death, and in a final judgment.[70]

Perry Miller, in his analysis of Williams's writing, emphasized the point that Williams's primary motivation was spiritual rather than secular:

> He did not conceive of the prohibition of a state church to be a negative device, but as a positive gesture, strengthening human reason with the immeasurable grace of God. He was not a humanitarian outraged by the cruelties of fanaticism, but a "seeker" after an unattainable perfection. He would build a wall of separation between state and church not to prevent the state from becoming an instrument of "priestcraft," but in order to keep the holy and pure religion of Jesus Christ from contamination by the slightest taint of earthly support. He beheld in

the ecclesiastical order of New England not what its apologists claimed for it, a primitive Christianity purified of the last remnants of Popery and restored to the simplicity of the New Testament, but rather a prostitution of the churches to the foul embraces of the civil power. To him, "The Way of the Churches in New England" was more insidious than Rome had ever been, because it was more fiendishly hypocritical.[71]

Williams based his ideas on the belief that there had been an apostasy from the true church of Christ shortly after the death of the apostles, and that the true church was no longer upon the earth. Nor were there any who could, with the authority of God, administer the sacraments, or even baptism. There were "no Churches of our Lord Jesus Christ" on earth, he insisted.[72] A new apostolic restoration would have to be established before legal ordinances could be rightfully performed. The true church would not be restored until the "begetting Ministry of the Apostles . . . according to the first institution of the Lord Jesus, are yet restored and extant."[73] And most certainly, reasoned Williams, Christ's authority would not be restored to the anti-Christ.[74] What he was talking about was a *restoration*, not a *reformation*. Only God could select new apostles. Ordinary men could not legally assume spiritual authority. God's annointed must act first.[75] In the meantime, men had no choice but to seek God and attempt to emulate the Master. Men were still inspired by the outpouring of the Spirit of God, even though no one was qualified to reestablish Christ's true church. In the absence of such a church, religious pluralism was to be defended and fostered.

THE SEPARATION OF CHURCH, AND STATE, AND THE FOUNDING

The ideas of Roger Williams and others were part of the political and religious heritage of James Madison and the other Founders. The examples of Rhode Island, Pennsylvania, and other colonies that practiced religious tolerance provided an important basis for the idea of the separation of church and state. It had become accepted by a number of Americans that religion could flourish free from direct governmental sponsorship, and that government could rely on a plurality of religions and a common core of beliefs without establishing religious beliefs and practices through formal edict.

Madison and the Role of Religion in Republican Government

James Madison, in providing for the constitutional separation of religion and the state, built upon other efforts in that direction that had taken place in America. He embraced the Puritan idea that religion and morality were essential to republican government. The disestablishment of religion from the state, however, would aid, not diminish, religious observance. In discussing the effect of disestablishment in Virginia, he contended that "there is much more of religion among us now than there ever was before the change; and particularly in the Sect which enjoyed the legal patronage. This proves rather more then, that the law is not necessary to support religion."[76] Far from attacking religion," writes Reichley, "Madison wrote as a Christian believer addressing other Christians, and argued that the principle of religious liberty stems from the inmost nature of Christianity."[77]

Madison did not assume that religion would have no impact on government, nor that government would be removed from the support of religious values or republican morals derived therefrom. According to Madison, there were certain aspects of the moral law that fell within the purview of public concern, and that government had a certain responsibility to encourage virtue among its citizens. The government, for instance, was obliged to enforce justice, and this was a justice that had been molded in its modern form by much influence of the Judeo-Christian ethic.

Madison believed that government was responsible to establish *"laws to cherish virtue."*[78] At the same time, other institutions in society, especially family, religion, and education, would help promote virtue, freedom, and stability among the citizens. "Learned institutions ought to be favorite objects with every free people," admonished Madison. "They throw that light over the public mind which is the best security against crafty and dangerous encroachments on the public liberty. They are the nurseries of skillful teachers for the schools distributed throughout the community. They are themselves schools for the particular talents required for some of the public trusts, on the able execution of which the welfare of the people depends. They multiply the educated individuals, from among whom the people may elect a due portion of their public agents of every description; more especially of those who are to frame the laws; by the perspicuity, the consistency, and the stability, as well as by the just and equal spirit of which the great social purposes are to be answered."[79]

In removing himself from the stringent classical and Medieval concept of civic virtue, Madison contended that prior to the citizen's obligation to civil society, was his obligation to God, and that that prior obligation ought to be recognized. Madison believed civil society would recognize individual devotion to God. There was no inconsistency between what is a duty to God and what is owed to other individuals. Religious liberty was an especially sacred right and duty, however, because of its divine origins.[80]

From Religious Toleration to Religious Freedom

The *Virginia Declaration of Rights* of 1776 contained a clause illustrative of Madison's thought on religion. Madison had rejected Mason's phrase dealing with religious "toleration." To Madison, the word "toleration" gave the connotation of classical and medieval civic direction, a concession or a gift from government rather than an inherent natural right of the individual. Although Madison agreed with Harrington that civil liberty must include liberty of conscience, he unequivocally rejected Harrington's reasoning that to achieve that liberty of conscience, an *established* national religion was necessary. His argument was much like de Tocqueville's admonition to the French: the disestablishment of the Catholic Church would not harm but benefit it. He also went beyond Locke's broadly based doctrine of religious toleration. He agreed with Price's contention, in his *Observations on the American Revolution*, that in order to have religious toleration, there must of necessity exist a civil religion to express that "toleration."

Madison's version removed the word toleration and substituted "full and free exercise," to be limited only when "under color of religion the preservation of equal liberty, and the existence of the State be manifestly endangered." Thus, Madison shifted from the theory of "toleration" to that of "rights". The final form adopted by the Convention read: "That religion, or the duty we owe to our Creator, and the manner of discharging it, can be directed only by reason and conviction not by force or violence, and therefore all men are equally entitled to the free exercise of religion, according to the dictates of conscience; and that it is the Mutual duty of all to practice Christian forbearance, love, and charity toward each other."[81] Here again is implied the *primacy* of a higher allegiance and duty one owed to God, and the moral obligation to practice what had come to be accepted as the Christian virtues—duties arising from, and inherent in, belief in a Creator. According to Professor Landi, "Madison consistently and emphatically held that [religion] is to be 'wholly exempt' from government. His doctrinaire position on the separation of church and state was based partly on a thin-edge-of-the-wedge argument: once admit the principle that government may 'intermeddle' in religion, and the way is opened to an established church or even an Inquisition."[82] "Distant as [establishment] may be in its present form from the Inquisition," reasoned Madison, "it differs from it only in degree. The one is the first step, the other the last, in the career of intolerance."[83] His motivation was certainly not to diminish the moral power of religion, nor to frustrate its growth; rather he was undoubtedly attempting to steer the republic away from the morbific experience of the past where the state had been viewed as a religious institution and where religious and political authority were interconnected.

Freedom of religion, then, was paramount in the thinking of Madison, and its release from both ecclesiastical and political chains occupied much of his attention. "To James Madison," argued Irving Brant, "freedom of religion was the fundamental item upon which all other forms of civil liberty depended. Its maintenance would not automatically preserve the entire liberty of the citizen. But without it the other rights were sure to be destroyed. In the area of religion, as Madison saw it, the basic element was freedom of conscience."[84] "The sacred obligations of religion," stated Madison, "flow from the due exercise of opinion, in the solemn discharge of which man is accountable to his God alone."[85]

Madison's views on this subject are clearly expressed in his "Memorial and Remonstrance Against Religious Assessments, 1785," offered to counter "A Bill Establishing a Provision for Teachers of the Christian Religion," which had been sponsored by Patrick Henry in the Virginia Legislature. (Henry's bill would have provided financial support by a general assessment and an equal distribution of taxes among the more well-established churches.) Madison argued that "the religion . . . of every man must be left to the conviction and conscience of every man," and that this right "is in its nature an unalienable right. . . . Whilst we assert for ourselves a freedom to embrace, to profess and to observe the religion which we believe to be of divine origin, we cannot deny an equal freedom to those whose minds have not yet yielded to the evidence which has convinced us. If this freedom be abused, it is an offense against God, not against man."

He reaffirmed that man's obligation to God superseded his allegiance to the state: "It is unalienable . . . because *what is here a right towards men, is a duty towards the Creator. It is the duty of every man to render to the Creator such homage, and such only, as he believes to be acceptable to him. This duty is precedent both in order of time and degree of obligation, to the claims of Civil Society. Before any man can be considered as a member of Civil Society, he must be considered as a subject of the Governor of the Universe: And if a member of Civil Society, who enters into any subordinate Association, must always do it with a reservation of his duty to the general authority; much more must every man who becomes a member of any particular Civil Society, do it with a saving of his allegiance to the Universal Sovereign.*"[86]

Madison expanded his contention with the claim of a benevolent

God who does not force men's beliefs, and a vital Christianity that can hold its own without "the powers of this world . . . [it] is known that this Religion both existed and flourished, not only without the support of human laws, but in spite of every opposition from them; and not only during the period of miraculous aid, but long after it had been left to its own evidence, and the ordinary care of Providence."

Madison described the interrelationship of the fundamental rights of citizens:

> [The Bill] will destroy that moderation and harmony which the forbearance of our laws to intermeddle with Religion, has produced amongst its several sects. Torrents of blood have been spilt in the old world, by vain attempts of the secular arm to extinguish Religious discord, by proscribing all difference in Religious opinions. . . .
>
> 'The equal right of every citizen to the free exercise of his Religion according to the dictates of conscience' is held by the same tenure with all our other rights. If we recur to its origin, it is equally the gift of nature; if we weigh its importance, it cannot be less dear to us; if we consult the Declaration of those rights which pertain to the good people of Virginia, as the 'basis and foundation of government,' it is enumerated with equal solemnity, or rather studied emphasis. Either then, we must say that the will of the legislature is the only measure of their authority; and that in the plenitude of this authority, they may sweep away all our fundamental rights; or, that they are bound to leave this particular right untouched and sacred: either we must say that they may control the freedom of the press, may abolish the trial by jury, may swallow up the Executive and Judicial Powers of the State; nay that they may dispoil us of our very right of suffrage, and erect themselves into an independent and heredity assembly: or we must say, that they have no authority to enact into law the Bill under consideration. We the subscribers say, that the General Assembly of this Commonwealth have no such authority; And that no effort may be omitted on our part against so dangerous an usurpation.[87]

Jefferson and Religious Liberty

These sentiments were quite similar to those of Thomas Jefferson. As a Virginia legislator, Jefferson had introduced legislation to disestablish the Church of England in that state in 1776. Although he was only partially successful, Madison was able in 1786 to secure passage of a "Bill for Establishing Religious Freedom in Virginia" in only a slightly different form than Jefferson had originally penned it. Madison's famous *Memorial and Remonstrance* had cleared the way for its passage. As with Madison, the obvious motivation of Jefferson was not religious suppression but religious freedom.[88] In terms of religious *belief*, Jefferson, like Madison, held that man was answerable to God alone. He would hold religious *practice* accountable only to the peace and good order of society. "Almighty God," he affirmed, "hath created the mind free, and manifested his supreme will that free it shall remain by making it altogether insusceptible of restraint; that all attempts to influence it by temporal punishments . . . are a departure from the plan of the holy author of our religion, who being lord both of body and mind, yet chose not to propagate it by coercions on either, as was his Almighty power to do, but to extend it by its influence on reason alone. Almighty God," he insisted, "hath created the mind free." Therefore, "to suffer the civil magistrate to intrude his power into the field of opinion and to restrain the profession or propogation of principles, on supposition of their ill tendency is a dangerous fallacy which at once destroys all religious liberty . . . that it is time enough for the rightful purposes of civil government offices to interfere when principles break out into overt acts against peace and good order. . . . We, the General Assembly, do enact, that no man shall be compelled to frequent or support any religious worship, place, or ministry whatsoever, nor shall be enforced, restrained, molested, or burdened in his body or goods, nor shall otherwise suffer, on account of his religious opinions or belief; but that all men shall be free to profess, and by agreement maintain, their opinion in matters of religion, and that the same shall in no wise diminish, enlarge, or affect their civil capacities."[89]

In his letter of January 1, 1803, to the Danbury Baptist Association, Jefferson charged that religion was "a matter which lies solely between man and his God, that he owes account to none other for his faith or his worship, that the legislative powers of government reach actions only and not opinions."[90] And reference to natural or higher law is unmistakable. In his "Notes on Virginia," he insisted that "our rulers have no authority over such natural rights, only as we have submitted to them. The rights of conscience we have never submitted; we could not submit. We are answerable for them to our God."[91] As did Madison, Jefferson believed that religious freedom was intertwined with other freedoms, making it essential that the Constitution not impose a national religion or belief. The First Amendment guarded "in the same sentence, and under the same words, the freedom of religion, speech, and of the press insomuch that whatever violates either throws down the sanctuary which covers the others; and . . . libels, falsehood and defamation, equally with heresy and false religions are withheld from the cognizance of federal tribunals."[92]

It was Jefferson, among others, who influenced Madison to write and introduce the Bill of Rights as an amendment to the Constitution. Jefferson contended that the First Amendment created a "wall of separation" between church and state. "I contemplate with sovereign reverence," Jefferson wrote, "that act of the whole American people which declared that their legislature should *'make no law respecting an establishment of religion or prohibiting the free exercise thereof,'* thus building a wall of separation between church and state."[93] So tightly did he hold to this doctrine, that while President of the United States, he refused to declare a national holiday of prayer and fasting. However, as a legislator for the state of Virginia, Jefferson sponsored a "Bill for Appointing Days of Public Fasting and Thanksgiving," which gave the Governor such power. Other bills dealing with religion sponsored by Jefferson were "A Bill for Saving the Property of the Church Heretofore by Law Established" (to protect the property rights of the disestablished Church of England); "A Bill for Punishing Disturbers of Religious Worship and Sabbath Breakers" (which outlawed working on Sunday but left church attendance optional); and "A Bill Annulling Marriages Prohibited by the Levitical Law" (where church and state interacted to "legalize" marriage).[94] In his letter to a Presbyterian clergyman in 1808, Jefferson made it clear that in his opinion the Constitution did not prohibit the states from dealing with matters of religion.[95]

Similarly, as president, Madison vetoed a bill for the incorporation of the Episcopal Church in the District of Columbia and denied relief to the Baptist Church in the Mississippi territory. In contrast, he had voted for the incorporation of the Episcopal Church in Virginia, "for the purpose of holding and managing the property of the church," in order to ward off "a general assessment [at some later time]."[96]

Jefferson and Madison appear not to have been averse to allowing some interaction between the local state and religion. Robert L. Cord reminds us that "the elimination of established churches in the several states continued after the ratification of the Federal Constitution in 1788 and culminated in disestablishment of the Congregational Church in Connecticut in 1818, in New Hampshire in 1819, and in Massachusetts in 1833;" and all under the auspices of state rather than national institutions.[97] Jefferson, for example, considered the public courthouse as a fit meetinghouse for the various religious sects of the community. The national government, however, was not to be involved in fostering specific religious activity. It was to be a government of limited powers; it assumed a virtuous citizenry and virtuous leaders, and it was to impose no national dogma or religious practice so that religious freedom could be assured.

Religion, Education, and Morality

For Jefferson, religion was an essential element of education. He authored an "Act for Establishing Elementary Schools" in 1817 which permitted religious activity in the classroom. As founder of the

University of Virginia, Jefferson declared that the aim of the curriculum of that institution would be "to develop the reasoning faculties of our youth, cultivate their morals, and instil into them the precepts of virtue and order."[98] He "planned to include religious teachings in the University of Virginia's curriculum in a way calculated to encourage morality and a belief in God while at the same time avoiding a preferential establishment of one sect's beliefs over those of another."[99] He made provision for religious instruction but with a "professor of ethics" rather than a sectarian clergyman. Courses were required that were to teach the students "the proofs of the being of a God, the supreme ruler of the universe, the author of all the relations of morality, and the laws and obligations these infer," and the "moral obligations, of those in which all sects agree," and that are "common to all sects."[100]

In 1822 Jefferson proposed the establishment of religious "Schools of Confines" on the University of Virginia campus. In his proposal one sees again the idea that religion, and the virtue and morality it engenders, is important. "It was not, however, to be understood," he wrote, "that instruction in religious opinions and duties was meant to be precluded by the public authorities as indifferent to the interests of society; on the contrary, *the relations which exist between man and his Maker, and the duties resulting from those relations, are the most interesting and important to every human being, and the most incumbent on his study and investigation.*" Jefferson, in his 1824 "Regulations for the University," therefore suggested that religious seminaries of various denominations be established "on the confines of the University, so as to give their students ready and convenient access and attendance."[101] Jefferson made it clear that should any religious organization so choose to locate itself on the campus "the students of the University will be free, and expected to attend religious worship at the establishment of their respective sects." Furthermore, Jefferson offered the facilities of the University for these seminaries.[102] In effect, Jefferson offered his approval for religious instruction in a state-owned university by a "minister-professor." And he further indicated that the University would do whatever necessary to encourage and accommodate such a program.[103]

ESTABLISHMENT OF RELIGION

There is also ample reason to believe that Jefferson, Madison, and at least those who cast their vote for the First Amendment, did not intend an *absolute* separation of the Federal Government from the *general* religion which they believed supported republican institutions, and that they were not in absolute opposition to nondiscrimnatory aid to religion. Religion was to be a friend, not an enemy to the republic. Madison's first draft of the Establishment Clause read: "The Civil rights of none shall be abridged on account of religious belief or worship, nor shall any national religion be established, nor shall the full and equal rights of Conscience be in any manner, or any pretext infringed."[104] According to Cord, "This version indicates that Madison was concerned *not* about nondiscriminatory aid to religion but rather about the establishment of a national religion by the Federal Government. In the Madison proposal the word 'established' is clearly synonymous with 'created,' 'organized,' or 'instituted,' and this interpretation is substantiated in the subsequent debate in which Madison explained that his proposal was generated, in part, by the resolutions of several of the State Ratifying Constitutional Conventions."[105]

At the same time, Madison's proposed fifth amendment in his list of nine *was* directed at the states. It provided that "No state shall violate the equal rights of conscience," but it avoided the language of disestablishment; it did not specify that the states, along with the nation, be prohibited from establishing a church.[106] Nor did it appear in the proposed first amendment. It seems to have implied protection against arbitrary action by a state rather than the fact of establishment. It passed the House without debate.[107]

In rejecting the national establishment of religion, the Framers did not mean to prohibit any cooperation between the state and religion. As Reichley has argued, "Madison's own description during the debate in the House on the objective of the part of the amendment dealing with establishment . . . indicates an idea of establishment much more narrow than that conceived by those who would interpret the clause to prohibit all forms of nondiscriminatory cooperation between government and religion." Reichley concedes that "some ambiguity was no doubt present in the meaning of the establishment clause from the start. But there is nothing in it inconsistent with the virtually unanimous view among the founders that functional separation between church and state should be maintained without threatening the support and guidance received by republican government from religion. . . . As the leaders of the generation of the Revolution passed gradually from the scene, they left a nation that saw no contradiction between the concept of separation of church and state and that the legitimacy of republican government must ultimately be rooted in religion."[108]

Cord contends that not only is it "extremely clear" that the First Amendment "left the entire issue of governmental involvement to the States," but that those who have suggested that the First Amendment intended an absolute separation of religion and the national state have erred.[109] Cord insists that the First Amendment was intended to accomplish three purposes:

> First, it was intended to prevent the establishment of a national church or religion, or the giving of any religious sect or denomination a preferred status. Second, it was designed to safeguard the right of freedom of conscience in religious beliefs against invasion solely by the national Government. Third, it was so constructed in order to allow the States, unimpeded, to deal with religious establishments and to aid religious institutions as they saw fit. *There appears to be no historical evidence that the First Amendment was intended to preclude Federal government aid to religion when it was provided on a non-discrimnatory basis. Nor does there appear to be any historical evidence that the First Amendment was intended to provide an absolute separation or independence of religion and the national state. The actions of the early Congresses and Presidents, in fact, suggest quite the opposite.*[110]

Neither Jefferson, nor Madison, nor the delegates to the Philadelphia Convention wished to make government and religion adversaries; they did not wish to see irreligion triumph over religion; they believed freedom of religion to be salutary to the republic. "I have," stated Madison, "ever regarded the freedom of religious opinions and worship as equally belonging to every sect, and the secure enjoyment of it as the best human provision for bringing all either into the same way of thinking, or into . . . mutual charity."[111] As Michael J. Malbin points out in his analysis of the First Amendment, "What should be emphasized here is the broad area of agreement between Madison and the others in the First Congress. *They all wanted religion to flourish, but they all wanted a secular government. They all thought a multiplicity of sects would help prevent domination by any one sect. All of them also thought religion was useful, perhaps even necessary, for teaching morality. They all thought that a free republic needed citizens who had a moral education.* They all thought the primary responsibility for this education lay with the states. And they all agreed that Article I gave Congress no direct power to deal with the subject."[112]

Malbin argues that even the selection of the words in the establishment clause demonstrates this point—the use of "*an* establishment of religion" rather than "*the* establishment of religion." Accordingly, he reasons, "had the framers prohibited *the* establishment of religion, which would have emphasized the generic word 'religion,' there might have been some reason for thinking they wanted to prohibit all official preferences of religion over irreligion. But by choosing '*an* establishment' over '*the* establishment,' they were showing that they wanted to prohibit only those official activities that tended to promote the interests of one or another particular sect. Thus, through the choice of 'an' over 'the,' the conferees indicated their intent." Malbin further insists that the First Congress "did not expect the Bill of Rights to be inconsistent with the Northwest Ordinance of 1787, *which the Congress reinacted in 1789.* One key clause in the Ordinance explained why Congress chose to set aside some of the federal lands in the territory for schools: 'Religion, morality, and knowledge,' the clause read, 'being necessary to good government and the happiness of mankind, schools, and the means of learning shall forever be encouraged.' This clause clearly implies that schools, which were to be built on federal lands with federal assistance, were expected to promote religion as well as morality. In fact, most schools at this time were church-run sectarian schools."[113]

According to Malbin, by adding the word "respecting," the Framers simultaneously prohibited Congress from passing laws *with respect to* the establishment of religion, thereby also protecting state sovereignty over religious establishment. The establishment clause had two major purposes: "It prohibited the government from giving aid to religion if the aid in question could tend to establish *a* religion . . . but it was not so broad as to forbid such forms of nondiscriminatory assistance to religion as were found in the Northwest Ordinance. At the same time, the Clause prohibited Congress from tampering with the state religious establishments."[114]

Establishment of Religion and the States

Perhaps, then, Jefferson's metaphor that the First Amendment had built "a wall of separation between church and state," carried with it a "federalist" connotation; that is, it appears that both his and Madison's reasoning involved both the *First* and the *Tenth* Amendments. "A careful study of Jefferson's actions and utterances over the span of his life," submits Malbin, "reveals that the Master of Monticello saw in the religious clauses of the first amendment more than a wall of separation between church and state; to him, they constituted a study of federalism."[115] As Jefferson repeated in the Kentucky-Virginia Resolution of 1798, since power over freedom of religion, speech, or press had not been delegated to the United States by the Constitution, nor prohibited by the Constitution to the States, these rights were by law reserved to the states or to the people. The First Amendment, then, was in keeping with Jefferson's and Madison's understanding of federalism, and in keeping with the apparent intent of the Tenth Amendment. The intent of the First Amendment was to *prevent the national government from showing preference to particular sects, not to place it in an adversary position toward religion;* not to nullify state sovereignty over the issue of religious establishment, nor to usurp an important segment of state sovereignty. Although Madison clearly favored the disestablishment of religion, he would have proved philosophically inconsistent indeed, if he had sought to release that general power to the central government. If there was to be disestablishment, it was to be accomplished at the state level. The Bill of Rights was originally written to limit Congress, as the legal reasoning in *Barron v. Baltimore* was to reinforce, not to limit the states.

The consensus of the First Congress was that the new government should be inhibited from establishing a national religion, and that it should be denied power to deliberately favor one religion over another. However, the delegates "also seemed to agree that the Bill of Rights should not prevent the federal government from giving non-discriminatory assistance to religion, as long as the assistance is incidental to the performance of a power delegated to government." Some of the delegates—Sylvester and Huntington in particular—argued that "the failure to extend this kind of assistance would be the equivalent of active hostility to religion. Madison, even though he . . . questioned the efficacy of governmental assistance to religion, accepted the Sylvester-Huntington view throughout the First Congress Debates."[116]

The intent of the members of the First Congress may also be inferred by the general condition of religion in the states. According to Matthew Collette, in his review of state constitutions in effect during the time of the adoption of the Bill of Rights, "many states had a large amount of involvement with religion. . . . Those states prohibiting the establishment of religion required only that government show no preference to one denomination over others." Collette's examination of religious provisions prohibiting the establishment of religion in the states demonstrates that "These clauses were not . . . vague . . . and can therefore give a good indication of what establishment meant to those in power at the time. . . . These provisions clearly show that establishment, to the early Americans, referred to a preference of one religion over another, and not to governmental aid to all religions. It is important to point out that nearly every state constitution contained some kind of guarantee for the freedom to worship according to the dictates of conscience. Apparently, the freedom of conscience was not thought to be infringed upon by aid to religion, or even by taxes in support of it."[117] Mark deWolfe Howe has argued that "the early state reports are full of cases in which decisions were effected, and sometimes controlled, by the thesis that Christianity is a part of the common law which we have inherited from England. This fact seems . . . to constitute persuasive evidence that it was a common assumption in the first decades of the nineteenth century that state governments may properly become supporters and friends of religion."[118]

Significantly, Justice Joseph Story, whose tenure included

Madison's Presidency, reiterated in his *Commentaries on the Constitution*, the opinion that the purpose of the First Amendment was not to make government the adversary of religion:

> Probably at the time of the adoption of the Constitution, and of the amendment to it now under consideration [the First Amendment], the general if not the universal sentiment in America was, that Christianity ought to receive encouragement from the State so far as was not incompatible with the private rights of conscience and religious worship. An attempt to level all religions, and to make it a matter of state policy to hold all in utter indifference, would have created universal disapprobation, if not universal indignation. . . . The real object of the First Amendment was not to countenance, much less to advance, Mahometanism, or Judaism, or infidelity, by prostrating Christianity: but to exclude all rivalry among Christian sects, and to prevent any national ecclesiastical establishment which should give to a hierarchy the exclusive patronage of the national government. It thus cut off the means of religious persecution (the vice and pest of former ages), and of the subversion of the rights of conscience in matters of religion which had been trampled upon almost from the days of the Apostles to the present age.[119]

Establishment and Free Exercise of Religion

The efforts of Jefferson and Madison, then, as well as other Framers, were not engendered by a desire to end the influence of religion or religious principles. There was no inference that religion did not play a highly utilitarian role in society. There was no attempt to promote irreligion over religion. Indeed, public opinion of the time would not have countenanced such an effort. The "very structure of the First Amendment's prohibitions [demonstrate]," insists Howe, "that it sought to do something more than secure the people from ecclesiastical deprivations. For the prohibition is not only against the enactment of laws respecting an establishment of religion; it is against the making of laws prohibiting its free exercise. The specificity of this second assurance makes it clear beyond controversy that the framers could not have intended the policy of separation, enunciated in the prohibition of establishment, to frustrate or inhibit the religious experience. . . . [T]he rule of separation was no less a postulate of faith than it was an axiom of doubt."[120]

Long before Thomas Jefferson had issued his statement on the "wall of separation," Roger Williams in his "Mr. Cotton's Letter Lately Printed, Examined, and Answered," had used the term.[121] Like Jefferson, Williams's "wall of separation" does not appear to shut out the growth of the church or religion. Rather it is to protect religion from external corruptions and intrusions. The "free exercise" clause seems to encourage this interpretation. Disestablishment had long been argued by some as a necessity to protect the church from political corruption. According to Howe, the "ultimate strength of our establishment is derived not from the favoring acts of government, but, in large measure, from the continuing force of the evangelical principle of separation . . . ; throughout our history the evangelical theory of separation has demanded that the *de facto* establishment be respected. The hold of that theory is so strong that it is almost inconceivable that any branch of government, whether local, state, or national, could today acknowledge that its objective is the destruction of this establishment." The wording of the First Amendment reflects, Howe argues, "the evangelical temper of the times":

> The phrasing and the imagery of Roger Williams' metaphor were derived, of course, from the religious faith of the seventeenth century. Yet the figure of speech luminously reflects the political theory of the eighteenth century—that theory which left its mark not only on the federal constitution but on the declarations and bills of rights enacted in the states. It was a theory which excluded much more than religion from the competence of government, for it contained at its center the concept of inalienable rights—the thesis, that is, that the law of nature renders wholly void any turning over of private liberty or immunity to the rule of public authority. The principle function of a bill or declaration of rights was to define the areas of personal autonomy wherein the writ of government could not run. Within such protected areas of immunity, private liberties would freely grow and flourish. . . . For sceptics and believers alike . . . the prohibitions of the First Amendment served the same purpose. They safeguarded the spiritual realm from the encroachments of government.
>
> . . . [B]y and large, American opinion in 1790 accepted the view that religious truth is identifiable and beneficent. It was, in large part, because that was the prevailing view that it seemed peculiarly appropriate to safeguard that truth from the rough and corrupting hand of government. I take it, in other words, that the predominant concern at the time when the First Amendment was adopted was not . . . fear that if it were not enacted the federal government would aid religion and thus advance the interest of impious clerks but rather the evangelical hope that private conscience and autonomous churches, working together and in freedom, would extend the rule of truth. [122]

DE TOCQUEVILLE AND THE SEPARATION OF CHURCH AND STATE

De Tocqueville confirmed the hypothesis of Madison and others that religion would flourish under a constitutional separation of church and state, where freedom of religion was emphasized.

While de Tocqueville was willing to concede that an aristocracy needed an *established* "civil religion" to maintain its legitimacy and continuity, he argued that such an arrangement was not compatible with democracy, particularly the American version. The freedom of choice inherent in democratic government would be inimical to an *established* "civil religion." Much more consistent with the idea of democracy was a common or general "civil religion" which, in a very real sense, bound the people to general moral principles which supported and were supported by the political and social systems and by the individual churches. De Tocqueville recognized that it was the climate of "general" Christianity together with the separation of church and state that allowed the various religious sects to operate on relatively common ground. "I found that they differed on matters of detail alone," he observed, "and that they all attributed the peaceful dominion of religion in their country mainly to the separation of church and state. I do not hesitate to affirm that during my stay in America I did not meet a single individual, or the clergy or the laity, who was not of the same opinion on this point."[123]

The leaders of the organized religions in a democracy, de Tocqueville believed, "ought more cautiously than at any other [time] to confine themselves within their own precincts; for in attempting to extend their power beyond religious matters, they incur a risk of not being believed at all. The circle within which they seek to restrict the human intellect ought therefore to be carefully traced, and beyond its verge the mind should be left entirely free to its own guidance." Using Mohammed (who "professed to derive from heaven, and has inserted in the Koran, not only religious doctrines, but political maxims, civil and criminal laws, and theories of science") as an example, the French philosopher offered that "the Gospel, on the contrary, speaks only of the general relations of men to God and to each other, beyond which it inculcates and imposes no point of faith." The former religion, insisted de Tocqueville, would "never long predominate in a cultivated and democratic age." Therefore, in such an age, he emphasized, religions must "confine themselves strictly within the circle of spiritual matters."[124]

De Tocqueville believed that the American clergy functioned well in the democratic setting. "All the American clergy know and respect the intellectual supremacy exercised by the majority: they never sustain any but necessary conflicts with it. They take no share in the altercations of parties, but they readily adopt the general opinions of their country and their age, and they allow themselves to be borne away without opposition in the current of feeling and opinion by which everything around them is carried along. They endeavor to amend their contemporaries, but they do not quit fellowship with them. Public opinion is therefore never hostile to them; it rather supports and protects them, and their belief owes its authority at the same time to the strength which is its own and to that which it borrows from the opinions of the majority. Thus it is that by respecting all democratic tendencies not absolutely contrary to herself and by making use of several of them for her own purposes, religion sustains a successful struggle with that spirit of individual independence which is her most dangerous opponent."[125] He concluded that, in America, "religion perceives that civil liberty affords a noble exercise to the faculties of man, and that the political world is a field prepared by the Creator for the efforts of mind. Free and powerful in its own sphere, satisfied with the place reserved for it, religion never more surely establishes its empire than when it reigns in the hearts of men unsupported by aught beside its native strength."[126]

The power of these religions, de Tocqueville argued, "also depend very much on the nature of the belief they inculcate, on the external forms they assume, and on the obligations they impose." He warned that the emergence of equality in democratic ages "leads men to very general and vast ideas," and this is "principally to be understood in respect to religion. Men who are similar and equal in the world readily conceive the idea of the one God, governing every man by the same laws and granting to every man future happiness on the same conditions. The idea of the unity of mankind constantly leads them back to the unity of the Creator; while on the contrary in a state of society where men are broken up into very unequal ranks, they are apt to devise as many dieties as there are nations, castes, classes, or families, and to trace a thousand private roads to heaven."[127]

However, de Tocqueville cautioned that while democratic religions must take care that their "external forms" and the "obligations they impose" are not too stringent, he was not arguing for the demise of the organized religions of Christianity. *Rather, he was attempting to demonstrate under what conditions they might remain legitimate in a modern democracy.* He maintained that they played an important role in supporting democracy and making it functional. Although he believed that the religions in a democracy ought to be careful lest they "allow homage paid to secondary agents to be confused with the worship due to the Creator alone;" and while he advocated that the "religions ought to have fewer external observances in democratic periods than at any others," he cautioned that these sects not disarm themselves of the "sacred" manifestations which made them a positive force in the democracy." They are "obliged to hold fast to [their articles of faith], whatever be the peculiar spirit of the age."[128]

For de Tocqueville, religion assumed a fragile, tenuous role in democratic society; yet a conundrum exists in the fact that if religion gives up its basic doctrines to public opinion it also ceases to be an influence on society. "The more the conditions of men are equalized, and assimilated to each other," continues de Tocqueville, "the more important it is for religion, while it carefully abstains from the daily turmoil of secular affairs, not needlessly to run counter to the ideas that generally prevail or to the permanent interests that exist in the mass of the people. For as public opinion grows to be more and more the first and most irresistable of existing powers, the religious principle has no external support strong enough to enable it long to resist its attacks. This is not less true of a democratic people ruled by a despot than of a republic. In ages of equality, kings may often command obedience, but the majority always commands belief; to the majority, therefore, deference is to be paid in whatever is not contrary to the faith."[129]

Yet religion must also maintain some insulation from public opinion in order to be the viable, vibrant source of morality and public virtue that de Tocqueville claimed it was. *"Religious institutions,"* he wrote, *"have remained wholly distinct from political institutions, so that former laws have been easily changed whilst former belief has remained unshaken. Christianity has therefore retained a strong hold on the public mind in America."*[130]

NOTES

1. Sidney E. Mead, *The Lively Experiment: The Shaping of Christianity in America* (New York: Harper and Row, 1963), p. 35. See also Glenn T. Miller, *Religious Liberty in America: History and Prospects* (Philadelphia: Westminster Press, 1976); and David Little, *Religion, Order, and Law* (New York: Harper and Row, 1969).

2. A. James Reichley, *Religion In American Public Life* (Washington, D.C.: The Brookings Institution, 1985), p. 366. "If Puritanism was the most important intellectual and cultural force shaping the American mind the the second half of the eighteenth century, The Enlightenment itself had important roots in the individualism and rationalism fostered by Puritanism," p. 85.

3. Sidney E. Mead, "Christendom, Enlightenment, and the Revolution," in Jerald C. Brauer, *Religion and the American Revolution* (Philadelphia: Fortress, 1976), p. 47.

4. See Robert T. Miller's analysis in "Religious Conscience in Colonial New England," *Journal of Church and State*, Vol. 1 (November 1959), especially pages 19–23.

5. Edmund S. Morgan, *Roger Williams: The Church and the State* (New York: Harcourt, Brace, 1967), p. 68.

6. Richard Reinitz, "The Typology Argument for Religious Toleration: The Separatist Tradition and Roger Williams," *Early American Literature*, Vol. 5, No. 1, Part 1 (Spring 1970), p. 74. *Ibid.*, see Sacvan Bercovitch, "Selective Check-List on Typology," Part 2, pp. 1–76.

7. Perry Miller, "Roger Williams: An Essay in Interpretation," *The Complete Writings of Roger Williams* (New York: Russell and Russell, 1963), Vol. 7, p. 6.

8. *Ibid.*, p. 11.

9. Robert Ashton, ed., *The Works of John Robinson* (Boston: Doctrinal Tract and Book Society, 1851), Vol. 2, p. 95.

10. George Selement, "The Covenant Theology of English Separatism and the Separation of Church and State," *Journal of the American Academy of Religion,* Vol. 41 (March 1973), p. 68.

11. Richard Reinitz, "The Typology Argument for Religious Toleration," p. 77.

12. Selement, "The Covenant Theology of English Separation," p. 68.

13. See William Haller, *The Elect Nation: The Meaning and Relevance of Fox's Book of Martyrs* (New York: Harper and Row, 1963).

14. Albert Peel and Leland H. Carlson, eds., *The Writings of Robert Harrison and Robert Browne* (London: Allen and Unwin, 1953), p. 165; Henry Ainsworth, *A True Confession of the Faith* (1596; facsimile ed., New York: Walter J. Johnson, 1969), paragraph 7; Henry Ainsworth and Francis Johnson, *An Apologie or Defense of Brownists* (1604; facsimile ed., New York: Walter J. Johnson, 1970), p. 8; Michael E. Moody, "A Man of a Thousand: The Reputation and character of Henry Ainsworth, 1569/70–1622," *Huntington Library Quarterly* (Summer, 1982) Selement, "The Covenant Theology of English Separatism," pp. 68–69.

15. Reinitz, "The Typology Argument for Religious Toleration," p. 83.

16. Selement, "The Covenant Theology of English Separatism," p. 70.

17. *Ibid.*, pp. 70–71.

18. Reinitz, "The Typology Argument for Religious Toleration," p. 88.

19. Rosalie L. Colie, *Light and Enlightenment: A Study of the Cambridge Platonists and the Dutch Arminians* (Cambridge: Cambridge University Press, 1957), p. 3. There is evidence, for example, that there was communication between the Arminians in Holland and the Cambridge Platonists, and that Locke was acquainted with the thought of both these groups of Latitude Men. Arminius himself debated English theology by means of pamphlets with the celebrated Cambridge Puritan William Perkins. According to Professor Colie, "It is not surprising, then, to find among the papers of the Dutch Arminian Philippus van Limborch, minister and professor at Amsterdam, record of correspondence with Henry More and with Ralph Cudworth carried on over two decades, from 1667 to 1687, the year of Cudworth's death. Examination of the extant correspondence and of the writings of Limborch and the Platonists reveals a genuine connection between the aims of the Platonists in England and the Arminians in Holland, a closeness of purpose indicative of an astonishingly similar mental attitude and outlook upon the spiritual and physical worlds." pp. 6–7.

20. Ernst Cassirer, *The Platonic Renaissance in England*, translated by James P. Pettegrove (Austin: University of Texas Press, 1953), p. 7.

21. Mintz, *The Hunting of Leviathan*, p. 80. While one cannot measure the impact of the Cambridge Platonists on the growth of religious tolerance, their influential positions at Cambridge would indicate that their contribution may have been significant. See Richard Ward, *The Life of the Learned and Pious Dr. Henry More* (London, 1710), p. 188; Ralph Cudworth, *A Sermon Preached before the Honourable House of Commons at Westminster, March 31, 1647* (Cambridge, 1647), "Introduction."

22. Henry More, *An Explanation of the Grand Mystery of Godliness . . .* (London, 1660), "Book 10," p. 521 (italics in original).

23. *Ibid.*, pp. 525–26 (italics in the original).

24. *Ibid.*, pp. 522–23.

25. *Ibid.*, p. 523.

26. *Ibid.*, p. 522.

27. *Ibid.*, p. 526; Benjamin Whichcote, *Several Discourses . . .* (London, 1701), "Book 4," p. 109.

28. Henry More, *Enchiridion Ethicum: An Account of Virtue; or Dr. Henry More's Abridgement of Morals*, put into English at London, 1690; reproduced by the Facimile Text Society (New York, 1930), p. 6.

29. *Ibid.*, pp. 6–7 (italics in the original).

30. *Ibid.*, p. 12 (italics in the original).

31. *Ibid.*, p. 13.

32. *Ibid.*, p. 15.

33. *Ibid.*, p. 24.

34. *Ibid.*, p. 26.

35. *Ibid.*, p. 31.

36. *Ibid.*, p. 28.

37. *Ibid.*, Discourse 2, p. 37.

38. *Ibid.*, Discourse 6, p. 168.

39. *Ibid.*, Discourse 2, p. 48.

40. Colie, *Light and Enlightenment*, pp. 20–21.

41. H. R. Fox Bourne, *The Life of John Locke*, Vol. 2 (London: H. S. King, 1876), pp. 5–16.

42. Richard I. Aaron, *John Locke*, 2nd ed. (Oxford: Clarendon, 1955), p. 21.

43. Patrick Romanell, "Introduction" to John Locke, *A Letter Concerning Toleration* (New York: Macmillan, 1955), p. 5.

44. John Locke, *The Reasonableness of Christianity* (Stanford: Stanford University Press, 1958), pp. 57–59. See Reichley's discussion in *Religion in American Public Life*, pp. 90–92.

45. John Locke, *A Letter on Toleration*, English translation with Introduction and Notes by J.W. Gough (Oxford: Clarendon, 1968), p. 59. This version of Locke's *Letter* includes also the Latin translation, including commentary. Reichley points out that "Locke cites biblical sources more than eighty times in the *First Treatise*, and twenty-two times in the *Second Treatise*." *Religion in American Public Life*, p. 368.

46. *Ibid.*, pp. 113–15.

47. *Ibid.*, p. 79.

48. *Ibid.*, p. 59.

49. *Ibid.*, p. 65.

50. *Ibid.*

51. *Ibid.*, p. 67.

52. *Ibid.*, p. 69.

53. *Ibid.*, p. 77.

54. *Ibid.*, p. 79.

55. *Ibid.*

56. *Ibid.*, p. 133, 135.

57. Geoffrey F. Nuttall, "The Influence of Arminianism in England," in Gerald O. McCulloh, *Man's Faith and Freedom: The Theological Influence of Jacobus Arminius* (New York: Abingdon, 1962), pp. 49–50; Hillel Schwartz, "Arminianism and the English Parliament, 1624, 1629," *Journal of British Studies*, Vol. 12 (May 1973), pp. 41–68; Godfrey Davies, "Arminian Versus Puritan in England, ca. 1620–1640," *Huntington Library Bulletin*, Vol. 5 (April 1943), pp. 157–79; Carl Bangs, "All the Best Bishoprics and Deaneries, The Enigma of Arminian Politics," *Church History*, Vol. 42 (March 1973), pp. 5–16.

58. Reichley, *Religion in American Public Life*, p. 39.

59. John Courtney Murray, *We Hold These Truths* (New York: Sheet and Ward, 1960), p. 56; Reichley, *Religion in American Public Life*, p. 68.

60. Reichley, *Religion in American Public Life*, p. 68.

61. *Ibid.*, p. 107 (italics added).

62. Aaron B. Seidman, "Church and State Reconsidered," in Hall, ed., *Puritanism in Seventeenth-Century Massachusetts*, p. 84.

63. *Ibid.*, p. 83.
64. *Ibid.*, p. 78.
65. Perry Miller, *The Complete Writings of Roger Williams*, Vol. 7, p. 23.
66. *Ibid.*, Vol. 1, pp. 347–48.
67. *Ibid.*, Vol. 3, p. 3.
68. *Ibid.*, Vol. 3, p. 4.
69. *Ibid.*, Vol. 6, p. 266.
70. Letter to Daniel Abbot, January 15, 1681, in Edmund S. Morgan, ed., *Puritan Political Ideas* (Indianapolis: Bobbs-Merrill, 1965), p. 224.
71. Perry Miller, *The Complete Writings of Roger Williams*, Vol. 7, pp. 6–7.
72. Quoted in Cotton Mather, *Magnalia Christi Americana, or, The Ecclesiastical History of New England*, Vol. 2 (Hartford: Silas Andrus, 1853), p. 497.
73. Perry Miller, *The Complete Writings of Roger Williams*, Vol. 7, p. 160.
74. *Ibid.*, p. 162.
75. Mather, *Magnalia Christi Americana*, Vol. 2, p. 498.
76. Hunt, ed., *The Writings of James Madison*, Vol. 9, p. 127.
77. Reichley, *Religion in American Public Life*, p. 88.
78. Hunt, ed., *The Writings of James Madison*, Vol. 6, p. 90 (italics added).
79. Padover, ed., *The Complete Madison*, p. 313.
80. Alexander Landi, "Madison's Political Theory," *The Political Science Reviewer*, Vol. 6 (Fall 1976), pp. 77–78.
81. George Mason's version read: "That religion, or the duty which we owe to our Creator, and the manner of discharging it, can be directed only by reason and conviction, not by force or violence; and therefore, that all men should enjoy the fullest toleration in the exercise of religion, according to the dictates of conscience, unpunished and unrestrained by the magistrate, unless under color of religion any man disturb the peace, the happiness, or safety of society, and that it is the mutual duty of all to practice Christian forebearance, love and charity toward each other." The Madison version read: "That religion, or the duty we owe to our Creator, and manner of discharging it, being under the direction of reason and conviction only, not of violence, or compulsion, all men are entitled to the full and free exercise of it, according to the dictates of conscience; and therefore, that no man or class of men ought on account of religion to be invested with particular emoluments or privileges, nor subjected to any penalties or disabilities, unless under color of religion the preservation of equal liberty, and the existence of the State be manifestly endangered." These texts may be found in Gaillard Hunt, "Madison and Religious Liberty," *American Historical Association Annual Report* (1901), pp. 163, 166–67. See commentary on these versions in Michael J. Malbin, *Religion and Politics: The Intentions of the Authors of the First Amendment* (Washington, D.C.: American Enterprise Institute, 1978), pp. 20–22.
82. Landi, "Madison's Political Theory," p. 78.
83. James Madison, "Memorial and Remonstrance Against Religious Assessments," in Padover, *The Complete Madison*, p. 303.
84. Irving Brant, "Madison on the Separation of Church and State," *The William and Mary Quarterly* Vol. 8 (1951), p. 3.
85. Padover, ed., *The Complete Madison*, p. 296.
86. *Ibid.*, pp. 299–301.
87. *Ibid.*, p. 300 (italics added).
88. See discussions in Sanford Kessler, "Jefferson's Rational Religion," in Sidney A. Pearson, Jr., *The Constitutional Polity* (Washington D.C.: University Press of America, 1983); and Joel F. Hansen, "Jefferson and the Church-State Wall: A Historical Examination of the Man and the Metaphor," *Brigham Young University Law Review*, Vol. 1978, No. 3, pp. 645–74.
89. Padover, ed., *The Complete Jefferson*, pp. 946–47.
90. *Ibid.*, pp. 518–19.

91. *Ibid.*, p. 675.

92. Thomas Jefferson in "The Kentucky Resolutions," in Mortimer J. Adler, et al., eds. *The Annals of America*, Vol. 4 (Chicago: Encyclopedia Britannica Educational Corp., 1968), p. 63.

93. Padover, ed., *The Complete Jefferson*, p. 946.

94. Joel F. Hansen, "Jefferson and the Church-State Wall," pp. 665–66.

95. Quoted in Robert L. Cord, *Separation of Church and State*, p. 40.

96. Hunt, *The Writings of James Madison*, Vol. 8, pp. 132–33; Vol. 9, p. 100; and Vol. 2, p. 113.

97. Cord, *Separation of Church and State*, p. 5.

98. Padover, *The Complete Jefferson*, p. 1098.

99. Hansen, "Jefferson and the Church-State Wall," p. 669.

100. J. Randolph, ed., *Early History of the University of Virginia as Continued in the Letters of Thomas Jefferson and Joseph C. Cabell* (New York, 1856), p. 441; Hansen, "Jefferson and the Church–State Wall," p. 670.

101. *Ibid.*, p. 474; Hansen, "Jefferson and the Church–State Wall," pp. 670–71 (italics added).

102. Padover, ed., *The Complete Jefferson*, p. 1110.

103. See Hansen's discussion under "Schools on the Confines–An Example of Jefferson's Approach," "Jefferson and the Church–State Wall," pp. 669–72. See the difference in interpretation between Henry Steele Commager, "The Significance of Freedom of Religion in American History," and Robert N. Bellah, "Cultural Pluralism and Religious Particularism," in Henry B. Clark, II, ed., *Freedom of Religion in America: Historical Roots, Philosophical Concepts and Contemporary Problems* (New Brunswick: Rutgers University, 1982), pp. 13–52.

104. Jonathan Elliot, *Debates on the Constitution*, Vol. 1 (Philadelphia: J. B. Lippencott, 1901), p. 434. Cord, *Separation of Church and State*, p. 7.

105. Cord, *Separation of Church and State*, p. 25.

106. Irving Brant, Madison's most thorough biographer, and Walter Berns have interpreted this language as a proposal for eliminating the remaining state establishments. This interpretation seems doubtful, however, particularly because none of the defenders of the state establishments, who were numerous in the House, raised the point when the amendment was debated (though the order of the clause was reversed, and the word 'violate' was changed to 'infringed'). Reichley, *Religion in American Public Life*, pp. 108–9. [Here Reichley quotes from *Annals of the Congress of the United States*, ed., Joseph Gales, Vol. 1 (Washington, D. C., 1834), pp. 444, 451–52.] Reichley also refers to Walter Berns, *The First Amendment and the Future of American Democracy* (New York: Basic, 1970), p. 5; and Irving Brandt, *James Madison: Father of the Constitution* (Indianapolis: Bobbs-Merrill, 1950), p. 273.

107. *Ibid.*, p. 110.

108. *Ibid.*, pp. 111–13.

109. Leo Pfeffer, *Church, State, and Freedom* (Boston: Beacon, 1967), and Anson Phelps Stokes and Leo Pfeffer, *Church and State in the United States*, Vol. 1 (New York: Harper and Row, 1964) give an opposition viewpoint. See also Leonard W. Levy, "The Original Meaning of the Establishment Clause of the First Amendment," in John E. Wood, Jr., ed., *Religion and the State: Essays in Honor of Leo Pfeffer* (Waco: Baylor University Press, 1985), pp. 43–84.

110. Cord, *Separation of Church and State*, pp. 14–15. It should be noted that Madison was a member of the Congressional Committee in the First Congress, which recommended the Chaplain system, and as President, he issued at least four Thanksgiving Day executive proclamations. Five years after he left the Presidency, he justified these actions to Edward Livingston on the grounds that these proclamations were "recommendatory; or rather mere *designations* of a day, on which all who thought proper might *unite* in consecrating it to religious

purposes, according to their own faith and forms." The letter is reprinted in Padover, ed., *The Complete Madison*, p. 308. However, earlier, in what was referred to as the "Detached Memoranda," which is said to be a document in Madison's handwriting written after his presidency and found in the papers of William C. Rives in 1946, he claims the appointment of chaplains to the Houses of Congress and religious proclamations to be inconsistent with the Constitution, and argues that the Constitution "forbids everything *like* an establishment of a national religion." Elizabeth Fleet, ed., "Madison's 'Detached Memoranda,' " *William and Mary Quarterly*, Vol. 3 (1946), pp. 535–36. And although Pfeffer holds this document to be of substantial significance, Cord counters with the argument that "Madison should be judged on his behavior, statements, and actions while he was a public servant in the House and in the Presidency making policy and [being] accountable for it. See Pfeffer concerning Cord's response in *Separation of Church and State*, pp. 29–36.

For his part, Thomas Jefferson, as President of the United States, requested the Senate to ratify a treaty—called the "Catholic Church Building Treaty" with the Kaskaskia Indians in 1803—that required the use of federal moneys to support a Catholic priest and build a church on lands that became part of the United States by the same treaty. Professor Cord's research points out that at least Presidents James Monroe, John Quincy Adams, Andrew Jackson, and Martin Van Buren followed Jefferson in committing federal money to the building of churches under treaty arrangements. Also, during Jefferson's Administration three different public land grants were awarded by the Federal Government that included religious purposes. James D. Richardson, *A Compilation of the Messages and Papers of the Presidents, 1789–1879*, Vol. 1 (Washington, D.C., 1901), pp. 59, 62, 79; Cord, *Separation of Church and State*, pp. 38–46, 58–82. However, Jefferson was the only one of the first four presidents who refused to issue Thanksgiving Proclamations.

111. Padover, ed., *The Complete Madison*, p. 347.
112. Malbin, *Religion and Politics*, p. 17 (italics added).
113. *Ibid.*, pp. 14–15 (italics added).
114. *Ibid.*, p. 16. With regard to Madison's statements elsewhere regarding a *strict* separationist position, it may be true, as Malbin suggests, that Madison was willing to compromise in order to get the Bill of Rights passed and the Constitution ratified. However, given the strict constitutional restraints that would be imposed by the Constitution, Madison may well have been quite satisfied with the wording and the intent of the establishment clause. As Malbin points out, nondiscriminatory aid "would be circumscribed very narrowly. It had to be given in pursuit of a legislative end specified in the Constitution [the 'necessary and proper' clause], and it could not discriminate among sects. Together, these requirements would produce practical results only slightly different from the ones that would flow from his preferred notion of separation."
115. *Ibid.*, p. 9. See also Kissler, "Jefferson's Rational Religion," p. 63. ". . . Some commentators suggest that [Jefferson's] attempt to prevent the national government from aiding religion as President was more the result of concern for the prerogatives of the states than of a desire to create an absolute breech between religion and government."
116. *Ibid.*, p. 28.
117. Matthew Collette, "Tearing Down the Wall: A Look at the Meaning of the First Amendment," *The Thetean*, Brigham Young University (April 1983), pp. 35, 37. Collette refers to Francis Thorpe, comp., *The Federal and State Constitutions, Colonial Charters and Other Organic Laws of the States, Territories, and Colonies Now or Hereafter Forming the United States of America*, 7 Vols., (Washington, D.C.: Government Printing Office, 1909).
118. "It is evident that the New England Mind of 1780, unlike its Virginia contemporary, did not conceive it to be an infringement of rights of conscience to

spend the taxes paid for a backslider or nonbeliever for the support of the parish minister. . . . [My analysis] suggests that, at least in New England, this view of government prevailed which not merely permitted but required a state's public power to be exercised for the advancement of religion. Nothing in the materials with which I am familiar would indicate, however, that any New England statesman or churchman saw that power as one appropriate to the federal government . . . but there was much logic and tradition to support the thesis of the orthodox that because state governments have a responsibility to secure happiness by promoting morality, they cannot escape the obligation to aid religion and its enterprises." Mark deWolfe Howe, *The Garden and the Wilderness: Religion and Government in American Constitutional History* (Chicago, 1965), pp. 26–28.

119. Story, *Commentaries on the Constitution*, Vol. 1, pp. 593, 594; Cord, *Separation of Church and State*, p. 13.

120. Howe, "The Garden and the Wilderness," p. 10.

121. "[T]he faithful labors of many witnesses of Jesus Christ, extant to the world, abundantly proving that the church of the Jews under the Old Testament in the type and the Church of the Christians under the New Testament in the antitype were both separate from the world; and that when they have opened a gap in the hedge or *wall of separation* between garden of the Church and the wilderness of the world, God hath ever broke down the wall itself, removed the candlestick, and made His garden a wilderness, as at this day. And that therefore if He will ever please to restore His garden and paradise again, it must of necessity be walled in peculiarly into Himself from the world; and that all that shall be saved out of the world are to be transplanted out of the wilderness of the world, and added unto His church or garden." Perry Miller, *Roger Williams: His Contribution to the American Tradition* (Indianapolis: Bobbs-Merrill, 1953) (italics added).

122. Howe, *The Garden and the Wilderness*, pp. 18–19.

123. Tocqueville, Vol. I, pp. 319–20.

124. *Ibid.*, Vol. 2, p. 24.

125. *Ibid.*, p. 29.

126. *Ibid.*, Vol. 1, p. 46.

127. *Ibid.*, Vol. 2, pp. 24–25.

128. *Ibid.*, pp. 26–27.

129. *Ibid.*, Vol. 2, pp. 27–28.

130. *Ibid.*, p. 6 (italics added).

6

Factions, Republican Virtue, and Constitutional Government

THE IDEAL OF A COMMONWEALTH has rested upon a foundation of civic virtue to assuage the effects of man's factious temperament and to assure a balance between classes or political factions, so that societal and political equilibrium is maintained and the continuity of the system assured. Even in religious societies, where common beliefs and traditions provide a sense of unity and social control, factionalism is a problem. In the biblical history of human society, there are, from the beginning, repeated stories of leaders' attempts to keep order in small, primary communities, and to prevent violence brought about as the expression of unbridled self-interest. The problem of order in a community confronted by divisive self-interest and factional disorder has troubled philosophers, prophets, kings, and magistrates from the beginning of social life. While much of their attention was directed to the structure of government and the governing process, the Framers of the Constitution held a sober view of human nature and its consequences for the prospects of self-government. They were keenly aware of the interaction of the framework of government and the people who were to serve in it and be governed by it. The structure of the government they fashioned assumed at least a minimum measure of public virtue in those who would fill the constitutional offices they provided for, and in those who would select those leaders. The constitutional structure, the separation of powers, checks and balances, federalism, and enumerated powers cannot be understood without recognizing the expectation of public virtue on which they were built.

162

These constitutional elements were "auxiliary precautions," designed in response to the limitations of human nature. Since men were not "angels," as Madison put it, the structure of government was important. It was designed to channel and check the ambition and factionalism that they believed to be inherent in human nature and social life. But they did not believe that structure was sufficient, that process alone could produce effective and restrained government. The Constitution was ultimately nothing more than "parchment barriers" to tyranny if there was not at least some commitment to self-restraint, to making the constitutional checks and balances work in a way that constrained power and made self-government possible.

THE PLAGUE OF FACTIONS

Examples of the problem of maintaining social order are evident in every age. The ancient Greeks and Romans were conversant with the term "faction." It eventually came to signify a seditious political group and had economic and class overtones.[1] It expressed the ubiquitous fear of social conflict in classical thought. Suggested means of controlling factional and class conflict ranged from the promotion of civic virtue energized by a civil religion, to Plato's concept of virtuous philosopher-kings managing the commonwealth with paternal devotion, to Aristotle's idea of a "mixed" system of monarchy, aristocracy and democracy. Plato, Aristotle, Polybius, and Cicero all expressed an overriding concern with the disruptive impact of factious and class conflict and the need for equilibrium in the republic.[2]

Plato, for example, saw a threat to the equilibrium of the small republic from commerce and foreigners. He denigrated the "erotic love of wealth" and the obsession to gratify every "lust." In *The Laws*, Plato presents the highest virtue as, first, the defense of the city, and then the neighborhood, the family, and finally the individual. Nevertheless, Plato warned that if the human soul were to lose the battle against appetite, the entire war would ultimately be lost. Goodness and peace would emerge with justice and the absence of internal factious conflict. He argued that it was "necessary for [the] city just as for a single human being, to live well. Now those who live happily must first avoid doing injustice to others and suffering injustice themselves at the hands of others. . . . This very same thing applies to a city: if it becomes good it lives a life of peace, but it lives a life of external and internal [factious] war if it is evil." Plato considered democracy, oligarchy, and tyranny to be "nonregimes," which should "most correctly be termed 'factions.' For none of them constitutes a voluntary rule over voluntary subjects, but instead a voluntary rule, always with some violence, over involuntary subjects."[3]

Much later, and from a much different perspective, Sir Thomas More struggled with the relationship between virtue, self-interest, and the orderly commonwealth. His *Utopia* was far more than a satire, although it has been difficult for More's critics to decide whether More actually believed in the possibility of the type of "benevolent" communitarianism presented in *Utopia*.[4] He wrote of the conflict between self-interest and the common interest and the place of private property and commerce, and searched for an alternative to the selfishness, avarice, and envy that plagued the classes in the England of his day.

One prominent answer to this dilemma has been the idea that private, factional, and class interests might be controlled or eliminated by a regulated social and economic system devoid of private wealth, private property, and private means of production. Machiavelli had lamented the factional strife that had plagued the Italian republics. He saw factions, stimulated by economic divisions, as the main source of instability in society. In his *Discourses* and in *The Prince*, he described man as primarily motivated by self-love. Although man's emotions and interests were mixed and ranged widely from public spiritedness or virtue, to greed and avarice, the dominant and controlling element in man's personality was self-interest or self-love. Since rich and poor alike were ruled by self-interest, the struggle for wealth and power was inevitable. His advocacy of a "mixed" system, which had been revived from the ancient Greeks, was in the hope for some unity and equilibrium in society.[5]

Other political theorists have focused on the problems related to factions, classes, parties and what are now called "special interest groups." Much of Karl Marx's writing addressed factional and class conflict as he sought a solution to the problem of the conflict between self-interest and the common interest. Marx argued that a rearrangement of the material environment (including the socio-economic-political system) would transform the nature of man. He called for the violent expunging of all interests and classes except for the "proletariat," who, having been freed from all class antagonism and individual self-interest, are expected to attain a virtually superhuman (Marx called it a truly "human") level of civic virtue—a communal order of common interest that will produce sufficient unity and cohesion so that the state can wither away.

Factions, Self-Interest, and Human Nature

Other philosophers, struggling with essentially the same problems, came to different conclusions concerning the remedy for republican degeneration. David Hume, contemporary of Adam Smith and a student of Machiavellian thought, was a devotee of the "new science of politics" and has been credited with having had substantial influence on the thinking of James Madison.[6] In his *Inquiry Concerning Human Understanding*, he accepted man in all his shades of darkness and light, as he attempted to develop a science of human behavior. As did Madison, he saw the nature of man stimulated by many motives—"ambition, avarice, self-love, vanity, friendship, generosity, public spirit [or virtue]: these passions, mixed in various degrees, and distributed through society, have been, from the beginning of the world, and still are, the source of all actions and enterprises, which have ever been observed among mankind."[7]

Hume wrote with invective concerning factions. While he used the term to identify economic cleavages and class antagonism, he was particularly concerned with the emotion generated by personal and ideological factions. These he saw as most dangerous. Yet he had misgivings concerning the idea of a "mixed" system. The success of such a tenuous juxtaposition, he reasoned, would depend upon the virtue of the members of each group, and his interpretation of human nature told him that there was no possibility of that. Eventually, one element would usurp the powers of the others in the system. He rejected Plato's *Republic* and More's *Utopia* as visionary in their inference that the nature of men could be transformed. Whether in an aristocracy or a democracy, he insisted, the most powerful faction would eventually oppress the weaker. When it came to political power, Hume suggested that all men be considered knaves, even if in actuality this might not be true.

Hume envisioned an extensive republic with a fragmented system of representation made up of artificial electoral districts as a means of preserving equilibrium. He supposed, however, that an extended republic would require an exceptionally wise leader who would enforce unity and give legitimacy to the system. He became resigned to the idea that sooner or later the republic would need a powerful king as the personification, the symbolic center, of that unity.

Checking the Mischief of Faction

In their search for a republic, the American Founders addressed these same issues. Their writings portray the same concern with peace and order in society, the conflict between virtue and self-interest, the problem of factions, and the structure of republican government. Time and again *The Federalist* laments the turbulence of democracies with their historical "perpetual vibration between the extremes of tyranny and anarchy";[8] and the "instability, injustice, and confusion," which had inevitably been introduced into their "public councils." These maladies, insisted Madison, have "been the mortal diseases under which popular governments have everywhere perished."[9] John Adams's lengthy dissertation concerning the fate of fifty historic republics gave a disheartening picture,[10] while Madison's treatises on ancient and modern federal republics, which became two memoranda entitled "Notes of Ancient and Modern Confederacies," and "Vices of the Political System of the United States," gave little cause for optimism. It was Hamilton who warned that republics of the past were prone to disorder,[11] had a penchant for war,[12] and were susceptible to foreign corruption.[13]

History taught the American Founders that man's primary motivation was self-interest. Unless self-interest could be tempered and the common interest—which came to be called "virtue"—strengthened, the commonwealth would face serious problems from within. The situation was exacerbated by the nature of liberty. The heady experience of freedom tended to thrust the self-interest of men and their factions to such heights of passionate expression and expectation as to undermine social unity. As the American Founders reviewed the democracies of the classical period forward, they came to believe that there was an ominous self-destructive force within them. They found little in history to give them encouragement that men in general could withstand the impact of liberty without self-interest and passion overruling all moderation, common sense, and reason.

Yet, James Madison believed that a viable republic *could* be established that would "break and control the violence of faction . . . and could provide a proper cure" for the "instability, injustice and confusion . . . under which popular governments everywhere have perished."

Madison and the Dilemma of Factions

By faction, Madison meant "a number of citizens whether amounting to a majority or minority of the whole, who are united and actuated by some common impulse of passion, or of interest, adverse to the rights of other citizens, or to the permanent and aggregate interests of the community."[14]

In attempting to diffuse the potential disruptive force of factions, Madison and his colleagues faced a dilemma: If they were to construct an open and free society, that freedom would prove a catalyst to the growth of both the number and variety of factions. In an open society people possess the right to express their various views and the opportunity to energize and expand their individual self-interests. They may organize into groups and petition government to promote certain causes and political ideologies and to pursue a variety of economic self-interests. If government were to attempt to abolish or strictly contain self-interest, that government would be forced to curtail freedom of action and choice. Furthermore, the regime would have to forbid the free expression of political views. The only alternative for modern republicanism was to accept the relationship between freedom and factions, and to find the means to maintaining order and concord without relying on tyranny. Freedom, however, was Madison's first priority.

In *The Federalist* No. 10, Madison acknowledged the dilemma and discussed two means that might be considered to cure "the mischiefs of faction": "removing its causes," or "controlling its effects." Madison argued that "there are again two methods of removing the causes of factions: the one, by destroying the liberty which is essential to its existence; the other, by giving to every citizen the same opinions, the same passions, and the same interests."

Madison believed the first option to be "worse than the disease. Liberty," he reasoned, "is to faction what air is to fire, an aliment without which it instantly expires." He warned that "it could not be less a folly to abolish liberty, which is essential to political life because it nourishes faction than it would be to wish the annihilation of air, which is essential to animal life, because it imparts to fire its destructive agency." At the same time, the second method, was "as impracticable as the first would be unwise. . . . The diversity in the faculties of men," and their subsequent varieties of self-interest would make such an attempt fruitless; especially so, since "the latent causes of faction are . . . sown in the nature of man." Therefore, since the *causes* of faction cannot be removed, one must look for relief from the "mischiefs" of faction by attempting to *control its effects.*[15]

How, then, would Madison assuage the problems of faction? Madison was not going to attempt to change what he believed to be the nature of man. Apparently, he did not believe that man's material environment was the sole determinant of human nature or behavior. There was something else to man; a "spiritual" something that transcended the physical and material, that allowed at least the possibility of a democratic republic. Madison believed that the foundation of a viable democratic republic required not only a *particular kind of governmental form,* but at least as important, *a certain kind of people.*

"IF MEN WERE ANGELS"

The Founders understood well the nature of man. Madison, Hamilton, and others viewed man as possessing a dual nature of both good and corruption, with corruption predominant. It was man's fallen nature that made government necessary, and yet made a lasting democracy impossible. "Why has government been instituted at all?" asked Hamilton. "Because the passions of men will not conform to the dictates of reason and justice without constraint."[16] "If men were angels," Madison concurred, "no government would be necessary. . . . But what is government itself but the greatest of all reflections on human nature?"[17] Madison typically referred to "the caprice and wickedness of men,"[18] and Franklin was convinced that men "are generally more easily provok'd than reconcil'd, more disposed to do Mischief to each other than to make Reparation, much more easily deceiv'd than undeceiv'd, and having more Pride and even Pleasure in killing than in begetting one another."[19]

Hamilton warned of "how often the great interests of society are sacrificed to the vanity, to the conceit, and to the obstinacy of individuals."[20] In *The Federalist* No. 6, Hamilton asserted that "momentary passions, and immediate interests, have a more active and imperious control over human conduct than general or remote considerations of policy, utility, or justice." Men are too often "ambitious, vindictive and rapacious—subject to the impulses of rage, resentment, jealousy, avarice and of other irregular and violent propensities." History, reasoned Hamilton, is filled with illustrations of man's evil nature, and to assume otherwise would be to "set at defiance the accumulated experience of the ages."

Benjamin Franklin admonished that lack of civic virtue led to abuse of power and war: "There are two passions which have a powerful influence in the affairs of men. These are *ambition* and *avarice;* the love of power and the love of money. Separately, each of these has great force in prompting men to action, but when united in view of the same object, they have in many minds the most violent effects. Place before the eyes of such men a post of *honor,* that shall at the same time be a place of *profit,* and they will move heaven and earth to obtain it." In reference to England, Franklin remarked, "The vast Number of such Places [of honor and profit] it is that renders the British Government so tempestuous. The Struggles for them are the true Sources of all those Factions which are perpetually dividing the Nation, distracting its Councils, hurrying it sometimes into fruitless and mischievous Wars, and often compelling a Submission to dishounorable Terms of Peace."[21]

Nor would the Founders concede that multiplying individuals into groups would necessarily improve their virtue. Thus, queried Hamilton, "Has it been found that bodies of men act with more rectitude or greater disinterestedness than individuals? The contrary of this has been inferred by all accurate observers of the conduct of mankind; and the inference is founded upon obvious reasons. Regard to reputation has a less active influence when the infamy of a bad action is to be divided among a number than when it is to fall singly upon one. A spirit of faction, which is apt to mingle its poison in the deliberations of all bodies of men, will often hurry the persons of whom they are composed into improprieties and excesses for which they would blush in a private capacity."[22] Madison reminded the readers of *The Federalist* that "the history of almost all the great councils and consultations held among mankind for reconciling their discordant opinions, assuaging their mutual jealousies and adjusting their respective interests, is a history of factions, contentions, and disappointments, and may be classed among the most dark and degrading pictures which display the infirmities and depravities of the human character. If in a few scattered instances a brighter aspect is presented, they serve only as exceptions to admonish us of the general truth; and by their luster to darken the gloom of the adverse prospect to which they are contrasted."[23] "The mild voice of reason, pleading the cause of an enlightened and permanent interest," he added in *The Federalist* No. 42, "is but too often drowned before public bodies as well as individuals, by the clamors of an impatient avidity for immediate and immoderate gain."

The Founders were ever concerned about the use and abuse of political power in the hands of the ever-fallible human being. Samuel Adams spoke for many of his compatriots when he insisted that all men were fond of power and that even public or elected bodies were prone to aggrandize that power at the public's expense. The term "tyranny of the majority" was used often. In *The Federalist* No. 51, Madison expressed his concern with the "gradual concentration of the several powers" into one dominant governmental organization, and the absolute necessity to counter personal ambition among the rulers of the people. He believed that the people were in greater danger of losing their freedoms to a developing tyranny through gradual usurpation than by violent or sudden revolution. Hamilton agreed, adding that the people are in the greatest danger of losing their rights through usurpation, when they have placed too much trust in their leaders. And Jefferson emphasized that "it would be a dangerous delusion were a confidence in the men of our choice to silence our fears for the safety of our rights."[24] "We assemble parliaments and courts, to have the benefit of their collective wisdom," added Franklin, "but we necessarily have, at the same time, the inconvenience of their collected passions, prejudices and private interests. By the help of these, *artful* men overpower their wisdom, and dupe its possessors."[25] And in a similar vein, Madison warned that the more "sagacious" will often promote their own interests at the expense of "the industrious farmers and tradesmen who are ignorant of the means of taking such advantages."[26]

The American Founders had no illusions about man and virtue. They avoided the temptation, typical of utopians, to glorify man, creating expectations that were impossible to fulfill. If, however, the American Founders had stopped here in their evaluation of man, their response would undoubtedly have been that, after all, an attempt to establish a democratic republic would be futile and they would have been driven, in desperation, to return to the idea of monarchy. Yet, inherent in their religious tradition was the belief, similar to that of the Renaissance or Christian humanists, that while man was "fallen," and as such prone to depravity, he was capable of regeneration and virtue, and therefore possessed the potential for self-government. Perhaps in this new land, man could rise above himself. "As there is a degree of depravity in mankind which requires a certain degree of circumspection and distrust," Madison argued, "so there are other qualities in human nature which justify a certain portion of esteem and confidence."[27] Hamilton suggested that one should be disposed "to view human nature as it is, without either flattering its virtues or exaggerating its vices."[28]

Jefferson, Adams, and Paine were among those who believed that God had created man with the necessary qualities to live in a social environment. "The Almighty has implanted in us these unextinguishable feelings for good and wise purposes," wrote Paine at the conclusion of his *Common Sense.* "They are the guardians of his image in our hearts. They distinguish us from the herd of common animals." According to Adams, men were "intended for society," and therefore the Creator had "furnished them with passions, appetites, and propensities . . . calculated . . . to render them useful to each other and in their social connections."[29] Man had a dual nature. His "passions and appetites are parts of human nature," but so are "reason and the moral sense."[30] "It would have been inconsistent in creation," confirmed Jefferson, "to have formed man for the social state, and not to have provided virtue and wisdom enough to manage the concerns of society."[31] "The Creator would indeed have been a bungling artist, had he intended man for a social animal, without planting in him social dispositions."[32] Jefferson emphasized that this "moral sense" or "conscience" was not left by the Creator to the wiles of men's intellect; it was rather part of their makeup. "I believe," he argued, "that it is instinct, and innate, that the moral sense is as much a part of our constitution as that of feeling, seeing, or hearing; as a wise Creator must have seen necessary in an animal destined to live in society."[33] "This sense," continued Jefferson, "is submitted, indeed, in some degree, to the guidance of reason; but it is a small stock which is required for this; even a less one than we call common sense. State a moral case to a ploughman and a professor.

The former will decide it as well and often better than the latter because he has not been led astray by artificial rules."[34]

The Founders accepted the necessity of a "science of politics," one which would, without sacrificing "the spirit and the form of popular government," provide a working republic free of the infectious diseases that had forever prostituted and destroyed republics, "a republican remedy for the diseases most incident to republican government,"[35] a "defense against the inconveniences of democracy consistent with the democratic form of government."[36] What was needed was a structure and program that would help check the vices of men while allowing and promoting the development of virtue and talents; a firm basis to overcome the baseness in man without destroying his spirit, energy, and freedom; a rejuvenating principle that would have the tendency to elevate man to a higher plane of existence. As Clinton Rossiter has put it, "If man was a composite of good and evil, of ennobling excellencies and degrading imperfections, then one of the chief ends of the community, an anonymous Virginian advised, was 'to separate his virtues from his vices,' to help him purposefully to pursue his better nature. The achievement of this purpose called for two types of collective action: establishing or encouraging institutions, especially religious and political institutions, that would give free play to his virtues while controlling or suppressing his vices; educating him to recognize the sweet harvest of the one and bitter fruits of the other. True religion encouraged man to suppress his savage impulses; constitutional government forced him to think before acting; sound education taught him the delights of virtue and liberty."[37]

Virtue and a Natural Aristocracy

The scheme of government envisioned by the Framers accepted as given a moderately virtuous people and moderately virtuous officeholders. Some of the American Founders were so concerned that "men of talents and virtue" be selected to manage republican government that they perceived the necessity of a particular kind of "elite"—a *natural* aristocracy, one that was compatible with "modern" virtue. Edmund Burke had written of a "natural aristocracy" of men possessing extraordinary wisdom, talents, and virtue who emerged to leadership in society by means of their excellence. Without this "natural aristocracy" Burke had reasoned, "there is no nation."[38] And John Adams wrote that "although there is a moral and political and natural Equality among Mankind, all being born free and equal, yet there are other Inequalities which are equally natural, such as Strength, Activity, Industry, Genius, Talents, Virtues, Benevolence."[39] Such men, it was often suggested, gained their "aristocracy" neither by wealth, birth, nor title, but through talent, capability, and performance. Hamilton agreed that "there are strong minds in every walk of life that will rise superior to the disadvantages of situation and will command the tribute due to their merit, not only from the classes to which they particularly belong, but from the society in general."[40] "There are men," he emphasized, "who, under any circumstances, will have the courage to do their duty at every hazard."[41]

Like Burke, Hamilton believed that these highly qualified and virtuous individuals served in political office in a form of stewardship, where they might at times hold opinions different from those of their constituents. In that case, responded Hamilton, while "the republican principle demands that the deliberate sense of community should govern the conduct of those to whom they [the people] intrust the management of their affairs, . . . it does not require an unqualified complaisance to every sudden breeze of passion, or to every transient impulse which people may receive from the arts of men who flatter their prejudices to betray their interests." Since the people will constantly be faced with "the wiles of parasites and sycophants, by the snares of the ambitious, the avaricious, the desperate, by the artifices of men who possess their confidence more than they deserve it, and of those who seek to possess rather than to deserve it," the natural aristocracy must hold its ground. "When occasions present themselves in which the interests of the people are at variance with their inclinations, it is the duty of the persons whom they have appointed to be the guardians of those interests to withstand the temporary delusion in order to give them time and opportunity for more cool and sedate reflection. Instances might be cited in which a conduct of this kind has saved the people from very fatal consequences of their own mistakes, and has procured lasting monuments of their gratitude to the men who had courage and magnanimity enough to serve them at the peril of their displeasure."[42]

"Though I prize as I ought the good opinion of my fellow citizens," concurred George Washington, "yet, if I know myself, I would not seek or retain popularity at the expense of one social duty or moral virtue. While doing what my conscience informed me was right, as it respected my God, my country, and myself, I could despise all the party clamor and unjust censure, which must be expected from some, whose personal enmity might be occasioned by their hostility to the government . . . and certain I am, whensoever I shall be convinced the good of my country requires my reputation to be put at risk, regard for my own fame will not come in competition with an object of so much magnitude."[43]

Jefferson expressed his belief that "there is a natural aristocracy among men. The grounds of this," he submitted, "are *virtue* and *talents. . . .* The natural aristocracy I consider as the most precious gift of nature, for the instruction, the trusts, and government of society. And indeed, it would have been inconsistent in creation to have formed man for the social state, and not to have provided virtue and wisdom enough to manage the concerns of society. *May we not even say, that that form of government is the best, which provides the most effectually for a pure selection of these natural aristo into the offices of government?"* Here Jefferson saw republicanism as the best possible form of government to secure men of virtue and wisdom for these offices. "I think the best remedy is exactly that provided by all our constitutions, to leave to the citizens the free election and separation of the aristo from the pseudo-aristo, of the wheat from the chaff. In general they will elect the really good and wise. . . . *It suffices for us, if the moral and physical condition of our own citizens qualifies them to select the able and good for the direction of their government,* with a recurrence of elections at such short periods as will enable them to displace an unfaithful servant, before the mischief he mediates may be irremediable."[44]

On the other hand, Jefferson warned of an *"artificial aristocracy, . . .* founded on wealth and birth, without either virtue or talents." In rejecting the traditional concept of a "mixed" constitution where one branch of government is in the hands of the aristocratic class, he chided Adams for his suggestion "to put the pseudo-aristo into a separate chamber of legislation, where they may be hindered from doing mischief by their coordinate branches, and where, also, they may be a protection to wealth against the Agrarian and plundering enterprises of the majority of the people." Jefferson contended that the existing means of selection and the existing constitutional checks are better methods. "I think that to give them power in order to prevent them from doing mischief, is arming them for it, and increasing instead of remedying the evil. For if the coordinate branches can arrest their action, so may they that of the coordinates. Mischief may be done negatively as well as positively. . . . Nor do I believe them necessary to protect the wealthy; because enough of these will find their way into every branch of the legislation, to protect themselves. From fifteen to twenty legislatures of our own, in action for thirty years past, have proved that no fears of an equilization of property are to be apprehended from them."[45]

The Framers themselves provided examples of the kind of virtuous leaders required for republican government. Madison marveled that the Convention expressed "in a very singular degree, an exemption from the pestilential influence of party animosities—the disease most incident to deliberative bodies and most apt to contaminate their proceedings"; and that "the deputations composing the convention were either satisfactorily accommodated by the final act, or were induced to accede to it by a deep conviction of the necessity of sacrificing private opinions and partial interests to the public good, and by a despair of seeing this necessity diminished by delays or by new experiments."[46] Madison marvelled that there never had been "an assembly of men . . . who were more pure in their motives, or more exclusively or anxiously devoted to the object committed to them"—that of "devising and proposing a constitutional system . . . to best secure the permanent liberty and happiness of their country."[47] John Jay praised the "convention, composed of men who possessed the confidence of the people, and many of whom had become highly distinguished by their patriotism, virtue, and wisdom, in times which tried the minds and hearts of men. . . . In the mild season of peace, with minds unoccupied by other subjects, they passed many months in cool, uninterrupted, and daily consultation; and finally, without having been awed by power, or influenced by any passions except love for their country, they presented and recommended to the people the plan produced by their joint and very unanimous councils."[48]

Nor did the extraordinary nature of the American Founders escape the perceptive de Tocqueville. "The chief cause of the superiority of the Federal Constitution," he observed, "lay in the character of the legislators who composed it. At the time when it was formed, the ruin of the Confederation seemed imminent, and its danger was universally known. In this extremity the people chose the men who most deserved the esteem rather than those who had gained the affections of the country. . . . [D]istinguished as almost all legislators of the Union were for their intelligence, they were still more so for their patriotism. They had all been nurtured at a time when the spirit of liberty was braced by a continual struggle against a powerful and dominant authority. . . . They had the courage to say what they believed to be true, because they were animated by a warm and sincere love of liberty."[49]

Virtue and The Mixed System

While Madison, as had Montesquieu, acknowledged the importance of virtue, he did not share the philosopher's optimistic view of the viability of a strict classical virtue. He did not countenance "political man" in the classical interpretation. "[A] nation of philosophers," he wrote, "is as little to be expected as the philosophical race of kings to be wished for by Plato."[50] He did not entertain the age-old interpretation that the individual must live in perpetual subordination of personal interest to the common welfare as distinguished by the state. He did not envision a public virtue that made man essentially dependent upon the state at the sacrifice of private rights and justice.[51] To Madison, the "modern" virtuous republican citizens would be "equally the friends of public and private faith and of public and personal liberty."[52]

Although Montesquieu was praised for his ideas concerning the "mixed system" and separation of powers,[53] Madison and the Federalist philosophers came to reject the concept of the "mixed system" as being incompatible with the culture and the "genius" of the American people.[54] However, according to Douglass Adair, for a time, a number of prominent Americans accepted Montesquieu's interpretation of republicanism. "Hamilton along with Madison, Adams, Jefferson, and every educated eighteenth-century statesman . . . knew from history that the mortal disease of democratical republics was and always would be the class struggle that had eventually destroyed every republican state in history." "In 1787," insists Adair, "the authority of scholars, philosophers, and statesmen was all but unanimous in arguing (from the experience of history) that no republic ever could be established in a territory as extended as the United States— that even if established for a moment, class war must eventually destroy every democratic republic." For a period, both Adams and Hamilton advocated a "mixed" government—balancing elements of monarchy, aristocracy and "democracy"—as the only possible solution in establishing a viable republic.[55] This was a common belief among the English Whigs.

Yet, as Madison contemplated the modern socio-political phenomenon that had evolved in America, he, as had Hume before him, came to the conclusion that the common contention that an extended republic was impossible was at least outdated. Furthermore, he came to believe that an extended republic had a better chance of survival than the alternative. It was the small, rather than the extended republic, that held the seeds of its own destruction, he reasoned. As Wills, Lutz, Pocock, and Wood have pointed out, the traditional concept of the "mixed system," which dated back through antiquity to Aristotle, Polybius, and Cicero, was not compatible with the modern republican system. According to Lutz, this became apparent in the American state constitutions before the Constitutional Convention. And Wood has reminded us that the "mixed system" assumed the existence of a class system that did not exist in America. Traditionally, writes John Paynter, "'the people' referred not to the whole, but only to the many or majority (and usually the poor majority) and the problem of political unity was treated, not in terms of 'sovereignty' and 'representation,' but with sole attention to 'ruling' the city. Aristotle, for instance, viewed the city as a composite of qualitatively diverse classes, of which 'the people' was only one ('DEMOS' or

'PLETHOS')." Therefore, concludes Professor Paynter, "The several classes, on their own terms, had nothing in common; each made an exclusive claim to rule based on its own vision of justice absolutized."[56] The American people, on the other hand, had become increasingly homogeneous in sharing the same rights, and had become politically indistinguishable.[57] Furthermore, they considered themselves to be collectively virtuous, while holding that individual virtue must be independent of other men. And the concept of a "natural elite" meant something different to the American Founders than it had to the ancients. Nor did they interpret the ideals of duty, courage, honor, and manliness in precisely the same way as had the warrior states of antiquity. The Christian humanists such as More, Colet, and Erasmus, had long since pointed out how these terms had been prostituted into the language of war and conquest, confiscation, and brutality. In effect, the humanist's attack on that particular form of "virtue," and their espousal of a Christian moral theology, was thoroughly repugnant to Machiavelli. Hamilton attempted to point out in *The Federalist*, No. 8, that the ancient ideal of virtue prevalent in the commonwealths of warriors was not suited to modern republics. "The industrious habits of the people of the present day, absorbed in the pursuits of gain and devoted to the improvements of agriculture and commerce, are incompatible with the condition of a nation of soldiers, which was the true condition of the people of those republics." After referring to the above statement, Gary J. Schmitt wrote that to equate "the term 'republic' as it is used by Montesquieu with how it is employed in *The Federalist*," is to mix "ancient apples with modern oranges."[58]

In the traditional doctrine of "balanced government," the "balance was defined as a relationship between 'virtues' no less than between classes or powers, so that 'virtue' consisted not merely in the exercise of one's own virtue—the mode of intelligence and action proper to membership in the one [Monarchy], the few [Aristrocracy], or the many [Democracy]—but also in respect for the virtues of the two categories to which one did not belong, and in the maintenance of the constitutional structure in which the balance of virtues was institutionalized." "But the Americans," argues Pocock, "simply did not differentiate along trinitarian lines. If the people could not be differentiated into separately-characterized groups, there could be no ascribing to them the higher virtue of deferring to the . . . virtues of others who in their turn defer, which is at the root of both the Polybian concept of mixed government and the Aristotelian concept of citizenship. The entire classical tradition of man the political animal seemed at the point of breaking down." In response to this dilemma, "the masters of Federalist theory" ceased regarding "the 'people' as trinitarian . . . , regarding them instead as an undifferentiated unity which elected to be represented in many ways, by a complex of assemblies, legislative, judicial and executive bodies, entrusted by them with a diversity of powers." The people were regarded "as sovereign rather than as simply constituent," and added the original "proposition that each mode of exercising political power constituted a separate 'representation' of the people, who chose to be represented in a diversity of ways, and to entrust diverse organs with a diversity of powers."[59] In effect, writes John Paynter, the American Founders had come to see "the people" as "directly linked to the emergence of the distinction between *sovereign* people and *representative* government."[60] The traditional "monarchical and aristocratic principles were not to be introduced into the American scheme," adds Wills, "even as partial or balancing factors. . . . There were no constitutional organs for the one or the few in America, no legal power all their own to be checked. . . . In America, difference of function is not a difference of interest, as in the mixed theory."[61]

In considering the above, one must include among the influences that made the "mixed system" redundant in America the religious heritage that, along with other social, political, and economic forces, played an important role. The general victory of freedom of the will over determinism in the Western world gave spiritual life to the ideals of individual human dignity and freedom; the doctrine of universal, conditional salvation based upon works, as announced in the casuistry of moral theology, in essence made all men—even priest and commoner—responsible for similar virtuous behavior, and provided a barrier against the idea that different classes inherently expressed different virtues. In addition, the development of the idea, garnered from the Bible, that all men were created equal before God and were to be treated with benevolence, could not help but have contributed to a sense of individual importance, and the belief that all men enjoyed certain inalienable rights and obligations ordained by a power superior to government. This would not suggest that great and different social groupings in society would inherently maintain broad, perpetual, and mutually exclusive interests. As so often was the case, the evolution of religion and the development of the Judeo-Christian ethic impacted on the political and social realms.

Virtue and the Anti-Federalists

The attachment to small republics died hard. While the anti-Federalists shared the Federalists' concern for virtue, they feared that Madison's extended republic would be inimical to its strength. They had a tendency to accept the classical ideal, and generally came to the conclusion that only in small republics could public virtue and hence popular government have a chance for survival. Many believed, with Montesquieu, that republican government could thrive only in a relatively small, geographic unit with a limited and homogeneous population, where public interest would be more pronounced, obvious, and acknowledged, and where abuse would be more quickly identified and exposed. They argued that a large republic would be unable to adjust to the cultural diversity and the sectional and economic differences of the people in the new thirteen states, that human wisdom was incapable of controlling or administering a continental republic, that local concerns and interests would be sacrificed, and that the close relationship between the citizens and their representatives would be forfeit. A large republic, they feared, would diminish civic virtue and would lead to factional conflict, corruption, and tyranny. It would be more difficult to select sensitive representatives of the people the further removed those representatives were from their electoral source and the sentiments of the people.[62] A large republic, reasoned James Winthrop of Massachusetts, would prohibit the people from enjoying the same "standard of morals, of habits, and of laws."[63]

Like the Federalists, many anti-Federalists argued that the virtue of rulers could not be counted upon. Federalists were frequently charged with excessive optimism in human nature, and for not fitting into the proposed Constitution adequate safeguards against corruption and tyranny, such as a Bill of Rights. While Madison argued that a large republic, rather than a small one, was more conducive to the selection of virtuous political leadership, anti-Federalists such as George Mason and Patrick Henry proposed the very opposite view. Both Federalists and anti-Federalists were concerned about the dangers inherent in trusting men with political power, and how virtue in the people and their rulers might be perpetuated.

Madison believed "that the level of virtue necessary to make small republics and by extension the state constitutions work was unrealistically high. Madison and other leading framers sought to establish a constitution, still republican in character, that could be founded on a more realistic level of virtue."[64] At the same time he apparently believed that there was a greater chance of electing men of character and virtue to a national legislature than was generally possible in the state systems characterized by "factious" tempers and "local prejudices." The anti-Federalists countered with the proposition that representatives close to and similar to their constituencies would best share their moral sensibilities, their character, and their needs; and hence a greater influence would be exerted upon those representatives to be virtuous spokesmen.[65]

Virtue, Corruption, and the Republic

Both the Federalists and anti-Federalists were searching for the best way to promote virtue, for neither side believed that a corrupt people could sustain a republic, large or small. With Montesquieu, Americans of the Revolutionary era had concluded "Fear is the principle of a despotic, honour of a kingly, and virtue is the principle of a republican government."[66] Writing in 1775, Samuel Williams concurred: "In a *despotic government*, the only principle by which the Tyrant who is to move the whole machine, means to regulate and manage the people, is Fear; by the servile dread of his power. But a *free government*, which of all others is far the most preferable, cannot be supported without Virtue."[67] Thus, the importance of both the quality of the republican structure and the character of the republican people was paramount to both Federalist and anti-Federalist.

If virtue was essential to a popular republic, then immorality and corruption could be looked upon as forerunners of tyranny.[68] Benjamin Franklin, in the Constitutional Convention of 1787, voiced his concern that although the new government would likely "be well administered for a course of years," it would "end in despotism, as other forms have done before it, when the people shall have become so corrupted as to need despotic government, being incapable of any other."[69] "Only a virtuous people," he said in another place, "are capable of freedom. As nations become corrupt and vicious, they have more need of masters."[70] In a letter to Lafayette in 1778, Washington reasoned that when a corrupt people have lost the ability to govern themselves and have become fit only for a master, "it is of little consequence from what quarter he comes."[71] "Free suffrage of the people," he continued, can be assured only "so long as there shall remain any virtue in the body of the people."[72] In giving his assent to the Constitution in the Massachusetts Ratifying Convention, John Hancock expressed his belief that the people would be secure under the new government "until they themselves become corrupt."[73] Before the Virginia Ratifying Convention, Madison stated: "To suppose that any form of government will secure liberty or happiness without any virtue in the people, is a chimerical idea."[74] Samuel Adams agreed that "neither the wisest constitution nor the wisest laws will secure the liberty and happiness of a people whose manners are universally corrupt."[75] "If we are universally vicious and debauched in our manners," he warned, "though the form of our Constitution carries the face of the most exalted freedom, we shall in reality be the most abject of slaves."[76] To Richard Henry Lee he wrote that whether or not America was to be able to enjoy its hard won "independence and freedom . . . depends on her virtue."[77]

Thomas Paine, in his *Common Sense* argued that society and government had different origins, the former produced by wants and needs and the latter by the wickedness of people needing a restraint upon their vices. Government was made necessary in the first place because of the paucity of moral virtue in the world. The inference was clear: the less virtue there is in the people, the greater the amount of government coercion is needed to maintain order in society.

REPUBLICAN VIRTUE AND THE EXTENDED REPUBLIC

Madison's answer to the ubiquitous problem of self-interest and factions was bound up in his concepts of republican virtue, and the extended republic. He argued that not only was the classical-medieval concept of republicanism dysfunctional, but that an extended republic could at least assuage some of the major problems that in the past, had proved fatal to republics. While praising the performance of the new state republics, Madison attempted to demonstrate that, as small republics, they were facing similar morbific tendencies as the republics of old. "The valuable improvements made by the American constitutions on the popular models, both ancient and modern, cannot certainly be too much admired," he acknowledged, "but it would be an unwarrantable partiality to contend that they have as effectively obviated the danger on this side as was wished and expected."[78]

Madison was especially concerned with the state legislatures, for he had seen legislative tyranny emerge. If there had been any questions in his mind whether small republics could emerge and prosper primarily by a unified virtue of the people, the events following the Revolution had expunged them from his mind. In *The Federalist*, he sought to justify the idea that an extended republic with a national legislature would provide men who had more virtue and were less under the control of interest than the more vulnerable state legislators. It appeared painfully evident to him that the susceptibility of small republics to the tyranny of a majority faction was real.

Factions and The Extended Republic

As did Hume, Madison believed that in an extended republic, based upon *representation*, the "effects" of factions might best be controlled. In a small democracy or republic, with relatively *fewer* factions, it would be easier for a large faction or class, or a corrupt coalition of factions, to become a tyrannous majority and thus the oppressors of the minority faction or factions. But an extended republic, insisted Madison, with its system of representation, would open promises for "the cure we are seeking." First of all, the system of representation would allow the republic to grow both in terms of its geographical size and its population, thus allowing the republic to absorb a large population and multiple interests. In a further turnabout of traditional republican theory, Madison suggested that *multiple* factions in an extended republic might well be a *stabilizing* force, which would allow the expression of self-interest without endangering public liberty. Not only would these factions tend to check and balance each other, but each representative would have to take into consideration the fact that he represented multiple interests, a phenomenon that would tend to moderate his performance if not his views. For, to be elected, he would necessarily have to gain the support of multiple factions and interests. He would have to pull himself in from extreme political fringes to what Ivan Hinderaker has called "the big reasonable middle" of public attitudes and expectations.

Madison believed that the selection of representatives by the people whose responsibility would generally extend to a comparatively large population with multiple interests would better tend to promote men of virtue. He championed the idea that the citizens would be more likely to select men of virtue at the national than at the state level, since "the former will present a greater option, and consequently a greater probability of a fit choice . . . , [and that since] each representative will be chosen by a greater number of citizens in the large than in the small republic, it will be more difficult for unworthy candidates to practice with success the vicious arts, by which elections are too often carried; and the suffrages of the people being more free, will be more likely to center on men who possess the most attractive merit and the most diffusive and established characters."[79] In pure democracies and small republics, "men of factious tempers, of local prejudices, or of sinister designs, may by intrigue, by corruption, or by other means, first obtain suffrages, and then betray the interests of the people." On the other hand "extensive republics are most favorable to the election of proper guardians of the public weal . . ."; that is, men of substantial civic virtue. "It follows," reasoned Madison, "that if the proportion of fit characters be not less in the large than the small republic, the former will present a greater option, and consequently a greater probability of a fit choice."[80]

In a large republic, encompassing a vastly greater number of interests and variety of factions, it would be more difficult for one faction, or even a coalition to grasp and maintain power over the rest. In the representative republic, the greater number of factions, representing a wider range of interests would, in effect, act as a check upon each other—a kind of "countervailing power." It was Madison's purpose to counter ambition with ambition, interest with interest, power with power, faction with faction, thus helping to control the *effects* of factions.

Madison was especially concerned with the possibility of a majority faction or a majority coalition of factions organizing on the basis of an interest to gain control of the system and creating a structure of oppression. He thought this highly probable in the small republics, and even possible, although far less likely, in an extended republic. In a republic, "If a faction consists of less than a majority, relief is supplied by the republican principle, which enables the majority to defeat its sinister views by regular vote. It may clog the administration, it may convulse the society; but it will be unable to execute and mask its violence under the forms of the Constitution." However, warned Madison, "when a majority is included in a faction, the form of popular government, on the other hand, enables it to sacrifice to its ruling passion or interest both the public good and the rights of other citizens." As Madison put it, "To secure the public good and private rights against the danger of such a faction, and at the same time to preserve the spirit and the form of popular government, is then the great object to which our inquiries are directed. Let me add that this is the great desideratum by which alone this form of government can be rescued from the opprobrium under which it has so long labored and be recommended to the esteem and adoption of mankind." And how was this monumental endeavor to be realized? Madison saw but two reasonable means: "Either the existence of the same passion or interest in a majority at the same time must be prevented, or the majority, having such coexistent passion or interest, must be rendered, by their number and local situation, unable to concert and carry into effect schemes of oppression."[81]

Madison emphasized his belief that it was not only important "to guard the society against the oppression of its rulers, but to guard one part of the society against the injustice of the other part." Here the variety of interests and the multiplicity of factions in the new republic come into play, nurturing in society "so many separate descriptions of citizens as will render an unjust combination of a majority of the whole very improbable, if not impracticable." Although "all authority in [the federal republic] will be derived from and dependent upon the society," reasoned Madison, "the society itself will be broken into so many parts, interests and classes of citizens, that the rights of individuals, or of the minority, will be in little danger from interested combinations of the majority." The pluralistic, multi-faceted society, then, would support so many different interests, from the economic to the religious, as to support the civil rights of each. "In a free government," continued Madison, "the security for civil rights must be the same as that for religious rights. It consists in the one case in the multiplicity of interests, and in the other in the multiplicity of sects; . . . and this may be presumed to depend on the extent of country and number of people comprehended under the same government." Madison expressed the belief that in an extended republic, a coalition of a majority would necessarily involve and incorporate so many interests that a high level of moderation would result. *"In the extended republic of the United States, and among the great variety of interests, parties, and sects which it embraces,"* he wrote, *"a coalition of a majority of the whole society could seldom take place on any other principles than of those of justice and the general good."*[82]

The extended republic would, by its nature, tend to frustrate the building up of a national majority faction. "Extend the sphere and you take in a greater variety of parties and interests; you make it less probable that a majority of the whole will have a common motive to invade the rights of other citizens; or if such a common motive exists, it will be more difficult for all who feel it to discover their own strength and to act in unison with each other. *Besides other impediments, it may be remarked that, where there is a consciousness of unjust or dishonorable purposes, communication is always checked by distrust in proportion to the number whose concurrence is necessary."*[83]

VIRTUE AND THE REPRESENTATIVE REPUBLIC

Throughout *The Federalist*, one finds the argument that the elaborate constitutional structure the Federalists proposed would provide structural and functional "filters" that would tend to sift out the least virtuous while allowing the more virtuous to gain political power. In this, Madison hoped to avoid the loss of virtue that had plagued earlier republics.

In *The Federalist* No. 76, Madison and Hamilton suggest that *"the institution of delegated powers implies that there is a portion of virtue and honor among mankind."* And in *The Federalist* No. 55, Madison contends that *"Republican government presupposes these qualities in a higher degree than any other form."* Indeed, if man were not in possession of these "other qualities of human nature," a Hobbesian monarchy rather than a democratic republic would be a necessity. "Were the pictures which have been drawn by the political jealousy of some of us faithful likeness of the human character," continued Madison, "the inference would be that there is not sufficient virtue among men for self-government; and that nothing less than the claims of despotism can restrain them from destroying and devouring one another." In his *Address to the States* of April 1783, Madison saw virtue as synonymous with true liberty: *"If justice, good faith, honor, gratitude, and all the other qualities which enoble the character of a nation and fulfill the ends of government, be the fruits of our establishments, the cause of liberty will acquire a dignity and luster which it has never yet enjoyed, and an example will be set which cannot but have the most favorable influence on the rights of mankind. If on the other side,"* warned the statesman, *"our governments should be unfortunately blotted with the reverse of these cardinal and essential virtues, the great cause which we have engaged to vindicate, will be dishonored and betrayed; the last and fairest experiment in favor of the rights of human nature will be turned against them."*[84] Madison left no doubt that the future of the republican system would depend to a significant degree upon the amount of virtue displayed by the people of the republic.

It was Madison's belief that reason had "clearly decided in favor of" a large republic, where the greatest possibility existed for the selection of *virtuous* men as the representatives of the people, "whose *enlightened views* and *virtuous sentiments* render them superior to local prejudices and to schemes of injustice." He believed that the scheme of representation announced in *The Federalist* would not only make the extended republic possible, but would, in the process, elicit a more virtuous representative than would be the case in small republics. In such a representative republic, argued Madison, "it may well happen that the public voice pronounced by the representatives of the people will be more consonant to the public good than if pronounced by the people themselves convened for the purpose."[85] According to Madison, a large republic would have a greater number of fit men to be selected as representatives by extended constituencies. The "greater sphere," he argued, would tend to engender better representation. The election of "proper guardians of the public weal" is therefore much more likely in an "extensive Republic" than in a small one. "In the first place . . . the number of Representatives . . . being proportionately greatest in the small republic, it follows that if the proportion of fit characters be not less in the large than in the small republic, the former will present a greater option, and consequently a greater probability of a fit choice. In the next place, as each representative will be chosen by a greater number of citizens in the large than in the small Republic, it will be more difficult for unworthy candidates to practice with success the vicious arts by which elections are too often carried; and the suffrages of the people being more free, will be more likely to center on *men who possess the most attractive merit and the most diffusive and established characters."*[86] He believed that the system of representation as announced in *The Federalist* would be more likely to seat in political office men *"whose wisdom may best discern the true interest of the country and whose patriotism and love of justice will be least likely to sacrifice it to temporary or partial consideration.*"[87]

Jay agreed with Madison that an extended republic provided the greatest opportunity for the selection of men of virtue and quality to political power. "When once an efficient national government is established," he reasoned, "the best men in the country will not only consent to serve, but also will generally be appointed to manage it; for, although town or country, or other contracted influence, may place men in State assemblies, or senates, or courts of justice, or executive departments, yet more general and extensive reputation for talents and other qualifications will be necessary to recommend men to offices under the national government—especially as it will have the widest field for choice, and never experience that want of proper persons which is not uncommon in some of the States. Hence, it will result that the administration, the political counsels, and the judicial decisions of the national government will be more wise, systematical, and judicious than those of individual States, and consequently more satisfactory with respect to other nations, as well as more safe with respect to us."[88]

Virtue, The People, and The Republic

Madison contended that the citizens of the republic would be more likely to elect proper guardians at the national level than at the state level. Yet even here, the personal virtue of those who ruled, which was so necessary to the republic—the probability of its existence in a large republic being greater than in other forms of government—could not simply be assumed. The interim period between the Revolution and the Constitution had taught the bitter lesson that virtue in government cannot be taken for granted.

Madison was also concerned with *keeping* men virtuous once they had obtained political power. "The aim of every political constitution," he reasoned, "is, or ought to be, first *to obtain for rulers men who possess most wisdom to discern, and most virtue to pursue, the common good of the society;* and in the next place, to take the most effectual precautions *for keeping them virtuous* whilst they continue to hold their public trust."[89] One of the most effectual means to secure this in republican government, he surmised, was limited terms of office and periodic elections—"a limitation of the term of appointments as will maintain a proper responsibility to the people."[90]

Madison clearly recognized both the limits and necessity of structural arrangements and emphasized the importance of the spirit of the people. Representatives, according to his view, "will have been distinguished by the preference of their fellow citizens. We are to presume that, in general, they will be somewhat distinguished also by those qualities which entitle them to it, and which promise a sincere and scrupulous regard to the nature of their engagements." These representatives "will enter into the public service under circumstances that cannot fail to produce a temporary affection at least to their constituents. There is in every breast a sensibility to marks of honor, of favor, of esteem, and of confidence, that, apart from all considerations of interests, is some pledge for greatful and benevolent returns. Ingratitude is a common topic of declamation against human nature; and it must be confessed that instances of it are but too frequent and flagrant, both in public and private life. *But the universal and extreme indignation which it inspires is itself a proof of the energy and prevalance of the contrary sentiments."*

At the same time, the "pride and vanity" of the representative will generally "attach him to a form of government which favors his pretensions and gives him a share in its honors and distinctions. Whatever hopes or projects might be entertained by a few aspiring characters, it must generally happen that a great proportion of the men deriving their advancement from their influence with the people would have more to hope from a preservation of the favor than from innovations in the government subversive of the authority of the people. . . . [T]he real check upon oppression at any level or branch of government was bound up in the *"the genius of the whole system; the nature of just and constitutional laws; and above all, the vigilant and manly spirit which actuates the people of America—a spirit which nourishes freedom, and in return is nourished by it."*[91]

Finally, Madison reasoned that in a large republic the traditional bane of past republics—factions of selfish and designing men seeking purely their own interests—could be minimized through the size and diversity of the country. The process of coalition building would moderate demands and produce actions that were consistent with the public good. Members of Congress would not merely reflect the interests of their constituents but would be sufficiently insulated from them so that independent judgments concerning the common good would also serve as an influence on legislation.[92]

The Federalists emphasized that in their proposed federal republic the final depository of power would remain in the people. Madison wrote that "the people are the only legitimate fountain of power, and it is from them that the constitutional charter, under which the several branches of government hold their power, is derived."[93] Madison had successfully argued that ratification of the Constitution ought to be consummated by special conventions in each state rather than by the state legislatures. As far as Madison was concerned, the

Constitution became a compact not between the states, but by the people. "Our government system," he wrote, "is established by a compact not between the Government of the United States and the State governments, but between the States as sovereign communities, stipulating each with the other a surrender of certain portions of their respective authorities to be exercised by a common government, and a reservation, for their own exercise, of all their other authorities."[94]

In Madison's concept of the people being "the only legitimate fountain of power," he assumed a people possessed of sufficient virtue to support a republic. He embraced the idea that a republic required a special people. To the Virginia Ratifying Convention at Richmond, he observed that the people could express *their* virtue by electing men of virtue and wisdom. *"I go on this republican principle,"* he stated, *"that the people will have the virtue and intelligence to select men of virtue and wisdom. Is there no virtue among us? If there be not, we are in a wretched situation. No theoretical checks—no form of government can render us secure. To suppose that any form of government will secure liberty or happiness without any virtue in the people, is a chimerical idea. If there be sufficient virtue and intelligence in the community, it will be exercised in the selection of these men. So that we do not depend on their virtue, or put confidence in our rulers, but in the people who are to choose them."*[95] The Republic, he reasoned, would supply "a process of elections as will most certainly extract from the mass of society the purest and noblest characters which it contains; such as will at once feel most strongly the proper motives to pursue the end of their appointment, and be most capable to devise the proper means of attaining it."[96]

At the same time, the want of "better motives" of human nature dictated that this moderately virtuous people would need "auxiliary precautions" to help maintain a certain "equilibrium" in the republic. Since the citizens were the only proper objects of government, it was to be the responsibility of government to regulate their "common concerns" and preserve "the general tranquility. . . . A dependence on the people," wrote Madison, "is no doubt, the primary control on the government; but experience has taught mankind the necessity of auxiliary precautions." Madison taught that the "policy of supplying [compensating for], the defect of better motives [in the people] might be traced through the whole system of human affairs, private as well as public. We see it particularly displayed in all the subordinate distributions of power, where the constant aim is to divide and arrange the several offices in such a manner as that each may be a check on the other—that the private interest of every individual may be a sentinel over the public rights. These inventions of prudence cannot be less requisite in the distribution of the supreme powers of the State."[97] The major "auxiliary precautions"—federalism, separation of powers, and checks and balances"—were inextricably intertwined with the Founder's beliefs concerning human nature. In *The Federalist*, No. 10, Madison warned that "Enlightened statesmen will not always be at the helm." This statement not only emphasizes the need for "auxiliary precautions," but illustrates the point that writers such as Willmoore Kendall and George Carey have tried to make; namely, that the Founders still believed in the need for virtuous leaders as well as citizens—government and society could survive lapses in virtue, but not its complete disappearance.[98]

Cato, Virtue, and the Problems of Self-Interest and Factions

As previously discussed, important sources of information and inspiration for Madison and other Founders came from the radical republican tradition and the philosophy of Renaissance humanism and the Puritan Revolution. Their concern with moral theology and the conflict between virtue and faction had substantial influence on American republicans. The later commonwealthmen, especially John Trenchard and Thomas Gordon, brought many of these concerns together as they provided a powerful and clear expression of radical republican ideology and were an important source of ideas for the American Founders.

For the Commonwealthmen, unbridled self-interest or self-love posed great danger to man's equilibrium. "Self-love," they wrote, "beguiles Men into false Hopes, and they will venture to incur a hundred probable Evils, to catch one possible good; nay, they run frequently into distracted Pains and Expenses to gain Advantages, which are purely imaginary, and utterly impossible. Were the Passions properly balanced, Men would act rationally; but by suffering one Passion to get the better of all the rest, they act madly or rediculously."[99] Man is a Mixture of Contrarieties; imperious and supple, sincere and false, fearful and bold, merciful and cruel: He can sacrifice every Pleasure to the getting of Riches, and all his Riches to a Pleasure: He is fond of his Preservation, and yet sometimes eager after his own Destruction: He can flatter those whom he hates, destroy those whom he loves."[100]

This "Picture of Mankind" depicted by Trenchard and Gordon was very similar to the concept of the dual nature of man that was finally expressed by the American Founders. Just as did Madison and others of the Founders, Trenchard and Gordon came to the conclusion that reason, or even the power of religion, were not sufficient to tame man's penchant to magnify his self-interest, or to moderate the lust for power both in government and church. They wrote of "the little Power that Reason and Truth have over the Passions of Men, when they run high."[101] "It shews the violent Bent of human Nature to evil," they wrote in the *London Journal* in 1721, "that even the Christian Religion has not been able to tame the restless appetites of Men, always pushing them into Enormities and Violences, in direct Opposition to the Spirit and Declarations of the Gospel, which commands us to do unto all Men what we would have all men do unto us."

Trenchard and Gordon believed that a commonwealth of freedom required a special kind of people. Both the governed and the governors had to be motivated in some degree by personal and public virtue. They saw a "Christianized" virtue as the cornerstone to a happy commonwealth: the greatest danger to the commonwealth was factious self-interest and the passions. How was the former to be promoted and the latter to be controlled and mitigated? First, they believed that the character of virtue was set by religion. "Religion was designed by Heaven, for the Benefit of Men alone," they wrote in January of 1720, "It teaches us to moderate our Desires, calm our Passions, and be useful and beneficient to one another; and whatever does not contribute to those Ends, ought not to be called by that Name."[102] They spoke of religion in terms of "Mercy, Wisdom, and Truth."[103] They expressed gratitude to the "Creator and Preserver of Mankind," for having "brought Life and Immortality to Light."[104]

However, they warned, religion and its companion virtue involved more than just restraint of negative actions; positive behavior is advocated as well. "Religion and Virtue consist in doing good Actions, or in a disposition to do them. These being in our Power, as we perform or neglect them, we merit Praise or Blame." In the tradition of the Christian Humanists and the "Latitude Men," they reminded their readers that "Faith without works . . . is said to be dead; and we all know that what is dead is useless. If you would know any Man's Affections towards God, consult his Behavior towards men. . . . What is the use of Belief, but to govern our Practice, and beget good Deeds?"[105] "To the true Patriot," wrote Cato in the *London Journal*, "the pleasure of doing Good, is superior to any Praise resulting from it."[106] "Morality, or Moral Virtues," continued Cato, "are certain rules of mutual Convenience or Indulgence, conducive or necessary to the well-being of Society," and carry with them the onus of God's judgment.[107]

To the Commonwealthmen, "Publick Honour and Honesty," the great expressions of virtue, had to be supported by "ready Remedies for private Injustice and Oppression, and to protect the Innocent and Helpless from being devour'd by Fraud and Rapine."[108] Political power had to be checked, and the people protected from its unbridled misuse. It was not enough for people to be able to select those who would rule over them; there had to be some means to keep even their representatives in check beyond dependence on their virtue alone.

It was necessary for societies "to lay Restraints upon their Magistrates or publick Servants, and to put Checks upon those who would otherwise put Chains upon them." Trenchard and Gordon perceived that some means of checking interest with interest, faction with faction, and power with power, while channeling interest in such a way as to be salutary for the commonwealth, made the difference between free and arbitrary governments. They anticipated, though more crudely, the theoretical puzzle that Madison struggled with in his advocacy of an extended republic. The ideal was to "model and form national Constitutions with such Wisdom and Art, that the Public Interest should be consulted and carried at the same Time, when those entrusted with the Administration of it were consulting and pursuing their own." The difference between governments, they suggested, was "not that more or less Power was vested in the one than in the other; nor that either of them lay under less or more Obligations, in Justice, to protect their Subjects, and study their Ease, Prosperity, and Security, and to watch for the same. But the Power and Sovereignty of Magistrates in free Countries was so qualified, and so divided into different Channels, and committed to the Direction of so many different Men, with different Interests and Views, that the Majority of them could seldom or never find their Account in betraying their Trust in fundamental Instances. Their Emulation, Envy, Fear, or Interest, always made them Spies and Checks on one another."[109]

Trenchard cautioned his readers that were all power lodged in one governmental department, a centralized tyranny would result. He suggested that English history gave ample testimony of this proclivity. "If the House of Commons," he wrote, "was fixed and indissolvable, the Government would soon devolve into an ill-contrived Democracy, and the Crown would have no Remedy but Acquiescence or Force. Such a body of Men would soon find and feel their own Strength, and always think it laudable to encrease it: and there are so many Emergencies happen in all States, that there can never be wanting favourable Opportunities to do it, when the Ambition of some, the Resentment of others, and the Appearance of Publick Good, spur them on, till at last by insensible and unobserved degrees, even to themselves, they would engross and possess the whole power of the State."[110]

THE REPUBLICAN STRUCTURE: A BRIEF OVERVIEW

Federalism

The Federalists believed that acknowledging more than one level of government and sovereignty would serve to inhibit the concentration of power, ensure stability, and protect the freedoms of the people while uniting the states in an indissoluble union. The two major levels of government would ensure the citizens double security, especially since at both the state and the national level a separation of powers was the norm. "In the compound republic of America," Madison insisted, "the power surrendered by the people is first divided between two distinct governments, and then the portion allotted to each subdivided distinct and separate departments. Hence a double security arises to the rights of the people. The different governments will control each other, at the same time that each will be controlled by itself."[111]

In the geographic separation of powers of the federal system, Madison also saw the relationship of the model to the various interests that would be ignited or stimulated as the result of an extended republic. "The federal Constitution," he urged, would form "a happy combination" of "great and aggregate interests being referred to the national, [with] the local and particular [interests] to the State legislatures."[112] Hamilton emphasized "the additional security that," the adoption of the Constitution "will afford to republican government, to liberty, and to property." The federal system, he reasoned, would be of great benefit to the individual states, since it would assure unity, domestic tranquility, interstate peace, and a republican form of government. "The additional securities to republican government, to liberty, and to property, to be derived from the adoption of the plan under consideration," he wrote, "consist chiefly in the restraints which the preservation of the Union will impose on local factions and insurrections, and on the ambition of powerful individuals in single States who might acquire credit and influence enough from leaders and favorites to become the despots of the people."[113] In answer to the charge that the national government in the proposed extended republic would usurp the prerogatives of the states, Madison argued that any attempts at usurpation would "be easily defeated by the State governments, who will be supported by the people,"[114] and Hamilton expressed his faith in the civic virtue of the people—"the prudence and firmness of the people; who, as they will hold the scales in their own hands, it is to be hoped will always take care to preserve the constitutional equilibrium between the general and the State governments."[115]

Separation of Powers

A primary means to prevent the concentration of power was to divide government's basic functions—legislative, executive, and judicial—into three separate departments or branches administered by three different groups of public servants, who may not simultaneously serve in any other branch. This definite separation of the powers of government again moves the modern republic beyond the traditional concept of a "mixed" political system.

Madison was particularly concerned should any division or branch of government be allowed to usurp the powers and prerogatives of any other. One of his major arguments for a national government based on a constitutional separation of powers was that in the individual state governments, the legislature had often usurped powers from the other branches. He was insistent that the mere designation on paper of a separation of powers would be worthless, if constitutional limitations and powers were not so designed as to make the system operable. "A mere demarcation on parchment of the constitutional limits of the several departments," warned Madison, "is not a sufficient guard against those encroachments which lead to a tyrannical concentration of all the powers of government in the same hands."[116] "The great security against a gradual concentration of the several powers in the same department consists in giving to those who administer each department the necessary constitutional means and personal motives to resist encroachments of the others."[117]

Checks and Balances

Perhaps the most unique concept of the Constitution was that of checks and balances. This multifaceted principle solved a number of problems that were inherent in a republican and separation-of-powers system. First, checks and balances operate to insure that the branches of government do not surpass their delegated powers. The possibility of usurpation of one branch over another or the others was one which preoccupied those who wrote the Constitution, as it did those who opposed its ratification. As Madison observed, "power . . . ought to be effectually restrained from passing the limits assigned to it. After discriminating, therefore, in theory, the several classes of power, as they may in their nature be legislative, executive, or judiciary, the next and most difficult task is to provide some practical security for each, against the invasion of the others."[118]

Second, the system of checks and balances eliminated what might otherwise have been institutionalized deadlocks, exclusions, and stagnancy in the operation of government, by making the several branches mutually dependent as an operational whole, while still allowing them to retain their essential independence. In effect, checks and balances laced the branches together by a complex formula, to the extent that the process could provide a dual service: one, to allow each branch to check the power of the other so "that its several constituent parts may, by their mutual relations, be the means of keeping each other in their proper places";[119] and two, require them to cooperate in order to serve their multiple interests.

In their advocacy of the system of checks and balances, the Federalists once again demonstrated that their work in constitution building was influenced to a great extent by their conception of human nature. In Hamilton's defense of "the trial of impeachments of high government officials," for example, he argued that "the powers relating to impeachments are . . . an essential check in the hands of [Congress] upon the encroachments of the executive." The involvement of both houses in the process, he suggested, had a number of salutary designs. The division of the responsibility between them— "assigning to one the right of accusing, to the other the right of judging, avoids the inconvenience of making the same persons both accusers and judges; and guards against the danger of persecution, from the prevalency of a factious spirit in either of those branches." Furthermore, "as the concurrence of two-thirds of the Senate will be requisite to a condemnation, the security to innocence, from this additional circumstance, will be as complete as itself can desire."[120]

VIRTUE, SELF-INTEREST, AND THE VIABILITY OF REPUBLICAN GOVERNMENT

In constructing the Constitution of the United States, the American Founders dealt with problems that were ancient in origin and yet still problematic. The authors of *The Federalist Papers* assumed that passion, self-interest, ambition, and faction would have to be dealt with by "auxiliary precautions" and "safeguards." Yet, at the same time, the Founders assumed that there was a measure of virtue in man, especially the American, which, balanced against his less praiseworthy characteristics and motives, provided a foundation upon which a republic could be built and maintained.

Structures, separations of power, and checks and balances are simply not enough to maintain equilibrium or order in a democratic republic whose citizens are not supportive of the system, or who are motivated purely by crass self-interest and contentious and factious ambition. Even more importantly, government officials must place some restraints on the pursuit of their own individual and political interests in order to maintain the viability of constitutional government. Officers of the government must have some personal commitment to making the constitutional system work. Madison, in a well-known phrase in *The Federalist* No. 51 argued that "ambition must be made to counteract ambition." The next sentence explains how that is to take place: "The interest of the man must be connected with the constitutional rights of the place." This assumes that elected officials will be virtuous, that they will be selected by the people because of their virtue, and that they will be possessed of "enlightened views and virtuous sentiments" that would "render them superior to local prejudices and to schemes of injustice."

However, it is not necessarily in the self-interest of the individual to attempt to counter ambition in others so as to protect the integrity of a constitutional institution. Constitutional "safeguards" can be circumvented, as well as protected by self-interest. When government officials work to protect the integrity of their offices, that is, when they merge their interests with the rights and obligations of their offices—which in turn protects the integrity of the Constitution—they reflect the kind of civic virtue essential for republican government. The Constitution is not simply a mechanical device, but requires a careful balance between the structure of government and the nature of the people who are required to make it work.

NOTES

1. An outstanding study of factions in historical perspective may be found in Grant James Hansen, "The Origins of Madison's Thought on the Problem of Faction as Discussed in His Tenth Federalist," thesis, department of political science, Brigham Young University (April 1976).

2. "Cicero was not the first to mourn the loss of concord. The idea of concord as the groundwork of society had been hackneyed since Aristotle." Jose Ortega y Gasset, *Concord and Liberty* (New York: Norton, 1946), p. 17.

3. *The Laws of Plato*, translated with notes and an interpretive essay by Thomas L. Pangle (New York: Basic Books, 1980), Book 8, 831c–832d, 829a.

4. Christopher Hollis, warns that critics should not give the impression that Utopia was a "futile book" in which "More was merely writing down everything that came into his head, indifferent to whether it was true or false," and that "what he wrote was not of great significance." Hollis contends that More intended to make a statement. *St. Thomas More* (London: Burns and Oates, 1961), pp. 60–61. More, in his *Utopia*, as well as in other writings, dealt with problems of great moment, not only of the age in which he lived, but problems that faced and were to face those who devoted their energies in search of the stable commonwealth or republic.

5. For example, see Niccolo Machiavelli, *The History of Florence*, Vol. III, edited with an introduction by Myron P. Gilmore, translated by Judith A. Rawson (New York: Twayne, 1970), and *The Discourses of Niccolo Machiavelli*, translated with an introduction by Leslie J. Walker (New Haven: Yale University Press,

1950), especially Book 1, Chapters 2, 9, 10, 27, 42, 56, and 58; and Book 2, Introduction.

6. Douglass Adair, "That Politics May be Reduced to a Science," *Fame and the Founding Fathers* (New York: Norton, 1974), pp. 93–105; Grant James Hansen, "The Origins of Madison's Thought on the Problem of Faction as Discussed in His Tenth Federalist," pp. 36–74; Garry Wills, *Explaining America*.

7. David Hume, "Of Liberty and Necessity," *An Enquiry Concerning Human Understanding* (Chicago: Open Court, 1909), p. 85.

8. *The Federalist*, No. 9.

9. *The Federalist*, No. 10.

10. John Adams, "A Defense of the Constitutions of Government of the United States of America . . . ," in Charles Francis Adams, ed., *The Works of John Adams, Second President of the United States . . .* , Vol. IV (Boston: Little, Brown, 1850–1856).

11. *The Federalist*, No. 28; No. 63.

12. *The Federalist*, No. 6.

13. *The Federalist*, No. 22.

14. *The Federalist*, No. 10.

15. *Ibid.* (Italics added).

16. *The Federalist*, No. 15.

17. *The Federalist*, No. 51.

18. *The Federalist*, No. 57.

19. Smyth, ed., *Writings of Benjamin Franklin*, Vol. 8, pp. 451–52.

20. *The Federalist*, No. 70.

21. Smyth, ed., *The Writings of Benjamin Franklin*, Vol. 9, p. 591.

22. *The Federalist*, No. 15.

23. *The Federalist*, No. 37.

24. "The Kentucky and Virginia Resolutions, 1798, *"The Annals of America, Britannica*, Vol. 6 (Chicago: Encyclopedia Britannica, 1968–74), pp. 65–66. "In questions of power," continued Jefferson, "let no more be said of confidence in man, but bind him down from mischief by the chains of the Constitution."

25. Smyth, ed., *Writings of Benjamin Franklin*, Vol. 9, p. 241 (italics added).

26. Jonathan Elliot, ed., *The Debates in the Several State Conventions on the Adoption of the Federal Constitution* (Philadelphia: Lippincott, 1890), Vol. 3, p. 261.

27. *The Federalist*, No. 55.

28. *The Federalist*, No. 76.

29. C. F. Adams, *Writings of John Adams*, Vol. 6, p. 232.

30. *Ibid.*, p. 115.

31. Lester J. Cappon, ed., *The Adams-Jefferson Letters* (Chapel Hill: University of North Carolina Press, 1959), p. 388.

32. Lipscomb and Bergh, *Writings of Thomas Jefferson*, Vol. 14, p. 142.

33. Cappon, ed., *The Adams-Jefferson Letters*, p. 492.

34. Julian P. Boyd, et al., *The Papers of Thomas Jefferson*, Vol. 12, (Princeton, N.J.: Princeton University Press, 1950), p. 15. See Garry Wills's discussion of the concept of "moral sense" among the scholars of the Scottish Enlightenment in his *Inventing America*, especially pp. 121–228. See also Adrienne Koch, *The Philosophy of Thomas Jefferson* (New York: Columbia University Press, 1943), Chapter 3, "Moral Sense," pp. 15–22. Koch sees the philosohy of Scots Hume, Price, Clarke and Reid in Jefferson's concept of "moral sense," but especially that of Hutcheson as expressed in his *Introduction to Moral Philosophy*, and *Beauty and Virtue*.

35. *The Federalist*, No. 9 and No. 10.

36. Hunt, *The Writings of James Madison*, Vol. 3, p. 103.

37. Rossiter, *Political Thought of Revolution*, p. 99. But see Richard Hofstadter, *The American Political Tradition and the Men Who Made It* (New York: Vintage, 1974); *The American Republic* (Englewood Cliffs, N.J.: Prentice-Hall, 1959).

38. "Appeal from the New to the Old Whigs," in Beaconsfield, ed., *The Writings and Speeches of Edmund Burke* (Boston: Little, Brown, 1901), Vol. 4, pp. 174–75. The theory that an "elite" will, in fact, rule in any social or political organization is one of long standing. According to Harold J. Laski, "What is a matter of history can alone be predicted of the state is that it has always presented the striking phenomenon of a vast multitude owing allegiance to a comparatively small number of men." Harold J. Laski, *Grammar of Politics* (London: Allen and Unwin, 1925), p. 21. ". . . Every people," according to Vilfredo Pareto, "is governed by an elite, by a chosen element in the population." Vilfredo Pareto, *Mind and Society* (New York: Harcourt, Brace, 1935), p. 169. Harold D. Lasswell and Abraham Kaplan insist that "whether a social structure is democratic depends not on whether or not there is an elite, but on the relations of the elite to the mass—how it is recruited and how it exercises its power." Harold D. Lasswell and Abraham Kaplan, *Power and Society: A Framework for Political Inquiry* (New Haven: Yale University Press, 1965), p. 202.

39. John R. Howe, Jr., *The Changing Political Thought of John Adams*, p. 137; quoted from John Adams, "Literary Notes and Papers."

40. *The Federalist*, No. 36.

41. *The Federalist*, No. 73.

42. *The Federalist*, No. 71.

43. Worthington Chauncey Ford, ed., *The Writings of George Washington*, Vol. 11 (New York: G. P. Putnam, 1889), p. 326.

44. Lipscomb and Bergh, *The Writings of Thomas Jefferson*, Vol. 14, pp. 487–93 (italics added).

45. *Ibid.*

46. *The Federalist*, No. 37.

47. Hunt, ed., *The Writings of James Madison*, Vol. 2, pp. 411–12.

48. *The Federalist*, No. 2.

49. Tocqueville, *Democracy in America*, Vol. 1, pp. 158–59.

50. *The Federalist*, No. 49.

51. *The Federalist*, No. 51. See discussion in David Epstein, *The Political Theory of the Federalist* (Chicago: University of Chicago Press, 1984), p. 92.

52. *The Federalist*, No. 10, No. 51.

53. "The oracle who is always consulted and cited on this subject of separation of powers is the celebrated Montesquieu. If he be not the author of this invaluable precept in the science of politics, he has the merit at least of displaying and recommending it most effectively to the attention of mankind." *The Federalist*, No. 47.

54. *The Federalist*, No. 51; No. 58.

55. Douglass Adair, "Experience Must be Our Only Guide," *Fame and the Founding Fathers*, pp. 115, 116, 117.

56. John Paynter, "John Adams: On the Principles of Political Science," *The Political Science Reviewer*, Vol. VI (Fall, 1976), p. 43.

57. Wood, *The Creation of the American Republic*, p. 18. See Lutz's analysis of Wood on this subject in his "Bailyn, Wood, and Whig Political Theory," pp. 119–21.

58. Gary J. Schmitt, "Sentimental Journey: Gary Wills and the American Founding," *The Political Science Reviewer*, Vol. XII (Fall, 1982), p. 117. But see Hamilton's comments quoting from the *Spirit of the Laws*, Vol. I, Book IX, Chapter One, where Montesquieu does discuss the idea of a "Confederate Republic" in *The Federalist*, No. 9.

59. J. G. A. Pocock, "Virtue and Commerce," pp. 124–25.

60. Paynter, "John Adams: On the Principles of Political Science," p. 43.

61. Wills, *Explaining America*, pp. 104–5.

62. Jackson Turner Main, *The Anti-Federalists: Critics of The Constitution,*

1781–1788 (New York: Norton, 1974); Herbert J. Storing, *The Complete Anti-Federalist* (Chicago: University of Chicago Press, 1981).

63. Quoted in Paul Leicester Ford, *Essays on the Constitution of the United States*, p. 65.

64. Paul Peterson, "Republican Virtue and the Federalist: A Consideration of the Wills Thesis," paper presented before the American Political Science Association, Chicago, Illinois (September 1–4, 1983), p. 18.

65. Hamilton argued that the criteria advocated by Montesquieu for small states had already been outgrown by the American states, leaving only "the alternative either of taking refuge at once in the arms of monarchy, or of splitting outselves into an infinity of little, jealous, clashing, tumultuous commonwealths, the wretched nurseries of unceasing discord and the miserable objects of universal pity or contempt." (*The Federalist*, No. 9.)

66. Rossiter, *Political Thought of the American Revolution*, p. 199.

67. Samuel Williams, *A Discourse on the Love of Our Country*, pp. 13–14.

68. "American colonists of the latter part of the eighteenth century readily identified the English Church and government with corruption—the Church with its pampered hierarchy and impoverished parish priests, and the government with its rotten boroughs and members of Parliament whose votes were bought by the monarch with sinecures." Clarence B. Carson, *The Rebirth of Liberty* (New York: Arlington House, 1973), p. 23.

69. Max Farrand, ed., *The Records of the Federal Convention of 1787*, Vol. 2, pp. 641–42.

70. Smyth, ed., *Writings of Benjamin Franklin*, Vol. 9, p. 569.

71. John C. Fitzpatrick, ed., *The Writings of George Washington* (Washington Bicentennial Commission, 1931), Vol. 29, p. 479.

72. Saul K. Padover, ed., *The Washington Papers*, p. 244.

73. Elliot, ed., *The Debates in the Several State Conventions on the Adoption of the Federal Constitution*, Vol. 2, p. 175.

74. Hunt, *The Writings of James Madison*, Vol. 5, p. 223.

75. William V. Wells, *The Life and Public Services of Samuel Adams* (Boston: Little, Brown, 1865), Vol. 1, p. 22.

76. *Ibid.*, pp. 22–23.

77. *Ibid.*, Vol. 3., p. 175.

78. *The Federalist*, No. 10.

79. *Ibid.*

80. *Ibid.*

81. *Ibid* (italics added).

82. *The Federalist*, No. 51 (italics added).

83. *The Federalist*, No. 10 (italics added).

84. Hunt, *The Writings of James Madison*, Vol. 1, pp. 459–60.

85. *The Federalist*, No. 10 (italics added). In his *The Authority of Publius* (Ithaca, N.Y.: Cornell University Press, 1984), Albert Furtwangler contends that *The Federalist* should be read first and foremost as political propaganda and not necessarily as a clear expression of political ideology. While this may have some merit, we believe that *The Federalist* makes a statement that both explains the basic philosophy of the writers and masterfully elicits the acceptance of the readers essentially on the basis of that philosophy. We agree with a statement from the Preface of *The Federalist Papers*, ". . . an authoritative analysis of the Constitution of the United States and an enduring classic of political philosophy that takes its place in history beside the Constitution itself." (The New American Library of World Literature, Inc., 1961).

86. *Ibid* (italics added).

87. *Ibid* (italics added). "The American Republic needs a substitute for the

direct concern with the public good which Montesquieu claimed for small republics. Madison finds this substitute in the possibility of selected men being wise enough to see what is necessarily remote in a large republic." Epstein, *The Political Theory of the Federalist*, p. 94.

88. *The Federalist*, No. 3. One of the great tasks facing the Federalists was to assuage the general fear in the people of a national executive. In the Declaration of Independence, it was the British Crown that had been condemned for tyranny. The election of the president by the Electoral College was championed as a way to constrain executive power, and of opposing the "most deadly adversaries of republican government"—"cabal, intrigue, and corruption." Hamilton argued that the electors would not compose "any pre-established body," but would be "men chosen by the people for the special purpose, and at the particular conjuncture." The quality of these men, selected by the people in each state for such an important purpose, would tend to be high, and it could be expected that their choice would be a man of ability and virtue. "It was equally desirable that the immediate election should be made by men most capable of analyzing the qualities adapted to the station and acting under circumstances favorable to deliberation, and to a judicious combination of all the reasons and inducements which were proper to govern their choice. A small number of persons, selected by their fellow citizens from the general mass, *will be most likely to possess the information and discernment requisite to so complicated an investigation.*"

The process would tend to "afford as little opportunity as possible to tumult and disorder. . . . The choice of several [electors] to form an intermediate body of electors will be much less apt to convulse the community with any extraordinary or violent movements. . . . And as the electors, chosen in each State, are to assemble and vote in the State in which they are chosen, this detached and divided situation will expose them much less to heats and ferments, which might be communicated from them to the people, than if they were all to be convened at one time, in one place." For Hamilton, "*This process of election affords a moral certainty that the office of the President will seldom fall to the lot of any man who is not in an eminent degree endowed with the requisite qualifications. . . . It will not be too strong to say that there will be a constant probability of seeing the station filled by characters pre-eminent for ability and virtue.*" *The Federalist*, No. 48.

89. *Ibid.*

90. *Ibid.*

91. *The Federalist*, No. 68 (italics added).

92. See Garry Wills, *Explaining America*, Chaps. 27–28, for a detailed development of this idea.

93. *The Federalist*, No. 49.

94. *Letters and Other Writings of James Madison*, Vol. 3, published by order of Congress (New York: Lippincott, 1865), p. 223; Martin Hickman, "Double Majesty: Madison's Middle Ground," unpublished manuscript, Brigham Young University, p. 27.

95. Elliot, ed., *The Debates in the Several State Conventions on the Adoption of the Federal Constitution*, Vol. 2, p. 175.

96. *The Federalist*, No. 16, and No. 51.

97. *The Federalist*, No. 51.

98. Willmoore Kendall and George Cary, *The Basic Symbols of the American Political Tradition* (Baton Rouge: Louisiana State University Press, 1970). See also Epstein, *The Political Theory of the Federalist*.

99. John Trenchard and Thomas Gordon, "The Independent Whig," (June, 1721), in *A Collection of All the Political Letters in the London Journal* (London: Printed for J. Roberts in Warwick-Lane, 1721), p. 259.

100. *Ibid.*, (May 27, 1721), p. 237.

101. *Ibid.*, p. 50.

102. *Ibid.*, (January 27, 1720), p. 8.

103. John Trenchard and Thomas Gordon, *Cato's Letters: or Essays on Liberty, Civil and Religious*, 3rd ed., Vol. 2 (New York: Russell and Russell, 1733), November 4, 1721, No. 51, p. 130.

104. Trenchard and Gordon, "The Independent Whig" (January 27, 1720) in *Political Letters*, p. 8.

105. *Ibid.*, (July 13, 1720), p. 193.

106. Trenchard and Gordon, *Political Letters*, p. A.

107. *Ibid.*, (January 21, 1720), p. 38.

108. *Ibid.*, pp. 38–39.

109. Trenchard and Gordon, *Cato's Letters*, Vol. 2 (January 6, 1721), No. 60, pp. 230–31.

110. Trenchard, "The Thoughts of a Member of the Lower House," in *Political Letters*, p. 5.

111. *The Federalist*, No. 51

112. *The Federalist*, No. 10

113. *The Federalist*, No. 85

114. *The Federalist*, No. 46

115. *The Federalist*, No. 31

116. *The Federalist*, No. 48

117. *The Federalist*, No. 51

118. *The Federalist*, No. 48

119. *The Federalist*, No. 51

120. *The Federalist*, No. 66

7

Public Virtue and
the Commercial Spirit

As THE AMERICAN FOUNDERS clearly recognized, economic and commercial activity assumed a central role in individual and social life. They saw parallels between the preconditions for social, political, and economic life in a society dedicated to freedom. Restraints on the pursuit of wealth were just as essential as they were on political and social spheres. Virtue, as developed in Puritan notions of covenant and calling, and radical republican ideas of justice and benevolence, were understood and championed as the basis of economic life. This chapter examines the relationship between virtue and economics, *not as a comprehensive study of political economy*, but as an additional means of demonstrating the critical role of personal and public virtue in the founding of the American republic.

THE PURITAN ETHIC AND ENTERPRISE

From the very beginning of European colonization of America, the ideal of the covenant was prominent. The Puritan emphasis on covenant led to the Mayflower Compact, to the colonial and state constitutions (both of which acknowledged God as the founder and protector of the enterprise), and to the Constitution of the United States. From the earliest times, one can find evidences of the concept of calling and stewardship deeply embedded in the Puritan culture. The covenant was the Puritans' central affirmation of participation in God's purposes in ordering a corrupt world. It was not just an agreement; it was a legal and binding contract, a judge, and a teacher.

The Puritans believed that God had called every man to service in church and commonwealth as a stewardship. By serving himself and society in a useful and productive manner, man was in turn serving God. *Thus, the calling necessarily incorporated man's economic occupation.* "Before entering on a trade or profession, man must determine whether he had a calling to undertake it. If he had talents for it, if it was useful to society, if it was appropriate to his station in life, he could feel confidence that God had called him to it." Diligence, thrift and frugality were watchwords. Sloth and idleness were to be avoided. With his property and talents the Puritan looked upon himself as a steward of his possessions: "If he needlessly consumed his substance, either from carelessness or from sensuality, he failed to honor the God who furnished him with it."[1]

This concept of the "calling" produced numerous fruits for the colonies and later the Republic. The impact of the Puritan ethic was such that even as the religious aspects became dimmed, the influence of the ethic remained. "Whether they derived their ideas from history thus interpreted or from the Puritan tradition or elsewhere," Edmund Morgan has written, "Americans of the Revolutionary period in every colony and state paid tribute to the Puritan Ethic and repeated its injunctions."[2]

The Puritan ethic contributed much to the energy, enterprise and production of the colonies and the new Republic. The stress on individual initiative and enterprise fostered sentiments of individualism and personal worth that contributed to the growth of and demand for freedom. Thomas Jefferson is a case in point. In March and in May of 1787, he wrote to his daughter Martha: "It is your future happiness which interests me, and nothing can contribute more to it (moral rectitude always excepted) than the contracting a habit of industry and activity. Of all the cankers of human happiness, none corrodes it with so silent, yet so baneful a tooth, as indolence. . . . Determine never to be idle. No person will have occasion to complain of the want of time, who never loses any. It is wonderful how much may be done, if we are always doing."[3]

When the first permanent merchants arrived in New England in 1630, they were influenced by the strength of Puritan concepts of virtue. Commerce and economic exchange were expected to be guided by the idea of virtue, which had evolved in such a way as to include nearly all forms of human intercourse. Virtue, and hence man's salvation, were intimately entwined with human welfare. Some of the clergy moved to an increasingly theoretical application of virtue that had the result of reference to almost everything man did that could have an impact on others. To some, the practice of virtue affirmed the "Golden Rule." Jonathan Edwards was to see "true virtue" as "love, or a disposition to love"; a "habit or frame of mind" that was expressed in a "generally benevolent disposition."[4] In his

Election Sermon of 1702 in Boston, Increase Mather spoke of "The Excellency of a Publick Spirit." While condemning "the great Evil which is in being a private self-seeking Spirit," he promised that "the Lord Jesus Christ will take notice of them before all the world at the last day, who have with a sincere heart sought the welfare of his people."[5]

So, while seeking his own self-interest, each member of the community was cautioned to remember that he was also a social being, charged with the responsibility to contribute to the whole, and, when the occasion required it, to sublimate his self-interest to that of the community. Thus, those whose activities influenced the welfare of others—religious, political, or economic—bore a special responsibility, often carrying with it an extraordinary temptation. The moral temptation that underlaid trade and economic exchange was seen as especially dangerous and an effort was made to place some rule of moral conduct on economic exchange. Usury was at first condemned, as it had been for generations, and there was concern over the payment of a "just wage," and exchanges at a "just price." These ideas, Bernard Bailyn has written, "were put into use the very first years of the Puritan settlements and helped shape the development of institutions and traditions from the start. Nowhere else did Calvinist doctrines of social ethics find such full application. In Geneva, Scotland, and the Netherlands, theory had always to be qualified to some extent by pre-Calvinistic practices. In New England, doctrine literally preceded practice."[6]

This system of virtuous economic exchange, with all its elements and ramifications, proved somewhat erratic in application. The heavy weight of social disapproval and indignation in the community against alleged economic indiscretions was perhaps the most effective deterrent to economic chicanery. There were the inevitable clashes between merchants and the public authorities, and where the merchant was concerned, strict adherence to a code of business ethics "required an amount of self-discipline that only great faith could sustain."[7] The high expectations would not always be maintained, and self-interest was perhaps often the primary motivation. Yet, as the economy developed, many began to perceive, as Madison later did, that self-interest, multiplied by increasing numbers of participants in the marketplace, need not necessarily be inimical to the overall benefit of the community.

The overall impact of Puritan economic philosophy was to energize the citizen, inure him to hard work, reinforce his commitment to virtue, and extend his expectations. The "mind set" engendered by Puritanism, which was both spiritual and philosophical, was critical. It was this "mind set" that rationalized hard work and economic progress as a "calling" replete with "virtuous" overtones. Thus, the "Puritan spirit" was at least a contributor to the rise of the "commercial spirit in the colonies," and, as a concomitant, helped provide a foundation for the rise of an energetic, stubborn, and forward-looking middle class, which was manifested in a zeal for enterprise, adventure, and progress. Burke's tribute to New England whalers describes this explosion of energy that was characteristic of the New World: "No sea but what is vered by their fisheries. No climate that is not witness to their toils. Neither the perseverance of Holland, nor the activity of France, nor the dexterous and firm sagacity of English enterprise, ever carried this most perilous mode of hard industry to the extent to which it has been pushed by this recent people who are still, as it were, but in the gristle and not yet hardened to the bone of manhood."[8]

The Impact of Puritanism

Much has been written concerning the emergence of capitalism and its relationship with puritanism;[9] the religious environment in colonial America served as an important influence in economic affairs, and the evolving concept of virtue was brought to bear on men's acquisitive nature and the economic means used to pursue that impulse. The metamorphosis of such concepts as covenant and stewardship had an impact on men's thoughts and actions with regard to enterprise, particularly in the seventeenth and eighteenth centuries. In following this conduit one finds a relationship to the idea of what has been referred to as the "radical commercial republicans," and, ultimately, to James Madison's "extended commercial republic."

Puritanism neither inaugurated commerce nor created the "Spirit of Capitalism." What Puritanism probably did accomplish was to energize and stimulate the enterprise motive among many of its adherents to an unusually high degree, which coincided with an age of economic stimulation.[10] As the concepts of *covenant* and *calling* became increasingly involved with "works"; as sentiments more amenable to freedom of the will began to nudge out the hopelessness of determinism, and as the very *pursuit* of excellence began to be acknowledged as a sign of grace; and as one's earthly calling increasingly came to be seen as a "stewardship" for which man would one day be obliged to give an accounting before God, an enterprising spirit was unleashed among the true believers that contributed to the development of modern freedom, the decline of feudal aristocracy, the development of the middle class, and the releasing of man from economic and class servitude. Furthermore, it found a working compatibility with the intensity of the acquisitive spirit, which emerged reinvigorated and "democratic" with the commercial age, and which really was different from the avarice and greed, the hoarding of wealth and the general economic stagnancy and selfishness that so exasperated Sir Thomas More and other Christian humanists in their day.

Puritanism, as it came to be an influence in its world, evolved toward a doctrine of voluntary virtue, the idea that order and equilibrium could be established spontaneously—both within the individual soul and the community—without force and coercion (or at least with a minimum of it). Perry Miller and others have shown how Puritanism came to be conspicuous in the development of the idea that freedom and voluntarism, and even self-interest, were not necessarily inimical to either private or civil virtue and hence, order. According to David Little, Puritan theology eventually developed an "individualism" that came to be associated with "a differentiated social order containing the principles of voluntarism, consensualism, private initiative and toleration. . . . When Puritanism appears," continues Little, "there will be special pressure toward voluntary, self-initiated economic behavior."[11]

The emerging idea that free men could find happiness in *this* world—a concept many were surprised to find both explicitly and implicitly flowing through the passages of their Scriptures—also added to the sense of meaning and of worth of virtue, and the excitement and enticement of the earthly "calling." This can be seen in the writings of Benjamin Franklin, both in his "Poor Richard"-type of success casuistry and in his religious declarations. According to Franklin, God "delights in the happiness of those he has Created," and "since without Virtue Man can have no happiness in this World, I firmly believe he delights to see me Virtuous, because he is pleased when he sees me Happy. . . . I love him therefore for his Goodness, and I adore him for his Wisdom."[12] When the American Founders championed the principle of "the pursuit of happiness," they were not acting contrary to modern Puritan doctrine.

As the evolution of Puritanism continued, certain factors basic to the founding doctrines began to lead inexorably toward ideals of human dignity and freedom, in spite of what might have been the stultifying doctrine of predestination. For this dogma, too, passed through a transformation, and its *original* idea of the "elect" was pushed into the background by the concepts of *covenant* and *calling* until it became more or less innocuous. To Clinton Rossiter, the result was a "reconstituted Puritanism," a "system of practical ethics, which called upon responsible, rational, virtuous, self-reliant men to pursue their busy lives within a system of ordered liberty." This, declared Rossiter, "was the first and, it may certainly be argued, the greatest of all American ways of life."[13] Perry Miller, among others, called the new doctrine "covenant theology." At last, a "reconstituted" Puritan theology came to be an enemy of all forms of determinism and the generator of a highly motivating source of psychic energy. "Covenant theology" inferred man's free will and action, or works, in the process of salvation; and suggested that man, freed from fatalistic dogmas, could experience a kind of spontaneous order through the exertion of free will.[14]

The Doctrine of a Dual Calling

One of the most significant factors in the evolution of Puritan doctrine and influence was the emergence of the concept of a "dual calling," especially in its relationship with the concept of the Covenant. As ancient Israel had made covenant with God, so the modern "Israelite" in his Protestant form, came to covenant with his God to bring forth righteousness and truth in return for salvation. When it became accepted that man could covenant with God, and that man's works were related to the fulfillment of the covenant, and hence, with salvation, it became necessary, after some twists and turns in doctrine, to downplay the idea of a few elect destined for salvation, and to emphasize the developing doctrine of the calling, which, in effect, had led to the potential of including virtually everyone.

The calling came to be a closely coordinated duality—the *general* calling, in which man was to love, worship and glorify God, and the *personal* calling, through which man gained a particular employment or "vocation," that would benefit him and his community—"so he may glorify God, by doing of *Good* for *others*, and getting of *Good* for himself"[15]—an obligation that inferred a high level of civic virtue. Man's talents were to be used in a beneficial way. More than anything else, it was this doctrine, in its dual yet interrelated admonitions, that lies at the core of the unusual spiritual and economic energy of the believing Puritan.

As Puritan theology developed, some of the most prominent and influential Puritan divines carried the doctrine of salvation beyond that envisioned by either Luther or Calvin; and the concept of works—beyond sacraments and penance—came to mean energetic and outward manifestations of dedication in one's life to the Glory of God, an enlivening rather than passive humility generated by faith in an atoning Christ, and the sense of spiritual rejuvenation stimulated through the concepts of repentance and forgiveness. It was this sense of personal participation, indeed responsibility, in the process of regeneration that formed the basis of the energy within the evolving Puritan community. The believer, given hope for salvation through a combination of his faith in an atoning Christ and his energy in works, sought the feeling of an "indwelling" relationship with God, a sign to him that his calling and election were sure. There was within Puritanism an awakening, enlivening stimulus, an inner force, that affected every aspect of their lives, including their economic impulses.

Crucial to the understanding of the development of Puritanism is the motivating activism that encompassed its theology and its practical application. The Puritan God was an activist, demanding God, just as had been the God of the Israelites; and the individual Puritan was charged with purposeful and energetic behavior in every aspect of his life. In a practical way, faith *and* works were reenthroned in religious life. In his remarkable study of one of the great Puritan leaders William Ames, Professor Keith L. Sprunger writes, "The theology of Ames is God-centered. His God is a creating, predestining, sustaining, and governing God. At the center of all existence, God is. Every activity of man, whether intellectual or physical, cannot escape the primary fact 'that God himself is our true chief good'; he is 'absolutely the chiefest good.' Theology's mission, according to [Ames], is to teach men first about faith in God and then about Christian living, that is 'a living to God, or a working to God, as well as a speaking of God.'"[16]

Salvation to the Puritans was an activist process that combined faith and the active participation of the one seeking grace. To the Puritans neither sacraments nor penance were enough. "The price of our redemption," wrote William Gouge, included "Christ's blood, and the special fruits thereof, as *Reconciliation*, Adoption, *Remission of Sins, imputation of righteousness.*" And the means of election and redemption were to be applied—"namely the effectuall operation of God's spirit: under this head are comprised effectuall *vocation, regeneration, sanctification,* and all those particular sanctifying graces, which *we* find and feele to be wrought in us, as *Knowledge, Faith, Hope, Love, Repentance, Patience, new Obedience,* etc., together with the blessed fruits of them, as *peace of conscience, joy in the spirit, holy security,* with the like."[17] In fine, "Man's workes are the rule of God's reward."[18]

Puritan doctrine called for its adherents always to be found in a good cause. "Good done to God's people is most acceptable."[19] Far from engendering contempt for the poor, the unsuccessful, and the unfortunate, Puritanism demanded of its adherents prayerful intercession and compassion on behalf of those in distress. They were charged with works of virtue and mercy; they were expected to be hospitable. In times of particular stress they were even expected to forego their own interests for appeasement of others' misfortune. According to Gauge, "They therefore that feare the Lord will . . . not over-strictly stand upon their right, especially in times of necessity and cases of extremity. Over-strict standing upon right may prove a great oppression."[20] Gouge urged his listeners to "take speciall notice of the particular cases of such as are in distress. . . . Goe to prisons, visit the sicke, cast your eyes on miserable objects. . . .[21] Ye that justly have obtained the names of good Patriots, and have begun to redress many grievances, goe on in that good worke, till through God's blessing and your endeavours it be brought to some good perfection."[22]

Charity was an expression of love and an activist Puritan faith. Puritans were urged to "take off the heavy burdens which others had laid upon the backs of their poore brethren," so that they might be "positively relieved with money, corne, and other necessaries, and that *gratis*, such as were in need."[23] And the regenerate should actively encourage others to join them in their acts of charity. "Put courage into others, ye that are men of courage,"[24] admonished Gouge, "stir up others to be aiding and assisting to you. This justifies your Protestation, your Subsidies, Pole-money, Land-rate, Loanes, and other meanes used for assistance from others in the weighty works you have in hand."[25]

Man's first responsibility was to glorify God and then to seek the welfare of others.[26] Of vital importance was the idea that man's calling was in the form of a stewardship; that is, men were to be judged as in the "parable of the talents"; it was not the degree of wealth or poverty that was important, but how men used the talents and blessings God had bestowed upon them. According to Ames, "Riches as they are considered absolutely and in themselves, are morally neither good nor bad, but things indifferent which men may use either well or ill."[27] "We are stewards," Sibbes observed, "and we must give a strict accounting ere long how we have used them";[28] and William Chillingworth wrote, "God hath placed us here in this World as his Stewards, has put into our Hands his Goods, his riches, to be dispensed for his Use and Advantage."[29] "The resulting Ethic," writes J. Wayne Baker, was a new approach related to the commercial world, "based on the Love Commandment."[30]

The personal "calling" carried with it a definite moral connotation for what was believed the benefit, betterment, and progress of the individual and thereby of the commonwealth. To the taboos of idleness and sloth were added pride, vanity, licentiousness, covetousness, maliciousness, hypocrisy, deceit, dishonesty, and irreverance. In short, one's "calling," to be worthy of the name, would have the result of contributing in an important way to the growth and character of the individual. The calling was expected to be a means of exercising virtuous discipline. Ames taught that every vocation ought to be performed in honesty, wisdom, and diligence. According to

Sibbes, God had "sanctified" the "particular callings" in order to "subdue the excess of corruptions. Men without callings," he wrote, "are exceedingly vicious, as some gentlemen and beggars."[31] The man of enterprise was expected to be a virtuous example of God's disciple in every way. Labor, then, was more than an economic means; its end was a spiritual one. Work, it was believed, was the God-ordained means whereby the individual established dominion over the earth and realized his calling, and with it, his self-realization as a unique human being as he reached his full potential.

The moral theology that encompassed the doctrine of the calling was concerned with man's character. However men might individually view the commercial process and the acquisitive impulse, Christianity had placed upon economic activity, just as it had on political and social endeavors, moral obligations and restraints. As the medieval dual system of morality gave way to universal moral principles; as the importance of the covenant became increasingly pronounced; and as the concept of stewardship became infused with the doctrine of salvation, the moral responsibility of the individual became increasingly pronounced. The growing belief that man would be judged by his actions in this life, not by a process of arbitrary selection, had a monumental impact on religion, especially in England and America. And we suggest that the impact was no less revolutionary on the thinking of men with regard to human dignity, freedom, and individual responsibility. Indolence, sloth, conspicuous consumption, greed, avarice, vanity, on the one hand, and diligence, energetic work, personal development, honesty, charity, and love of one's fellowman on the other hand, were not only intimately related to civic virtue, but to personal virtue, including the growth of the individual to his full functioning potential as a command from God.

Virtue, Covenant, and Calling

The idea of the personal calling brought individuals into the concept of covenant. The writings of Richard Baxter, perhaps the most widely cited and important spokesman of Puritan economic casuistry, reflect a consistent and ubiquitous insistence on the guiding direction of virtue—both individual and civil—as a motivator of energy and dedication, and at the same time a moral restraint upon pride, selfishness, and greed. The personal callings, insisted Baxter, though relating to mundane tasks, remained as an integral part of man's stewardship on earth for which he was answerable to God. Self-interest, properly applied, need not be a sin, since it could be directed at both the betterment of the individual, his family, his neighbor, and the community. There was nothing wrong with success if it bred philanthropy rather than avarice and greed—and since

rich and poor alike through all ages had suffered from these indications of lack of character, the problem was related to personal virtue,
not the mode of production.[32]

For the Puritan, the primary purpose of his "calling" was to serve
God. Therefore, Baxter found no difficulty with laboring "to be rich
for God. . . . Though it is said, 'Labour not to be rich,' the meaning is
that you make not riches your chief end." Riches, on the other hand,
might be sought "in subordination to higher things . . . that is, you
may labour in that manner as tendeth most to your success and
lawful gain: you are bound to improve all your master's talents: but
then your end must be, that you may be the better provided to do
God service, and may do the more good with what you have. If God
shew you a way in which you may lawfully get more than in another
way (without wrong to your soul, or to any other), if you refuse this,
and choose the less gainful way, you cross one of the ends of your
calling, and you refuse to be God's steward, and accept his gifts, and
use them for him."[33]

Inherent in the concept of the calling is the admonition that one
use his time, energy and largess for the benefit of the community—
the commonwealth in Puritan terms—and for the good and well-
being of others. This is the Puritan manifestation of civic virtue
incorporated with the biblical ideal of benevolence and the Golden
Rule. The difference between the "calling" and the ancient concept of
civic virtue, is not only in the rejection of the classical demand to
sacrifice self-interest completely to what the state considers the common good, but in the increasingly and vastly broadened base of the
biblicalized "calling" and its evolution to the championing of free
choice in the Puritan metamorphosis. "It is a great satisfaction to an
honest mind, to spend his life in doing the greatest good he can,"[34]
wrote Baxter. If "religion is our obligation to obey God," he continued, then we must understand that "God bindeth us to do all the
good we can to others."[35]

A major difference in the metamorphosis of the "calling," as
Puritanism matured, existed between the Calvinistic interpretation
and that of the Catholics or the Lutherans. According to Tawney,
Luther and the medieval theologians looked upon "vocation" or the
"calling" as that "state of life in which the individual had been set by
heaven and against which it was impious to rebel." On the other
hand, the "calling" that finally developed under Puritanism was "not
a condition in which the individual was born, but a strenuous and
exacting enterprise to be chosen by himself, and to be pursued with a
sense of religious responsibility."[36] Not only was it acceptable for a
man to change "callings," but also to diversify his labour. "May a man
have divers trades or callings at once? Yes, no doubt, if it be for the

common good or for his own, and no injury to any other; nor so inconsistent, as that one shall make him unfaithful in the other."[37] The only moral cautions in the independent selection of one's calling or callings beyond that indicated—that they be in the service of God, the public good, and to the laborer's good—were that they be selected with consultation and care. "Choose no calling (especially if it be of public consequence) without the advice of some judicious, faithful persons of that calling"[38]—take not "the work of other men's callings out of their hands."[39]

So, the concept of the calling, as it developed through the metamorphosis of Puritanism, did not ignore the spiritual, emotional, psychological, and economic needs of the individual. Considering the nature of the "calling" in relation to service to others and the development of self, Puritan practicality was far from being wholly "other worldly" where the individual withdrew from the vicissitudes of life into rapt contemplation of the eternal world. Puritanism was a philosophy of action, of energy, indeed, of enthusiasm. Baxter's God was called a God of "action." "It is for action that God maintaineth us and our abilities; work is the moral as well as the natural end of power. It is the act by the power that is commanded us. It is action that God is most served and honoured by: not so much by our being able to do good, but by our doing it."[40] Thus, Baxter, as a spokesman of Puritan moral doctrine, admonished his flock to "abhor a sluggish habit of mind: go cheerfully about what you have to do: and do it diligently, and with your might. Even about your lawful, worldly business, it is a time-wasting sin to be slothful. If you are servants or labourers you rob your masters and those that hire you; who hired you to work and not be idle. Whatever you are, you rob God of your service, and yourselves of your precious time, and all that you might get therein."[41]

Baxter saw idleness and sloth affect every facet of man's existence, frustrating or ruining his "calling" and his life and impoverishing him in every way. "Idleness and sloth are consumers of all the mercies of God. You are the barren ground where he soweth his seed, and none comes up. You return him but a crop of thorns and briars. . . . Will you accuse your Maker of so great imprudence, and your Redeemer of more, as if he created and redeemed you to do nothing, or that which is as bad or worse than nothing?" Idleness, insists Baxter, is a thief. It "is a robbing of God, who is the Lord of us and all our faculties, and all our service is his due. You rob him of the honour and service that you might have done him by your diligence. And it is a robbing yourselves of all the good to soul or body, which by your labour and industry you might have got. The slothful man lieth wishing till he perish. And it is a robbing of the commonwealth, and of all those to whom your labours, or the fruit of them was due. You are burdens to the commonwealth; like drones in the hive."[42]

THE RADICAL REPUBLICAN TRADITION

Puritanism had a fundamental impact on the attitudes of seventeenth and eighteenth century Americans. It was, however, only part of the intellectual fountain from which the Founders of the nation drank.The radical republican tradition, discussed in earlier chapters, also addressed economics and commerce, although, it must be conceded that this tradition was also influenced by Puritanism. Radical republicans believed that self-interest would be man's primary motivation in a commonwealth. They were not unaware that the individual freedom, which they championed, would, in effect, prove a catalyst to an even greater unleashing of expressions of self-interest as former restraints on individual expression, individual and group interests, and freedom of choice were relaxed.

One of the more radical changes affecting the concept of civic virtue was the gradual transfer of ultimate sovereignty from the state to God; and equally important, the decline of the belief that the state was the expression of the will of God. This change, of course, helped undermine the idea that the greatness of the state or the regime was to be served at the expense of the happiness and comfort of the people.[43] At the same time, the ideal of freedom continued to make inroads into the philosophy of the marketplace. The concept of self-interest found increasing compatibility not only with notions of common interest, but with biblical interpretation as well. The onus was being removed from intensive labor and specialization. Enterprise, it was argued, stimulated the virtues of frugality and self-restraint, and the rigor of active lives toward positive ends, while the rights of enterprise and property energized a middle class at the expense of the once-dominant and decadent aristocracy, thereby promoting freedom in all its forms and simultaneously benefiting society with its largess. Thus emerged a radical difference from classical and medieval virtues of unproductive asceticism and the honor of war. The new aquisitiveness which stimulated and gave virtue to the pursuit of well-being through commerce, trade, the professions, and the management of land, it was argued, began to replace or sublimate hoarding, greed, and avarice, while freeing growing numbers of the masses to seek their betterment in an increasingly open economic climate. The poor might escape the land and their aristocratic masters.

212 IN SEARCH OF THE REPUBLIC

Locke on Virtue and Commerce

Isaac Kramnick has argued that Locke had been influenced by
the Puritan ethic, a tradition with which he certainly was not unaware, having come from Puritan stock and having been in contact
with its doctrines both in England and while in exile in Holland. As
such, his ideas were to be included with those that influenced the
later radical reformers. "Locke," writes Kramnick, "had often written
on the themes of industry and talent and was perceived as a crucial
part of the Protestant tradition that so informed much of this reform
movement. In the libraries of the dissenting academies, Locke's
works were standard references not only for psychology and education, but also for politics and commerce. The praise of industry,"
continues Kramnick, "of what the seventeenth and eighteenth centuries considered 'skill, assiduity, perseverance and diligence,' and the
denunciation of idleness were, of course, by no means unique to
Locke. Protestant writers, especially Puritans like Baxter, had long
made them a crucial part of their notions of work, of the obligation to
labor, and of the importance of one's calling. What Locke did was
wed these earlier views to a political theory of private rights and
individualism with his argument that property was an extention of
self, the injection of personality into nature through work."

Kramnick reminds us that there were "other Lockean texts read in
these dissenting academy libraries [which] spoke to the themes of
industry, idleness, and the glory of work. Indeed, so concerned with
these themes was Locke that it is little exaggeration to suggest that he
saw industriousness as the central characteristic of the human personality, of personal behavior, and of social and personal activity."[44]
Locke, in his *Essay Concerning Human Understanding*,[45] linked activity
to anxiety, a connection not unfamiliar to later readers of Weber and
Tawney; a desire for some as yet unachieved good, which impelled
men to unrelenting activity. And, Locke's *Thoughts Concerning Education*, is, as expressed by Kramnick, "a veritable diatribe against
idleness," where emphasis is placed on the inculcation of a futuristic
attitude as a primary virtue in the young.[46] "The well Educating of
their Children is so much the Duty and Concern of Parents, and the
Welfare and Prosperity of the Nation so much depends on it," wrote Locke,
"that I would have *every one* lay it seriously to Heart; and after having
well examined and distinguished what Fancy, Custom or Reason
advises in the Case, set his Helping Hand to promote everywhere
what way of training up Youth, with regard to their several Conditions, which is the easiest, shortest, and likeliest to produce *vertuous*,
useful, and able Men in their distinct Callings."[47]

Locke's Puritan heritage is demonstrated no more conclusively than the influence of the Scriptural command to subdue the earth is evident in his concept of property. "Whether we consider natural *Reason*, which tells us that men, being once born, have a right to their preservation, and consequently to meat and drink, and such other things as Nature affords for their Subsistence: Or *Revelation*, which gives us an account of those Grants God made of the world to *Adam*, and to *Noah*, and his *Sons*. 'Tis very clear, that God, as King David says, Psal. CXV. xvi, *has given the Earth to the Children of Men*, given it to Mankind in common."[48] "God, who hath given the World to Men in common, hath also given them reason to make use of it to the best advantage of Life, and convenience. The Earth, and all that is therein, is given to Men for the Support and Comfort of their being."[49] "Every Man has a *Property* in his own Person."[50]

However, also evident in Locke's concept of government and property is the ancient concern with order and peace in society. "God hath certainly appointed *Government* to restrain the partiality and violence of men."[51] "By entering into Society and Civil Government," he wrote, men "have excluded force, and introduced Laws for the preservation of Property, Peace, and unity amongst themselves . . ."[52] rather than becoming "a confused Multitude, without Order or Connection."[53] "The Reason why men enter into Society, is the preservation of their Property; and the end why they chuse [sic] and authorize a Legislative, is, that there may be law made, and rules set as Guards and Fences to the Properties of all the Members of the Society to limit the Power, and moderate the Dominion of every Part and Member of the Society." However, should the Legislative, having been established by the consent of the people act contrary to their Trust, and *"endeavour to take away, and destroy the Property of the People,* or to reduce them to Slavery under Arbitrary Power, they put themselves into a state of War with the People, who are thereupon absolved from any further Obedience and are left to the Common Refuge, which God hath provided for all Men, against Force and Violence." When the Legislative *"endeavour to grasp themselves, or put into the hands of any other an Absolute Power* over the Lives, Liberties, and Estates of the People: By this breach of Trust they *forfeit the Power,* the People had put into their hands, for quite contrary ends, and it devolves to the People, who have a Right to resume their original Liberty, and, by the Establishment of a new Legislative (such as they shall think fit) provide for their own Safety and Security, which is the end for which they are in Society."[54]

Locke, Virtue, and Property

There is, in Locke's economic doctrines, a compatibility with the radical republican tradition, an emphasis on the importance of private property, economic freedom, and the expectation of a certain trust or moral behavior in the conduct of economic enterprise and in the relationship of property to political power. As much as Locke loved freedom and however he viewed the sanctity of private property, he did not espouse either political or economic anarchy. Here, as in the political marketplace, was needed the restraining influence of an ordered community and established law. As far as Locke was concerned, men had left the state of Nature and united into commonwealths because they needed "the Regulating and Preserving of Property."[55] The "great and chief end . . . of Men's uniting into commonwealths, and putting themselves under Government," he wrote, "is the Preservation of their Property."[56]

By property, Locke, as did the radical republicans, meant more than material possessions. He included "Lives, Liberties and Estates, which I call by the general name, Property."[57] (Madison was to include the liberty of conscience under the term.) According to Laslett, "except in the chapter on property and in other cases where it is clear that material possessions are meant, the word 'property' in the Second Treatise is usually to be read in this sense. It is the sense in which Locke's contemporaries could talk of the Protestant religion established by law as their 'property,' and Richard Baxter maintained that 'men's lives and Liberties are the chief parts of their property' though he, like Locke, sought the origin of 'property in man's industry.' "[58]

With all his emphasis on the sanctity of property and the importance of labor, Locke's religious beliefs did not allow economic activity to escape biblical injunctions of justice, mercy, and benevolence. Man is morally restrained from making a "perverse . . . use of God's Blessings poured on him with a liberal Hand."[59] According to Locke, the "Law of Nature," and "Reason, which is that Law, teaches all Mankind, who will but consult it, that being all equal and independent, no one ought to harm another in his Life, Health, Liberty, or Possessions. For Men being all the Workmanship of one Omnipotent, and infinitely Wise Maker; All the Servants of one Sovereign Master, sent into the World by his order and about his business, they are his Property, whose Workmanship they are, made to last during his, not another's Pleasure. . . . Every one as he is bound to preserve himself . . . , ought he, as much as he can, to preserve the rest of Mankind, and may not unless it be to do Justice to an Offender, take away, or impair the life, or what tends to the Preservation of the Life, Liberty, Health, Limb or Goods of Another."[60]

According to Locke, "God, [who] has given us all things richly, I Tim. vi. 17 is the voice of Reason confirmed by Inspiration"; but, that which was bestowed by God carried with it moral obligations. "Nothing was made by God for Man to Spoil or destroy."[61] When "God and his Reason commanded [man] to subdue the earth," he was obliged to "improve it for the benefit of Life . . . ,"[62] not at the expense of "another's Pains,"[63] not by entrenching "upon the right of another," or "to the Prejudice of his Neighbour," or by "Injury to any body;"[64] rather, "to increase the common stock of mankind."[65] For God "gave it to the use of the Industrious and Rational, (and *Labour* was to be *his title* to it); not to the Fancy or Covetousness of the Quarrelsom and Contentious."[66]

Locke and the Radical Republicans

As Professor Kramnick has pointed out—paraphrasing Mark Twain—"the scholarly consensus on Locke's death in the late eighteenth century is greately exaggerated." According to Kramnick, "Late eighteenth-century English reformers dramatically worked Lockean themes into the heart of their critique of traditional England, turning to Locke because The *Second Treatise of Government* was uniquely appropriate to their peculiar problem. . . . Locke's belief in the residual power of the people against their governors legitimized the reformers' campaign against the unreformed House of Commons. Locke's political theory legitimated their demands, both substantive and procedural, for a reform of the suffrage and of parliamentary representation. His concept of a limited secular magistrate legitimated their demand for the separation of church and state." These reformers found significant compatibility in Locke's ideology with their own. "No one," insists Kramnick, "had better expressed their economic and social convictions than Locke had. His socioeconomic vision was perfectly compatible with—indeed, had helped shape—their image of a world peopled by hard-working, industrious property owners."[67]

The radical republicans were not in the process of resurrecting or reconstructing the ancient past, but, rather, in creating a modern liberal-republican ideal—an ideal that presented a more realistic understanding of the nature of man, and a political philosophy encompassing principles that they believed were both universal and timeless. It is not that the ideal of virtue had ceased to be a necessary ingredient for republican government, but that it had gone through an evolutionary process that had made it more compatible with the nature of man in a "modern" world. Again, it is not a question of "either-or." Unfortunately, some who have seen the incompatibility of *classical* civic virtue with the modern republican state and with the modern system of commerce, have rejected the idea of virtue altogether. Thus, theoretically, they leave modern man in the maelstrom of crass self-interest, void of any concern with interests, problems and possibilities beyond his own immediate world of self-gratification; indeed, in a form of modern cannibalism, which would sooner or later put an end to civilized life.[68]

Kramnick insists that there was a deep "theoretical bond the reformers constructed between themselves and such Lockean themes as contract, state of nature, and natural rights and government as a trust in all of their writing on taxation and representation." Burgh began and ended his works with Locke, and in Richard Price's *Observations on the Nature of Civil Liberty* printed in 1776, the influence of Locke is unmistakable. It was with the Lockean world view that Price and others of the British radical reformers looked to America with great admiration for its maintenance of freedom, its devotion to hard work and its practice of limited government.[69]

A New Economic Ethic

Economic concepts were an integral part of the writings of the radical British reformers. It would be an anomaly had not their thinking included the economic universe, for their ideals of freedom and human dignity would certainly have been drawn to the growing involvement with man's relationship to the marketplace and the Puritan philosophy of economic endeavor. Much in line with the thinking of Protestant dissenters, the radical reformers lamented idleness and unproductiveness. Among the nonindustrious selected for criticism were those "who made money in the funds or through the manipulations of the credit system, . . . the nobility, most landed gentlemen, and the nonworking poor. The talented men of the middle class were unknowingly revising the classical, Thomistic dichotomy between a natural and artificial economy. No longer was a subsistence economy 'natural' and a market economy for profit 'artificial.' A natural economy was now characterized by productive hard work and industry, profit notwithstanding; the artificial economy was characterized by idleness and nonproductivity, and its practitioners were the useless aristocrats by birth and the equally useless parasites by profession, the money men who lived off the national debt. Protestant dissenters looked with little favor on the ill-gotten gains of gaming, whether at the table or in the funds."[70]

Among the radical republicans, both freedom and individual worth were related to the free and open marketplace. And as such, they perceived the economic phenomenon in terms of virtue—virtue that replaced sloth, beggary, idleness and covetousness on the one hand, and avarice, greed, and unproductive luxury on the other. They tended to see economics in terms of freedom from the severist restraints of class, a greatly expanded opportunity for growth by an energetic middle class (indeed, a "vision of a moral middle-class society"),[71] the encouragement of frugality, honesty, industry, and the spread of wealth, while counteracting the corruption of the aristocracy. Many radical republicans believed the free marketplace to be coterminous with political and economic decentralization, and a means by which political freedom might break the shackles of tyranny. "Freedom," confirms Joyce Appleby, "could now be construed as a universal liberation, wherein men . . . were free to define and pursue their own goals."[72]

Thus, a new economic ethic was developing in the West as a result of religious and philosophical responses to and influences upon significant changes in the social, political, and economic world. The philosophies of the Commonwealthmen, including John Locke, and the radical republicans were to contribute not only in a significant way to the struggle for freedom and the emergence of modern republicanism, but also to the rise of freedom of enterprise. These momentous events demonstrated a break from the classical experience and medieval world in a number of ways. A new emphasis on the dignity of man, on natural law and rights, on consent and dissent, on individual liberty, all spread to the world of economics. At the core of the new economics was an ideal of the dignity of labor; labor, traditionally viewed as a curse, was theoretically transformed radically to become a positive religious duty and a salutary social and personal function. In the new religious world of Europe, the ideal of a strenuously virtuous life was, in effect, becoming democratized; that is, virtuous behavior, once reserved only for the cloister was, to a significant degree, through the maturity of moral theology, becoming the responsibility of all men, thus challenging a double standard of morality. At the same time, the hard ascetic life of the Monks, which was confined to monastic orders, appeared to be, at least symbolically, transformed into a general work ethic.[73]

The absolute prohibition of usury by the Church was gradually modified and adjusted to fit the growth of the marketplace. The acquisitive motivation of man began to lose its unvirtuous connotation in the ecclesiastical condemnation of avarice, conspicuous waste, hoarding, on the one hand, while on the other, concern for finding sufficiency in this life gained greater acceptance. Capital meant reinvestment and was coincidental with free labor. The gaining of wealth in a proper manner, especially if it was accompanied by philanthropy, came to be seen as proper and as an expression of civic virtue. New emphasis was placed on the care of and duty to one's family. The Puritans were not contemptuous of the energetic poor, or those who were consigned to poverty through no fault of their own. The poor were not despised, nor was their condition considered indicative of lack of grace. And while charity was considered no less an obligation, indiscriminate alms-giving came to be seen as a possible means of perpetuating poverty and idleness. It was hoped that honest labor would diminish beggary and vagabondage, and bring man into productive activity.

Virtue, Law, and Commerce

So it was that the concept of virtue was integral to the philosophical discussion that came to surround the growth and impact of commerce. And, it should be noted, the discussion was not always on the positive side. Drew R. McCoy, in his remarkable book, *The Elusive Republic*, points out that "the eighteenth century marked a watershed in the economic as well as the intellectual history of Western Europe, for the leading thinkers of that era had to assess the impact of a commercial revolution that had transformed nearly every aspect of European society since the fifteenth century."[74] The great question, according to George Mason, was this: "If virtue is the vital principle of a republic, and it cannot long exist, without frugality, probity and strictness of morals, will the manners of populous commercial cities be favorable to the principles of our free government? Or will not the vice, the depravity of morals, the luxury, venality, and corruption, which invariably prevail in great commercial cities, be utterly subversive of them?"[75] Vigorous debates raged over "the question of whether some kind of fundamental decay was curiously inherent in social progress."[76] And although Professor Joyce Appleby correctly points out that, "the imagination of men who studied commerce was not imprisoned within the classical republican world view;" and while she has reason to write that, "Men [found] the means of talking about commerce that over time produced a language totally unassimilable to the social grammer of civic humanism,"[77] nevertheless, it should not be supposed that the idea of virtue was ejected from the philosophy or the language of the marketplace.

The discussion ranged through the extremes of thought such as the materialism and the hedonism expressed by Bernard Mandeville in his *The Fable of the Bees*, and the idea that out of the collectivity of private vices, the public benefit would actually be served; to the claim that commerce fertilized freedom, created a division of labor, and encouraged such virtues as frugality, honesty, and industriousness, including, as David Hume, Adam Smith, and Baron de Montesquieu, pointed out, a certain civilizing influence that promoted culture and made men less warlike; to the fear that the rise of modern commerce coterminously with "progress" would invariably engender wholesale corruption, vice, and all the venalities of luxury, which would prove inimical to society. Plato's warnings about luxury and Sparta's banishment of commerce were brought to mind, as was Rousseau's warning that the spread of the commercial spirit would not only destroy virtue, but stimulate inequality among men.[78]

Professor McCoy reminds us that, even among the champions of commerce, there were some misgivings, both with the potential impact of the system on virtue and the possibility that the results of a too rapid growth of the commercial phenomenon might bury traditional moral values in the maelstrom of progress. This latter possibility was of substantial concern to Thomas Jefferson.

In the contemplation of freedom and the role of virtue, the spectre of anarchy is always present. As de Tocqueville observed, when the power of the magistrate is relaxed, some other influence will be necessary to supplant his regulating power in the lives of the citizens. The same concern may be extended to the realm of economics. For Adam Smith and other commercial republicans, the idea of a spontaneous harmony of interests was not one that could be expected with perpetuity in practice. Economic intercourse did, by its very nature, develop certain norms and practices that became commonplace as a result of enlightened self-interest; that is, in commercial arrangements the need for cooperation, consistency and integrity was often an obvious and mutually beneficial one. These common practices and expectations often contributed to a more or less spontaneous order of commercial systems, especially those dealing with international exchange. And there is no doubt that many of these practices evolved into law.[79]

Nevertheless, as Adam Smith recognized, one could not count on pure spontaneous order in the economic system any more than one could expect enlightened public virtue alone to uphold the political system. In both areas there was also the need for legal process and restraint to ensure order, security, and consistency. So, while Smith, as with Hume and Montesquieu, was convinced that the commercial system of free economic exchange did, indeed, prove a catalyst to the expression of virtuous social character traits, he also feared that the new emerging commercial society might open up new, unforeseen, and unanticipated opportunities for unencumbered private interests to operate against the common or public good.

Again, even the most avid of the radical republicans did not rest their case solely on the checking of interest with interest. None of them believed that a commercial republic could be based upon an untempered and unrestrained expression of self-interest. There was needed as well the restraint and regularity of good law and the normative moral influence of other institutions of society, such as the family, the church, the school, and other voluntary organizations and associations. Certainly, the character of an economic system will be deeply influenced by a "common subscription to" certain "princi-ples," and "a higher-order identification of worthy objectives to be pursued in common."[80]

The marketplace was seen to function as a positive structure in society to the extent that it was fully integrated into the community and to the extent that its practices were regularized by law, thus restraining its most extreme expressions, while carefully preserving the core of its creative, competitive, and productive freedom and protecting the rights associated with it. However, as with all struc-tures of society—social, economic, religious, and political—the mar-ketplace was an institution that involved the interaction of men. Therefore, some other means of restraint was needed other than competition or legal regulations. In a republic, at least, men could abuse their freedoms, in spite of constitutions, laws, and courts. It was much the same in the market economic system of freedom of enterprise. In the case of the economic as well as other structures of society, continued abuses of freedom in the interactive process of men may well engender a counterforce by the state, characterized by increasingly restrictive laws, rules, regulations, and a compensating growth in its police function. Such a situation may also afford legiti-macy to the advocacy of those in every age who are uncomfortable with the vagaries of freedom and feel more secure in a centrally directed political system. And, since the state is the primary order-maintaining system of society, it can be expected to respond to threats against that order.

The free marketplace, in order to remain free and competitive over time, must have a further ingredient beyond legally sanctioned relationships, or the spontaneous order that appears as the output of a general and competitive self-interest. Adam Smith was among those who recognized this. If he accepted the inherent sociability of human beings or the naturalness of the political community, he did not believe that these two phenomena were wholly spontaneous. Another crucial ingredient contributing to a relatively spontaneous order in any social, economic or political context was absolutely essential—*virtue*.

Adam Smith, Virtue and Economics

Adam Smith's *The Theory of Moral Sentiments* was first published in 1759. It was based on his lectures in moral philosophy at the University of Glasgow, which also served as the basis for *The Wealth of Nations*, published in 1776.[81] Smith was greatly influenced by the writings of David Hume and others, and like Hume, sought to demonstrate that commercial activity promoted personal liberty.[82] His writings were well received in his day: *The Theory of Moral Sentiments* was highly praised by Hume, Burke, and others of his contemporaries. In *The Theory of Moral Sentiments*, Smith presented a blend of pragmatic and theoretical ideas, infused with the influence of Christianity, on ethics and the role of individuals in society. He sought to devise a "system of justice" or rules for human conduct; for Smith, the creation of political institutions was essential for a harmonious society. The purpose of a constitution was to develop and articulate a consensus in society. This did not require a unified, homogeneous population in the classical mode, but, rather, an effort at finding common values among diverse individuals.[83]

Smith's primary concern, however, focused on the nature of a virtuous life. A virtuous life included a balance between the values of prudence, justice, and benevolence and provided the basis for social order and social life. "The man who acts according to the rules of perfect prudence, of strict justice, and of proper benevolence," he wrote, "may be said to be perfectly virtuous."[84] Prudence rested on the necessity of self-preservation, as individuals naturally had to be concerned with survival. However, he rejected the view that "disinterested benevolence is the only motive which can stamp upon any action the character of virtue."[85] "Concern for our own happiness recommends to us the virtue of prudence," he argued. "[T]he first of those three virtues is originally recommended to us by our selfish, the other two by our benevolent affections. Regard to the sentiments of other people, however, comes afterwards both to enforce and to direct the practice of all those virtues."[86]

These three virtues were not inconsistent and were to be cultivated together. Justice, "the most important of all the virtues" according to Smith, "is no more than discreet and prudent conduct with regard to our neighbours." Justice involved both a negative and a positive perspective. Individuals were to "abstain from what is another's" since by doing otherwise they would "provoke the resentment and indignation of mankind" and destroy the "security and tranquility of [their] mind." Justice also "consists in doing proper good offices to different persons." "To act properly in all these different relations," Smith argued, "procures us the esteem and love of those we live with . . . to be amiable, to be respectable, to be the proper object of esteem, is by every well-disposed mind more valued than all the ease and security which love, respect, and esteem can procure us."[87]

Benevolence or beneficence relied on voluntary efforts to be concerned with others more than self, "to restrain our selfish, and to indulge our benevolent, affections constitutes the perfection of human nature; *and can alone* produce among mankind that harmony of sentiments and passions in which consists their whole grace and propriety."[88] "[P]roper benevolence," he wrote, "is the most graceful and agreeable of all the affections; that it is recommended to us by a double sympathy; that as its tendency is necessarily beneficent, it is the proper object of gratitude and reward; and that, upon all these accounts, it appears to our natural sentiments to possess a merit superior to any other."[89] Self-interest, the fair treatment of others, and benevolence were, for Smith, consistent and complementary ideals.

A virtuous citizenry made self-government possible. "The wise and virtuous man is at all times willing that his own private interest should be sacrificed to the public interest of his own particular order or society." "The administration of the great system of the universe," Smith argued, "is the business of God. . . . To man is alloted a much humbler department . . . the care of his own happiness, of that of his family, his friends, his country."[90] "The love of country seems," he wrote, "to involve it in two different principles; first, a certain respect and reverence for that constitution or form of government which is actually established; and secondly, an earnest desire to render the condition of our fellow-citizens as safe, respectable, and happy as we can. He is not a citizen who is not disposed to respect the laws and to obey the civil magistrate; and he is certainly not a good citizen who does not wish to promote, by every means in his power, the welfare of the whole society of his fellow-citizens."[91]

The motivation for beneficence comes, in part, according to Smith, from the "Impartial Spectator" or "internal spectator," a "guiding light" or "conscience." Man's inner feelings incline him to be sympathetic toward others; man is, by nature, a social animal, and moderates his passions and concerns as he lives with others. Individuals seek excellence as a result of a desire to increase their self-respect and merit the respect of others.[92] Religion, of course, assumed a central role in Smith's argument. Man's responsibility was to "cooperate with the Deity, and to advance as far as in our power the plan of Providence." All interests "should be sacrificed to the greater interest of the universe, to the interest of that great society of all sensible and intelligent beings, of which God himself is the immediate administrator and director." "The idea of that divine being," he wrote, "is certainly, of all the objects of human contemplation, by far the most sublime."[93] Mankind was expected to demonstrate "magnanimous resignation to the will of the great Director of the universe."[94]

The Wealth of Nations was written for a different purpose than was *The Theory of Moral Sentiments*, yet Smith's ideas are consistent across his writings. *The Wealth of Nations* was written to explain to members of Parliament and others the nature of a commercial society and what governments and others might do to foster economic growth and national prosperity. It does not provide a detailed statement of the moral qualities of people that were, for him, the preconditions for free enterprise or market economics. That explanation had already been provided in *The Theory of Moral Sentiments*.[95]

VIRTUE AND THE AMERICAN COMMERCIAL REPUBLIC

The radical republican sentiments concerning the freedom of property, both physical and philosophical or spiritual, came to be deeply ingrained into the sinews of American republicanism. Madison was among those "new men of commerce"—Montesquieu, John Adams, Adam Smith, Benjamin Franklin, David Hume, Benjamin Rush, etc.—who, according to Ralph Lerner, "were united at least in this: that they saw in commercial republicanism a more sensible and realizable alternative to earlier notions of civic virtue and a more just alternative to the theological-political regime that had so long ruled Europe and its colonial periphery. However much these advocates differed—in their philosophic insight, in their perception of the implications of their proposals for the organization of economic life, even in the degree of their acceptance of the very commercial republic they were promoting—for all of this, they may be considered a band of brethren in arms."[96]

The commercial republicans believed that the new commerce directed men's passions away from the conflict and cruelty once associated with class antagonism or with ideological or ecclesiastical conflict, toward the expending of energy in one's particular calling. This, it was believed, helped to maintain order and equilibrium while promoting freedom of the individual, and helped sponsor the development of standard commercial practices and *quid pro quo* relationships, legal precedence and expected practices, even a language of commerce that contributed to the regularity and consistency in the relations between nations. According to Professor Lerner, the commercial republic "tended to ignore or transcend the conventional divisions within nations and among them. Its eighteenth-century proponents could realistically urge men to consider their larger independence without expecting (or even desiring) the neglect of national interest and identity, for commerce, properly understood and reasonably conducted, would serve both man and citizen. . . . Even as each labored intently to satisfy his own wants, men would become commercial cousins, cool fellow-citizens of a universal republic."[97] As Hume put it, where traditionally men had "lived almost in a continual state of war with their neighbors, and of servile dependency upon their superiors," now there existed the possibility of "order and good government, and with them, the liberty and security of individuals," thus leading to an elevation of the whole.[98] So it was that "even the humblest man, by adopting and acting on commercial maxims, might serve himself and thereby the public good."[99]

The commercial republicans perceived the development of variety and opportunity and a breakdown of the severest class divisions in the commercial phenomenon. For the masses, this provided the potential of "escape from the mediocrity of one's station."[100] Here was an alternative to the traditional form of beggary, laziness, and poverty on the one hand, and extravagance, avarice, and vanity on the other. Indeed, "the commercial republicans thought they were returning to simple reason."[101] Instead of eternal conflict between irreconcilable class divisions, interest would be greatly splintered and decentralized as desperation over poverty and wide property inequalities would give way to an ever-expanding diversity of opportunity in the marketplace. At the very least, the passion born of desperation might give way to the normal unhappiness experienced by most people. At best, the new commercial system could both stimulate wants and to some degree satisfy them. And the icing on the cake was a quiet form of virtue resembling the Puritan ethic, which encouraged private energy and dedication in man—circumscribed to a reasonable degree by personal frugality and prudence—and a futuristic attitude whereby he "deferred present ease for greater enjoyment later." He would seek incremental gains; "The energies set in motion would bring forth an array of small comforts and conveniences beyond the reach or imagining of serf or savage, relieving miseries once thought fated."[102]

Thus, the rise of the modern commercial state allowed American statesmen to form their ideas in a time of decline in rigid class distinctions, with the simultaneous growth of an active and obstinate middle class, and the growing diversification and variety of property and economic or commercial pursuit. Hamilton argued that "The often-agitated question between agriculture and commerce has from indubitable experience received a decision which has silenced the rivalships that once subsisted between them, and has proved, to the entire satisfaction of their friends, that their interests are intimately blended and interwoven. It has been found in various countries that in proportion as commerce has flourished, land has risen in value. And how could it have happened otherwise?" he asked. "Could that which procures a freer vent for the products of the earth, which furnishes new enticements to the cultivators of the land, which is the most powerful instrument in increasing the quantity of money in a state—could that, in fine, which is the faithful handmaid of labor and industry in every shape fail to augment the value of that article, which is the prolific parent of far the greatest part of the objects upon which they are exerted?"[103]

Still, many of the American Founders were concerned with the negative potential of modern commercial economics. What would there be to restrain man from turning his new-found productivity into excess, vanity, gluttony? Would the growth of economic largess drive man to degeneracy, hedonism and, finally, loss of freedom? Would society be as bad off as, or worse than before? In his letter to Thomas Jefferson dated December 18, 1819, John Adams queried, "Will you tell me how to prevent riches from becoming the effects of temperance and industry? Will you tell me how to prevent riches from producing luxury? Will you tell me how to prevent luxury from producing effeminacy, intoxication, extravagance, vice and folly?"[104] It was Thomas Jefferson who had warned during the Revolution: "From the conclusion of this War, we shall all be going downhill and these people will forget themselves, but in the sole faculty of making money."[105]

These republicans, however, equated the new economics with freedom, their primary goal; in spite of their concern with the dangers of wealth and the abuse of property, they naturally accepted the concepts of freedom of choice and the right of property. They were clear advocates of Locke's theory that government should protect those rights. Without the guarantee of the right of property in the widest possible sense, political freedom could not be guaranteed. The task was to take the givens of the modern commercial system and the nature of man and provide a means whereby they might contribute to the republican system. They were forward rather than backward looking. For example, Appleby warns us not to make the rather common error of placing even the cautious, concerned Jefferson in the realm of "agrarian nostalgia." In spite of their concerns, Jeffersonian Republicans promoted commercial agriculture, international trade, and economic progress.[106]

Property and Freedom

Locke and the British radical republicans exerted a profound influence on the philosophies of Madison, Hamilton, Adams, and Jefferson. The American architects accepted private property as a basic condition of human freedom, that it was the responsibility of government to protect the possessions of its citizens and their persons from both foreign and domestic threats. "Property is surely a right of mankind as real as liberty," expounded John Adams. "The moment the idea is admitted into society that property is not as sacred as the laws of God, and that there is not a force of law and public justice to protect it, anarchy and tyranny commense. Property must be secured or liberty cannot exist."[107]

Madison, as had Locke, expanded the term "property" to embrace "everything to which a man may attach a value and have a right, and which leaves to everyone else the like advantage. In the former sense, a man's land or merchandise, or money, is called property. In the latter sense, a man has property in his opinions and the free communication of them. He has," continued Madison, "a property of peculiar value in his religious opinions and the free communication of them, and in the profession and practice dictated by them. He has a property very dear to him in the safety and liberty of his person. He has an equal property in the free use of his facilities, and free choice of the objects on which to employ them. In a word, as a man is said to have a right to his property, he may be equally said to have a property in his rights."[108] And, in the tradition of Locke, Madison also portrayed government as no less the protector of property than of persons. "Government," stated Madison, "is instituted to protect property of every sort. . . . This being the end of government, that alone is a just government, which impartially secures to every man, whatever is his own. . . . That is not a just government . . . nor is property secure under it, where the property which a man has in his personal safety and personal liberty, is violated by arbitrary seizures of one class of citizens for the service of the rest."[109] One of Madison's great concerns with the value of an extended republic over a small one was that "A rage for paper money, for an abolition of debts, for an equal division of property, or for any other improper or wicked project, will be less apt to pervade the whole body of the Union" in the former.[110]

The radical American republicans thus sought to keep government interference with commerce at a minimum. "Why should we fetter commerce?" asked Patrick Henry. "If a man is in chains, he droops and bows to the earth, for his spirits are broken . . . but let him twist the fetters from his legs and he will stand erect. . . . Fetter not commerce—let her be as free as air."[111] As this philosophy evolved, the retrenchment of both Madison and Jefferson over the suggestion by Hamilton that the federal government extend its fostering care in terms of financial support to America's still-infant industry is best understood. Hamilton, himself, explained his opposition's point of view as well as anyone: "To *endeavor*, by the . . . *patronage of government*, to accelerate the *growth* of *manufactures*, is in fact to endeavor, by force, . . . to transfer the *natural current* of industry from a *more* to a *less* beneficial channel. . . . Such a tendency must *necessarily* be unwise; indeed, it can *hardly ever be wise* in a government to attempt to give direction to the industry of the citizens. This, under the quick-sighted guidance of *private interest*, will, if left to itself, infallibly find its own way to the most profitable employment; and it is by such employment, that the public prosperity will be most effectually promoted. To leave industry to *itself*, therefore, is, *in almost every case*, the *soundest* as well as the simplest policy."[112]

Nevertheless, as had the radical republicans before them, the American Founders rejected, or probably never entertained, any ideas of economic anarchism. They believed that the commercial system, both for its own protection and for the protection of society, needed to be integrated into that society by settled practices, expectations, and the rule of law. The market for goods; the investment of capital and rules of honest exchange; the promulgation of contracts, patents, and titles to property; the integrity of weights and measures and the quality of goods; the reasonableness of taxes and duties; and the guarantee of the movement of goods across state boundaries, all came to be seen as fit measures to fall under the aegis of law. Nor should we lose track of the expectation of virtue in the citizen which the Founders entertained. *They did not suggest that an individual or a group should pursue its own self-interest to the injury of others, just as long as it did not violate the law. The individual was expected to be morally responsible for his social conscience and comportment as well.*

Neither did they believe that sheer competition between economic factions would engender a consistent and peaceful equilibrium. Nor did they suppose that the freedom of enterprise they supported meant the separation of the economic system from society. Professor McCoy reminds us of the term "political economy," which was used more extensively then than now. In a general sense, writes McCoy, "the concept . . . signified the necessary existence of a close relationship between the government, or the polity, and the social and economic order. Thus to the Revolutionaries in America, the notion of 'political economy' reinforced the characteristically republican idea of a dynamic interdependence among polity, economy, and society." Continuing, McCoy writes, "eighteenth-century thinkers also generally considered political economy under the broader rubric of moral philosophy. Before 'economics' achieved the dubious status of pure science, it was not common practice to separate economics and ethics. The Revolutionaries lived during an age when a consideration of the normative dimension of economic life had not yet been sacrificed to the hubris of those who would claim to make economics into a 'nonmoral' science."[113] McCoy's research has led him to the conclusion that, "above all, the Revolutionaries were acutely aware of the moral dimension of economic life, for they seemed obsessed with the idea that a republican polity required popular virtue for its stability and success:"

> Simply stated, they assumed that a healthy republican government demanded an economic and social order that would encourage the

shaping of a virtuous citizenry. In this sense, once the Revolutionaries succeeded in establishing independence from the British Empire, they had to do much more than merely define and put into practice the proper constitutional principles of republican government. They had to define, and then attempt to secure, a form of economy and society that would be capable of sustaining the virtuous character of a republican citizenry. They had to establish, in short, a republican system of political economy for America. . . . Because a commitment to republican government demanded attention to the more general question of the structure and character of society, American statesmen were intensely concerned with the broader social and moral implications of the policies they pursued. In their quest to build a republican economy and society, therefore, they could perceive intimate connections between such seemingly remote and discrete matters as, for example, the need to open export markets for American produce and the need to sustain the virtuous character of a republican people.[11]

THE EXTENDED COMMERCIAL REPUBLIC

The American Founders perceived the new republic in terms of the multiple differences in men; not just economic differences, but individual human differences as well, many of which overlayed those economic differences. If their system were to be based upon freedom, then human differences would not only have to be tolerated, they would have to be protected. The result would naturally be a substantial growth in the number and diversity of factions. Madison could not change the fact that the "latent causes of faction" were "sown in the nature of man," and that "we see them everywhere brought into different degrees of activity, according to the different circumstances of civil society. The regulation of these various and interfering interests," wrote Madison, would have to be "the principal task of modern legislation and involves the spirit of party and faction in the necessary and ordinary operations of government."

Madison saw clearly that a system of freedom must recognize the "diversity in the faculties of men, from which the rights of property originate," and that a government embodying that philosophy would have as its "first object," the "protection of these faculties." "From the protection of different and unequal faculties of acquiring property," he reasoned, "the possession of *different degrees and kinds* of property immediately results; and from the influence of these on the sentiments and views of the respective proprietors ensues a division of the society into different interests and parties." It was in the shift of conflict from the class struggle over great inequalities between "those who hold and those who are without property," i.e., between the rich and the poor, to "different degrees and kinds of property," that

Madison hoped a change in the character of factional conflict would emerge, whereby its "effects" might be controlled.[115]

Here Madison was writing not about the traditional factious and class conflict, but about a new stimulus for factions of a modern kind, related to the rise of the modern state and modern commerce. In effect, he was advocating "an economic system that allows all citizens freely to acquire, possess, and dispose of private property, and encourages them to devote themselves to the pursuit and enjoyment of wealth."[116] "To judge from the overall character of *The Federalist*," concurs Robert Horwitz, "it is evident that what Madison was pointing to here was the creation of a large commercial republic, one within which the widest possible range of interests would be fostered. No attempt would be made to restrain what Machiavelli bluntly described as 'man's natural desire to acquire.' On the contrary, acquisitiveness would be encouraged, and the citizenry given free scope in developing the abundant resources of a new country. Every form of agricultural, manufacturing, and commercial enterprise would be encouraged. The guiding and energizing principle of the community would be the vigorous pursuit of individual self-interest."[117]

In his efforts, Madison was not without some assistance, for a new era was dawning. By the time he began to form his constitutional ideas, he was able to draw not only upon the experience and the thought of Europe, particularly England and Scotland, but he could take account of the political and economic vagaries in his own world. Madison's greatness was not the result of his having created a political and an economic system, as it were, from scratch. His unmatched contribution to republican government, and hence to modern freedom, lay in his genius of perceiving the phenomenal forces already in motion, and then molding or directing them into practical manifestations. His lack of utopian fantasy, his grasp of the reality of the world in which he lived and the common nature of those who dwelt upon it, and the forces which motivated them, provided him with the background and the tools to design and bring forth a modern republic.

Basic to radical commercial thought was Locke's inference that men sought not only the protection of property, but the right and the opportunity to expand their possessions. Thus, not just the *having*, but the *getting* process itself was valuable. That Madison was in agreement with this concept is made obvious by *The Federalist* No. 10. "Moreover," suggests Professor Gary J. Schmitt, "it is plausible that Jefferson's substitution of 'pursuit of happiness' for 'property' was generated by the Virginian's own insight into what Locke's teaching on property really meant. Briefly stated, Locke taught that men leave the state of nature and seek the guarantees of society not only to keep what they have but to multiply it as well. The right to expand one's possessions, the right to acquire plenty, does not seem to be adequately captured by the static-sounding term 'property.' The essence of Locke's thought is more accurately reflected in Jefferson's use, intentional or not, of the dynamic word 'pursuit.' "[118]

It was in the multiplicity of factions—based on a modern economics that tames the blatant struggle over the *"inequality"* of property by replacing it with a modern system of factions based on a *"multiplicity of interests"* derived from a *variety* of property and enterprise and the pursuit thereof—that Madison saw the potential success of an extended commercial republic. Here the great number of factions would tend to act as a check upon each other; the greater the diversity of economic pursuits, the more difficult to form into a lasting political or class-based majority coalition at the expense of the minority factions. At the same time, the exigencies of freedom might be met and the "pursuit of happiness" guaranteed to an increasing number of citizens. And, after all, a moderately virtuous citizenry might instil within the system a spirit of moral expectation that would contribute both to its stability, and, its longevity.

NOTES

1. Edmund Morgan, "The Puritan Ethic and the American Revolution," *William and Mary Quarterly*, Vol. 24 (January 1967), pp. 4–5.

2. *Ibid.*, p. 7.

3. Julian Boyd et al., *The Papers of Thomas Jefferson*, Vol. 11 (Princeton: Princeton University Press, 1955), pp. 250, 349.

4. Clarence H. Faust and Thomas H. Johnson, eds., *Jonathan Edwards: Representative Selections* (New York: American Book, 1933), pp. 352–53.

5. The influence of this reasoning was later seen in Jefferson—"The essence of virtue is doing good to others" (Cappon, ed., *Adams-Jefferson Letters*, Vol. 2, p. 492.)—and in Hamilton who wrote in *The Federalist* No. 1 that philanthropy, or love of mankind, was an integral part of American patriotism.

6. Bernard Bailyn, *The New England Merchants in the Seventeenth Century* (Cambridge: Harvard University Press, 1955), p. 23. See also Bernard and Lottie Bailyn, *Massachusetts Shipping 1697–1714* (Cambridge: Harvard University Press, 1959).

7. *Ibid.*, p. 91.

8. Edmund Burke, *The Works of the Right Honorable Edmund Burke*, Vol. 2 (Boston: Little, Brown, 1889), pp. 30–31.

9. Some of the studies of capitalism and religion include: Max Weber, *The Protestant Ethic and the Spirit of Capitalism*, (trans. Talcott Parsons, New York: Scribner, 1930); Robert W. Green, *Protestantism and Capitalism* (Boston: Heath, 1959); Perry Miller and Thomas H. Johnson, eds., *The Puritans* (New York: Harper and Row, 1938); Max Savelle, *Seeds of Liberty: The Genesis of the American Mind*

(New York: Knopf, 1948); Aminatore Fanfani, *Catholicism, Protestantism, and Capitalism* (New York: Sheed and Ward, 1955); Sidney A. Burrell, "Calvinism, Capitalism, and Middle Classes," *The Journal of Modern History*, Vol. 32 (June, 1960); and R. H. Tawney, *Religion and the Rise of Capitalism* (New York: Harcourt, Brace, 1926). Irving S. Michelman, *The Roots of Capitalism in Western Civilization: A Socioeconomic Assessment* (New York: Frederick Fell Publisher, 1983); Winthrop S. Hudson, "Puritanism and the Spirit of Capitalism," *Church History*, Vol. 18 (March, 1949).

10. Tawney, *Religion and the Rise of Capitalism*, p. 69. "[T]he new world of the sixteenth century took its character from the outburst of economic energy in which it had been born." H. M. Robertson, *The Rise of Economic Individualism* (Cambridge: University of Cambridge Press, 1933); P. C. Gordon Walker, "Capitalism and the Reformation," *The Economic History Review*, Vol. 8 (November, 1937).

11. David Little, "The Protestant Ethic and the Puritan Experience of Order," *Harvard Theological Review*, Vol. 59 (1966), pp. 417, 421; *Religion, Order and Law* (New York: Harper and Row, 1969), pp. 222–23.

12. Franklin, *Autobiography*, pp. 330–31.

13. Rossiter, *The First American Revolution*, pp. 215–17.

14. Perry Miller, *The New England Mind: The Seventeenth Century*, pp. 398–99; David Little, "The Protestant Ethic," p. 421.

15. Cotton Mather, *A Christian at His Calling: Two Brief Discourses, One Directing a Christian in his General Calling; Another Directing him in his Personal Calling* (Boston: B. Green and J. Allen, 1701), p. 38 (italics in the original).

16. Keith L. Sprunger, *The Learned Doctor William Ames* (Urbana: University of Illinois Press, 1972), p. 144.

17. William Gouge, *The Whole Armor of God, or, The Spiritual Furniture Which God Hath Provided to Keep Safe Every Christian Soldier From All the Assaults of Satan* (London: John Beale, 1616), p. 392.

18. William Gouge, *The Saints Support, A Sermon Preached Before the Honorable House of Commons Assembled in Parliament at a Publick Fast* (London: Printed by G. M. for Joshua Kirkton, June 29, 1642), p. 13.

19. *Ibid.*

20. *Ibid.*, p. 27.

21. *Ibid.*, p. 21.

22. *Ibid.*, p. 24.

23. *Ibid.*, p. 25.

24. *Ibid.*, p. 23.

25. *Ibid.*, p. 21.

26. According to J. Wayne Baker, "The Covenant in all ages had taught faith in God and love of the neighbor, as evidenced in the Scriptures, the record of the Covenant. Gospel and law, then, played the same roles in the Covenant both before and after Christ." "Heinrich Bullinger and the Idea of Usury," *Sixteenth Century Journal*, Vol. 5 (April 1974), p. 68.

27. William Ames, *Conscience with the Power and the Cases Thereof* (Norwood, N.J.: Walter J. Johnson, 1975), p. 253; Timothy Hall Breen, "The Nonexistent Controversy: Puritan and Anglican Attitudes on Work and Wealth, 1600–1640," *Church History*, Vol. 35 (Sept. 1966), p. 283.

28. Richard Sibbes, *The Works of Richard Sibbes* (London: Nichol's Series of Standard Divines, 1862–1864), Vol. 4, p. 508; Breen, "The Nonexistent Controversy," p. 283.

29. *The Works of William Chillingworth*, Sermon VI (London: Printed for D. Medwinter, 1742), p. 68; Breen, "The Nonexistent Controversy," p. 283.

30. Baker, "Heinrich Bullinger and the Idea of Usury," pp. 58–59.

31. Sibbes, *Complete Works of Richard Sibbes*, Vol. 6, p. 251.

32. Richard Baxter, *A Christian Directory: or, a Body of Practical Divinity, and Cases of Consciences*, Vol. 2 (London: Richard Edwards, 1825). p. 73.
33. *Ibid.*, p. 585. Here Baxter quotes Proverbs 23:24.
34. *Ibid.*, p. 584.
35. *Ibid.*, p. 578.
36. Tawney, *Religion and The Rise of Capitalism*, p. 241.
37. Baxter, *A Christian Directory*, p. 583.
38. *Ibid.*, pp. 586–87.
39. *Ibid.*, p. 591.
40. *Ibid.*, p. 580.
41. *Ibid.*, p. 158.
42. *Ibid.*, p. 592.
43. Ralph Lerner, "Commerce and Character: The Anglo-American as New-Model Man," *William and Mary Quarterly*, Vol. 36 (January 1979), p. 12.
44. Kramnick, "Republicanism Revisionism Revisited," p. 657.
45. John Locke, *An Essay Concerning Human Understanding*, ed., A. C. Fraser, Vol. 2 (Oxford: Oxford University Press, 1894), Book 20, Section 6.
46. Kramnick, "Republican Revisionism Revisited," p. 658.
47. John Locke, *Some Thoughts Concerning Education* (Cambridge: Cambridge University Press, 1892), Sections 110–13 (italics added).
48. John Locke, *Two Treatises of Government*, with introduction and notes by Peter Laslett, "The Second Treatise," Vol. 2, Section 25 (Cambridge: Cambridge University Press, 1963).
49. *Ibid.*, Section 26.
50. *Ibid.*, Section 27 (italics in the original).
51. *Ibid.*, Section 13 (italics added).
52. *Ibid.*, Section 226.
53. *Ibid.*, Section 219.
54. *Ibid.*, Section 222 (italics in the original).
55. *Ibid.*, Section 3.
56. *Ibid.*, Section 124 (italics in the original).
57. *Ibid.*, Section 123. He also included money. See *ibid.*, Sections 37 and 49 (italics in the original).
58. *Ibid.*, "Introduction" by Laslett, pp. 115–16.
59. *Ibid.*, Vol. 1, Section 43.
60. *Ibid.*, Vol. 2, Section 6 (italics in the original).
61. *Ibid.*, Section 31 (italics in the original).
62. *Ibid.*, Section 32.
63. *Ibid.*, Section 34.
64. *Ibid.*, Section 36.
65. *Ibid.*, Section 37.
66. *Ibid.*, Section 34 (italics in the original).
67. Kramnick, "Republican Revisionism Revisited," pp. 655–57.
68. Among the most important of the radical republicans and their writings were James Burgh (*Political Disinquisitions: An Enquiry into Public Errors, Defects, and Abuses*, 3 vols., 1774); Richard Price (*Observations on the Nature of Civil Liberty, the Principles of Government, and the Justice and Policy of the War with America*, 1776; *An Appeal to the Public on the Subject of the National Debt*, 1771; and *Observations on the Importance of the American Revolution and the Means of Making It a Benefit to the World*, 1784); Tooke (*Causes and Effects of the National Debt and Paper Money in Real and Natural Property in the Present State of Civil Society*, 1795); and Joseph Priestly (*An Essay on the First Principles of Government and on the Nature of Political, Civil, and Religious Liberty*, 1771; and *Lectures on History and General Policy*, 1788).
69. Kramnick, "Republican Revisionism Revisited," p. 639.
70. *Ibid.*, p. 643.

71. *Ibid.*, p. 644.

72. Appleby, "Republicanism in Old and New Contexts," p. 31.

73. "Physical asceticism in all its forms is abandoned. More important, the ordinary domiciles and the usual occupations of the world are not to be fled or eschewed in the effort to achieve the utmost reaches of spiritual fulfillment. The intense forms of religious experience, instead of being isolated in monastic cells, are to be brought into the housewife's kitchen and carpenter's shop, the merchant's counting house, and the magistrate's palace." Charles and Katherine George," "Protestantism and Capitalism in Pre-Revolutionary England," *Church History*, Vol. 27 (December 1958), p. 354.

74. Drew R. McCoy, *The Elusive Republic: Political Economy In Jeffersonian America* (Chapel Hill: University of North Carolina Press, 1980), p. 17.

75. Robert A. Rutland, ed., *The Papers of George Mason, 1725–1792*, Vol. 2 (Chapel Hill: University of North Carolina Press, 1970), p. 862; Drew R. McCoy, "The Virginia Port Bill of 1784," *Virginia Magazine of History and Biography*, Vol. 83 (1975), pp. 228–303; McCoy, *The Elusive Republic*, p. 16.

76. McCoy, *The Elusive Republic*, p. 17.

77. Appleby, "Republicanism in Old and New Contexts," pp. 31, 33.

78. See discussion in McCoy, *The Elusive Republic*, p. 17, pp. 13–104; David Hume, *Writings on Economics*, edited with introduction by Eugene Rotwein (Madison: University of Wisconsin Press, 1955), especially the editor's introduction, pp. ix–liii; and Hume's Essays on "Commerce," and "Refinement in the Arts," pp. 3–32.

79. See Leon Trakman, *The Law Merchant: The Evolution of Commercial Law* (Littleton, Colorado: Fred Rothman, 1983); William Mitchell, *An Essay on the Early History of the Law Merchant* (New York: B. Franklin, 1969); Norman Barry, "The Tradition of Spontaneous Order," *Literature of Liberty*, Vol. V (Summer, 1982), pp. 7–58; Peter Stein, *Legal Evolution: The Story of an Idea* (New York: Cambridge University Press, 1980).

80. James P. O'Leary, "Political Regimes and Economic Markets," *The Intercollegiate Review*, Vol. 19 (Fall 1983), p. 43.

81. Adam Smith, *The Theory of Moral Sentiments*, with an introduction by E. G. West (Indianapolis: Liberty Classics, 1976), pp. 18–20; *An Inquiry into the Nature and Course of the Wealth of Nations*, edited by Edwin Cannan, with an introduction by Max Lerner (New York: The Modern Library, 1965), pp. vi–vii.

82. Edward J. Harpham, "Liberalism, Civic Humanism, and the Case of Adam Smith," *American Political Science Review*," Vol. 78 (1984), pp. 764–74.

83. Smith, *Moral Sentiments*, pp. 24–25.

84. *Ibid.*, p. 387.

85. *Ibid.*, p. 431.

86. *Ibid.*, p. 422.

87. *Ibid.*, pp. 471–72.

88. *Ibid.*, pp. 71–72 (italics added).

89. *Ibid.*, p. 477.

90. *Ibid.*, p. 386.

91. *Ibid.*, p. 377.

92. *Ibid.*, pp. 31–33.

93. *Ibid.*, pp. 384–85.

94. *Ibid.*, p. 384.

95. Smith's *Wealth of Nations* is often misinterpreted because of the lack of understanding *The Theory of Moral Sentiments*. See A. L. Macfie, "Adam Smith's *Moral Sentiments* as foundation for His *Wealth of Nations*," in A. L. Macfie, ed., *The Individual in Society* (London: Allen and Unwin, 1967), pp. 59–81; Glenn R. Morrow, *The Ethical and Economic Theories of Adam Smith: A Study of the Social Philosophy of the Eighteenth Century* (New York: A. M. Kelley, 1969).

96. Ralph Lerner, "Commerce and Character: The Anglo-American as a New-Model Man," p. 3.

97. *Ibid.*, pp. 10–11.

98. Hume, "Of Refinement in the Arts," Essays, pp. 280–81, 283–84; Lerner, p. 15.

99. Lerner, "Commerce and Character," p. 15.

100. *Ibid.*, p. 16.

101. *Ibid.*, p. 8.

102. *Ibid.*, p. 9.

103. *The Federalist*, No. 12.

104. Cappon, ed., *Adams-Jefferson Letters*, Vol. 2, p. 551. Paul Wilstach, ed., *Correspondence of John Adams and Thomas Jefferson, 1812–1826* (Indianapolis: Bobbs-Merrill, 1925), p. 170.

105. *The Works of Thomas Jefferson*, Vol. 4 (Federal Edition), pp. 81–82.

106. Joyce Appleby, "Commercial Farming and the 'Agrarian Myth' in the Early Republic," *Journal of American History*, Vol. 68 (1982). See analysis by Banning, "Jeffersonian Ideology Revisited," pp. 3–19.

107. C. F. Adams, *The Works of John Adams*, Vol. 6, pp. 8–9, 280.

108. Hunt, ed., *The Writings of James Madison*, Vol. 4, pp. 478–79.

109. Padover, *The Complete Madison*, pp. 267–68.

110. *The Federalist*, No. 10.

111. William Wirt, *Sketches of the Life and Character of Patrick Henry* (Philadelphia: Desilver, Thomas, 1836), p. 255.

112. Harold C. Syrett, ed., *The Papers of Alexander Hamilton*, Vol. 10 (New York: Columbia University Press, 1966), p. 232. The quote is taken from Hamilton's final version of "The Report on the Subject of Manufactures, 1791–1792." See Adrienne Koch's excellent discussion of this subject in *Jefferson and Madison: The Great Collaboration* (New York: Oxford University Press, 1964), especially Chapter 5, pp. 97–134. Jefferson and Madison "saw Hamilton's proposal as the culmination of a financial and political program that would give unconstitutional power to the general government to be used mainly for the protection of speculators, promotors, and moneyed merchants at the expense of more than nine tenths of the people. The logic of their protest was suited to a government of, by, and for the people and is a significant early phase of republican ideology in this country" (p. 134).

113. McCoy, *The Elusive Republic*, p. 6.

114. *Ibid.*, pp. 7–8.

115. *The Federalist*, No. 10 (italics added).

116. Marc F. Plattner, "American Democracy and the Acquisitive Spirit," in Robert A. Goldwin and William A. Schambra, eds., *How Capitalistic is the Constitution?* (Washington, D.C.: American Enterprise Institute, 1982), p. 2.

117. Robert H. Horwitz, "Locke and the Preservation of Liberty," *The Political Science Reviewer*, Vol. 6 (Fall 1976), pp. 328–29.

118. Schmitt, "Sentimental Journey," p. 112. See C. B. Macpherson, *The Political Theory of Possessive Individualism* (Oxford: Clarendon, 1962), especially pp. 194–262.

8

Self-Interest
Rightly Understood

A NEW VIRTUE AND A NEW SELF-INTEREST

Bʏ ᴛʜᴇ ᴇʀᴀ ᴏꜰ ᴛʜᴇ Fᴏᴜɴᴅɪɴɢ, the concept of virtue had taken a modern connotation that took it beyond the classical interpretation. The term had evolved with the development of modern Christianity, and had found a working compatibility with modern republican ideology as well as with the marketplace. Modern radical republicans administered the *coup de grâce* to a strict classical virtue when they, first, rejected the severity of its classical connotation by lowering the expectations for collective human excellence, and, second, when they made such a radical concession to what had for millenia been the foremost enemy by virtue—self-interest. When the idea was developed that self-interest could be humbled, that it could actually be directed both consciously and unconsciously toward the general good; in short, when the radical republicans wed virtue and self-interest, the Gordian knot with antiquity had been cut. A new republican philosophy emerged.

Eventually, the idea of self-interest would begin to lose its wholly negative connotation. As it merged with such concepts as human dignity, individualism, and freedom, it would come to be seen as increasingly complex—an important factor in freedom of choice and self-expression; indeed, a critical element in the development of personality, of being, and of self-actualization. Michael Novack insists that, "The real interests of individuals . . . are seldom merely self-regarding." If we are to fully understand the concept, we must see it in its full expression:

To most persons, their families mean more than their own interests; they frequently subordinate the latter to the former. Their communities are also important to them. In the human breast, commitments to benevolence, fellow-feeling, and sympathy are strong. Moreover, humans have the capacity to see themselves as others see them, and to hold themselves to standards which transcend their own selfish inclinations. Thus the "self" in self-interest is complex, at once familial and communitarian as well as individual, other regarding as well as self-regarding, cooperative as well as independent, and self-judging as well as self-loving. . . .

Under self-interest, then, fall religious and moral interests, artistic and scientific interests, and interests in justice and peace. The interests of the self define the self. In a free society, persons are free to choose their own interests. It is part of the function of a free economy to provide the abundance which breaks the chains of the mere struggle for subsistence, and permit individual persons to "find themselves," indeed, to define themselves through the interests they choose to make central to their lives.[1]

Virtue, Benevolence, and Modern Republicanism

Therefore, modern virtue was expressed in numerous ways and from more than one motive. To be sure, virtue still was expressed in terms of patriotism and public spiritedness, for without some degree of this, the days of a self-governing system will be numbered. But there was now more to the concept as a result of the generations of impregnation by biblical precepts until, at last, it had become coterminous with moral theology and had touched virtually the totality of men's endeavors. And in all of this was emphasized *most of all* the concept of love—love first of God, then of one's fellowman rather than the state. This concept developed in American republican philosophy through diverse contributions, including the influence of religion and the Bible, the tradition of *charity* as expounded by generations of theistic-humanists, including the ideals of *benevolence* and *moral sense* as taught by divines at Cambridge; and certain great minds of the Scottish Enlightenment. Without these closely interrelated concepts, often referred to as the *Golden Rule*, American republican philosophy, with its basis in modern virtue, would have been vacuous.

David Kirk Hart and H. George Frederickson remind us that while traditional civic virtue, expressed as "patriotism" or "the love of one's country, is important," it is, after all, "insufficient" for a vital republic. Modern republicanism "must be founded upon a knowledge of, and belief in, democratic values. . . . It requires the intentional inculcation, and practice of *benevolence*—which is the extensive and non-instrumental love of others."[2]

Enlightened Self-Interest

As the ideology of freedom and self-worth grew in the Western World, it was accompanied by the inevitable acquiescence to acquisitiveness and self-interest. Out of this metamorphosis of thought, combined with the emergence of modern concepts and practices of economics and politics, a modern idea of an *enlightened* self-interest began to emerge. That is, as the free and spontaneous interactions of men multiplied, participants came to see that to bend for the common interest, to consider with magnanimity the interests of those with whom they were involved, to moderate at times the intensity of their own self-interest, would bring greater rewards to all involved.

What this meant was that self-interest, properly expressed, need not at all be inimical to the common or public interest. This realization was crucial to a republican system where freedom and individualism might reign without succumbing to class hatred, factionalism, and anarchy. For example, *enlightened self-interest* might emerge from the desire of men for esteem, to be admired or well thought of by their fellow men. In seeking public approval or admiration, the officeholder might well find the promotion of the common or public interest to be salutary to his self-esteem and his favorable recognition, hence, his self-interest.

In his *Utopia*, Sir Thomas More suggested that men might turn to virtuous behavior so that their fellowmen would extend to them esteem, honor, and respect. Some men, he surmised, would value respect, or perhaps popularity, or the emoluments of high position to such a degree that they would perceive the public interest to be synonymous with their own. Based upon his belief that man possessed an innate moral sense, Adam Smith suggested that nature had endowed man, "not only with a desire of being approved of, but with a desire of being *what ought to be approved of;* or of being what he himself approves of in other men. The first desire could only have made him appear to be fit for society. The second was necessary in order to render him anxious to be really fit. The first could only have prompted him to the affection of virtue, and to the concealment of vice. The second was necessary in order to inspire him with the real love of virtue, and with the real abhorrence of vice. In every well-informed mind this second desire seems to be the strongest of the two."[3] "Man naturally desires, not only to be loved, *but to be lovely; or to be that thing which is the natural and proper object of love. . . .* He desires not only praise, *but praise-worthiness; or to be that thing which, though it should be praised by nobody, is, however, the natural and proper object of praise.*" Furthermore, he offered, "The love of praise-worthiness is by no means derived altogether from the love of praise." There is in man, he believed, a real desire to be or become admirable, a need to believe that he is admirable, to see himself as admirable. "The most sincere praise can give little pleasure when it cannot be considered as some sort of proof of praise-worthiness."[4] According to Smith, men, when they are praiseworthy, feel good about themselves. Their positive self image becomes an integral part of the benefit they receive from being praise-worthy. "We are pleased to think that we have rendered ourselves the natural objects of approbation. . . . The man who is conscious to himself that he has exactly observed those measures of conduct which experience informs him are generally agreeable, reflects with satisfaction on the propriety of his own behavior. . . . This self-approbation, if not the only, is at least the principal object, about which he can or ought to be anxious. *The love of it is the love of virtue.*"[5]

John Adams posited that men were in need of esteem and respect, that some possessed a veritable passion for distinction, popularity and reputation. In turn for the self-interest of being thought significant by his fellow members of the republic, he would seek distinction in service to his community or country, thus merging his self-interest with that of the whole.[6] Alexander Hamilton agreed with Adams. In attempting to promote the principle of re-election to political office, he wrote, "*the desire of reward is one of the strongest incentives of human conduct; or that the best security for the fidelity of mankind is to make their interest coincide with their duty.*" On the other hand, he surmised, "the love of fame, the ruling passion of the noblest minds, which would prompt a man to plan and undertake extensive and arduous enterprises for the public benefit, requiring considerable time to mature and perfect them, if he could flatter himself with the prospect of being allowed to finish what he had begun, would, on the contrary, deter him from the undertaking, when he foresaw that he must quit the scene before he could accomplish the work, and must commit that, together with his own reputation, to hands which might be unequal or unfriendly to the task. The most to be expected from the generality of men, in such a situation," concluded Hamilton, "is the negative merit of not doing harm, instead of the positive merit of doing good."[7]

James Madison concurred that "there is in every breast a sensibility to marks of honor, of favor, of esteem, and of confidence, which, apart from all considerations of interest, is some pledge for greatful and benevolent returns." Concerning the relationship of the "representative to his constituents," Madison reasoned that "his pride and vanity attach him to a form of government which favors his pretentions and gives him a share in its honors and distinctions. Whatever hopes or projects might be entertained by a few aspiring characters, it must generally happen that a great proportion of the men deriving their advancement from their influence with the people would have more to hope from a preservation of the favor than from innovations in the government subversive of the authority of the people." Furthermore, wrote Madison, the people's representatives "can make no law which will not have its full operation on themselves and their friends, as well as on the great mass of society. This has always been deemed one of the strongest bonds by which human policy can connect the rulers and the people together. It creates between them that communion of interests and sympathy of sentiments of which few governments have furnished examples; but without which every government degenerates into tyranny." And finally, Madison predicted that the relationship between the national representatives and their constituents would be influenced by "duty, gratitude, interest, ambition itself, [which] are the cords by which they will be bound to fidelity and sympathy with the great mass of the people."[8]

In their thoughts concerning moral sense and esteem, Smith, Hume, Adams, and Madison assumed at least two important factors: one, that there was something more to man than animal instincts—something transcendent, inbred in man by his Creator; and two, that they were referring to a specific body of values associated with Western civilization, values which acted as indicators of man's true nobility, and a standard by which man's actions might be judged by himself and by others.

Virtue and Liberty

By the time of the Revolution, the American people were active and knowledgeable recipients of a long heritage in the development of modern freedom, one that extended far beyond colonization. They were conversant with interrelated terms which formed the warp and the woof of modern republicanism—virtue, human dignity, natural law, natural rights, covenant, resistance, freedom. Thomas Jefferson had remarked that the principles he had announced in the Declaration of Independence were already the settled opinion of the American people. As he put it, the object of the Declaration was "not to find out new principles, or new arguments never before thought of . . . but to place before mankind the common sense of the subject. . . . [I]t was intended to be an expression of the American mind, and to give to that expression the proper tone and spirit called for by the occasion."[9] And John Adams referred to the principles of the Declaration as "hackneyed."

Sermons and political writings of the period were replete with references to virtue, liberty, higher law, and natural rights. Time and again British corruption was seen as a primary threat to American virtue. An example can be taken from a sermon delivered by Samuel Langdon, President of Harvard College before the "Congress of the Colony of the Massachusetts-Bay" in May of 1775. Though delivered over a year before the Declaration, the address contained many of the points Jefferson was later to include in it. Langdon condemned a Britain without virtue for compelling "us to submit to the arbitrary acts of legislators who are not of our representatives." He lashed out against political sycophants sent from Britain "whose principles are subversive of our liberties—whose aim is to exercise lordship over us and share among themselves the public wealth—men who are ready to serve any master and execute the most unrighteous decrees for high wages—whose faces we never saw before and whose interests and connections may be far divided from us by the wide Atlantic . . . counselors and judges . . . to be set over us . . . at the pleasure of those who have the riches and power of the nation in their hands, and whose noblest plan is to subjugate the colonies first and then the whole nation to their will."[10] The firmness of colonial "opposition to the establishment of an arbitrary system" was dictated by the fact that "submission to the tyranny of hundreds of imperious masters firmly embodied against us and united in the same cruel design of disposing of our substance and lives at their pleasure, and making their own will our law in all cases whatever, is the vilest slavery, and worse than death."[11] Langdon excoriated Britain's "pretense for taxing America," a controversy "which now threatens a final separation of the Colonies from Great Britain."[12]

Although he expressed longing for a reconciliation "so that the colonies may again enjoy the protection of their sovereign with perfect security of all their natural rights and civil and religious liberties,"[13] he remained pessimistic. With the "blessing of the most High . . . we are using our best endeavours to preserve and restore the civil government of this Colony, and defend America from slavery."[14] He reviled the mercenaries sent from England "who know no distinction betwixt an enemy and a brother," who had "plundered and massacred" the protectors of freedom,[15] and whose officers have held "our brethren" captive.[16] Nevertheless, "we have used our utmost endeavors, by repeated humble petitions and remonstrances—by a series of unanswerable reasonings published from the press in which the dispute has been fairly stated, and the justice of our opposition clearly demonstrated—and by the mediation of some of the noblest and the most faithful friends of the British Constitution, who have powerfully pled our cause in Parliament. . . . But our king, as if impelled by some strange fatality, is resolved to reason with us only by the roar of his cannon and the pointed arguments of muskets and bayonets," for refusing "submission to the despotic power of a ministerial parliament."[17]

Therefore, separation from a corrupt England was inevitable. In point of doctrine, President Langdon expounded on the right of self-defense. In order to protect "property and life . . . we have taken up arms in our own defense, and all the colonies are united in the great cause of liberty,"[18] and for "natural and constitutional rights."[19] And with the dissolution of union with the mother country, "thanks be to God that he has given us, as men, natural rights independent of all human laws whatever. . . . By the law of nature any body of people, destitute of order and government, may form themselves into a civil society according to their best prudence and so provide for their common safety and advantage."[20] "Every nation, when able and agreed," emphasized Langdon, "has a right to set up over themselves any form of government which to them may appear most conducive to their common welfare."[21]

Indeed, the general acceptance of the principles that appeared in the Declaration, as evidenced by Clinton Rossiter's research, convinced him to make the following remarkable declaration:

> Had ministers been the only spokesmen of the American Cause, had Jefferson, the Adamses, and Otis never appeared in print, the political thought of the Revolution would have followed almost exactly the same line—with perhaps a little more mention of God, but certainly no less of John Locke. In the sermons of the patriot ministers, who were responsible for fully one third of the total output of political thought in these years, we find expressed every possible refinement of the reigning secular faith. The leading thinkers among the ministers, for the most part sons of the Puritan churches, were Jonathan Mayhew, Charles Chauncy, Samuel Cooper, Stephen Johnson, Jonas Clarke, Samuel Webster and Samuel Cooke. A step behind this select band of prophets was a small army—'the black Regiment,' as Peter Oliver labeled it—of staunch expounders of English and natural rights: William Gordon, Samuel West, Samuel Langdon, Judah Champion, Ebenezer Devotion, Simeon Howard, Amos Adams, John Cleaveland, Phillips Payson, Isaac Skillman, John Allen, Thomas Allen, Gad Hitchcock, John Tucker, Charles Turner, Ebenezer Bridge, Eliphalet Williams, Edward Barnard, Jason Haven, Sameul Lockwood, and literally hundreds of others hardly less skilled than Mayhew or Cooper in expounding the doctrines of resistance, unalienable rights, and consent.
>
> Outside New England the Clergy was less accustomed to find its way into print on political matters, but such names as John Wither-

spoon, William Smith, Jacob Duché, John Joachim Zubly, John Hurt, and William Tennent are evidence that there, too, men of God were keen participants in political argument."[22]

By the time of the Founding, Americans had become conversant with the great advocates of republican liberty both at home and abroad, including Locke, Trenchard, Gordon, Price, Priestly, Blackstone, to mention but a few. The Americans had been through generations of practical experience in constitution building, from the early compacts and through some rather sophisticated state constitutions. They had experienced the growth of religious pluralism and toleration on the road to religious freedom and separation of church and state, without rejecting God or religion, or expunging moral theology. They had earned that measure of virtue or excellence detected by Madison that made self-government possible.

Virtue and Republican Structure

The American Founders believed that the republican government hammered out at Philadelphia and argued so eloquently in *The Federalist* would tend to stimulate and draw out certain admirable qualities that were already part of the "spirit" and "character" of the people, and that would have the effect of supporting and helping preserve the system. Under these favorable conditions, republican government might instruct an enlightened people in the virtues of self-government, where traditional political systems would, in effect, mute this spirit.

As Martin Diamond has pointed out, it is an easy error to be "concerned only with the foundation [of the Republic] and to settle for a form of liberty that consists only in the free play of raw self-interest. *But this is to ignore the subtle ethical demands of the American political order.*" According to Diamond, "we must accept that [it] had its foundation in the human interests and passions; but we must appreciate also that their political order presupposes certain enduring qualities that can and should be achieved in the American character."[23]

Diamond finds in the American constitutional structure an impetus to public and individual virtue, born in the protection and encouragement of individual freedom. The very nature of the system summons "forth the capacity of a people to govern themselves." Thus, "the American political order advances beyond mere self-interest toward that full self-governance which is the very idea of virtue."[24] Diamond admits that "the idea of what is advantageous and just for humans . . . is clearly less elevated than that of the classical teaching." Therefore, "the ethical aim of the American political order being less lofty, the kinds of human characters to be politically formed are likewise less lofty and, hence, less difficult of formation. Such human beings may be produced by softer means, subterranean in their operation and indirect, thereby rendering unnecessary the strenuous and penetrating political authority characteristic of the ancient regime. It has in fact proved possible to raise human character to the American height in the gentler, less demanding fashion." According to Diamond, the formation of what some might call bourgeois virtues "does not require the severity and constant statesmanship of the classical political outlook; it suffices that a modern regime generate that 'spirit' and then the desired virtues tend naturally to form themselves."[25] In fact, "the American Republican virtues . . . arise from the habit and practice of self-government. Like the bourgeois virtues, these too are formed in the milder modern way. The American republican virtues arise primarily from political arrangements that accept and seek to channel the force of human passion and interest rather than to suppress or transcend them. And these republican virtues likewise arise primarily from the original Founding and not from subsequent statesmanship shaping the character of the citizenry." Diamond insists that "the constitution, and, thanks to federalism, the state constitutions as well, establish a basic framework of institutions that elicit ethical qualities of citizenship such as independence, initiative, a capacity for cooperation and patriotism." The "republican decencies in the American character do not depend decisively upon constant constraint or encouragement by statesmanship but tend to flow from the operation of the political institutions as originally founded."[26]

In referring to his handiwork, the Bill of Rights to the Constitution, James Madison reflects a similar analysis. "The political truths declared in that solemn manner," observed the Father of the Constitution, "acquire by degrees the character of fundamental maxims of free government, and as they become incorporated with the national sentiment, counteract the impulses of interest and passion."[27]

Professor Hart argues that although the "Founders generally believed that the ultimate measure of a state was the level of virtue achieved by its citizens, . . . they rejected the argument that the government should use its power to produce such virtue." They therefore "took the bolder and riskier path of moral individualism, understanding that virtue had no meaning if it was not achieved through the voluntary efforts of a free people," rather than their being forced "into some predefined and artificial character. *The responsibility of democratic government was to elicit rather than to command appropriate actions from a virtuous people.*"[28]

Virtue and the Republican Spirit

To be sure, the American Founders were clearly aware of the shortcomings of mankind, and believed that self-interest was at the root of man's motivations. Yet, they never denied for a moment the maxim that a true democratic republic needed at least a measure of virtue in the people and the rulers they would select, or the final outcome would be either anarchy or tyranny. Furthermore, their writings leave no doubt that they believed that, of all peoples, the American people might possess sufficient virtue to make self-government possible. As both Madison and Hamilton pointed out, this people, whatever their level of virtue, would show, perhaps once and for all, whether, given the nature of man, self-government was really possible. Their cautioned respect for mankind stands starkly against others, such as Hobbes, who believed that only the restrictive, omnipotent state could control the rebellious nature of man. The possibility of channelling that energy in a system of freedom was apparently beyond the thinking of Hobbes, as was the proposition that men might have the virtue necessary to sustain self-government.

Hamilton and Madison were talking of a modern republican form of spontaneous virtue, not so structured as in the classical or medieval understanding. Here, even the term "honor" possessed a special connotation. There is the inference, too obvious to ignore, that the honor and respect that men sought in that form of republic championed by the above statesmen would be extended to them by a modern "republican people" in response to their being judged against those moral and civil virtues, values, and standards that had become commonplace in their thinking and in their beliefs. This concept lies at the basis of Madison's deep concern that the people of the new republic would possess sufficient virtue and common sense to honor and select men to rule over them who were possessed of wisdom and virtue; for the heroes of society, to be extended the accolades, must express the image of conformance to, or the illumination of, the values already held dear by the community. One means by which the great men of society may merge their self-interest with that of the whole is related to the extent to which there is a coincidence of basic values held in common. In the case of the American republic, these values, to a great extent, had been either formed or nurtured by the influence of the Judeo-Christian heritage.

Beyond that, it was widely believed that God had implanted in man what some called "reason," others a "conscience" or "moral sense" and—using Locke's interpretation of the term—"trust," which enticed men toward virtue. This "sense of moral good and evil" offered John Witherspoon, "is as real a principle of our nature, as either the gross external or reflex senses."[29] Men were more than animals; they could reason; they could be motivated by other than fear to moral behavior and concern with the higher interests of the community; their intelligence could merge private and common interest; religion could stimulate a natural conscience, a propensity to act in a certain way, that could bring forth justice, benevolence, and philanthropy. According to Thomas Jefferson, God "has made us moral agents . . . that we may promote the happiness of those with whom he has placed us in society, by acting honestly towards all, benevolently to those who fall within our way, respecting sacredly their rights, bodily and mental, and cherishing especially their freedom of conscience as we value our own."[30]

Indeed, the modern theses, which show the American Founders turning completely away from virtue and moral theology to allow the entirety of men's interaction to be based solely on the collision of competitive self-interest, energized by an introverted selfishness, are far too narrow in context and theory. For, as Diamond insists, the American Founders began their adventure with the belief that in spite of their failings, the American people possessed "certain enduring qualities" that made self-government possible; and secondly, that the nature of the new constitutional system itself would nourish and elicit these qualities.

Christianity, then, as integral to the Judeo-Christian heritage of Western civilization, had evolved to a moral system supported by moral theology, and had become, on the one hand, a force whereby men would restrain their own passions of their own free will; and, on the other hand, a source of active moral behavior that was stimulated in the individual conscience.

If the constitutional system was to "summon forth" virtuous behavior from its citizens, it must be assumed that the citizens possessed an *anterior* image of the world—a moral belief or value system that was penetrating and enduring enough to be stimulated on a more or less continual basis by their participation in it. Otherwise, they would hardly be responsive to its needs nor amenable to its expectations. As Robert A. Goodwin has written, both "then and now" the system, which includes the sentiments of the people, "does not ignore or condone immorality. In fact, it holds morality very high in public esteem." There has remained "a strong sense of morality, of fairness, or aversion to unfairness."[31] No constitutional system can be expected to be the *author* of virtue in the people, though one structure and formation might well be more conducive to the expression of that virtue than another.

What made the American system "work" was that its structure tended to "summon forth" an *already existing* "ethic" that had previously become part of the "character" or "spirit" or "genius" of the people; that is, that it had become internalized to the point that its impact could influence people favorably toward a self-governing system to which they found themselves amenable. One could venture the proposition that few of the millions of people who dwelt upon the earth in the eighteenth century would have, or even could have, had the same response to the new Republic. The extended commercial republic, neither in its political nor in its economic character, was the generator of first instance of virtue. According to Professor Diamond, "the American Founders seem simply to have taken for granted that the full range of the higher human virtues would have suitable opportunity to flourish, so to speak, privately. They presumed that man's nature included a perhaps weak but nonetheless natural inclination to certain virtues. Although they did not rely upon these 'better motives' . . . as the basis for the political order, they were apparently confident that, privately and without political tutelage in the ancient mode, these higher virtues would develop from religion, education, family upbringing, and simply out of the natural yearnings of human nature."[32]

To be sure, the modern republicans had matured beyond the ideal belief that civic and personal virtue among men could be counted upon with consistency. The American Founders had ceased to have any illusions about man and virtue. It became obvious to them, even to the once-enthusiastic John Adams, that a classical type of civic virtue was out of the question in a modern republic. They were going to have to lower the horizon on their expectations. "There is reason to fear," John Jay admitted to a concurring Thomas Jefferson, "that too much has been expected from the Virtue and the good Sense of the People."[33] Adams's love affair with classical civic virtue during the revolutionary period turned to caution as he perceived and experienced the practical politics of the new states. The great accolades he had heaped upon the quality of American civic virtue came to include concerns about immorality, uncontrolled passions and selfishness, of democracy turning into anarchy, liberty into license. As with others of the Founders, he came to the realization that the new republic or republics were not going to run on a classical-type civic virtue alone. He became increasingly concerned with the political means to control and regulate society—"auxiliary precautions" as Madison was to call them. He became increasingly aware of the need for stable, mediating institutions, and the need for a modern republican virtue energized by moral theology. As Professor Howe put it, "Adams, while praising American virtue, recognized that Americans, like other men, were also creatures of passion, and if left uncontrolled, would too often act selfishly against each other. Provision had to be made for this, even in the American political system."[34] Still, he confirmed to Jefferson that "without virtue there can be no political liberty," and that "no effort in favor of virtue is lost."[35]

Having brought man into what they believed to be proper perspective, the American Founders were just as certain that self-government required a measure of civic and personal virtue in the people, and that the American people, at least, possessed sufficient "excellences" of nature to make the attempt worthwhile. "However angrily they might argue over points of constitutional structure," concludes Rossiter, "the American spokesmen agreed unanimously that it would take more than a perfect plan of government to preserve ordered liberty. Something else was needed, some moral principle diffused among the people to strengthen the urge to peaceful obedience and hold the community on a even keel."[36] Add to these sentiments the "better motives," along with a belief that God has been the founder, the shield and buckler of the nation, and has nourished its progress, and is the author of its rights and freedoms, and the nation then possesses all the accoutrements of a public philosophy or an "unestablished" civil religion. Without such a public philosophy or religion, any nation, especially one which depends on the free and spontaneous "personal" and "civic" virtue of its citizens and political leaders as well, will likely atrophy. As Brookings Institution's A. James Reichley offers, "the founding fathers after all were right: republican government depends for its health on values that over the not-so-long run must come from religion. Through theistic-humanism, human rights are rooted in the moral worth with which a loving Creator has endowed each human soul, and social authority is legitimized by making it answerable to transcendent moral law."[37]

Virtue and the Acquisitive Spirit

As indicated in previous chapters, the radical republicans believed that a proper republic would stimulate sentiments of patriotism—"public spiritedness" (*virtus civitas*)—indeed, civic virtue. The practice of self-government, combined with the emotive impact of public documents, shrines, symbols, etc., would tend to "teach" public virtue; and what is more, enlightened self-interest might bring the citizen to the realization that in supporting the republic he was also benefiting himself. Notwithstanding, the American Founders also clearly believed that a republic also depended upon the quantity and quality of moral virtue in the people, which owes its origins to other sources that are prior to and apart from the political system, and which have traditionally been nurtured at the breast, the hearth, the pulpit, the classroom, and in private associations for public ends. Therefore, when a republican symbol stimulates a virtuous response, it is primarily because that symbol has attained legitimacy—even perhaps the aura of the sacred—from an energizing, complimentary source beyond its sphere. There is no political constitution, whatever its checks and balances, immune from wholesale corruption, or that can call up a moral or virtuous response from a corrupt citizenry. The American Founders knew this, and they were well aware that a special kind of people was needed to sustain a republic.

The radical republicans also believed that a *commercial* republic could stimulate certain virtues and "excellences" in men. The opportunities offered by the open market-system taught persistence, frugality, cooperation with others, and willing adherence to generally accepted practices that helped engender a kind of automatic and spontaneous order and a system of mutually beneficial expectations.

Montesquieu was not the only one who argued that "frugality, economy, moderation, labor, prudence, tranquility, order and rule," were human virtues that tended to emerge in a "democracy founded on commerce."[38] Nor was Franklin alone in his conjecture that "industry and constant Employment are great preservatives of the Morals and Virtue of a Nation."[39] According to Martin Diamond, who uses Montesquieu as his text on this point, "These may be put down as 'bourgeois virtues,' *but they are virtues, or human excellences nonetheless. They reach at least to decency if not to nobility; they make life at least possible under the circumstances of modern mass society.*"[40]

Professor Diamond makes a special point that the modern commercial society generally replaced "avarice" with "acquisitiveness." "Avarice," he explains, "is a passion centered on the things themselves, a narrow clutching to one's self of money or possessions; it has no built-in need for any limitation of itself, no need for moderation or for the cultivation of any virtues as instrumental to the satisfaction of the avaricious passion." Acquisitiveness, on the other hand, "teaches a form of moderation to the desiring passions from which it derives, because to acquire, is not primarily to have and to hold but to get and to earn, and, moreover, *to earn justly*, at least to the extent that the acquisition must be the fruit of one's own exertions or qualities." This process, according to Diamond, "requires the acquisitive man to cultivate *certain excellences*, minimal ones perhaps from the classical perspective, but excellences nonetheless, as means to achieve his ends. He wants enlargement and increase and these require of him at least venturesomeness, and hard work, and the ability to still his immediate passions so as to allow time for the ripening of his acquisitive plans and measures." It is in this context that we can best understand Hamilton's statement in *The Federalist* No. 12 that the commercial republic nurtures "the assiduous merchant, the laborious husbandman, the active mechanic, and the industrious manufacturer." "And," continues Diamond, "it is not only excellences like assiduity, labor, activity, and industry that a commercial society nurtures. 'Honesty is the best policy' is not acceptable prudence to the avaricious man, but it is almost natural law to the 'assiduous merchant.' *Acquisitiveness may not be the highest motive for honesty, but if it produces something like the habit of honesty in great numbers, is not that a prodigious accomplishment?"*[41]

Nevertheless, although the commercial system may well stimulate positive character traits that emerge from acquisitiveness and enlightened self-interest, the premier *source* of these virtues springs *from an already active value system.* Such virtues as loyalty, honor, honesty, benevolence, dependability, and tenacity are not solely the product of the vagaries of the commercial system, not solely the result of practical experience, not entirely the product of self-interested hopes and benefits, any more than they are solely the issue of political structures, practices, and symbols; but they are, as well, the product of the influence of moral sentiments, expectations, and attitudes, learned and inherited through a separate conduit of human development. This value system, with its core in the Judeo-Christian ethic, effectively makes the commercial republic possible in the first place. There is no economic system which will, by its own mechanical devices or competitive checks, hold its balance when dishonesty, greed, envy and lack of benevolence become the rule.

De TOCQUEVILLE AND SELF-INTEREST RIGHTLY UNDERSTOOD

De Toqueville was conversant with the modern form of virtue as compared to the classical and medieval concept, and he understood that modern freedom and equality would multiply men's opportunities and wants, stimulating a great variety of economic pursuits, factions, and private organizations. However, he believed that certain factors within the system would help moderate and direct these unleashed forces in ways that would simultaneously benefit both the individual and the community as a whole. The existence of freedom and a legal system bent on justice would, he believed, draw forth from the American a general sense of appreciation, a patriotism, for the protections and opportunities offered. Also included in the idea of enlightened self-interest was the understanding that support of public interest, in this case, contributed in the end to one's self-interest. De Tocqueville incessantly reminded his readers that the unruly and acquisitive nature of the American was tempered by the restraining and mediating institutions of family, school, and church. He was particularly impressed with the women of America, whom he described as "the protectors of morals." Furthermore, he opined that "there is no country in the world where the tie of marriage is more respected than in America or where conjugal happiness is more highly or worthily appreciated."[42] All together, these factors provided a political, economic and social ecology that could support an extraordinary freedom and at the same time experience a spontaneous moral restraint.

According to de Tocqueville, the exceptional morality of the American people, comparatively speaking, was obvious. "Although the travelers who have visited North America differ on many points, they all agree in remarking that morals are far more strict there than elsewhere. It is evident that on this point the Americans are very superior to their progenitors, the English." De Tocqueville determined that "the great regularity of American morals was due to a number of factors, including the qualities of country, race, and religion," but not excluding the "principle of equality," which "does not of itself produce regularity of morals, but it unquestionably facilitates and increases it."[43]

De Tocqueville was able to see, as had Madison, that the freedom of the individual, combined with the muting of strict class lines simultaneous with the growth of the middle class, and the emergence of variety and opportunity in the modern commercial system, would redirect the intensity of class conflict and poverty against wealth, which had been paramount in "aristocratic times," to a different level and a more extended and fragmented character. "The love of well-being is there displayed as a tenacious, exclusive, universal passion," reasoned de Tocqueville, "but its range is confined. To build enormous palaces, to conquer or to mimic nature, to ransack the world in order to gratify the passions of a man, is not thought of, but to add a few yards of land to your field, to plant an orchard, to enlarge a dwelling, to be always making life more comfortable and convenient, to avoid trouble, and to satisfy the smallest wants without effort and almost without cost."

De Tocqueville assured his readers that this acquisitive character associated with democracy in America was different from the "sumptuous depravity and splendid corruption" of aristocratic systems. "The special taste that men of democratic times entertain for physical enjoyments is not naturally opposed to the principles of public order; nay, *it often stands in need of order that it may be gratified.* Nor is it adverse to regularity of morals, for good morals contribute to public tranquility and are favorable to industry. It may even be frequently combined with a species of religious morality; men wish to be as well off as they can in this world without forgoing their chance of another. Some physical gratifications cannot be indulged in without crime; from such they strictly abstain."[44]

"As wealth is subdivided and knowledge diffused," continued de Tocqueville, "no one is entirely destitute of education or of property; the privileges and disqualifications of caste being abolished, and men having shattered the bonds that once held them fixed, the notion of advancement suggests itself to every mind, the desire to rise swells in every heart, and all men want to mount above their station; ambition is the universal feeling." "But," he emphasized, "if the equality of conditions gives some resources to all the members of the community, it also prevents any of them from having resources of great extent, which necessarily circumscribes their desires within somewhat narrow limits. Thus, among democratic nations, ambition is ardent and continual, but its aim is not habitually lofty; and life is generally spent in eagerly coveting small objects that are within reach."[45]

As was Madison and the other commercial republicans, de Tocqueville was aware that a free society where men were able to pursue their self-interest and enjoyed freedom of choice, great variety in enterprise would likely develop, stimulating not only individual differences but multiple factions as well. Too, de Tocqueville perceived that with the multiple opportunities available in a commercial society the pursuit of wealth would be widespread. No longer would there be a few and isolated mighty rich, contrasting their lives with the ubiquitous poor; no longer the greed of the upper classes arrayed against the coveting of the lower classes. A new vital, industrious middle class had emerged with an acquisitiveness that energized a new era.

"When men living in a democratic state of society are enlightened," offered de Tocqueville, "they readily discover that they are not confined and fixed by any limits that force them to accept their present fortune. They all, therefore, conceive the idea of increasing it. If they are free, they all attempt it, but do not succeed in the same manner." With the law of entail and primogeniture abolished, there is prevented "the establishment of wealthy families, but it does not prevent the existence of wealthy individuals. It constantly brings back the members of the community to a common level, from which they as constantly escape; and the inequality of fortunes augments in proportion as their knowledge is diffused and their liberty increased."[46] Here all "classes mingle together because they live so close together. They communicate and intermingle every day; they imitate and emulate one another. This suggests to the people many ideas, notions, and desires that they would never have entertained if the distinctions of rank had been fixed and society at rest."[47]

Therefore, modern republican freedom, especially that related to the commercial republic, would stimulate the growth of a variety of interests and factions. De Tocqueville reasoned that "men who live in ages of equality have continual need of forming associations in order to procure the things they desire; and . . . political freedom improves and diffuses the art of association.[48] In aristocracies," he suggested, "men are separated from each other by lofty stationary barriers; in democracies they are divided by many small and almost invisible threads, which are constantly broken or moved from place to place. Thus whatever may be the progress of equality, in democratic nations a great number of small private associations will always be formed within the general pale of political society; but none of them will bear any resemblance in its manners to the higher class in aristocracies."[49] Freedom, including freedom of enterprise, would multiply individual opportunity and stimulate individual endeavor in a great variety of ways, providing some acquisition for most while directing the intensity of one's acquisitiveness to generally and relatively small proportions. "The principle of equality," wrote de Tocqueville, "does not destroy the imagination, but lowers its flight to the level of the earth."[50]

"What most astonishes me in the United States," expressed de Tocqueville, "is not so much the marvelous grandeur of some undertaking as the innumerable multitude of small ones."[51] Democracy, he wrote, "not only swells the number of working men, but leads men to prefer one kind of labor to another."[52] Furthermore, he reasoned, men are "led to engage in commerce, not only for the sake of the profit it holds out to them, but for the love of the constant excitement occasioned by that pursuit."[53]

De Tocqueville agreed with the radical commercial republicans that there was "a close bond and necessary relationship between these two elements, freedom and productive industry."[54] "Give democratic nations education and freedom," he suggested, "and leave them alone. They will soon learn to draw from this world all the benefits that it can afford; they will improve each of the useful arts and will day by day render life more comfortable, more convenient, and more easy. Their social condition naturally urges them in this direction."[55]

Religion and Self-Interest Rightly Understood

De Tocqueville repeatedly asserted that there is no possibility of a democratic republic without virtue and morality and that virtue and morality will not persist without religion. He considered religion a veritable "political institution which powerfully contributes to the maintenance of a democratic republic."[56] North America had been peopled by immigrants who had "brought with them into the New World a form of Christianity which I cannot better describe than by styling it a democratic and republican religion."[57] This general religion was supported by a multitude of sects to which "Christian morality [was] common."[58]

De Tocqueville also pointed out that religion and patriotism in the United States had a reciprocal relationship, for while religion nurtured patriotism there, feelings of patriotism garnered from the just laws and the political, social, and economic freedoms the Americans enjoyed also significantly affected the climate of general religion. "Thus, religious zeal is perpetually warmed in the United States by the fires of patriotism. These men do not act exclusively from a consideration of a future life; eternity is only one motive of their devotion to the cause."[59] He insisted that unity in a democratic society required the sustenance of patriotism and religion. "Do what they may," he emphasized, "there is no true power among men except in a free union of their will; and patriotism and religion are the only two motives in the world that can long urge all the people towards the same end."[60] "The Anglo-Americans," he continued, "have been allowed by their circumstances, their origin, their intelligence, and especially by their morals to establish and maintain the sovereignty of the people."[61]

He took great care to emphasize that the tempering force of religion was vital in democratic times, when men sought after riches and equality with such intensity. "Of all the passions which originate in or are fostered by equality," he wrote, "there is one which it renders peculiarly intense, and which it also infused into the heart of every man; I mean the love of well-being. The taste for well-being is the prominent and indelible feature of democratic times." He was aware that a reliance on classical virtue to curb the intensity of self-interest in a modern democratic republic was futile, for any attempt "to destroy so deep-seated a passion would in the end be destroyed by it."[62]

Nevertheless, de Tocqueville reminds us that the self-interest nurtured by equality and freedom needs a tempering religious influence. *"The chief concern of religion,"* he wrote, *"is to purify, to regulate, and to restrain the excessive and exclusive taste for well-being that men feel in periods of equality;* but it would be an error to attempt to overcome it completely or to eradicate it." In this sentence he gives us his understanding of "modern" virtue, as it were, "rightly understood." It was not the intense virtue of classical times, but a more quiet and realistic variety more in tune with human nature as he understood it. "Men cannot be cured of the love of riches," he continued, "but they may be persuaded to enrich themselves by none but honest means."[63] The French philosopher applauded the wisdom of the American clergy for grasping this concept, else man might turn from religion altogether. "The American ministers of the Gospel," he observed, "do not attempt to draw or to fix all the thoughts of man upon the life to come; they are willing to surrender a portion of his heart to the cares of the present, seeming to consider the goods of this world as important, though secondary, objects. If they take no part themselves in productive labor, they are at least interested in its progress and they applaud its results; and while they never cease to point to the other world as the great object of the hopes and fears of the believer, they do not forbid him honestly to court prosperity in this."[64]

De Tocqueville points out that while equality of condition "brings great benefits into the world," nevertheless it had a tendency to promote some "very dangerous propensities" among men, such as isolating "them from one another," and laying "open the soul to an inordinate love of material gratification." He insisted that religion had the tendency of providing a necessary balance of self-interest with virtue. "The greatest advantage of religion," he offered "is to inspire diametrically contrary principles. There is no religion that does not place the object of man's desires above and beyond the treasures of the earth and that does not naturally raise his soul to regions far above those of the senses. Nor is there any which does not impose on man some duties towards his kind and thus draw him at times from the contemplation of himself." He claimed it to be of great importance "for men to preserve their religion as their conditions become more equal."[65] According to de Tocqueville, if "the soul . . . were . . . left stripped of all belief, the love of physical gratifications [would] grow upon it and fill it wholly."[66] Since the "passions, . . . wants, . . . education, and everything about . . . the native of the United States . . . seems to unite in drawing [him] earthward; his religion alone bids him turn, from time to time, a transient and distracted glance to heaven."[67]

Thus, de Tocqueville held tenaciously to his belief that religion must play a part in the life of men in a democracy; that the concept of self-interest rightly understood fully incorporated the force of religion. *"If the principle of self-interest rightly understood had nothing but the present world in view, it would be very insufficient,* for there are many sacrifices that can find their recompense only in another; and whatever ingenuity may be put forth to demonstrate the utility of virtue, it will never be an easy task to make that man live aright who has no thought of dying [and of facing judgment]." According to de Tocqueville, "religions give men a general habit of conducting themselves with a view to eternity; in this respect they are not less useful to happiness in this life than to felicity hereafter, and this is one of their chief political characteristics." On the other hand, when men lose "the habit of placing their chief hopes upon remote events, they naturally seek to gratify without delay their smallest desires; and no sooner do they dispair of living forever, than they are disposed to act as if they were to exist but for a single day. . . . It is only by resisting a thousand petty selfish passions of the hour that the general and unquenchable passion for happiness can be satisfied."[68]

De Tocqueville came to the conclusion that the principle of self-interest rightly understood would not "undermine the religious opinions of men; it seems to be more easy to show why it should strengthen them." He believed that religion and self-interest rightly understood were reciprocal:

> Let it be supposed that in order to attain happiness in this world, a man combats his instincts on all occasions and deliberately calculates every action of his life; that instead of yielding blindly to the impetuosity of first desires, he has learned the art of resisting them, and that he has accustomed himself to sacrifice without an effort the pleasure of a moment to the lasting interest of his whole life. If such a man believes in the religion that he professes, it will cost him but little to submit to the restrictions it may oppose. Reason herself counsels him to obey, and habit has prepared him to endure these limitations. If he should have conceived any doubts as to the object of his hopes, still he will not easily allow himself to be stopped by them; and he will decide that it is wise to risk some of the advantages of this world in order to preserve his rights to the great inheritance promised in another. "To be mistaken in believing that the Christian religion is true," says Pascal, "is no great loss to anyone; but how dreadful to be mistaken in believing it to be false!"

"The Americans," continued de Tocqueville, "do not affect a brutal indifference to a future state; they affect no purile pride in despising perils that they hope to escape from. They therefore profess their religion without shame and without weakness; but even in their zeal there is something so indescribably tranquil, methodical, and deliberate that it would seem as if the head far more than the heart brought them to the foot of the altar."[69]

As with Locke, de Tocqueville could not bring himself to suggest that all men practiced virtuous behavior only out of pureself-interest. There must also be, he suggested, conversion, belief, a love of God, an innate moral sense or inspired urge to do good on its own merits. "I cannot believe," he reasoned, "that all those who practice virtue from religious motives are actuated only by the hope of a recompense. . . . Christianity, indeed, teaches that a man must prefer his neighbor to himself in order to gain eternal life; but Christianity also teaches that men ought to benefit their fellow creatures for the love of God! A sublime expression! Man searches by intellect into the divine conception and sees that order is the purpose of God; he freely gives his own efforts to aid in prosecuting this great design, and, while he sacrifices his personal interests to this consummate order of all created things expects no other recompense than the pleasure of contemplating it."[70]

Virtue and Self-Interest Rightly Understood

Particularly in the United States, observed de Tocqueville, "the inhabitants . . . almost always manage to combine their own advantage with that of their fellow-citizens." What enables them to do this? "In the United States hardly anybody talks of the beauty of virtue, but they maintain that virtue is useful and prove it every day. The American moralists do not profess that men ought to sacrifice themselves for their fellow creatures *because* it is noble to make such sacrifices, but they boldly aver that such sacrifices are as necessary to him who imposes them upon himself as to him for whose sake they are made. . . . They therefore do not deny that every man may follow his own self-interest, but they endeavor to prove that it is in the interest of every man to be virtuous." As de Tocqueville perceived the situation, the Americans were conversant with this concept, indeed, to the point of perhaps not giving "natural" philanthropy its just dues. "The Americans . . . are fond of explaining almost all the actions of their lives by the principle of self-interest rightly understood; they show with complacency how an enlightened regard for themselves constantly prompts them to assist one another and enclines them willingly to sacrifice a portion of their time and property to the welfare of the state. In this respect I think they frequently fail to do themselves justice; for in the United States as well as elsewhere people are sometimes seen to give way to those disinterested and spontaneous impulses [of benevolence] that are natural to man."[71]

De Tocqueville was among those who believed that the commercial republic would help teach men the virtue of sacrificing present satisfactions for greater accomplishments at some future time, thereby teaching moderation, perseverence, and a futuristic attitude. As de Tocqueville described his concept of "self-interest rightly understood" in detail, one can again perceive the influence of radical republican thought on his thinking. We see the rejection of a strictly classical form of virtue, for a "modern" one more in keeping with a particular idea of the nature of man. "The principle of self-interest rightly understood is not a lofty one, but it is clear and sure. It does not aim at mighty objects, but attains without exertion all those at which it aims." De Tocqueville's concept, having lowered the expectations concerning man, included the concept so dear to Madison of checking faction with faction, interest with interest. "By its admirable conformity to human weaknesses it easily obtains great dominion; nor is that dominion precarious, since the principle checks one personal interest with another, and uses, to direct the passions, the very same instrument that excites them."

Of seminal importance to de Tocqueville's thought on this subject, is its conformity with that of the American Founders with regard to the concept of virtue. While the heights of virtuous expectations with regard to natural man were lowered to more realistic levels, de Tocqueville was no more willing to accept the possibility of a republican system without virtue than were the American Founders. "The principle of self-interest rightly understood," he reasoned, "produces no great acts of self-sacrifice, but it suggests daily small acts of self-denial. By itself it cannot suffice to make a man virtuous; but it disciplines a number of persons in habits of regularity, temperance, moderation, foresight, self-command; and if it does not lead men straight to virtue by the will, it gradually draws them in that direction by their habits. If the principle of interest rightly understood were to sway the whole world," suggested de Tocqueville, "extraordinary virtues would doubtless be more rare; but I think that gross depravity would then also be less common. The principle of interest rightly understood perhaps prevents men from rising far above the level of mankind, but a great number of other men, who were falling far below it, are caught and restrained by it. *Observe some few individuals, they are lowered by it; survey mankind, they are raised.*"[72]

De Tocqueville was certain that this concept was most appropriate for the nature of man in modern times. "I am not afraid to say that the principle of self-interest rightly understood appears to me the best suited of all philosophical theories to the wants of the men of our time, and that I regard it as their chief remaining security against themselves. Towards it, therefore, the minds of the moralists of our age should turn; even should they judge it to be incomplete, it must nevertheless be adopted as necessary."[73]

De Tocqueville left a warning to his readers. He believed his concept of self-interest rightly understood to be a leavener against the potential excesses associated with the lust for equality and love of physical gratification. "It remains to be seen," he wrote, "how each man will understand his personal interest. If the members of a community, as they become more equal, become more ignorant and coarse, it is difficult to forsee to what pitch of stupid excess their selfishness will lead them; and no one can fortell into what disgrace and wickedness they would plunge themselves lest they should have to sacrifice something of their own well-being to the prosperity of their fellow creatures." Therefore, in his consistent caution that democracy must be tempered, de Tocqueville saw the concept of self-interest rightly understood as one means by which this might be brought about. And while the fruits of it may not always be self-evident, de Tocqueville was impressed by the need for men to be educated. "I do not think," he stated, "that the system of self-interest as it is professed in America is in all its parts self-evident, but it contains a great number of truths so evident that men, if they are only educated, cannot fail to see them. Educate, then, at any rate, for the age of implicit self-sacrifice and instinctive virtues is already flitting far away from us, and the time is fast approaching when freedom, public peace, and social order itself will not be able to exist without education."[74]

Again, de Tocqueville was well aware of the differences between classical and modern concepts of virtue. "The American," for instance, "lauds as noble and praiseworthy ambition what our own forefathers in the Middle Ages stigmatized as severe cupidity, just as he treats as a blind and barbarous frenzy that ardor and martial temper which bore them to battle." To such a people as the Americans "the inactivity and sloth of the community at large would be fatal. . . . Boldness of enterprise is the foremost course of its rapid progress, its strength, and its greatness."[75] The modern ideal of honor was less an expression of martial valor—although such bravery was still admired—than "the courage which is best known and most esteemed . . . which emboldens men to brave the dangers of the ocean in order to arrive earlier in port, to support the privations of the wilderness without complaint, and solitude more cruel than privations, the courage which renders them almost insensible to the loss of a fortune laboriously acquired and instantly prompt to fresh exertions to make another. Courage of this kind is peculiarly necessary to the maintenance and prosperity of the American communities, and is held by them in peculiar honor and estimation; to betray a want of it is to incur certain disgrace."[76] Furthermore, "the point of honor . . . has changed quite around and has been turned . . . against idleness." The modern concept of virtue "condemns that laxity of morals which diverts the human mind from the pursuit of well-being and disturbs the internal order of domestic life which is so necessary to success in business." According to de Tocqueville, "to earn the esteem of their countrymen, the Americans are therefore forced to adapt themselves to orderly habits; and it may be said in this sense that they make it a matter of honor to live chastely."[77] So it was that while the ideal of honor can be found in both aristocratic and democratic ages, "it assumes a different aspect" in the latter.[78] And in dealing with self-interest rightly understood in the modern setting, de Tocqueville continues to remind us that the concept of virtue is not abandoned; nor are morality and religion made obsolete. People need more than material gratification. "It must not, then, be supposed that at any period or under any political condition the passion for physical gratification and the opinions which are superinduced by that passion can ever content a whole people. The heart of man is of a larger mold; it can at once comprise a taste for the possession of the earth and the love of those of heaven; at times it may seem to cling devotedly to the one, but it will never be long without thinking of the other."[79] Man, de Tocqueville reminds us, is more elevated than an animal. "It is because man is capable of rising above the things of the body, and of scorning life itself, of which the beasts have not the least notion, that he can multiply these same goods of the body to a degree of which the inferior races cannot conceive." It is this "heart," or "soul," that places the "things of the earth" in proper perspective. It is the difference between the integrated individual and the brute. "If men were ever to content themselves with material objects, it is probable that they would lose by degrees the art of producing them; and they would enjoy them in the end, like the brutes, without discernment and without improvement."[80]

Through de Tocqueville's perceptive pen, we see the interplay of concepts and institutions that, together, produced modern virtue in an environment of freedom and enlightened self-interest, that sustained the new experiment in democratic republicanism. To suggest that "virtue" in all its forms ceased to be of importance with the "new science of politics," or that at the very least its importance ended after the Declaration of Independence and the Revolution, is to ignore the metamorphosis and rise of modern virtue, to misinterpret de Tocqueville's concept of "self-interest rightly understood," to ignore the statements of the American Founders themselves, and to deny modern man those inherited and acquired values and qualities that may lift him from meanness and avariciousness and preserve his freedom and personhood. If, indeed, a modern republic needs the aegis of virtue to sustain it in freedom, then the American Founders and de Tocqueville have left us a sobering message.

NOTES

1. Michael Novack, *The Spirit of Democratic Capitalism* (New York: Simon and Schuster 1982), pp. 93–94.

2. David K. Hart, "The Virtuous Citizen, the Honorable Bureaucrat, and 'Public' Administration," *Public Administration Review*, Vol. 44 (March 1984), pp. 111–19; H. George Frederickson and David K. Hart, "The Public Service and the Patriotism of Benevolence," *Currents and Soundings* (September–October 1985), p. 547.

3. Adam Smith, *The Theory of Moral Sentiments*, p. 212 (italics added).

4. *Ibid.*, pp. 208–9 (italics added).

5. *Ibid.*, pp. 211, 213 (italics added). See also David Hume, *An Inquiry Concerning the Principles of Morals*, eds., T. H. Green and T. H. Grose (London: Longmans, Green, 1882), p. 251. See discussion in Garry Wills, *Explaining America*, pp. 83–86.

6. Adams, *The Works of John Adams*, Vol. 6, pp. 241, 246–48. See discussion of this subject in John Paynter, "John Adams: On the Principles of Political Science," *The Political Science Reviewer*, Vol. 6 (Fall 1976), especially pp. 68–72.

7. *The Federalist*, No. 72 (italics added). See also Adair, *Fame and the Founding Fathers*.

8. *The Federalist*, No. 57. "It is possible that these may all be insufficient to control the caprice and wickedness of men. But are they not all that government will admit, and that human prudence can devise? Are they not the genuine and the characteristic means by which republican government provides for the liberty and the happiness of the people?"

9. Albert Ellery Bergh, *The Writings of Thomas Jefferson*, Vol. 16 (Washington, D.C.: Jefferson Memorial Association, 1907), pp. 118–19.

10. "A Sermon Preached Before the Honorable Congress of the Colony of the Massachusetts-Bay . . . by Samuel Langdon, D. D. . . ." A. W. Plumstead, ed., *The Wall and the Garden, Selected Massachusetts Election Sermons 1670–1775* (Minneapolis: University of Minnesota Press, 1968), p. 358.

11. *Ibid.*, p. 369.

12. *Ibid.*, pp. 365–66.

13. *Ibid.*, pp. 366–67.

14. *Ibid.*, p. 368.

15. *Ibid.*, pp. 360–61.

16. *Ibid.*, p. 368.

17. *Ibid.*, p. 360.

18. *Ibid.*, p. 369.

19. *Ibid.*, p. 360.

20. *Ibid.*, p. 369.

21. *Ibid.*, p. 362.

22. Rossiter, *Political Thought*, pp. 8–9.

23. Martin Diamond, "Ethics and Politics: The American Way," Horwitz, *The Moral Foundations of the American Republic*, p. 72 (italics added).

24. *Ibid.*, p. 67.

25. *Ibid.*, pp. 69–70.

26. *Ibid.*, pp. 70–71.

27. Hunt, ed., *The Writings of James Madison*, Vol. 5, p. 273; Diamond, "Ethics and Politics," p. 71.

28. Hart, "The Virtuous Citizen," p. 112.

29. John Witherspoon, *Lectures on Moral Philosophy*, 3rd ed. (Philadelphia: William Woodward, 1810), p. 17.

30. Dewey, *Living Thoughts of Thomas Jefferson*, p. 104.

31. Robert A. Goodwin, "Of Men and Angels," in Horwitz, *The Moral Foundations of the American Republic*, pp. 11–12.

32. Diamond, "Ethics and Politics," p. 71. Discussions concerning the necessity of "a system of beliefs, legitimizing the democratic system," may be found in Seymour Martin Lipset, "Some Social Requisites of Democracy: Economic Development and Political Legitimacy," *American Political Science Review*, Vol. 53 (March 1959); Joseph Schumpeter, *Capitalism, Socialism and Democracy* (New York: Harper and Row, 1975); Max Weber, *Essays in Sociology* (New York: Oxford University Press, 1946).

33. Letter of February 9, 1787 in Julian Boyd, *et al.*, eds., *The Papers of Thomas Jefferson*, Vol. 2, p. 129.

34. Howe, Jr., *The Changing Political Thought of John Adams*, p. 89.

35. Wilstach, ed., *Correspondence of John Adams and Thomas Jefferson, 1812–1826*, p. 170.

36. Rossiter, *The Political Thought of the American Revolution*, p. 199.

37. Reichley, *Religion in American Public Life*, p. 348.

38. Montesquieu, *The Spirit of the Laws*, Book 5, Chapter 6.

39. Smyth, ed., *The Writings of Benjamin Franklin*, Vol. VIII, p. 613.

40. Diamond, "Ethics and Politics," p. 65 (italics added).

41. *Ibid.*, p. 64 (italics added).

42. Tocqueville, *Democracy in America*, Vol. 1, p. 315. See also Vol. 2, Chaps. 8–12, pp. 205–25.

43. *Ibid.*, Vol. 2, p. 216.

44. *Ibid.*, pp. 139–40 (italics added).

45. *Ibid.*, pp. 257–58.

46. *Ibid.*, p. 39.

47. *Ibid.*, p. 40.

48. *Ibid.*, p. 148.

49. *Ibid.*, p. 227.

50. *Ibid.*, p. 219.

51. *Ibid.*, p. 166.

52. *Ibid.*, p. 163.

53. *Ibid.*, p. 165.

54. *Ibid.*, p. 148.

55. *Ibid.*, p. 153.

56. *Ibid.*, Vol. 1, p. 310.

57. *Ibid.*, p. 311. "If the Americans, who change the head of government once in every four years, who elect new legislators every two years, and renew the state officers every twelve months; if the Americans, who have given up the political world to the attempts of innovators, had not placed religion beyond their reach, where could it take firm hold in the ebb and flow of human opinions? Where would be that respect which belongs to it, amid the struggles of faction? And what would become of its immortality in the midst of universal decay." *Ibid.*, p. 323.

58. *Ibid.*, pp. 313–14.

59. *Ibid.*, p. 317.

60. *Ibid.*, p. 97.

61. *Ibid.*, p. 56.

62. *Ibid.*, Vol. 2, p. 27.

63. *Ibid* (italics added).

64. *Ibid.*, pp. 28–29.

65. *Ibid.*, p. 23.

66. *Ibid.*, p. 155.

67. *Ibid.*, p. 38.

68. *Ibid.*, pp. 158–59.

69. *Ibid.*, p. 134.

70. *Ibid.*, pp. 133–34.

71. *Ibid.*, p. 130.

72. *Ibid.*, p. 131 (italics added).

73. *Ibid.*, p. 131.

74. *Ibid.*, p. 132.

75. *Ibid.*, p. 248.

76. *Ibid.*, pp. 249–50.

77. *Ibid.*, pp. 248–49.

78. *Ibid.*, p. 250.

79. *Ibid.*, p. 156.

80. *Ibid.*, p. 157.

Index

Index